S0-BQW-477

## DATE DUE

|  |  |  |  |
|---|---|---|---|
|  |  |  |  |
|  |  |  |  |
|  |  |  |  |
|  |  |  |  |
|  |  |  |  |
|  |  |  |  |
|  |  |  |  |
|  |  |  |  |
|  |  |  |  |
|  |  |  |  |
|  |  |  |  |
|  |  |  |  |
|  |  |  |  |
|  |  |  |  |
|  |  |  |  |
|  |  |  |  |
|  |  |  |  |
|  |  |  |  |
|  |  |  |  |
|  |  |  |  |

# LAW AND RECOVERY FROM DISASTER:
## HURRICANE KATRINA

# Law, Property and Society

Series Editor:
Robin Paul Malloy

The Law, Property and Society series examines property in terms of its ability to foster democratic forms of governance, and to advance social justice. The series explores the legal infrastructure of property in broad terms, encompassing concerns for real, personal, intangible, intellectual and cultural property, as well as looking at property related financial markets. The series is edited by Robin Paul Malloy and addresses issues related to the work of the Center on Property, Citizenship, and Social Entrepreneurism sponsored by the Syracuse University College of Law. Contributions are requested from authors without regard to affiliation with the Center. Submissions are encouraged on all property-related topics.

**Robin Paul Malloy** is E.I. White Chair and Distinguished Professor of Law at Syracuse University College of Law, USA. He was Vice Dean of the College (through July 2008), and is Director of the Center on Property, Citizenship, and Social Entrepreneurism. He is also Professor of Economics (by courtesy appointment) in Maxwell School of Citizenship and Public Affairs, College of Law, Syracuse University. Professor Malloy writes extensively on law and market theory and on real estate transactions and development. He has published 12 books, more than 25 articles, and contributed to 12 other books. His recent books include: *Law and Market Economy* (Cambridge, 2000, in English and translated into Spanish and Chinese); *Law in a Market Context* (Cambridge, 2004); and *Real Estate Transactions 3rd* (with James C. Smith, Aspen, 2007).

# Law and Recovery From Disaster: Hurricane Katrina

*Edited by*

ROBIN PAUL MALLOY
*Syracuse University, USA*

## ASHGATE

Published by
Ashgate Publishing Limited
Wey Court East
Union Road
Farnham
Surrey, GU9 7PT
England

Ashgate Publishing Company
Suite 420
101 Cherry Street
Burlington
VT 05401-4405
USA

www.ashgate.com

**British Library Cataloguing in Publication Data**
Law and recovery from disaster : Hurricane Katrina. - (Law,
    property and society)
    1. Disaster relief - Law and legislation - United States
    2. Natural disasters - Law and legislation - United States
    3. Hurricane Katrina, 2005 - Economic aspects
    I. Malloy, Robin Paul, 1956-
    344.7'305348

**Library of Congress Cataloging-in-Publication Data**
Law and recovery from disaster : Hurricane Katrina / by Robin Paul Malloy.
    p. cm. -- (Law, property and society)
    Includes bibliographical references and index.
    ISBN 978-0-7546-7500-6
    1. Disaster relief--Law and legislation--United States. 2. Natural disasters--Law and
legislation--United States. 3. Hurricane Katrina, 2005--Economic aspects. I. Malloy,
Robin Paul, 1956-

    KF3750.L39 2008
    344.7305'348--dc22

                                                                2008033491

ISBN 978-0-7546-7500-6

Mixed Sources
Product group from well-managed
forests and other controlled sources
www.fsc.org Cert no. SGS-COC-2482
© 1996 Forest Stewardship Council
FSC

Printed and bound in Great Britain by
TJ International Ltd, Padstow, Cornwall

# Contents

# Series Editor's Preface

The book series on Law, Property, and Society, brings together experts from a variety of fields and institutions to discuss and explore issues related to modern Real Estate Transactions and Finance; Community Development and Housing; Global Property Law Systems; and Access to Ownership.

A core principle of the series is that a just and accessible property law system is the basis for both good citizenship and successful economic development. Therefore, the books in this series address all areas of property law and theory; including real, personal, intangible, intellectual, and cultural property. In doing this it is understood that property, in all its forms, addresses the fundamental relationships between the state and its citizens, and among the people themselves. For this reason the books in this series examine property in terms of its ability to foster democratic forms of governance, advance social justice, promote citizenship, build sustainable and supportive communities, and enhance the stewardship of our global environment and its natural resources.

In this book on *Law and Recovery from Disaster: Hurricane Katrina*, attention is focused on the way in which law functions and sometimes malfunctions under dramatic socio-legal stress. Contributors address a wide-ranging set of issues using Hurricane Katrina as a case study that can teach us many lessons in its own right as well as shed significant light on disaster situations globally.

In 2005, Hurricane Katrina hit the Gulf Coast of the United States killing more than 1,500 people and directly affecting 1.5 million people in a three-state region while destroying more than 300,000 homes. This took place within a year of the 2004 Indian Ocean tsunami that struck Ache, Indonesia, killing more than 200,000 people, displacing more than 2 million, and destroying or damaging more than 370,000 homes. Thankfully, events of this proportion are relatively uncommon. On the other hand, hurricanes, earth quakes, floods, and other natural disasters affect countless people every year. As forces of nature they are not limited to occurrences in any one community or any one country.

In this book, contributors address the ability of law and legal institutions not only to survive such disasters but to effectively facilitate recovery. They deal with both the frustrations and the opportunities that emerge in such circumstances.

In reviewing the table of contents for this book one can quickly grasp the extent of the rich collaboration undertaken by the scholars addressing this important subject area. Jim Chen introduces the book by making the seemingly controversial assertion in his chapter that there is no such thing as a "natural disaster." John A. Lovett, who was raised and currently teaches law in New Orleans, brings a special perspective to the subject as he explores the idea of property in conditions of radical change. Frank S. Alexander examines land use planning considerations; Debra Lyn Bassett in her chapter, and Janet E. Lord, Michael E. Waterstone, and Michael Ashley Stein in their chapter, contribute thoughts on implications for persons with disabilities. In considering the loss of life and property that accompany such disasters, Aviva Abramovsky and Robert Rhee each address the use of insurance as a risk spreading and risk protecting device. Rodney C. Runyan and Patricia Huddleston focus on the needs of small business owners and examine recovery efforts in this important segment of the economy. Olympia Duhart and Eloisa C. Rodriguez-Dod join together to explore problems for renters while Michèle Alexandre contextualizes opportunities for addressing past geographic segregation as part of a post-disaster rebuilding process. And, Erin Ryan evaluates the idea of New Federalism in the aftermath of the government's response to Katrina. Collectively, the contributors to this book provide a rich and critical analysis of law and legal institutions in the aftermath of a natural disaster.

The workshop that formed the basis for the contributions to this book was held in November 2006. Since the time of the workshop much has happened and the issues discussed herein have proven to be of great relevance and importance in understanding the role law plays in the process of recovery from disaster.

It has been my pleasure both to arrange the original workshop from which this work emerged and to work with each author in bringing this book to fruition. In editing this book I thank Nicholas D. Birck, Laura E. Gagnon, Geoffrey D. Korff, and Sheila Welch for their invaluable assistance.

All notes and sources used in this book are prepared in accordance with *The Bluebook: A Uniform System of Citation* (18th edition).

Robin Paul Malloy

E.I. White Chair and Distinguished Professor of Law

College of Law, Syracuse University

rpmalloy@law.syr.edu

Director, Center on Property, Citizenship, and Social Entrepreneurism (PCSE)

www.law.syr.edu/pcse

# List of Contributors

**Aviva Abramovsky** Associate Professor of Law, College of Law, Syracuse University.

**Frank S. Alexander** Professor of Law, Emory University School of Law, Director of Project on Affordable Housing and Community Development.

**Michèle Alexandre** Associate Professor of Law, University of Mississippi School of Law.

**Debra Lyn Bassett** Professor of Law and Judge Frank M. Johnson, Jr., Scholar, University of Alabama School of Law.

**Jim Chen** Dean and Professor of Law, University of Louisville Louis D. Brandeis School of Law.

**Eloisa C. Rodriguez-Dod** Professor of Law, Nova Southeastern University Shepard Broad Law Center; B.B.A., University of Miami; M.B.A., Florida International University; J.D., University of Miami Law School.

**Olympia Duhart** Assistant Professor of Law, Nova Southeastern University Shepard Broad Law Center; B.A. University of Miami; J.D., Nova Southeastern University.

**Patricia Huddleston** Professor, Advertising, Public Relations and Retailing, Michigan State University.

**Janet E. Lord** Partner, BlueLaw International LLP; Adjunct Professor of Law, University of Maryland School of Law.

**John A. Lovett** Associate Professor of Law, Loyola University New Orleans College of Law.

**Robert J. Rhee** Associate Professor, University of Maryland School of Law.

**Rodney C. Runyan** Assistant Professor, Retail and Consumer Science, University of Tennessee.

**Erin Ryan** Associate Professor, Marshall-Wythe School of Law, The College of William & Mary.

**Michael Ashley Stein** Cabell Research Professor, William & Mary School of Law; Executive Director, Harvard Project on Disability.

**Michael E. Waterstone** Professor of Law, Loyola Law School Los Angeles.

Dedicated to
our friends on the School of Law Faculties of
Loyola University, New Orleans
and
Tulane University

# Chapter 1

# Law Among the Ruins

## Jim Chen

### Hurricanes and Heartbreak

Hurricane Katrina broke America's collective heart. No previous natural disaster in the nation's history inflicted a grimmer toll. The legendary city of New Orleans all but sank when its levees failed and the resulting storm surge drowned much of the city and many of its feeblest, most vulnerable residents. The flood waters consumed the forlorn hope that the United States could rescue its citizens during their darkest and neediest hour. Although Katrina exposed flaws in virtually every aspect of disaster management at every level of government in the United States, the magnitude and senselessness of the loss indicted American society for its callous disregard of social vulnerability.

"The moral test of government," said Vice President Hubert H. Humphrey, "is how it treats those who are in the dawn of life, the children; those who are in the twilight of life, the aged; and those who are in the shadows of life, the sick, the needy and the handicapped."[1] The cloud of natural disaster puts government to an extreme test of its ability to protect those citizens who dwell in the dawn, the twilight, and the shadows of life. As Katrina demonstrated, social vulnerability profoundly affects the ability of governments to prepare for, respond to, mitigate, and recover from natural disasters.

Conservative estimates of Katrina's economic impact range in the hundreds of billions of dollars, measured strictly in terms of compensation, insurance, and reconstruction. Lawyers will continue to be heavily involved for years in disputes connected to recovery and resettlement after that storm. Despite Katrina's deep impact, we have no reason to believe that a single event in 2005 can provide the last word on disasters and what disasters demand of the law. Katrina merely represents one recent—albeit very dramatic—demonstration of serious gaps in the legal system's ability to respond to natural disasters and other catastrophic events.[2]

---

1 Arnold v. Arizona Dep't of Health Servs., 160 Ariz. 593, 775 P.2d 521, 537 (1989) (quoting Humphrey).

2 *See generally* DISASTERS AND THE LAW: KATRINA AND BEYOND (Daniel A. Farber & Jim Chen eds., 2006).

From the chaos of catastrophe, a form of legal order emerges. At first glance, disaster law seems to be nothing but a collection of legal rules that happen to come into play when communities have suffered severe physical damage. Upon deeper examination, however, we should regard disaster law as the enterprise of assembling the best portfolio of legal rules to deal with catastrophic risks. That portfolio should include strategies for prevention, emergency response, mitigation, compensation and insurance, and rebuilding.

The chapters in this volume focus Syracuse University's annual workshop on property, citizenship, and social entrepreneurship on the vital task of building the arsenal of legal tools for addressing and redressing natural disasters. Two chapters—Debra Lyn Bassett, *Place, Disasters, and Disability*, and Janet E. Lord, Michael E. Waterstone and Michael Ashley Stein, *Natural Disasters and Persons with Disabilities*—answer Hubert Humphrey's moral challenge very directly by examining the impact of disasters on the disabled. The combination of disaster and disability strains the law and other social systems to the utmost. Nearly half of the elderly population affected by Katrina, for instance, reported having at least one disability.[3] Erin Ryan, in *How the New Federalism Failed Katrina Victims*,[4] criticizes the United States' traditional commitment to federalism and the thorough delegation of police powers to state and local governments. Despite post-Katrina amendments of the Stafford Act, emergency response in the United States remains in the first instance the responsibility of state and local governments. Moreover, the federal law of emergency response retains the mark of the Homeland Security Act, which reorganized FEMA within a bureaucratic structure dedicated in the first instance to responding to terrorism and acts of war, and only secondarily to natural threats. Decisions such as *Sher v. Lafayette Insurance Co.*,[5] in which the Louisiana Supreme Court held that the standard policy exception for "flood" damage relieves insurance companies of liability for water damage caused by the failure of New Orleans's levees during Hurricane Katrina, highlight the importance of Aviva Abramovsky, *Insurance and the Flood*, and Robert J. Rhee, *Participation and Disintermediation in a Risk Society*.

Five additional chapters in this volume—Frank S. Alexander, *Land Use Planning by Design and by Disaster*; Michèle Alexandre, *Navigating the Topography of Inequality Post-Disaster: A Proposal for Remedying Past Geographic Segregation During Rebuilding*; Olympia Duhart and Eloisa C. Rodriguez-Dod, *Legislation*

---

3    *See* Thomas Gabe, Gene Falk & Maggie McCarty, Hurricane Katrina: Social-Demographic Characteristics of Impacted Areas 18 (Nov. 4, 2005) (CRS Order Code RL33141).

4    *See also* Erin Ryan, *Federalism and the Tug of War Within: Seeking Checks and Balance in the Interjurisdictional Gray Area*, 66 Md. L. Rev. 503 (2007).

5    2007-C-2441 & 2007-C-2443 (La. April 8, 2008) (rejecting the argument that a "flood" exclusion was ambiguous insofar as it might be limited to strictly "natural" events, as opposed to all instances of damage by water, and reducing a policyholder's recovery to damage from wind, lost rent, and other losses sustained during Katrina).

*and Criminalization Impacting Renters Displaced by Katrina*; John A. Lovett, *Property and Radical Change: Observations on Property Relationships from Post-Katrina New Orleans*; and Rodney C. Runyan and Patricia Huddleston, *Small Business Recovery from a Natural Disaster: Lessons from Katrina*—address the core issues of property law that Syracuse University's PCSE Center considers most closely related to citizenship and social entrepreneurship. No less central a figure in post-Katrina law and politics than Walter Isaacson, vice-chair of the Louisiana Recovery Authority, experienced the intensely personal nature of urban planning in the hurricane's wake.[6] Initially an advocate of aggressive, top-down urban planning as a precondition to the actual disbursement of Community Block Development Grants and other publicly controlled recovery funds, Mr. Isaacson reversed field when he learned that much of his family's neighborhood, Broadmoor, had been targeted for bulldozing and conversion into green space. One may applaud Mr. Isaacson's belated appreciation of the fact that a planning official's preferred "urban footprint" demands the bulldozing of someone else's neighborhood. From a broader perspective, though, the greater challenge lies in ensuring that recovery after disasters—to say nothing of prevention before they strike and mitigation and rescue efforts during a catastrophe—satisfies broader notions of social justice.

In this introduction, I wish to strike a single, unifying note. There is no such thing as a "natural" disaster. Understanding the interplay of environmental events with social conditions holds the key to the optimal application of legal tools for preventing, mitigating, and remedying natural tragedies—a grand social exercise that I call "law among the ruins."

## Disaster Is Never Natural: Social Vulnerability and Resilience

Natural disaster supposedly does not discriminate; it putatively strikes everyone in its path, without regard to race, class, age, sex, or disability. In more vivid terms, "poverty is hierarchic, smog is democratic."[7] Closer examination of the interplay between natural and social factors at work in any disaster, however, belies this assumption. Disaster does not so much erase as expose social vulnerabilities within the society it strikes. Although "'[n]atural disasters' such as hurricanes, earthquakes, and floods are sometimes viewed as 'great social equalizers'" in the sense that "they strike unpredictably and at random, affecting black and white, rich and poor, sick and well alike," Katrina bluntly demonstrated that "the harms

---

6   *See* Posting of Jim Chen to http://jurisdynamics.blog spot.com/2006/10/emergent-new-orleans-cybernetic-urban.html (Oct. 13, 2006, 8:38 EST) (blog entry entitled *Emergent New Orleans: Cybernetic Urban Planning and Some Self-Organizing Alternatives*).

7   ULRICH BECK, RISK SOCIETY: TOWARD A NEW MODERNITY 36 (1986); *accord* Scott Frickel, *Our Toxic Gumbo: Recipe for a Politics of Environmental Knowledge*, http:// understandingkatrina.ssrc.org/Frickel (Oct. 6, 2005).

are not visited randomly or equally in our society."[8] What is true of the disaster itself applies with even greater force to social responses to disaster. To name but one example as striking as it is embarrassing, "68 percent of [the] respondents" in a survey of Katrina evacuees "thought the federal government would have responded more quickly if people trapped in the floodwaters were 'wealthier and white rather than poorer and black.'"[9]

In short, disasters are never strictly "natural." Catastrophic losses invariably stem from social as well as environmental factors. Around the world, social injustice contributes so heavily to the incidence and intensity of natural disasters that the quest for domestic and global equality may be rightfully regarded as a valuable tool for refining the law's approach to disaster preparedness, response, mitigation, compensation, and recovery.

The first step in overcoming natural disaster lies in defining social vulnerability. According to one definition, social vulnerability means "the characteristics of a person or group in terms of their capacity to anticipate, cope with, resist, and recover from the impact of a natural hazard."[10] Geographer Susan Cutter has elaborated this definition in a very useful way: "Social vulnerability is partially a product of social inequalities—those social factors and forces that create the susceptibility of various groups to harm, and in turn affect their ability to respond, and bounce back (resilience) after the disaster."[11]

In other words, social vulnerability consists of two distinct components: the susceptibility of certain groups to harm and the resilience of these groups. Susceptibility is an ex ante quality; it is already in place when disaster strikes. Inequality in New Orleans and elsewhere throughout America has taken hundreds of years to build. Differences in living conditions, wealth, and political power rendered the poorest, often black victims of Katrina susceptible to disproportionate loss during the storm.

Resilience, by contrast, assumes importance after the fact. Rebuilding communities destroyed by natural disaster demands extraordinary human and material resources. Material resources available for recovery—and often taken for granted—in more affluent communities may simply not exist in poorer communities.

---

8   CENTER FOR PROGRESSIVE REFORM, AN UNNATURAL DISASTER: THE AFTERMATH OF HURRICANE KATRINA 34 (2005).

9   U.S. HOUSE OF REPRESENTATIVES, A FAILURE OF INITIATIVE: FINAL REPORT OF THE SELECT BIPARTISAN COMMITTEE TO INVESTIGATE THE PREPARATION FOR AND RESPONSE TO HURRICANE KATRINA 19 (2006).

10   PIERS BLAIKIE, TERRY CANNON, IAN DAVIS & BEN WISNER, AT RISK: NATURAL HAZARDS, PEOPLE'S VULNERABILITY AND DISASTERS 9 (1994).

11   Susan L. Cutter, *The Geography of Social Vulnerability: Race, Class, and Catastrophe*, http://understandingkatrina.ssrc.org/Cutter (Sept. 23, 2005).

Crucial physical and social infrastructure, often strained or undermined by disaster and its aftermath, is not as readily reestablished.[12]

Katrina played itself in media reports as a grand tragedy of race and class, of official incompetence and social injustice. If anything, the condemnation of a society that found itself unprepared for Katrina has not been severe enough. To prevent or at least to mitigate future disasters, we must confront social vulnerability in all its manifestations, from its racial and class-based dimensions to other vectors of discrimination laid bare by the storm, such as sex, age, disability, and immigrant status. All of these factors contribute to the susceptibility of specific individuals and groups to disaster. In addition to recognizing and making best efforts to ameliorate these sources of susceptibility to harm during disasters, government owes its weakest citizens a corresponding responsibility to maximize their resilience in disaster's wake.

In other words, the entire battery of legal tools designed to prevent and mitigate natural disaster might be profitably reimagined as a twofold challenge for the law. First, law must seek to minimize social susceptibility before the next natural event becomes a social catastrophe. Second, during times of relative tranquility, the law should strive to improve resilience within vulnerable communities so that they might recover more rapidly and effectively should disaster strike. By addressing both of these dimensions of social justice in times of disaster, the chapters in this volume represent a significant step toward the fulfillment of the highest calling in public governance, that of law—and love—among the ruins.

---

12   *See generally* Mapping Vulnerability: Disasters, Development and People (Greg Bankoff et al. eds., 2003).

# Chapter 2
# Property and Radical Change: Observations on Property Relationships from Post-Katrina New Orleans

John A. Lovett

## Sisyphus on the Levee

It is not always easy to understand how property relationships are responding to the devastation caused by Hurricane Katrina and the failure of New Orleans' levees. Every day in post-Katrina New Orleans brings a cascade of new developments—some encouraging, others deeply troubling. One day in August of 2007, as the city prepared to commemorate the second anniversary of Katrina, demographers released a new study suggesting that the City of New Orleans had regained sixty-eight percent of its pre-storm population, that the entire metropolitan area had recovered eighty-four percent of its population, and that the pace of repopulation was quickening even in some of the city's most damaged neighborhoods.[1] But just a few days later, another report documented that thousands of New Orleans homes are still abandoned, blighted or only partially repaired, depressing not only their neighbors' property values, but also their commitment to participating in the city's revival.[2]

Another day in August 2007, a well-known developer announced plans for a new high-rise condominium and retail development in the old warehouse section

---

[1]   Amy Liu & Allison Plyer, The New Orleans Index: Second Anniversary Special Edition, A Review of Key Indicators of Recovery Two Years After Katrina (Aug. 2007), *available at* http://www.gnocdc.org/. *See id.* at Addendum: Updated Population Statistics (Aug. 23, 2007). By April 2008, the population estimates had improved even more. According to one leading demographic report, the City of New Orleans had regained more than seventy percent of its pre-Katrina households (71.5% to be precise) and the six-parish New Orleans metropolitan area had regained almost eighty-seven percent (86.9%) of its pre-storm households. New Orleans Index, 6, tbl. 1 (April 16, 2008). Another leading demographer estimates that the city's population passed the 300,000 mark in January 2008. *See* GCR Metropolitan New Orleans Population Estimate, *available at* http://www. gcrprofessional.com/Pro_NewsRelease.htm?NewsID=18. Both of these studies suggest, however, that the pace of repopulation slackened considerably in the last quarter of 2007.

[2]   Michelle Krupa, *Doubt Next Door*, Times-Picayune (New Orleans), Aug. 26, 2007, at A1.

of the city next to the Mississippi River, promising a New Urbanist dreamscape of intermingled residential and commercial uses all connected by a new riverfront park stretching from the French Quarter to the Garden District. The city signaled it would cooperate by giving the developers generous property tax breaks to make the developments more profitable.[3] But at almost the same time, we learned that commercial property insurance rates in the region are still much higher than they were prior to Katrina, creating a substantial obstacle for any new ambitious real estate development as well as for established businesses struggling to prosper in the new market conditions created by the storm.[4]

Over the past two years we have heard repeated demands for more affordable housing in the region. Housing advocates have argued that we need more numerous and more generous federally subsidized rental housing vouchers and "one to one" replacement of all the public housing units that were damaged or closed after the storm. This is the only way, they contend, that low income renters will be able to return and cope with average monthly rents that are, by most accounts, somewhere between twenty to fifty percent higher than they were before the city flooded.[5] And yet others have criticized the way the State of Louisiana has allocated billions of dollars worth of federal housing tax credit incentives, claiming that the State risks re-creating the same landscape of concentrated poverty and segregated housing that plagued the city before Katrina and is doing nothing to insure that low income housing is spread throughout the entire region, bringing low income residents to middle-class neighborhoods with better schools, more job opportunities, and greater chances for social mobility.[6]

To live in New Orleans and to observe the city's struggle to rebuild after Katrina is like witnessing Sisyphus push his boulder up the mountainside only to see it roll

---

3　Greg Thomas, *Riverfront Power Plant Gets Initial OK for Tax Breaks*, TIMES-PICAYUNE (NEW ORLEANS), Aug. 15, 2007, at A1.

4　Rebecca Mowbray, *Insurance Outlook Gets Brighter*, TIMES-PICAYUNE (New Orleans), Sept. 3, 2007; Rebecca Mowbray, *Reason for Hope*, TIMES-PICAYUNE (New Orleans), Aug. 12, 2007.

5　ANNIE CLARK & KALIMA ROSE, POLICY LINK, BRINGING LOUISIANA RENTERS HOME (2007), *available at* http://www.policylink.org/Communities/Louisiana/resources.html; Stacy E. Seicshnaydre, *The More Things Change, The More They Stay the Same: In Search of a Just Public Housing Policy Post-Katrina*, 81 TUL. L. REV. 1263 (2007). *See also* Greg Thomas, *Rental Rates Fall with Demand*, TIMES-PICAYUNE (New Orleans), Sept. 9, 2007, at A1 (documenting recent softening in rental rates across the metro region and noting that in flooded parts of the city, rates are only ten percent higher than before the storm). HUD's fair market rent estimates show a similar pattern with rent levels now at approximately forty-six percent of their pre-storm levels. NEW ORLEANS INDEX (Nov. 13, 2007), *supra* note 1, at 7, app. tbl. 11; NEW ORLEANS INDEX (April 16, 2008), *supra* note 1, at app. tbl. 12 (showing only minor increase).

6　BUREAU OF GOVERNMENTAL RESEARCH, CEMENTING IMBALANCE: A POST-KATRINA ANALYSIS OF THE REGIONAL DISTRIBUTION OF SUBSIDIZED RENTAL HOUSING 2 (2007), *available at* http://www.bgr.org.

back down again just as he is about to reach the summit. The difference here is that there are no hills, only levees that need to be built higher and stronger, even as the muddy soils beneath them gradually subside, sea levels gradually rise due to global warming, and our coastal wetlands continue to erode. And yet despite the inevitable frustration, the sense that for every three steps forward we also take at least two steps backwards, there are unmistakable signs of hope. And just as important, there are lessons to be learned from the experience of watching and participating in this collective effort of recovery.

This chapter draws on insights I developed in writing a lengthier study of how property relationships respond to events like Hurricane Katrina[7] and from insights gained in other attempts to understand how particular relationships mediated by property law respond to other kinds of change.[8] The first major point of the Hurricane Katrina-inspired study is that most lawyers, judges, and legal academics think about property law as an institution that is designed to promote stability—stability of ownership, stability of value, and stability of markets to exchange the objects of property law. Whether we are defining the legal and physical parameters of an individual's claim of ownership, or protecting a lender's security interest in collateral or its ability to obtain repayment of a loan, or defining the rights of non-owners to gain access to valuable resources, stability, certainty, and predictability are consistently posited as key values for property law.

But if stability is so important, what happens to property law and property relationships when stability is dramatically undermined, when the world seems to be turned upside down by events that take us by surprise? Posing this question led me to appreciate that if we want to understand how property relationships respond to events like Hurricane Katrina—events which I characterize as producing *radically changed circumstances*—then we also need to examine what makes some of those relationships more resilient than others. Before going further, however, we need to define several key concepts: *property relationships*, *changed circumstances*, *radically changed circumstances*, and *resiliency*.

## Property Relationships: Short- and Long-Term, Finite and Infinite, Voluntary and Involuntary

Before we can begin to understand what events of radically changed circumstances might entail for property law, we should first briefly consider the concept of a *property relationship* itself. By using the term "property relationship," I am referring to any relationship of individuals, juridical entities, or institutions that

---

7    John A. Lovett, *Property and Radically Changed Circumstances: Hurricane Katrina and Beyond*, 74 TENN. L. REV. 463 (2007).

8    John A. Lovett, *Doctrines of Waste in a Landscape of Waste*, 72 MO. L. REV. 1209 (2007); John A. Lovett, *A Bend in the Road: Easement Pliability in the New Restatement (Third) of Property: Servitudes*, 38 CONN. L. REV. 1 (2005).

share some property claims to a common resource, whether in the form of shared ownership, shared or interrelated possessory use, future interests or security rights in the resource, or shared rights to participate in decision-making about the resource. One common example of a property relationship is between a tenant and landlord, the tenant holding a short-term right to possess and enjoy the leased premises for the duration of the lease while the landlord holds the long-term, reversionary interest in the land or building. Both the tenant and landlord will have rights to dictate how the property is used during the terms of the lease, and each will have rights to terminate the relationship prematurely, all of these determined either by the terms of the lease or by statutory or common law default rules. Because a lease has a defined term (even if it is capable of being renewed indefinitely by the tenant) and because parties enter into leases through some affirmative act of will, we can characterize a landlord and tenant relationship as primarily a *finite* and *voluntary* relationship. A residential lease will typically have a term lasting anywhere from a few months to a few years, while commercial leases can often have much longer terms, ranging anywhere from five to ten to thirty or even in some cases ninety-nine years. Thus, lease relationships can be both *short-term* and *long-term* in duration.[9]

Another example of a property relationship arising from the depths of the common law is between a life estate holder and the holder of a reversionary interest or remainder. The life tenant will have immediate possessory rights in the asset subject to the life estate and those rights can potentially endure until her death. But her ability to make significant changes in the use of the resource may be curtailed by the authority of the person holding the reversionary interest or remainder to protect the value of the asset either under express terms of the act creating the life estate relationship or under what has come to be known as the law of waste.[10] Just as with a basic lease, the relationship between the life tenant and future interest holder is *finite*. Even though no one knows when exactly the life tenant will die and even though the ensuing life estate relationship could last quite a long time if the life tenant is relatively young, her property interest will come to an end at some point in time. On the other hand, because most life estates are created as the result of a gratuitous disposition or grant from some other person (usually a decedent), rather than by mutual contract, a typical life estate relationship can be understood as being more or less *involuntary in origin*, even though in theory the recipient of the life estate could always renounce or reject the gift creating the relationship.

---

9   For a thorough discussion of landlord and tenant relationships under American common law, see WILLIAM A. STOEBUCK & DALE A. WHITMAN, THE LAW OF PROPERTY 241–433 (3d ed. 2000).

10   *See generally* STOEBUCK & WHITMAN, *supra* note 9, at 146–74; Lovett, *Doctrines of Waste*, *supra* note 8 at 1212–15. In Louisiana civil law, this same temporally disaggregated property relationship is regulated in great detail by the rules governing usufructuary and naked ownership interests. *See* LA. CIV. CODE ANN. arts. 535–629 (1980).

Yet another example of a crucial modern property relationship is between a mortgagor and mortgagee. The mortgagor of the property can be understood as holding either legal or equitable title but in almost all cases will be in possession of the mortgaged property, while the mortgagee can be understood as holding either a legal title to or a lien on the mortgaged property. Regardless of how we define the mortgagee's interest, though, in some fundamental sense it can be understood as a kind of contingent future interest in the property that will become possessory (or real) in the event the mortgagor defaults or a foreclosure proceeding becomes necessary. In this relationship, too, each party will typically have some rights to dictate how the property can be altered or used during the term of the mortgage, and these decision-making rights can be defined by contractual agreement or by background default rules established by statute or common law.[11] Like a lease or life estate, a mortgage relationship is primarily *finite* in a temporal sense in that the underlying mortgage loan will have a defined term. It is also *voluntary* in the sense that most mortgages are granted by property owners as a matter of choice. And like leases, they can be either *long-term* or *short-term*, depending on the length of the mortgage loan term.

A property relationship can also exist outside of these classic property law categories. In my Katrina-inspired article, I suggest that the relationship between a city itself and its residents can also be understood as a property relationship. Although a resident of a city like New Orleans does not have any formal ownership stake in municipal resources and cannot directly control how the common assets of a community are managed, developed, or deployed to respond to a community's needs, a resident does have a *vote* and a *voice*. And when residents combine their votes and voices together to demand changes in government policies, they can affect how a local or state government uses its assets, whether they are the tangible ones directly under the government's control, like its streets, parks and schools, or intangible ones like its ability to create new law or to decide how it will dispense funds that are made available to rebuild a community from other governmental sources. This relationship between a city and its residents is theoretically *voluntary* in the sense that no state or municipal government can legally compel residents to remain in the community or prevent an influx of newcomers.[12] At the same time, though, for residents who may enjoy family, community, cultural, and economic connections to a city or region that extend across many decades or generations, the ability to *exit* from a relationship with a city or town may be deeply constrained and thus the relationship might also be characterized as being

---

11   *See generally* GRANT S. NELSON & DALE A. WHITMAN, REAL ESTATE FINANCE LAW 130–55 (4th ed. 2001). *See also* ROBIN PAUL MALLOY & JAMES CHARLES SMITH, REAL ESTATE TRANSACTIONS: PROBLEMS, CASES AND MATERIALS 351–62 (3d ed. 2007).

12   *See* Saenz v. Rose, 526 U.S. 489, 500, 505–11 (1999) (addressing constitutional right to travel and unconstitutionality of citizen classifications based on residency duration); Shapiro v. Thompson, 394 U.S. 618, 629 (1989) (addressing unconstitutionality of durational residency requirements designed to inhibit migration of needy persons to a state).

*involuntary* in nature. Further, individuals seeking to *enter* or *return* to a city or community may be restrained, not so much by legal obstacles, but by practically insurmountable economic barriers such as moving costs, housing costs, lack of employment opportunities, and contractual obligations undertaken in other places. For all of these reasons, a city–resident relationship can be both *finite* or *infinite*, *long-term* or *short-term*, will be subject to constant revision and negotiation, and will be influenced by the city's formal and informal attempts to induce its residents to stay or to return or by its efforts to attract new residents.

### Changed Circumstances: Three Examples from Traditional Property Law

With this understanding of property relationships in mind, and before we contemplate what an event of *radically changed circumstances* might mean for these relationships, we should first consider how property law has understood and used the concept of *changed circumstances* itself. Property lawyers have long recognized that when the social, physical, environmental, or political circumstances in which a property relationship is situated changes dramatically, the participants in these relationships are sometimes entitled to alter the terms of what, in normal circumstances, would be considered a permanent and unchangeable contractually-based property arrangement. When individuals buy a lot and house in a neighborhood subdivision subject to a recorded scheme of restrictive covenants, for instance, they normally cannot alter the terms of those covenants or violate them unless they obtain the consent of all, or in some cases a majority or super-majority, of those who hold the right to enforce those covenants. But when circumstances have changed so radically that the initial purpose of the covenants can no longer be accomplished (usually because a once quiet residential neighborhood has gradually been infiltrated by commercial activity or other land uses), courts sometimes will allow a property owner burdened by such covenants to ignore them partially or entirely.[13] Although in England and Scotland this phenomenon of judicial alteration and termination of obsolete covenants was regularized and made much more common through twentieth-century statutes, American courts still do not allow this to occur lightly and thus recognize the "doctrine of changed conditions" more as a matter of principle than law in action.[14]

---

13   For the most recent attempt to state the case for the changed conditions doctrine in the context of servitude and covenants, see RESTATEMENT (THIRD) OF PROPERTY: SERVITUDES § 7.10 (2000). For critiques of the doctrine, see Glen O. Robinson, *Explaining Contingent Rights: The Puzzle of Obsolete Covenants*, 91 COLUM. L. REV. 546, 572–79 (1991); Richard Epstein, *Notice and Freedom of Contract in the Law of Servitudes*, 55 S. CAL. L. REV. 1353, 1364–68 (1982); Carol Rose, *Servitudes, Security and Assent: Some Comments on Professors French and Reichman*, 55 S. CAL. L. REV. 1403, 1412–13 (1982).

14   *See, e.g.*, City of Bowie v. MIE Props., 922 A.2d 509 (Md. 2007) (holding that restrictive covenant requiring land to be used as a science and technology research park

Another example of how property relationships can sometimes be altered in response to changing conditions arises in the law of easements, or what civil law trained lawyers call "servitudes of passage." Under traditional American common law, if a servient owner wishes to relocate an easement or right of way to another part of his estate in order to develop the land in a new way (perhaps because the once rural farm land or wooded forest is now in the middle of a burgeoning suburb and is ripe for subdivision into a housing track or commercial development), he normally cannot make this change unless he obtains the consent of the easement holder. When the drafters of the *Restatement (Third) of Property: Servitudes* changed this rule to allow a servient estate owner to relocate an easement as long as he paid for the change and as long as the new location and route were equally convenient for the easement holder,[15] a controversy broke out in this usually placid corner of American property law. Some American courts and legal commentators have passionately resisted the *Restatement*'s innovation, suggesting that it is an affront to the stabilizing purposes of property law itself.[16] A respectable handful of American courts, however, have begun to embrace this new rule, seeing in it perhaps a pragmatic response to the need for property law to be more adaptable to change.[17] Of course, the surrounding change of circumstances that provokes a dispute about easement relocation tends to be gradual in nature. Usually it is the encroachment of suburban development and a concomitant rise in property values, not any sudden or dramatic change like an earthquake or hurricane.

One final example of the connection between property law and changing conditions can be found in the traditional common law rules regarding life estates, future interests, and the doctrine of waste. At traditional English common law, a farmer holding a life estate was generally not permitted to cut any significant

---

remained valid and enforceable nineteen years after its recordation even though state university had withdrawn from original developer's contemplated project and other changes had occurred in the vicinity); River Heights Ass'n v. Batten, 591 S.E.2d 683 (Va. 2004) (refusing to terminate forty-five year old restrictive covenant requiring land fronting on road to be used for residences even though road had changed from two lanes to an eight to ten lane highway because of lack of change in interior of subdivision); Western Land Co. v. Truskolaski, 495 P.2d 624, 626–27 (Nev. 1972) (refusing to terminate single family use restrictive covenants despite increased traffic and commercialization in surrounding area); Rick v. West, 228 N.Y.S.2d 195, 34 Misc. 2d 1002, 1006–08 (N.Y. Sup. Ct. 1962) (same and emphasizing reliance interests of owner of benefited parcels).

15   RESTATEMENT (THIRD) OF PROPERTY: SERVITUDES § 4.8(3) (2000).

16   *See* Herren v. Pettengill, 538 S.E.2d 735, 736 (Ga. 2000); MacMeekin v. Low Income Hous. Inst., Inc., 45 P.3d 570, 577–79 (Wash. Ct. App. 2002); AKG Real Estate, LLC v. Kosterman, 717 N.W.2d 835, 844–47 (Wisc. 2006); John V. Orth, *Relocating Easements: A Response to Professor French*, 38 REAL PROP. PROB. & TR. J. 643 (2004).

17   *See* Stanga v. Hussman, 694 N.W.2d 716, 718–20 (S.D. 2005); M.P.M. Builders v. Dwyer, 809 N.E.2d 1053, 1057 (Mass. 2004); Lewis v. Young, 705 N.E.2d 649, 653–54 (N.Y. 1998); Roaring Fork Club LP v. St. Judes Co., 36 P.3d 1229, 1237 (Colo. 2001). *See generally* Lovett, *A Bend in the Road, supra* note 8.

amount of standing timber or otherwise alter land use patterns on the property subject to a life estate unless he obtained the consent of the persons holding the future interest. The usual justifications were that self-interested changes made by the life tenant might impair the value of the future interest holder's inheritance or might even make it difficult to determine the boundaries of the property. Any significant change in the use of the land by the life tenant that took place without the approval of the reversionary interest holder, even if it might improve the land's value, was thus said to constitute impermissible "waste" and could lead to forfeiture of the life tenant's interest in the land and other harsh sanctions.[18]

When this supposedly strict "English" rule on waste crossed the Atlantic, it gradually gave way to a new rule as American courts realized that a strict, purely consent-based approach to life tenant–reversioner conflicts might frustrate the ability of life tenants and other tenants (such as tenants for years) to develop the supposedly raw American wilderness into productive agricultural uses. And so, during the first half of the nineteenth century the English rule was left behind, and American courts began to approve of life tenants' land use changes by holding that they would constitute waste and lead to forfeiture and other penalties only if the change seriously impaired the value of the future interest holder's inheritance.[19]

Later in the late nineteenth and early twentieth centuries, the traditional English rule on waste was called into further question in two famous cases involving urban buildings. In the celebrated and often cited decision in *Melms v. Pabst Brewing Co.*,[20] the Wisconsin Supreme Court rejected a claim by reversioners that a life estate holder had committed voluntary waste by tearing down a once fine brick house that had become surrounded by a brewery and related businesses and re-grading the lot to ready it for commercial redevelopment. Noting that the once strict English conception of waste had already been significantly softened in actual application in England and in America, the court insisted that these kinds of conflicts between a life tenant and reversionary interest holder should be resolved by considering the effect of changing conditions on the interests of both parties. As the court put it:

> In the absence of any contract, express or implied, to use the property for a specified purpose, or to return it in the same condition in which it was received, a *radical and permanent change of surrounding conditions*, such as is presented in the case before us, must always be an important, and sometimes a controlling,

---

18   *See generally* Lovett, *Doctrines of Waste*, *supra* note 8; Jedediah Purdy, *The American Transformation of Waste Doctrine: A Pluralist Interpretation*, 91 Cornell L. Rev. 653 (2006).

19   *See, e.g.*, Jackson v. Brownson, 7 Johns. 227, 232–34 (N.Y. Sup. Ct. 1810). *See generally* Purdy, *supra* note 18.

20   79 N.W. 738 (Wisc. 1899).

consideration upon the question whether a physical change in the use of the buildings constitutes waste.[21]

In *Brokaw v. Fairchild*,[22] however, a New York court strictly enforced the traditional rule on waste when it enjoined the proposed demolition of another fine nineteenth-century mansion located on Fifth Avenue in New York City and its proposed replacement with a much more valuable thirteen-story apartment building. Here, although the court noted that changing land use patterns in New York City made the proposed apartment building a logical development for the property, it focused much more closely on the implied intent of the grantor of the life estate, and observed that the mansion was not completely valueless in its current condition and that it was still surrounded by three other palatial residences. It thus concluded that the life estate holder should not be able to make a unilateral decision to dramatically alter the nature of the property subject to the life estate.[23] What is most significant about *Brokaw*, though, is not so much the holding itself, but the outrage it provoked in the legal world. The decision was heavily criticized by academics,[24] repudiated in the *First Restatement of Property*,[25] and was soon statutorily overruled in New York.[26] What we see in these changing conceptions of the law of waste then is yet another recognition that sometimes a participant in a property relationship should be allowed to respond to a significant change in surrounding conditions by altering the physical condition or use of the property as long as the alteration does not harm other participants in the relationship. Put differently, concern for utilitarian progress can sometimes outweigh our concern for the contractual sanctity of property relationships. And society's desire for practical adaptability can sometimes trump the legal systems' professed interest in guaranteeing certainty and stability.

So it was my awareness of this possibility that property relationships can bend, or even end, as a result of "changing circumstances" that led me to question whether an event like Hurricane Katrina might produce similar kinds of alterations in some of the most fundamental property relationships that structure our lives. At this juncture it is still too early to tell whether Hurricane Katrina will produce changes in long-term servitude and covenant relationships or affect the relationships between present possessory interest holders and future interests holders (for instance usufructuaries and naked owners in Louisiana). But the more

---

21    *Id.* at 741.

22    237 N.Y.S. 6 (N.Y. Sup. Ct. 1929), *aff'd*, 245 N.Y.S. 402, *aff'd*, 177 N.E. 186 (1931).

23    *Brokaw*, 237 N.Y.S. at 14–20.

24    Marvin H. Niehuss, *Alteration or Replacement of Buildings by Long-Term Lessee*, 30 MICH. L. REV. 386, 397 (1932); 2 TIFFANY, REAL PROPERTY § 632 (3d ed. 1939); 5 AMERICAN LAW OF PROPERTY § 20.11 (ed. James Casner) (1952).

25    RESTATEMENT OF PROPERTY § 140 cmt.f (1936).

26    N.Y. REAL PROP. ACTS. LAW § 803 (McKinney 1979).

I thought about how Katrina was affecting the property relationships of my fellow residents of New Orleans, the more I realized I would have to look for examples where pressure for change was being applied right now. In addition, I needed to refine my conception of changed circumstances because Hurricane Katrina had produced a degree of change of an entirely different magnitude than in the changed conditions cases I have just described.

**Radically Changed Circumstances**

In thinking about the kind of change wrought by Hurricane Katrina—what I call *radically changed circumstances*—and in trying to distinguish this change from the often more gradual, but nonetheless profound, changes that can sometimes lead to alteration of property relationships in the covenant, easement, and waste cases I describe above, I concluded that there are at least four distinguishing characteristics of an event producing *radically changed circumstances*. Although no single one of these characteristics is necessary to produce such an event, they are all strong markers and help us understand why events like Hurricane Katrina provoke such a challenge to property law's core concern with stability and certainty.

First of all, an event like Hurricane Katrina is obviously *sudden*. Unlike the kind of gradual social transformations that spark typical controversies about restrictive covenants, easements, or life estates, events like Hurricane Katrina, the 1994 Northridge California earthquake, or the terrorist attack on the World Trade Center on September 11, 2001 can arrive instantly and can unfold in a matter of minutes, hours, or perhaps just a few days. This is not to say that gradually emerging transformations like those associated with global climate change or the complete overhaul of the political systems that have recently occurred in the countries of the former Soviet Union, in Eastern Europe, and in South Africa cannot be equally dramatic in their eventual scope or effect, but just that they are a different kind of phenomenon. The primary difference is that because these transformations occur somewhat more slowly (though they are not always easily detected by people living through them), individuals and institutions have somewhat more time to prepare and plan for the radical changes they portend.

Second, events of radically changed circumstances are *unexpected*. Although everyone knows that hurricanes, earthquakes, and even terrorist attacks can and will happen one day, none of us knows for sure when or where they will occur. Although we must and do try to prepare for these kinds of events by creating government agencies like FEMA and by creating our own private insurance networks, the unexpectedness of events like Hurricane Katrina still make them capable of producing change that takes us by surprise.

Next, events like Hurricane Katrina are *intensely disruptive*. They can change everything about our lives and communities, from where we live, to where and how we work, to how we recreate and care for each other. The severity of the change they bring about is so deep, so penetrating, that they tend to cleave our collective sense of time itself. They create a sense of before and after. Our community consciousness is shattered and altered for good.

Finally, events like Hurricane Katrina tend to be (but are not always) *geographically and demographically pervasive.* That is to say their destructive impact extends beyond a few individuals, a few homes or a few businesses and reaches out to affect the lives of people in entire communities and entire cities, or even, as with Hurricane Katrina or the Indian Ocean tsunami of 2004, entire regions. Rather than affecting the lives of dozens or even hundreds of individuals, these events will impact acutely and irrevocably the lives of thousands, and perhaps hundreds of thousands, of people across many social classes and ethnic and racial divides.

If these kinds of events are so devastating in their impact, and if they are likely to occur, as many studies indicate, with increasing frequency as our environment becomes increasingly fragile as a result of both global climate change and unresolved social, political, and religious tensions, then we all need to think much more carefully about how our property relationships can and should respond to these potentially destabilizing events. My first step was to try to map the recurring problems these events typically produce, both immediately and in the intermediate and long term, as individuals and institutions respond to radical change.

## Repeat Problems and Decision Trees

When participants in a property relationship are faced with an event of radical change that has damaged, destroyed, altered, or undermined the security of the common resource in which they are invested, they typically will face four basic problems. Each core problem will in turn raise a series of complex second order issues. The first and usually most pressing problem is that the participants must decide whether they want to preserve their shared property resource, and if so, how to accomplish this task. The answer to this basic question of resource *preservation* is not self evident. Some participants might decide there is no use in trying to rebuild, restore, or preserve the resource in light of the new circumstances that have emerged and instead might prefer to cut their losses and dissolve the property relationship altogether. Others will, of course, be committed to complete restoration of the common resource. The answers to the second order decisions stemming from the core preservation issues are not self evident either. If preservation is going to be undertaken, which participants will be responsible for initiating the conservatory acts? Will unanimous consent be required before conservatory action is undertaken? If not, can one participant or a subset of participants undertake the conservatory actions and demand contribution from passive participants? All of these decisions are fraught with complexity, and property law has often devised complex default rules to answer them.[27]

The second major problem that typically confronts participants in a property relationship after radical change has occurred is whether, rather than preserving the resource and restoring it to its previous condition and level of security, the participants should alter it substantially or improve it. The question of whether to undertake *substantial alteration and improvement* in turn leads to another set of complex second order issues. Once again, will unanimous consent be required to undertake major changes in the resource? Will reimbursement be owed to participants who undertake significant changes unilaterally or should they be penalized? Should some form of majority decision-making be used to resolve questions about substantial alterations and improvements of the resource?[28]

The final two dominant problems that will confront property relationships in the wake of an event of radical change involve the terms on which participants will be allowed to *exit* from or regain *entrance* to the property relationship. If a participant can no longer afford to participate in the relationship, how will her desire to exit be accommodated? Will she lose the value of the investments she may have previously made in the resource? Should she have the ability to transfer her property interest to a third party freely? Or should her ability to trade her property interest be constrained by the desires and interests of the remaining property participants? Should a participant be entitled to demand dissolution of the entire property interest in order to facilitate her ability to turn her share into a liquid asset? Or should other participants be able to block dissolution and preserve the basic structure of the property relationship even though this might reduce the value of the exiting member's interest?[29]

Similarly, when participants in a property relationship suddenly lose access to the shared resource or their place in the relationship, the questions which then arise regarding exit rights and limitations can be reframed in terms of *entrance*. This is an especially acute problem in post-Katrina New Orleans where thousands of residents with long and deep ties to the city and its closely knit neighborhoods were displaced in Katrina's wake. Will former participants or new individuals who would like to join a community or property relationship be allowed to re-enter or enter the fold? Should former participants be given a preference over newcomers? Should members of the community that stayed behind or came back early be given the right to select new participants based on their likelihood of being able

---

27    Lovett, *Property and Radically Changed Circumstances, supra* note 7, at 481–82; Hanoch Dagan & Michael Heller, *The Liberal Commons*, 110 YALE L. J. 549, 612 (2001).

28    Lovett, *Property and Radically Changed Circumstances, supra* note 7, at 482; Dagan & Michael, *supra* note 27, at 614.

29    Dagan & Michael, *supra* note 27, at 598–600; Thomas W. Mitchell, *From Reconstruction to Deconstruction: Undermining Black Landownership, Political Independence, and Community Through Partition Sales of Tenancies in Common*, 95 Nw. U. L. REV. 505 (2001).

to contribute to the community's revival? In short, we need to ask how legal rules and institutional structures regulate the desires of property participants to re-enter or enter a property relationship or re-establish themselves in a community.

## The Virtues of Resilient Property Relationships

By referring to the *resiliency* of a property relationship or property regime, I aim to describe the ability of the participants in that relationship to rebuild or renew their common resource after an event of radically changed circumstances damages, destroys, or undermines that resource in some significant way. Resiliency itself can be measured from a variety of perspectives, some focused on measuring economic efficiency and others guided by independent normative judgments about justice and fairness. My criteria for determining whether a property relationship demonstrates resiliency in the wake of an event of radically changed circumstances is fundamentally pluralist in perspective. I am interested in measures of both efficiency and fairness and do not necessarily view these goals as mutually exclusive. Indeed, as Michael Heller and Hanoch Dagan have shown, property relationships that employ rules emphasizing democratic decision-making can enhance trust and cooperation and often lead in a virtuous circle to greater long-term efficiency. Property regimes that demonstrate resiliency in the face of radical change, I believe, will be distinguishable because they share all or some of the following virtues.

*Resilient Property Relationships Facilitate Quick Action to Preserve Common Resources and Employ Democratically-Oriented and Trust-Enhancing Decision-Making to Substantially Improve or Alter Those Resources*

It should come as no surprise to anyone who has observed media accounts of the recovery of New Orleans and the Gulf Coast that many people around the nation consider the speed of decision-making about whether and how to restore property resources and the ability of local institutions and communities to implement these basic restoration decisions quickly to be a fundamental characteristic of resiliency. Almost every major study of hurricane recovery efforts on the Gulf Coast implicitly assumes that quick decisions and rapid restoration of as many raw assets as possible is at least one of the most significant criteria for judging the effectiveness of private and public recovery efforts. I do not quibble with this emphasis on speed itself except to note that many commentators who implicitly criticize Katrina recovery efforts as taking too long forget to acknowledge that recovery from widespread disasters like Hurricane Katrina typically unfolds on a logarithmic scale. In other words, recovery from major disasters like Katrina will typically take decades, not years, to complete.[30] Nevertheless, if decisions about what resources are going to be preserved can be made relatively quickly, these decisions can facilitate recovery by allowing people to plan for the future with some degree of certainty, even if it may take time to implement these decisions.

The manner in which decisions about resource preservation, substantial alteration and improvement of shared resources, and exit and entrance rights are made may in the long run, however, be just as important as the speediness of those decisions and their implementation. Here it is important to recall the range of options that are available. A property regime can require unanimous consent for decisions of this kind of long-term magnitude. It can empower one person or a small group of elite leaders to make decisions for the entire group of participants. Or it can employ mechanisms of democratic decision-making that give all individuals with a stake in the resource an opportunity to have a *voice* in the decision-making process without giving any single person or interest group veto power or control over the decision-making. Which decision-making structure makes most sense will, of course, depend on the number of participants in the relationship, on the size and relative importance of the individual participants' stakes in the common resource, and on the degree of change the decision would bring about. Models of decision-making structures abound in property law, from the emphasis on unanimous decision-making in tenancy-in-common and co-ownership regimes to the controversial trend toward quasi-democratic self-governance in common interest community decision-making structures.[31] The experience of post-Katrina recovery efforts in Louisiana so far strongly suggests that democratic decision-making processes that are capable of building consensus and trust are much more likely to produce long-lasting community cooperation and lead to resource regeneration.

*Resilient Property Relationships Encourage Parties to Spread Risk and to Enlist Exogenous Institutional and Financial Resources to Respond to Radical Change*

The next virtue of a resilient property relationship is a tendency to spread risk, not just among the members of the relationship itself, but to outsiders, and thus to enlist exogenous financial and institutional resources that can be called upon to rebuild, improve, or alter the damaged resource at the heart of the property relationship after an event of radical change. Where do these exogenous resources

---

30    Lawrence J. Vale & Thomas J. Campanella, The Resilient City: How Modern Cities Recover from Disaster 336–37 (2005).

31    *Compare* Mitchell, *supra* note 29, at 512–23, *with* Dagan & Heller, *supra* note 27, at 590–96. Some observers of the decision-making regimes currently used in developer designed common interest communities (CICs) find models of coercion, punishment and control rather than collaboration and mutual concern. *See* Paula Franzese & Steven Siegal, *Trust and Community: The Common Interest Community as Metaphor and Paradox*, 72 Mo. L. Rev. 1111 (2007).

come from? Private insurance markets will obviously be a major source of these resources, along with publicly supported insurance networks and direct governmental aid. In the wake of Hurricane Katrina, despite the innumerable disputes between property owners and their insurers, proceeds from private insurance policies covering residential and commercial property damage and from the National Flood Insurance Program have provided close to sixty billion dollars to fund rebuilding and restoration on the Gulf Coast.[32] Because this massive influx of private and quasi-private insurance proceeds was still not enough to rebuild all of the damaged or destroyed resources on the Gulf Coast, private and public property owners (state and local governments) have been able to call upon billions of dollars more of government grants and assistance to make up the gap between the cost of rebuilding and restoration and available insurance proceeds.[33]

Perhaps the biggest question that property owners and participants in property regimes will face in any place that has suffered catastrophic destruction resulting from an event like Hurricane Katrina is how will they be able to spread risk or enlist exogenous resources in the future. If exogenous institutions and market players will not or cannot insure against the risk of future catastrophic events occurring at affordable premiums, then communities and property regime participants will have to develop endogenous mechanisms to spread risk and create reserve pools that can be called on to respond to future events of catastrophic change.[34]

### Resilient Property Relationships Seek Economies of Scale and New Opportunities in Responding to Radical Change

A third major characteristic of resilient property relationships is that they seek the benefits of economies of scale in responding to events of radical change. If the participants in a property relationship are left to respond to the destruction of a resource completely on their own, or if their individual shares are small and fragmented, they may not be able to muster the money or expertise necessary

---

32    Commonly cited figures are $40 billion in private insurance payments and $15.7 billion in National Flood Insurance Program payments resulting from Hurricane Katrina alone. Michael Lewis, *The National Catastrophe Casino*, N.Y. TIMES MAG., Aug. 26, 2007, at 28.

33    The biggest components of this direct federal government assistance for the Gulf Coast areas impacted by the 2005 hurricane season include $7 billion in FEMA Public Assistance (used to rebuild local government infrastructure), $16.7 billion in HUD Community Development Block Grants, and $10.3 billion in Small Business loans. In addition, the federal government allocated $9.7 billion in IRS tax benefits to areas impacted by the 2005 hurricane season. *See* JENNIFER PIKE, GULF GOV. REPORTS: SPENDING FEDERAL DISASTER AID 2 (Nelson A. Rockefeller Inst. of Gov. and the Pub. Affairs Research Council of Louisiana 2007), *available at* www.rockinst.org/gulfgov.

34    This is the risky path that the State of Florida has recently embarked upon to respond to the state's property insurance crisis by creating a state-subsidized pool of $28 billion in catastrophe insurance coverage. Lewis, *supra* note 32, at 51.

to rebuild or restore that resource, let alone alter or adapt it creatively to new circumstances. On the other hand, if the property relationship applies to a large enough set of resources or if the resources of a number of property relationships or property owners can be pooled together, it is often easier to call upon exogenous resources to aid in recovery or to provide insurance against future risks. In short, scale itself can be a crucial factor in whether a property relationship can adapt to radical change. It is important to note here, though, that large size is not alone a guarantee of resilience. As the successes of some small businesses in post-Katrina New Orleans show, sometimes small, nimble property relationships are able to adapt to radically changed circumstances remarkably well, sometimes even more robustly than large, national or multi-national entities which fail to seize new local opportunities or cannot alter their traditional practices or other operations quickly enough to respond to new conditions.[35]

*Resilient Property Relationships Facilitate Exit in Ways That Encourage Trust and Cooperation and Honor Past Commitments*

The last two virtues of resilient property relationships reflect both utilitarian and justice based theories of property law. First, as property theorists Hanoch Dagan and Michael Heller have shown, one of the central characteristics of any property regime that hopes to promote core liberal values such as the protection of individual autonomy and liberty is that it offers robust protection of its participants' exit rights. This robust protection of exit is crucial because exit rights can serve as an invaluable defense mechanism against harmful, invasive and opportunistic actions of other participants or to discipline other participants and encourage trust and cooperation. At the same time, however, healthy property regimes do not have to protect exit absolutely. They can and often will impose some soft and flexible restraints on participants' exit rights if those restraints are designed to promote trust and cooperation among all members of the property regime.[36] Examples of these soft restraints on exit might include time delays that give participants a chance to think carefully about the consequences of exit (for example the waiting periods imposed on spouses seeking to obtain a divorce), rights of first refusal granted to non-exiting participants to buy out exiting participants' property interests (for example as some states require when a minority co-owner seeks partition of a co-owned asset),[37] or might even take the form of mild exit taxes. In the context of radically changed circumstances, well protected exit rights (and sometimes

---

35   MICHAEL A. TURNER ET AL., RECOVERY, RENEWAL & RESILIENCY: GULF COAST SMALL BUSINESSES TWO YEARS LATER, POLITICAL & ECONOMIC RESEARCH COUNCIL 4, 14 (2007) (reporting that one in four small businesses in Katrina-impacted areas of the Gulf Coast reported increased revenues since the 2005 hurricanes and that this strength was especially prevalent in the demolition and construction sectors).

36   Dagan & Heller, *supra* note 27, at 567–70, 597, 604–10.

37   *See, e.g.*, LA. REV. STAT. ANN. § 9:1113 (2007).

cooperation enhancing limitations on exit rights) can likewise play an important role in discouraging property relationship participants from opportunistically exploiting new conditions too easily and in protecting individual liberty interests when individual participants decide to leave but wish to preserve the economic value of their prior investments. At the same time, if exit rights are too absolute or too easily manipulated by a participant with much greater power in a property relationship (for example when a landlord seeks to evict a residential tenant), we will see that absolute and unfettered exit rights can be a source of instability and vulnerability.

*Resilient Property Relationships Facilitate Entrance for Those Who Wish to Re-enter and Spread Access to Resources More Widely and Equitably*

If resilient property relationships afford participants the opportunity to *exit* on terms that honor their prior investments and commitments and promote cooperation and trust, it may not come as a complete surprise that they also provide those who were forced to leave involuntarily meaningful opportunities to re-enter the relationship and provide opportunities for other individuals to gain access to property anew. Eduardo Peñalver and Joseph Singer have both written eloquently on this subject and their fundamental insights about the nature of property are important to remember when we consider how property regimes can and should respond to radical change.[38] In essence, Peñalver and Singer teach us that the vision of negative liberty that justifies protecting exit rights robustly is only half the story of property law. Human beings are rarely, if ever, entirely self-sufficient autonomous creatures. We need and depend on relationships with many other persons and institutions in order to live secure and meaningful lives. In fact, the social norms and commitments that underscore our social lives often make "exit" a very costly or impractical option for many individuals. Peñalver and Singer instead urge us to judge property relationships (and property regimes more broadly) by how well they facilitate entrance into community or promote access to vital resources. Not only will promoting entrance and access to property bestow undeniable individual benefits on the new participant in a property regime, but this will lead to numerous indirect benefits flowing to society at large. Property ownership, as many social commentators observe, tends to "anchor individuals" in what legal historians have called "the structure and power of virtue."[39] It also promotes strong social attachments to neighborhoods and community, leads to greater involvement in politics, and can lay the groundwork for numerous repeat beneficial transactions involving property.

---

38    Eduardo Peñalver, *Property as Entrance*, 91 Va. L. Rev. 1889 (2005); Joseph William Singer, *After the Flood: Equality and Humanity in Property Regimes*, 52 Loy. L. Rev. 243 (2006).

39    Gregory Alexander, Commodity & Property 31 (1979) (quoting Joyce Appleby, Capitalism and a New Order: The Republican Vision of the 1790's, at 9 (1984)).

But to realize the full benefits of this kind of virtuous cycle of property ownership, it is crucial that we give all members of society access to at least some minimum level of property in exchange for their commitment to participate as an active working member of society. An event that produces radically changed circumstances and destabilizes property relationships is a perfect opportunity to try to spread access to property more broadly because at such moments we are all reminded of just how vulnerable each of us would be if we were truly autonomous individuals unable to count on the support of friends, family, institutions, and government itself. As Joseph Singer in particular urges us to remember, our individual resiliency and the resiliency of our property relationships will be enhanced if we spread access to property more broadly and thus instill in more people the sense of power, virtue, and commitment to others that property ownership can entail.

With all these ideal characteristics of a resilient property regime in mind then, I have examined how several types of property relationships have fared under the pressure of radical change that Hurricane Katrina wrought in New Orleans and the Gulf Coast. Although a comprehensive study of the dialectic between property relationships and radical change would have to encompass many kinds of property relationships (including co-ownership, corporate ownership, life estates and future interests, common interest communities, and marital property relationships, just to name a few) my initial research has addressed two of the most common property relationships that a vast majority of Americans will encounter at some point in their lives. Those relationships are between a landlord and tenant and between a homeowner/mortgagor and a lender/mortgagee.

**Landlord and Tenant Relationships: Resiliency and Vulnerability**

As I discussed earlier, the relationship between a landlord and a tenant, a lessor and a lessee, is usually understood as an essentially *voluntary* and *finite* relationship. The duration may be relatively short—as in a month to month or year-long residential lease—or it might be much longer—as in a commercial or ground lease. Although there is always the possibility of renewal of the lease for another term, at common law, the tenant is understood as holding a finite possessory interest, either for the lease term, or, if the lease is at will, until either landlord or tenant elects to terminate. The landlord is understood as holding a kind of reversionary interest of some longer duration. In the civil law, leases are understood to be essentially contractual in nature, a bilateral agreement between lessor and lessee, rather than a transfer of a possessory estate in land. Regardless of how a lease is visualized in formal terms, its great advantage is that by decoupling possession from ownership it allows a tenant to obtain the benefits of actual physical use and possession of the leased premises without having to incur the costs and risks of purchasing a perpetual interest. The landlord can likewise obtain an immediate economic return by allowing someone else who values the use and possession of the property more than he currently does to have a short-term possessory interest while still preserving the potential for capital appreciation.

When a landlord and tenant encounter an event that produces radically changed circumstances, it is not easy to predict whether the relationship will survive. Resiliency will often depend on the degree of care the parties took to plan for such an event by engaging in detailed lease negotiation and drafting. Resiliency will also depend on the nature of the relationship itself and the surrounding market conditions.

My research into how landlord and tenant relationships have been affected by Hurricane Katrina reveals several broad trends.[40] First, in the commercial lease arena, it is important to observe that because of the uncertainties and frequently harsh consequences of common law and civil law default rules, the vast majority of commercial landlords and tenants will have drafted detailed lease clauses that address the rights and obligations of either party in the event that the leased premises is seriously damaged by a casualty causing event such as a hurricane. These provisions will typically assign responsibility for repair of the leased premises to one party depending on the level of destruction to the improvements, will often provide for rights of termination in the event of complete destruction, and will usually designate which party is responsible for maintaining commercial property insurance and specify how insurance proceeds are to be distributed in the event of a covered loss. This kind of private ordering tends to make common law principles or statutory default rules relatively unimportant.[41]

Moreover, as a result of this extensive private ordering, litigation and reported disputes about repair obligations and termination rights in the commercial lease context have been relatively rare post-Katrina. When such disputes have arisen, courts have tended to enforce contract terms strictly despite the radical change brought by Hurricane Katrina. In one recent case involving a commercial lease that specifically required the tenant—a regional cafeteria chain—to repair and reconstruct the leased improvements in the event of a casualty and provided for rent abatement while the premises were unfit for occupancy, the court held that the landlord was justified in evicting the tenant six months after Hurricane Katrina severely damaged the leased premises. The court found that the tenant had enjoyed more than enough time to decide whether to repair the premises and actually commence those repairs, even though it had been busy repairing forty-six out of its fifty-two other restaurants that had been damaged as a result of Hurricanes Katrina, Rita, and Jeanne in 2005.[42] In other cases, courts have similarly enforced contractual provisions of ground leases and required commercial tenants to repair

---

40  *See* Lovett, *Property and Radically Changed Circumstances*, *supra* note 7, at 495–515.

41  See 1 MILTON R. FRIEDMAN & PATRICK A. RANDOLPH, JR., FRIEDMAN ON LEASES §§ 9.1–9.12 (5th ed. 2004).

42  Carrolton Cent. Plaza Assocs. v. Piccadilly Rests., 952 So. 2d 756 (La. Ct. App. 2007).

or reconstruct major improvements that were partially or totally destroyed by Katrina.[43]

In commercial lease situations in which the leased premises were not damaged but landlord and tenant faced radically different market conditions as a result of Hurricane Katrina, we find another unexpected phenomenon—some landlords sought to accommodate long-term commercial tenants rather than terminate leases. In a market like New Orleans' French Quarter, for instance, where the post-Katrina decline in tourism caused many commercial tenants' revenues to fall dramatically, some landlords resisted terminating leases, even though their tenants were potentially in default on rent, because they were unsure that a replacement tenant could easily be found. Instead of terminating the leases, it appears that some landlords cut back on rent obligations to give their commercial tenants a chance to survive the downturn in the tourism industry. This was particularly true if the tenant could still be counted on to at least pay the quickly rising premiums for commercial property insurance.[44] In short, it seems that even when the rights and responsibilities of commercial landlords and tenants are carefully negotiated, these parties sometimes will try to accommodate each other's needs when they are both threatened by the economic dislocation caused by an event of radically changed circumstances.

In residential leases, we see an entirely different set of issues and trends. Here, careful *ex ante* negotiation about repair, reconstruction, and lease termination rights is much less likely to occur. Consequently, residential tenants in particular will often rely on statutory rules designed to offer them some minimal level of protection in the event that their apartments or rented homes are rendered uninhabitable because of some major casualty or if they are denied access because of some unexpected contingency such as a mandatory evacuation order. While a residential tenant is not likely to be responsible for repairing a damaged apartment or house, and in fact will likely be able to abandon the premises or terminate the lease if the apartment or house is no longer habitable, residential tenants may have little leverage to demand that a recalcitrant landlord make the repairs that would enable him to return to his home. In Louisiana (and to some extent in Mississippi as well), this predicament arises because even though a landlord has a statutorily implied duty to maintain the premises in a habitable condition, the tenant is not allowed to remain in possession of the leased premises and withhold rent from the lessor to put economic pressure on the lessor to make major necessary repairs. This leaves a residential tenant who cannot afford to make the repairs himself without any meaningful remedies other than to move out.[45]

---

43   Schwegmann Family Trust No. 2 v. KFC Nat'l Mgmt. Co., 2007 WL 60971, at *3–4 (E.D. La. Jan. 5, 2007); Tetra Techs. v. La. Fruit Co., 2007 WL 54814, at *6 (E.D. La. Jan. 5, 2007).

44   Lovett, *Property and Radically Changed Circumstances, supra* note 7, at 512.

45   *See* Lovett, *Property and Radically Changed Circumstances, supra* note 7, at 501– 07. In Louisiana, the tenant can stay in possession and withhold rent only if the landlord

Finally, as numerous journalists and legal academics have pointed out, summary eviction rules can be and have been quite easily manipulated by residential landlords eager to terminate leases for apartments that were not seriously damaged by Hurricane Katrina. Even though these rules are designed to provide some minimal due process protection for tenants, landlords' ability to manipulate them with relative ease allowed them to exit from their lease obligations and seize new market opportunities to charge higher rents to new tenants. Meanwhile their tenants, who were often displaced from New Orleans at great distances and often had trouble communicating with their landlords, could not gain access to their apartments to recover their belongings before they were removed and were frustrated in their attempts to renew their rent payments and revive their leases.[46] Of course, sometimes tenants are less than diligent in their efforts to find their landlords and maintain their lease payments even when their apartments become accessible. And often, and as one recent case shows, both the landlord and the tenant each share some blame for the collapse of their lease relationship.[47] What an examination of residential landlord and tenant relationships reveals in general, though, is that the residential landlord usually has considerably stronger opportunities to exit from an existing lease and enter new lease relationships, whereas residential tenants, especially low to moderate income ones, are particularly vulnerable to eviction and have trouble regaining access to affordable housing once it is lost.

## Mortgagor and Mortgagee Relationships: Surprising Resiliency

Just as with a lease, a mortgage creates a *voluntary* property relationship that normally has a well-defined *finite* duration, even though its term may be extended or may be subject to early termination in the event of pre-payment by the mortgagor or foreclosure by the mortgagee resulting from a borrower default. When an event brings about radically changed circumstances—for example, when

---

refuses to make requested necessary repairs *and* the tenant pays for the reasonable costs of the repairs himself. LA. CIV. CODE ANN. art. 2694 (2004). This remedy is of limited value, of course, if the cost of repairs are beyond the tenant's means. In Mississippi, the rule is essentially the same, but the tenant can only make repairs and deduct rent if the cost of repairs is less than one month's rent. MISS. CODE ANN. §§ 89-8-13(2), 89-8-15 (West 1999). Even in states that permit tenants to withhold rent more frequently for violations of the warranty of habitability, landlords sometimes will just absorb this loss, wait for a lease to terminate, and then charge a higher rent to another vulnerable tenant. *See* Mary Marsh Zulack, *If You Prompt Them, They Will Rule: The Warranty of Habitability Meets the New Court Information Systems*, 40 J. MARSHALL L. REV. 395 (2007).

46   See Erin Bohacek, *Comment, A Disastrous Effect: Hurricane Katrina's Impact on Louisiana Landlord-Tenant Law and the Need for Legislative and Judicial Action*, 52 LOY. L. REV. 877, 880–81, 898–904 (2006); Lovett, *Property and Radically Changed Circumstances, supra* note 7, at 507–10.

47   Sciacca v. Ives, 952 So. 2d 762 (La. Ct. App. 2007).

a hurricane destroys or damages the improvements that often constitute a large part of a mortgagee's collateral and causes widespread economic dislocation in a community—a number of problems may arise for both parties to the relationship. These questions can be relatively simple: What should happen if the borrower temporarily becomes delinquent in making her mortgage payments because she loses her job or because she has to rent another home in another city while her own community rebuilds its basic infrastructure? And they can be complex: Does the mortgagor have a duty to rebuild the damaged real estate? Who has control over insurance proceeds, the mortgagor or the mortgagee? Can a mortgagee insist that insurance proceeds be applied to pay down the mortgage instead of being used for rebuilding?

In the aftermath of the 2005 Hurricane season, many politicians and observers expected to see a veritable wave of mortgage foreclosures sweep across the Gulf Coast, especially in the areas of Southeast Louisiana and the Mississippi Gulf Coast hard hit by Katrina. The assumption was that borrowers, either due to job losses or the need to pay for replacement housing or to replace other essential items of personal property, would not be able to make their mortgage payments. In addition, it was assumed that foreclosing mortgage holders would end up with large inventories of heavily damaged mortgaged properties whose post-storm values would be far less than their pre-storm values. One of the most ambitious Gulf Coast recovery plans proposed in the United States Congress was largely premised on this fear of a crisis in mortgage relationships and was designed primarily to provide an equitable buy-out plan that would have benefited borrowers and lenders in roughly equal ways.[48]

In the end, this foreclosure and mortgage crisis never materialized even though the number of borrowers who became temporarily delinquent on their mortgage payments did shoot up dramatically in the first months after the hurricanes. In fact, despite the dramatic rise in mortgage loan delinquency in Louisiana and Mississippi, for the remainder of 2005 and for practically all of 2006, foreclosure rates in both states remained remarkably low—in fact, lower than, or at most equal to, their pre-Katrina foreclosure rates. In the greater New Orleans metropolitan area, in fact, the actual number of foreclosures that occurred in all of 2006 was only one-third of the lowest annual number of foreclosures in the last twenty years. In 2007 the greater New Orleans metropolitan area foreclosure rate continued to be quite modest by historical standards, recording only one fifth of the total number of foreclosures that occurred in the worst years of the late 1980's oil bust. In Orleans Parish, the foreclosure numbers in 2006 were even lower on a relative basis and continued to be moderate throughout all of 2007.[49] The surprising phenomenon

---

48    Louisiana Recovery Corporation Act, H.R. 4100, § 106(h), 109th Cong. (2005); John A. Lovett, *Rebuilding a Region: Housing Recovery Efforts in the Wake of Katrina and Rita*, 20 Prob. & Prop. 49, 51 (2006).

49    For detailed statistics, *see* Lovett, *Property and Radically Changed Circumstances*, *supra* note 7, at 517 & 520. *See also* A. Brooke Overby, *Mortgage Foreclosure in Post-*

of a sudden spike in mortgage debt delinquency and the concurrent remarkable stability in foreclosure rates and inventory in post-Katrina Louisiana through the end of 2007 is depicted in Figure 2.1 below. What accounts for this apparent resiliency in mortgage relationships?

One reason is simply the presence of large amounts of exogenous resources that could be called upon to rebuild damaged property. Recall that these resources came in three distinct forms: (1) billions of dollars of standard homeowner casualty insurance proceeds for damage attributable to wind destruction; (2) billions of dollars in federally-supported National Flood Insurance Program (NFIP) proceeds; and (3) billions of dollars in Community Development Block Grants (CDBG) funds provided by the federal government to Louisiana and Mississippi that were used to provide grants to assist individual homeowners who were either completely uninsured or underinsured for their hurricane-related losses.[50] It is true, of course, that numerous lawsuits have been filed against private insurers alleging that they underpaid homeowners, or denied claims, or sought to shift too much of their losses to the NFIP flood program. It is also true that Louisiana's Road Home homeowner assistance program, funded by CDBG funds, has been notoriously slow and inefficient in delivering grants to individual homeowners. But in the end, we should not lose sight of the huge sums of exogenous resources that were made available to homeowners—borrowers and mortgagors—to rebuild their damaged homes. And we should also not lose sight of the fact that homeowners who were mortgagors—and were thus contractually obligated to maintain standard homeowner's insurance policies and often flood insurance policies as well—were often able to call upon more exogenous resources than non-mortgagor homeowners who were more likely to find themselves underinsured or completely uninsured.

---

*Katrina New Orleans*, 48 B.C. L. Rev. 851, 859–61 (2007) (confirming this startlingly low foreclosure rates in Orleans Parish in the year after Katrina based on a detailed study of public records filings). In 2007, the number of completed foreclosures in both Orleans Parish and the greater New Orleans area did increase some, but the total numbers were still well below historical averages. In Louisiana the total number of households in foreclosure was also well below the national average, with Louisiana having the tenth lowest percentage of households in foreclosure according to one report. *See* Latter & Blum Inc. Realtors Report, *available at* http://www.realestate.uno.edu. (providing detailed numbers for Orleans Parish and Greater New Orleans and comparisons between Louisiana and other states); Kate Moran, *No Boom, No Bust*, Times-Picayune (New Orleans), Mar. 5, 2008, at C-8 (noting that Louisiana had one of the lowest foreclosure rates in the country in January 2008 and attributing this to the absence of a speculative real estate boom, a flood of insurance money into the state, and the mortgage industry's forbearance policies discussed below).

50   *See supra* note 33 and accompanying text.

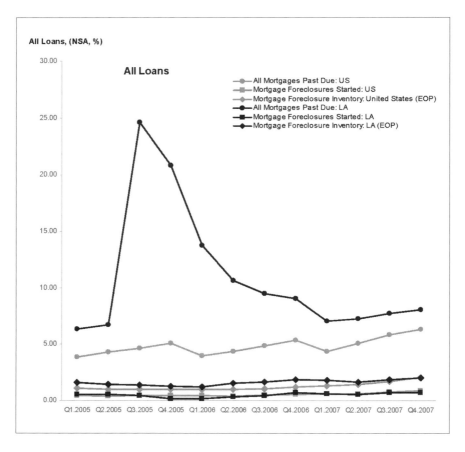

**Figure 2.1  Mortgage Delinquency Rates (U.S. and Louisiana)**
*Note*: All loans is not the sum of conventional and subprime.
*Source*: Mortgage Bankers Association, National Delinquency Survey. Reprinted with permission of the Greater New Orleans Community Data Center <gnocdc.org>.

Another reason for the relative stability and resiliency in mortgage relationships stems from an important, but probably underappreciated, change that occurred over the last thirty years regarding the rights and obligations of a mortgagor and a mortgagee with respect to rebuilding mortgaged property and the use of insurance proceeds. To appreciate this change, it is useful to ask first whether, after an event like Hurricane Katrina has caused its destruction, the mortgagor has a duty to rebuild damaged or destroyed improvements that might comprise the bulk of the mortgagee's collateral. Section 4.6 of the *Restatement of the Law of Property (Third): Mortgages (Restatement of Mortgages)* gives us an interesting answer: No! Although a mortgagor who fails to maintain and repair mortgaged real estate to prevent normal deterioration can usually be held liable for permissive waste and can thus face foreclosure or some other sanction, when repair of real estate is required because of "casualty damage or acts of third parties not the fault of the mortgagor," a failure to repair is *not* considered waste.[51] In this circumstance, the mortgagor is presumably left with a choice to repair the property or leave it in its dilapidated condition as long as he continues to make his mortgage payments. This surprising result might be explained by some deeply embedded altruistic instinct which recognizes that a mortgagor should not be penalized because some chance event beyond his control has damaged or destroyed the mortgaged property. More likely, though, it is explained by the fact that modern mortgage law and the *Restatement of Mortgages* assume that all reasonable mortgagees will require the mortgagor to carry some appropriate amount of casualty insurance to protect the value of the mortgagee's security interest in the case of an accidental casualty.

The next question then that arises in a mortgage relationship when an event like Katrina happens is what to do with the insurance proceeds. Is the mortgagor entitled to use the proceeds to rebuild the real estate or can the mortgagee insist that the proceeds be applied to pay off or pay down the principal debt? Under traditional American common law, the presumption was that the mortgagee could make the election. In fact, many mortgage documents reflected this common law presumption favoring mortgagee discretion and courts enforced any contractual discretion in favor of the mortgagee quite strictly. There were two primary rationales for this rule. First, forcing the lender to allow the mortgagor to use the proceeds to rebuild would effectively convert the mortgage holder into the position of a construction lender, a status full of new risks for which it never bargained. Second, allowing the lender to use insurance proceeds to pay down the principal debt does not really harm the borrower after all because he still receives the benefit of having his debt reduced or eliminated. In the case of commercial mortgages, these presumptions and rules probably still make a good deal of sense because commercial borrowers should be able to, and in many cases will actually, negotiate for specific contract language addressing potential casualty loss and the use of insurance proceeds. Indeed, when disputes about application of insurance proceeds arise in commercial mortgage contexts, courts routinely and properly enforce express contract language giving lenders wide latitude to dictate the application of insurance proceeds.[52]

---

51   RESTATEMENT (THIRD) OF PROPERTY: MORTGAGES § 4.6(2) (1997).

52   *See* Patrick Randolph, *A Mortgagee's Interest in Casualty Loss Proceeds, Evolving Rules and Risks*, 32 REAL PROP. PROB. & TR. 1, 1–20 (1997); Lovett, *Doctrines of Waste*, *supra* note 8, at 1224–25; Strouse Greenberg Properties IV Ltd. Partnership v. CW Capital Asset Management LLC, 442 F. Supp. 2d 313, 321 (E.D. La. 2006) (enforcing express contractual language granting a mortgagee absolute discretion to apply $5 million in mortgage proceeds to reduce outstanding loan balance after multi-family apartment complex was destroyed by Hurricane Katrina).

In the context of residential mortgage loans for single family homes, however, these presumptions and rules have been challenged from three directions. First, several prominent judicial decisions have challenged the majority rule and asserted that borrowers, especially residential mortgagors, should be able to use the proceeds to rebuild their property.[53] After all, these decisions reason, this is the benefit that most homeowners expected to receive in exchange for paying their homeowners insurance premiums. In addition, these courts recognize that allowing lenders to apply insurance proceeds to the outstanding principal balance could have serious collateral consequences for the borrower. The homeowner mortgagor might now have to borrow funds at a higher rate of interest to refinance the rebuilding of his home and might also incur other indirect costs, such as having to pay rent for substitute housing while he searches for refinancing and begins to rebuild.

In the second challenge to the majority rule, Section 4.7 of the *Restatement of Mortgages* recognizes the merits of these minority view policy arguments and proposes a new rule unless the mortgage documents specifically provide for mortgagee discretion. As long as restoration of the real estate is "reasonably feasible within the term of the mortgage with the funds available from the insurance proceeds, together with any additional funds made available by the mortgagor," and "if after restoration the real estate's value will equal or exceed its value at the time the mortgage was made," then the *Restatement* proposes that "the mortgagee holds the funds received subject to a duty to apply them, at the mortgagor's request and upon reasonable conditions, toward restoration."[54] In other words, absent an express declaration to the contrary, there will be a presumption in favor of allowing the mortgagor-owner to use insurance proceeds to rebuild. As the comments to the *Restatement* explain, the goal here is to encourage mortgagees to cooperate with mortgagors on the project of rebuilding the mortgaged property as long as it is "feasible to do so."[55] The *Restatement* drafters do recognize that rebuilding is not always practical for a variety of reasons—zoning laws may have changed or new market conditions might render the real estate, even if restored, much less valuable than at the time the mortgage was created. But the cornerstone principle is that lenders should not be able to seize upon the fortuity of an accidental casualty to force the borrower into an involuntary prepayment or into refinancing at a higher interest rate. In their boldest statement, the *Restatement* drafters even suggest that sometimes a court might justifiably refuse to enforce an express mortgage clause that gives the mortgagee the right to claim insurance proceeds or negates any duty to allow rebuilding on the ground that such a clause forms an unconscionable contract or because enforcement would violate the mortgagee's duty of good faith and fair dealing.[56] Although this may be a step that many courts will be unwilling

---

53  Schoolcraft v. Ross, 146 Cal. Rptr. 57 (1978); Starkman v. Sigmond, 446 A.2d 1249 (N.J. Super. Ct. 1982); Kreshek v. Sperling, 204 Cal. Rptr. 30 (1984).

54  Restatement (Third) of Property: Mortgages § 4.7 (1997).

55  *Id.* at cmt.d.

56  *Id.* at cmt.e.

to follow, the fact that it was suggested at all by the prominent drafters of the *Restatement of Mortgages* (Professors Grant Nelson and Dale Whitman) suggests the degree to which thinking about insurance proceeds in the context of mortgage relationships has changed.

The third major challenge to the majority rule comes from mortgage documents themselves, particularly from widespread use of the Fannie Mae/Freddie Mac Uniform Mortgage—Deed of Trust Covenants for single family residences. This instrument, which has been widely adopted by lenders who want to assure that the mortgages they originate will be acceptable for sale into the all important secondary mortgage market, provides that unless the borrower and lender agree otherwise, any insurance proceeds "shall be applied to restoration or repair of the Property, if the restoration or repair is economically feasible and Lender's security is not lessened."[57] The same section of this instrument also gives the lender an opportunity to inspect the property to make sure progress on repair or reconstruction is being completed and the right to disburse the insurance funds either in a lump sum or periodically as rebuilding progress is completed, just as in a typical construction loan.

When all three of these challenges to the common law assumptions regarding application of insurance proceeds are taken into account, it becomes apparent that a significant change in norms relating to mortgage relationships has occurred. The new norms, which encourage and favor practices of mutual accommodation and cooperation between mortgagor and mortgagee, probably helped to stabilize mortgage relationships in the wake of the 2005 hurricane season. In fact, one Florida judge deciding a mortgagee–mortgagor dispute about application of insurance proceeds in the wake of Hurricane Jeanne specifically noted how most borrowers and lenders in that court's community were able to work out an equitable process for allowing borrowers to use insurance proceeds to rebuild their damaged homes and how this practice facilitated recovery of the entire community affected by that hurricane.[58]

One more reason for the relative stability and resiliency of mortgage relationships in the wake of the catastrophic 2005 hurricane season can be found in the risk spreading structure of the current home loan industry itself. Even with the substantial insurance proceeds that eventually became available to repair damaged homes or pay down loan balances, many mortgagor-homeowners undoubtedly faced potential default situations in the immediate months after the hurricanes because they had lost their jobs or suffered other financial strains. Fortunately, though, mortgage holders generally did not seize on these defaults and commence foreclosure. Instead, the extraordinary risk-spreading capacity of the secondary residential mortgage market enabled mortgage holders to forbear on thousands

---

57  *Fannie Mae/Freddie Mac Uniform Mortgage—Deed of Trust Covenants—Single Family, Part* 5, *in* GRANT S. NELSON & DALE WHITMAN, REAL ESTATE TRANSFER, FINANCE AND DEVELOPMENT: CASES AND MATERIALS 1202, 1208 (7th ed. 2006).

58   Bean v. Prevatt, 935 So. 2d 557, 560 (Fla. Dist. Ct. App. 2006).

of technically delinquent mortgage loans. Both Fannie Mae and Freddie Mac, huge government-supported players in the secondary market, implemented year-long blanket moratoria on residential mortgage foreclosures in Louisiana parishes affected by Hurricanes Katrina and Rita and during this period also prevented or discouraged mortgage servicers from collecting prepayment penalties when borrowers paid off defaulted mortgages, regardless of the source of funds used.[59] These practices allowed mortgagors to make insurance claims and collect insurance payments, reestablish employment, and work out arrangements for resumption of their mortgage payments without having to face foreclosure or else permitted them to pay off mortgages with insurance proceeds or funds collected from government compensation programs without facing stiff prepayment penalties.

By recounting this story of surprising resiliency and stability in mortgage relationships, I do not mean to discount the likelihood that many homeowner-mortgagors did encounter serious hardships after Hurricane Katrina even if they managed to avoid an actual foreclosure. Undoubtedly, some borrower/homeowners who were underinsured or whose insurance settlements were insufficient to finance complete rebuilding may have been strong-armed by opportunistic mortgage holders to pay off or pay down their loan balances to avoid either foreclosure or onerous penalties and this may have left them with few resources with which to commence rebuilding. Furthermore, even though low cost SBA loans were available for some homeowners as a means of refinancing, and even though various CDBG funded homeowner grant programs (like Louisiana's infamous Road Home program) were designed to fill in the gap between the true cost of rebuilding homes and actual insurance proceeds, administrative delays in implementing these programs undoubtedly left many homeowners in difficult financial straits in which paying off a home mortgage debt may have seemed like the lesser of several evils.[60] But even taking into account these undoubted hardships, the overall story of mortgagor–mortgagee relationships in the wake of Hurricane Katrina is one of surprising resiliency rather than catastrophic failure.

---

59    Both Freddie Mac's and Fannie Mae's forbearance periods lasted until August 31, 2006—a full year after Katrina. *See generally* Lovett, *Property and Radically Changed Circumstances, supra* note 7, at 523–24; Overby, *supra* note 49, at 885–87, n.163 (providing even more detail on forbearance policies of the government supported entities). *See also* Robin Paul Malloy, *The Secondary Mortgage Market: A Catalyst for Change in Real Estate Transactions*, 39 Sw. L.J. 991 (1986).

60    For a more detailed account of these homeowner assistance programs, including Louisiana's Road Home program, see Lovett, *Property and Radically Changed Circumstances, supra* note 7, at 532–42.

**A Temporary Conclusion: The Enduring Stickiness of Property Relationships**

This brief sketch of how property relationships respond to events like Hurricane Katrina presents a more hopeful outlook than what some other commentators have discerned in the wreckage of the 2005 hurricane season. Not all property relationships are doomed to failure. If the participants manage to see each other as partners in a long-term relationship marked by mutual vulnerability and mutual need, they might be able to create practices and structures that emphasize accommodation, consensus building, and cooperation toward the goal of rebuilding and improving shared resources. On the other hand, if the participants view an event producing radically changed circumstances merely as an opportunity to exit from one property relationship and replace it with another, more profitable one, then weaker parties will continue to be vulnerable.

If we zoom out and focus on the health of an entire city that was devastated by Hurricane Katrina and the property relationship between the city and its residents, we also might see glimmers of hope. Although the core of New Orleans, Orleans Parish, has suffered a significant population loss, the fact that it appears to have regained more than two-thirds of its pre-Katrina households is still an amazing success story considering that the city was almost entirely depopulated for two months after the city flooded. Similarly, the fact that the entire New Orleans metropolitan area has somehow regained about eighty-seven percent of its pre-Katrina households suggests that talk of simply abandoning New Orleans and moving its citizens elsewhere was nothing more than an excuse for several prominent academics to show off their cold and dehumanizing theories.[61]

What accounts then for the city and region's recovery, incomplete as it still may be? Perhaps more than anything—more important than the billions of dollars in insurance proceeds and billions of dollars in federal rebuilding assistance and grants—is the inherent "stickiness" of so many New Orleans' residents' attachment to their city and region.[62] As geographer Richard Campanella has shown, New Orleanians have a remarkably high propensity for local nativity, that is, for remaining as residents in the city or state of their birth.[63] In fact, according to the 2000 census, seventy-seven percent of the City of New Orleans' residents were Louisiana-born. And, as anyone who has spent time in New Orleans beyond the tourist zone of the French Quarter knows, this deep attachment to community and place extends to many New Orleanians who were not born here, but who came to the city at some point in their lives and became so ensnared by its rich culture that they, too, have found it difficult to imagine living anywhere else.

---

61    See Lovett, *Property and Radically Changed Circumstances, supra* note 7, at 464 n.2; NEW ORLEANS INDEX (April 16 2008), *supra* note 1, at 6.

62    Peñalver, *supra* note 38, at 1922.

63    RICHARD CAMPANELLA, GEOGRAPHIES OF NEW ORLEANS: URBAN FABRICS BEFORE THE STORM 403 (2006).

One of the most bitter ironies of Katrina, though, was that the areas of New Orleans that flooded most extensively also tended to be the neighborhoods with the highest incidence of this local nativity. These included the heavily African American Lower Ninth Ward and Seventh Ward, but also the heavily white, largely working-class communities of St. Bernard Parish, the more affluent white neighborhood of Lakeview, the more racially-mixed neighborhoods of Broadmoor and Gentilly, and the black and Vietnamese middle-class neighborhoods of New Orleans East. All of these areas, despite their diverse ethnic and class demographics, had high local nativity rates. In contrast, the unflooded areas of the city—the French Quarter, the Garden District, the uptown University areas—all had the city's lowest levels of local nativity.[64] This was a bitter pill, but it is also a silver lining. For it is precisely in some of the hard hit communities with high levels of local nativity—in Broadmoor, in pockets of Gentilly, in the Holy Cross area of the Lower Ninth Ward, in the Versailles and Village de l'Est neighborhoods of New Orleans East—that we are now finding a remarkable resiliency, despite all the obstacles that their residents continue to face.

New Orleans and its property relationships suffered a terrible blow. But it and they did not die. Its residents, like participants in other kinds of property relationships who share long-standing bonds to each other and ties to common resources, both tangible and intangible, are struggling to help each other recover even when local government recovery efforts have been fitful at best. Like Sisyphus, we keep pushing the boulder up the levee. Perhaps out of sheer obstinacy, and just perhaps out of love as well.

---

64   *Id.*

# Chapter 3
# Land Use Planning by Design and by Disaster

Frank S. Alexander[*]

The goal of planning is to anticipate and to guide. Anticipating is a best guess based upon an understanding of the past. Guiding is making a set of choices about the good for the future. Anticipating tends towards the empirical; guiding tends towards the normative. To engage in planning is to make judgments as we anticipate and as we guide. Our judgments are rarely perfect, not just because we are human, but because the past is only a rough predictor of the future and our conceptions of the good are caught in the constant tension of "Good for Whom?" Nothing focuses our attention as much as a disaster, for a disaster is the quintessential misjudgment about the anticipation and guiding at the core of our planning.

Hurricane Katrina, on August 29, 2005, was an overwhelming tragedy in the loss of life, the injuries, the illness, and the suffering. It was an unparalleled challenge to an American metropolis, with devastation and paralysis across eighty percent of the City of New Orleans. With the sister hurricanes Rita and Wilma following in a matter of weeks, over 1.2 million housing units were damaged across the Gulf Coast.[1]

The City of New Orleans and other affected communities in Louisiana, Mississippi, Alabama, and Florida, their residents and their leaders, responded courageously in the immediate triage of disaster response. They moved rapidly to restore, rebuild, and recreate their communities. They once again began planning by anticipating and guiding. This time, however, the anticipation of the future is informed by the recent past, and the guiding poses new sets of choices.

Land use planning since the early twentieth century tends to be two dimensional in nature in each of the functions of anticipation and guidance. In both contexts the assumption is that there are two variables: market conditions (the relative

---

&ast;   Copyright 2007, Frank S. Alexander. Portions of this chapter also appear in Frank S. Alexander, *Louisiana Land Reform in the Storms' Aftermath*, 53 LOYOLA L. REV. (2008) (used here with permission).

1   U.S. Dept. of Hous. & Urban Dev., Office of Policy, Dev. & Res., *The Impact of Hurricanes Katrina, Rita and Wilma on the Gulf Coast Housing Stock*, *in* U.S. HOUSING MARKET CONDITIONS (2006), *available at* www.huduser.org/periodicals/ushmc/spring06/USHML_06Q1_ch1.pdf.

supply and demand for different uses) and governmental regulation of use through zoning. These may be amplified by other governmental requirements (housing and building codes) or by private land use controls (community associations), but the perspective remains just two dimensional—use governmental regulatory powers to guide anticipated market conditions. The experience of New Orleans both pre-Katrina and post-Katrina suggests the need for a third dimension in land use planning—that of controlling land for the future. In a manner first suggested by Professor Charles Haar in 1971,[2] the very process of anticipating and guiding needs to be enhanced by a land use structure that permits inventories of land to be held in reserve in order to respond to the shifts in market conditions and determinations of the social good. Land use planning in New Orleans would take a very different form if a "land bank" could provide a third dimension.

**New Orleans Pre-Katrina**

Land use planning in the City of New Orleans did not begin with Katrina recovery, and it will not end when public utility services are restored throughout its geographic area. This planning is inherently a dynamic process, and to anticipate the future requires a sense of New Orleans in the months and years prior to Katrina. With its centuries of history and richness of culture, New Orleans in 2004 and 2005 was already struggling with the lack of coordinated urban planning.

In the spring of 2004, the City of New Orleans and the New Orleans Neighborhood Development Collaborative solicited the assistance of the National Vacant Properties Campaign to identify strategies to address more effectively blighted and abandoned properties throughout the city.[3] The reports of the National Vacant Properties Campaign followed earlier reports recommending action on

---

2   *Wanted: Two Federal Levers for Urban Land Use – Land Banks and Urbank: Paper submitted to Subcomm. on Housing Panels, of H. Comm. on Banking and Currency*, 92d Cong. 927-940 (1971) (Charles M. Haar, Prof. of Law, Harvard Law School) [hereinafter Haar].

3   The National Vacant Properties Campaign was founded in 2002 by the Local Initiatives Support Corporation, the International City/County Management Association, and Smart Growth America. Its initial work in New Orleans took place between May 2004 and February 2005. Two reports were issued by the Campaign team composed of myself, Evelyn Brown, Lisa Mueller Levy, and Joe Schilling. The initial report was entitled *New Orleans Technical Assessment and Assistance Project – Draft Report*, October 28, 2004 (23 pages). The final report was entitled *New Orleans Technical Assessment and Assistance Report: Recommended Actions to Facilitate Prevention, Acquisition, and Disposition of New Orleans' Blighted, Abandoned, and Tax Adjudicated Properties*, February 21, 2005 [hereinafter *New Orleans Technical Assistance Report*]. Copies of each of these reports are on file with the author. Portions of this chapter are derived from these reports.

blighted and abandoned properties.[4] According to the 2000 Census, New Orleans had an estimated 27,000 vacant units (defined as unoccupied structures).[5] In 2000, its 485,000 residents[6] inhabited a city built for over 650,000 people, and the abandoned and blighted housing stock resulting from years of population decline was a significant factor in decreasing the quality of life in neighborhoods across the City. The City of New Orleans estimated in 2004 that there were roughly 7,000 properties that had been adjudicated to the City for failure to pay taxes. Despite the lack of consistent definitions and an accurate count of vacant, abandoned, and blighted properties in New Orleans, by any definition and any count, a significant challenge existed for the City even before the devastation caused by Katrina, Rita, and Wilma.

In hindsight, especially when looking through the prism of Katrina, it becomes much clearer that the two dimensions of market forces and government regulations combined in unfortunate ways to exacerbate the abandonment and deterioration of housing and neighborhoods in New Orleans. The decline in population and the decrease in the demand for housing have obvious correlations and are likely mutually causative in nature. What is less obvious, but equally correlated, is how the absence of marketable and insurable title to properties itself encouraged flight and disinvestment. The lack of marketable and insurable title in New Orleans took three forms: "heir property," tax adjudicated property, and property in noncompliance with housing and building codes.

Relative to other urban communities, New Orleans in 2004 had a high percentage of residential properties "owned" by the same families over several generations. The ownership of this property passed down from one generation to the next usually without the benefit of probate and with the presence of potential clouds on title from unknown heirs. This "heir property" is most commonly found in lower income neighborhoods that do not confront the pressures and incentives of new construction and new mortgage financing which serve as triggers for re-examining title, and for correcting defects that would otherwise render title unmarketable and uninsurable.

The numerous problems that are caused by heir property are small in relation to the title problems created by the system of property tax enforcement in New Orleans. As was true of a large number of jurisdictions throughout the United

---

4   *See, e.g.*, Committee for a Better New Orleans, A Blueprint for a Better New Orleans (2001); *Improving Housing Policy and Practice* (Mtumishi St. Julien, November 2001); *Blighted Housing Task Force Report* (Nagin Transition Team: R. Stephanie Bruno & Wayne Neveu, co-chairs, May 2002). Copies of each of these reports are on file with the author.

5   U.S. Census, GCT-H5. General Housing Characteristics: 2000, Data Set: Census 2000 Summary File 1 (SF 1) 100-Percent Data.

6   U.S. Census, GCT-PH1. Population, Housing Units, Area, and Density: 2000, Data Set: Census 2000 Summary File 1 (SF 1) 100-Percent Data.

States in the twentieth century,[7] Louisiana continues to follow a tax foreclosure—or tax adjudication—process which does not involve a judicial proceeding or a judicial ruling on the finality of a tax sale. Tax delinquent property is auctioned at a public nonjudicial sale and is subject to a constitutional three-year right of redemption.[8] Property located in the City of New Orleans is subject only to an eighteen-month redemption period[9] if it is classified as abandoned[10] or blighted,[11] but unfortunately the definitions of abandoned or blighted are underinclusive with respect to the inventory of tax delinquent properties and are not consistent with one another. Properties not sold at a tax sale for the minimum bid of taxes, costs, and interest are automatically transferred to the parish or municipality,[12] but physical possession of the property requires yet another action.[13] Even more problematic than the length of the redemption period (which runs only from the date of recording of a tax sale deed) is the fact that full notice as required by the federal constitution[14] to property owners of the potential loss of the property is not given until the expiration of the redemption period.[15] Because there is no judicial ruling on the adequacy of the tax sales as part of the adjudication process, additional legal proceedings usually in the form of a quiet title action are essential in order to render title to property marketable and insurable.[16] As a consequence, property that is tax delinquent usually remains immune from forced transfers or investment by third parties for years after the date of the initial delinquency.

The third hindrance to marketable and insurable title to properties in New Orleans which reinforces the negative ties between declining market demand and neighborhood deterioration is the inadequacy of code enforcement proceedings. Most urban areas in the United States have housing codes or building codes that prescribe minimum standards for the condition of improvements. Furthermore code enforcement activities tend to be reactive in nature, with public inspectors responding to complaints from neighbors rather than targeting neighborhoods or zones for systematic enforcement. When property owners fail to remedy

---

7   *See generally* Frank S. Alexander, *Tax Liens, Tax Sales and Due Process*, 75 IND. L.J. 747 (2000).

8   LA. CONST. art. VII, § 25(B).

9   LA. CONST. art. VII, § 25(B)(2).

10   LA. REV. STAT. ANN. § 33:4720.12 (2006) ("abandoned" is defined as tax adjudicated to a local government, vacant, and not lawfully occupied).

11   LA. REV. STAT. ANN. § 33:4720.59 (2006) ("blighted" is defined as vacant, uninhabitable, or hazardous).

12   LA. REV. STAT. ANN. §§ 47:2186, 47:2251 (2006). Direct acquisition of tax adjudicated properties by the City of New Orleans is governed by LA. REV. STAT. ANN. § 47:2254 (2006).

13   LA. REV. STAT. ANN. §§ 33:2862, 47:2185 (2006).

14   U.S. CONST. amend. XIV.

15   *See* Jones v. Flowers, 547 U.S. 220 (2006); Mennonite Bd. of Missions v. Adams, 462 U.S. 791 (1983).

16   LA. REV. STAT. ANN. § 47:2228 (2006).

code violations local governments may use their own funds to cure the defects or demolish the improvements. Governmental action to remedy code violations becomes prohibitively expensive in the absence of an efficient and effective means of force repayment of the costs or a transfer of the property. In 2004, the year prior to Katrina, statutory amendments were enacted granting the City of New Orleans clearer authority to enforce a public lien for code enforcement expenditures as a senior priority lien on the property.[17]

Land use planning in the face of declining market demand and inefficient and ineffective governmental regulations is a daunting task. When the responsibilities for addressing blight and decay and fostering potential redevelopment are spread across separate agencies, departments, and authorities, coherent planning is virtually impossible. In the years prior to Katrina, New Orleans was a city suffering from population decline and the lack of a functioning real estate market in many core neighborhoods. The City did possess a strong toolbox of methods for individuals and organizations to acquire surplus property for redevelopment, and reclaiming these properties was a high priority. The multitude of existing programs, however, had evolved into a maze of inconsistent programs guided by contradictory policies applied to differing definitions of applicable property that could be acquired or transferred in fundamentally different ways for radically different purposes. The sheer complexity of these programs became a major barrier to a functioning market. The existing land acquisition and disposition programs and policies required potential developers to go through time-consuming and costly steps to acquire and develop tax delinquent, blighted, and adjudicated properties in the City. There were at least five different City programs that originated in four different agencies[18] to deal with property acquisition and disposition, and no central place to obtain information about properties, programs, or neighborhood plans. Further, while the City had selected seven strategic investment neighborhoods, there was no larger vision guiding and connecting these disparate programs and the investment they should stimulate. Ultimately, the structure and functioning of land use and redevelopment systems in New Orleans discouraged investment.[19]

---

17    LA. REV. STAT. ANN. §§ 13:2575(B)(2)(f), 13:2575(C) (2006).

18    The lead agencies in 2004 with authority or responsibility for aspects of land use included the Department of Housing and Neighborhood Development, the New Orleans Redevelopment Authority, the City Law Department, the New Orleans Affordable Housing Corporation, the Housing Authority of New Orleans, and the Finance Authority of New Orleans.

19    These findings of the National Vacant Properties Campaign were presented to city agencies and community development corporations in the spring of 2005 and were scheduled to be presented to Mayor Nagin in September 2005 until Katrina redefined New Orleans.

**The Katrina Response**

The sheer magnitude of the devastation wrought by Katrina and her sister storms can never be fully grasped. Tragic deaths, displaced families, and destroyed communities change us all for generations, if not forever. The homes and the properties, the land and the land use, are symbols of both destruction and the possibility of re-creation. The three hurricanes damaged 1.2 million housing units across the Gulf Coast region with Louisiana being the hardest hit. Almost one-third of all occupied housing units in Louisiana sustained some damage, and in metropolitan New Orleans, 182,000 housing units—38.8 percent of *all* occupied housing units—sustained serious damage.[20] The number of vacant and abandoned housing units in New Orleans reached over 100,000.[21]

Within ten months of Katrina, the federal government had appropriated $16.7 billion in emergency recovery funds for the Gulf Coast region.[22] Of this amount, an aggregate of $10.4 billion was made available for recovery in Louisiana.[23] By mid-October, 2005, Governor Kathleen Blanco created the Louisiana Recovery Authority (LRA) as the lead state agency to administer recovery efforts and receive the federal funds.[24]

The primary recovery initiative of the LRA was The Road Home, the largest single-housing recovery program in United States history.[25] It anticipated using the $10.4 billion in federal funds by allocating $7.5 billion for homeowner assistance, $1.6 billion for workforce housing, and $1.7 billion for mitigation activities. Homeowners are eligible to receive up to $150,000 in compensation depending on whether they elect to pursue one of three options available to them under the program: (1) they could remain in their homes and apply the compensation toward rebuilding; (2) they could convey their damaged property and relocate to another

---

20    U.S. Dep't of Hous. & Urban Dev., *supra* note 1.

21    New Orleans Redevelopment Authority, http://www.noraworks.org/post_katrina. htm.

22    In December 2005, Congress appropriated $11.5 billion, and in June, 2006 it appropriated an additional $5.2 billion in Community Development Block Grant Assistance. U.S. Dep't of Hous. & Urban Dev. Office of Policy Dev. & Res., *Funding for Recovery in the Hurricanes' Wake, Part I*, Research Works (Oct. 2006), *available at* www.huduser. org/periodicals/Researchworks.html.

23    U.S. Dep't of Hous. & Urban Dev., Office of Policy Dev. & Res., *Funding for Recovery in the Hurricanes' Wake, Part II*, Research Works (Oct. & Nov. 2006), *available at* www.huduser.org/periodicals/Researchworks.html.

24    The Louisiana Recovery Authority was initially created by Exec. Order KBB 2005-63 (2005) and subsequently codified by the state legislature. La. Rev. Stat. Ann. § 49:220.1 – 49:220.7 (2006). The Louisiana Office of Community Development is the state agency that essentially provides the administrative staff of the LRA. La. Rev. Stat Ann. § 49:220.5.C(4) (2006).

25    Louisiana Recovery Authority, The Road Home Program, http://www.road2la. org/about-us.

residence in Louisiana; or (3) they could convey their property and relocate to another state.[26] As initially designed, the Road Home Homeowner Assistance Program contemplated payments to individuals who elected to rebuild and remain in their homes with funds held in escrow and disbursed as approved construction proceeded, coupled with a covenant to remain in the home for at least three years following completion of reconstruction.[27] The Louisiana recovery legislation also authorized the creation of the Road Home Corporation as a nonprofit corporation acting under the direction of the LRA to acquire, hold, manage, and convey properties.[28]

Given the level of devastation and the availability of compensation, it was anticipated that there would be a substantial number of homeowners who would elect the second or third options that were available—receipt of a payment from the LRA in exchange for conveyance of property interests to the LRA, or more specifically to the Road Home Corporation. In this vision, the Road Home Corporation would quickly become one of the largest landowners in southern Louisiana, and certainly in New Orleans, and would be able to function as the equivalent of a land bank, holding and conveying properties for strategic land use planning purposes. The LRA cautioned that funds might be limited if too many homeowners elected to sell.[29]

Two things, however, stood in the way of this land banking function. First, the overwhelming majority of the applicants for recovery assistance elected to receive compensation to rebuild and remain in their homes. Of the first 36,000 completed assistance applications, 84.8 percent of the applicants chose to rebuild and remain.[30] The second event which rendered a land banking function for the LRA (or the Road Home Corporation) less likely was the decision by the federal government to insist that lump sum payments be made to applicants instead of transferring the assistance funds to escrow accounts, or disbursement accounts.[31]

The perhaps surprising decision by the majority of homeowners to rebuild and remain in New Orleans rather than relocate elsewhere, coupled with the

---

26    Louisiana Recovery Authority, Homeowners, http://www.road2la.org/homeowner. John A. Lovett, *Rebuilding a Region: Housing Recovery Efforts in the Wake of Katrina and Rita*, 20 PROB. & PROP. 49, 52 (2006).

27    *Id.*

28    LA. REV. STAT. ANN. § 40:600.63 (2006).

29    Lovett, *supra* note 26, at 53.

30    Louisiana Recovery Authority, The Road Home Program: Latest Statistics, *Weekly Detailed Statistics as of April 30, 2007, available at* http://www.road2la.org/newsroom/stats. htm (last visited May 8, 2007). As of this date, the LRA had received 130,828 applications and held initial appointments with 101,140 applicants. The total benefit calculation for 70,053 applicants was $5.31 billion. Closings had occurred for 13,753 applicants, with 2,952 closings pending. Updated numbers are now available at this website.

31    Louisiana Recovery Authority, *The Road Home Homeowner Policies* (Version 4.0, April 15, 2007), *available at* http://www.road2la.org/homeowner/resources.htm#policies (last visited May 8, 2007).

governmental decision to provide cash assistance without requiring conveyances (or even the imposition of servitudes to ensure rehabilitation of the property), has the clear advantage of maximizing the delivery of cash assistance to affected parties. Unfortunately, these decisions do little to change the functioning of the two dimensional paradigm (market forces and governmental regulation), and miss the opportunity to move to a third dimension—that of land banking.

The infusion of cash will allow rebuilding to occur to the extent that construction capacity and the permitting process are capable of handling a significant volume of activity. In this sense it does invigorate market demand, but almost exclusively for those properties on which a homeowner elects to rebuild. In theory, the homeowner is required to remain on the property for a period of three years, but this is a covenant creating personal liability and is most likely not a covenant that burdens the land or that is binding upon purchasers. Homeowners are also expected to have "clear title" prior to closing,[32] which will exclude the overwhelming majority of possessors of "heir property" and most properties that fall within the multi-year time frame of tax adjudication.

As part of the recovery legislation, the Louisiana legislature enacted several amendments to the New Orleans Community Improvement Act, the basic legislation creating and empowering the New Orleans Redevelopment Authority (NORA).[33] The amendments increased the size of the Board of Commissions from seven to eleven, permitted requests for designation of specific properties as blighted to be submitted by community-based organizations, and expanded its capacity for revenue bond financings.[34]

During the eighteen months that followed the flooding of New Orleans, a broad range of land use planning and urban redevelopment proposals were prepared, largely by public and private entities acting in cooperation with the City of New Orleans. The first set of proposals emanated from the "Bring New Orleans Back" Commission (BNOB) created by Mayor Nagin in October, 2005.[35] Its report, prepared with the assistance of the Urban Land Institute, recommended redevelopment only in certain portions of the City. It received such widespread public criticism that it was not accepted. The second major plan resulted from a collaborative effort of the City of New Orleans and the Greater New Orleans Foundation—the "Unified New Orleans Plan."[36] By the end of March 2007, the City designated seventeen specific "Target Recovery Zones" in different portions

---

32   *Id.*

33   LA. REV. STAT. ANN. § 33:4720.55 (2006).

34   2006 LA. ACTS 666.

35   THE ROCKEFELLER FOUNDATION, NEW ORLEANS: PLANNING FOR A BETTER FUTURE 3 (2006), http://www.rockfound.org/library/no_better_future.pdf.

36   The Unified New Orleans Plan, http://unifiedneworleansplan.com. The final draft of the Unified New Orleans Plan was released in January, 2007.

of the City, classified according to the level of destruction and the capacity for redevelopment.[37]

## Sidesteps

The City's first land use planning decision post-Katrina was to make fundamental decisions about where to rebuild and how to rebuild. It finessed the politically charged issue of whether to ban rebuilding in certain low-lying flood prone areas by proactively choosing "target zones" which included a range of neighborhoods, leaving unaddressed questions of areas in which rebuilding could not occur. Virtually all rebuilding and restoration initiatives, however, quickly confront the fundamental issue of ownership of the individual parcels of property. If there were 27,000 vacant and abandoned properties prior to Katrina and over 100,000 such properties in its aftermath, such a huge inventory plays a key role in the success of any and all recovery efforts.

Market demand for redevelopment and reinvestment activities may be stimulated by increased financial resources made available through the LRA Road Home Homeowner Assistance Program, and local governmental regulations may facilitate access in the Target Recovery Zones. The New Orleans context, however, demonstrates how these two conventional approaches to land use planning are not sufficient as planning tools. The large inventory of properties lacking meaningful "ownership" remains a major barrier. In two very different ways the immediate post-Katrina recovery legislation failed to further the possibility of land banking as a third dimension to land use planning in New Orleans: constitutional amendments were passed limiting the use of expropriation, and no legislation was enacted to redress the inefficiencies of tax adjudication.

### The Kelo Reaction

Intense storms are rarely anticipated fully, and so with intense public reactions to Supreme Court decisions. Louisiana had both. Just two months prior to Katrina's landfall, the United States Supreme Court rendered its decision in *Kelo v. City of New London*.[38] In *Kelo*, the Court sustained the use of eminent domain power for acquisition of non-blighted properties located within an economic redevelopment project. Though this decision did not alter existing constitutional doctrine,[39] a widespread public outcry arose resulting in new restrictions on the exercise of

---

37    Press Release, City of New Orleans, Mayor's Office of Comm'ns, City Announces First 17 Target Recovery Zones (March 29, 2007).

38    545 U.S. 469 (2005).

39    *See* Hawaii Hous. Auth. v. Midkiff, 467 U.S. 229 (1984) (determining that the "public use" clause of the Constitution is effectively co-terminus with the scope of the police powers of the government).

eminent domain in numerous states across the county. In early 2006 the Louisiana legislature approved for submission to the voters a series of twenty different constitutional amendments, four of which pertained to hurricane protection.[40] Two of these amendments were directly in response to *Kelo*, and both received voter approval on September 30, 2006. One of the two *Kelo* amendments (known as Amendment #5 because of its position on the ballot) placed limits on the use of the power of expropriation.[41] The other (known as Amendment #6) placed restrictions on the subsequent transferability of expropriated property.[42]

Prior to these constitutional amendments, NORA served as the lead entity for the City of New Orleans in the exercise of expropriation of blighted properties. The passage of Amendments #5 and #6, however, raises serious questions for NORA expropriations. Amendment #5 created a very specific list of permitted purposes for which expropriation could be exercised, limiting it primarily to acquisitions for traditional public purposes such as transportation and public buildings. As amended, the constitution expressly prohibits using economic development or enhancement of tax revenues in determining a public purpose.[43] The acquisition of "blighted" properties for community redevelopment, which is traditionally the primary purpose of NORA's activities, must now fall within the express constitutional authorization of expropriation for "[t]he removal of a threat to public health or safety caused by the existing use or disuse of the property."[44] Because Amendment #5 also contains an express prohibition on expropriations for predominantly private use and on expropriation for subsequent transfers to private entities,[45] the question arises as to what rights NORA has with respect to further disposition of such properties. If NORA uses expropriation to acquire property in order to remove "a threat to public health or safety caused by the existing use or disuse of the property," is it barred from subsequently transferring this property to a new owner? A strict textualist interpretation is that this clause is found within the paragraph setting forth the definition of "public purpose" which is the point of Amendment #5.[46] An expropriation for "public purpose" is limited by a prohibition of expropriations for use by or transfers to third parties. The problem with this

---

40    *See* Press Release, Pub. Aff. Res. Council of La., Guide to the Constitutional Amendments (Sept. 8, 2006).

41    2006 LA. ACTS 851 (amending LA. CONST. art. I, § 4(B), art. VI, 21(A), and adding art. VI, § 21(D)).

42    2006 LA. ACTS 859 (adding LA. CONST. art. I, § 4(H)). Because there was a third constitutional resolution, 2006 LA. ACTS 853 (amending LA. CONST. art. I, § 4(G)), the section originally designated 4(G) by Acts 859 was re-designated 4(H).

43    LA. CONST. art. I, § 4(B)(3).

44    LA. CONST. art. I, § 4(B)(2)(c).

45    LA. CONST. art. I, § 4(B)(1). The prohibition on expropriations for use by or transfers to third parties expressly exempts expropriations for industrial plants, public ports, and pollution control facilities. LA. CONST. art. VI, § 21.

46    LA. CONST. art. I, § 4(B)(2) provides that the limiting definition of "public purpose" in § 4(B)(2) refers to "public purpose" as used in § 4(B)(1).

strict textualist approach is that it creates the entirely anomalous situation where NORA can expropriate blighted properties, but never transfer them to any third party. An alternative policy-based interpretation of Amendment #5 would construe the key word "for" in the limiting clauses as indicative of prohibited dominant purposes of the expropriation and not as a limitation on subsequent use when the dominant purpose for acquisition is public health and safety.

The uncertainty with respect to NORA's expropriated blighted properties is made even more confusing by Amendment #6. This amendment provides that the original owners of expropriated property have rights to reacquire the property when it is no longer needed for the public purpose. If a plausible policy-based interpretation of Amendment #5 is that NORA can expropriate blighted property, and can dispose of it to third parties, is such a disposition subject to the constraints of Amendment #6? On its face, Amendment #6 applies to all expropriated property interests.[47] The separate subsections all contain references to "project" and "surplus," providing an argument that these particular subsections are not applicable to blighted property acquisitions.[48] That still leaves open, however, the question of whether the basic thrust of Amendment #6 is applicable to expropriations of blighted property justified as threats to public health and safety.

*Marketable Title for Adjudicated Properties*

Property tax foreclosure laws in Louisiana are among the most complex, lengthy, and convoluted of any state in the country. Properties sold at tax auctions are subject to multi-year rights of redemption and inevitably fail to convey marketable and insurable title because of the lack of judicial process and the inadequacy of constitutionally required notice to interested parties. Properties not purchased by private third parties at the tax auctions default to the local government as "adjudicated" properties. They are then subject to even more statutory procedures and time periods before they can be conveyed to third parties.

The reports of the National Vacant Properties Campaign in early 2005 identified a dozen possible statutory amendments which would increase the efficiency and effectiveness of the tax adjudication process. With the crush of other legislative initiatives post-Katrina, none of these recommendations has been enacted though several have been introduced.[49]

---

47  LA. CONST. art. I, § 4(H)(1).
48  LA. CONST. art. I, §§ 4(H)(2), (3), and (4).
49  *See, e.g.,* H.B. 516, 2006 Reg. Sess (La. 2006).

## Land Banking as Affirmative Planning

The third dimension of land use planning is the concept of using a governmental entity to acquire, manage, and hold properties for both short- and long-term strategic uses in the face of contractions and expansions of normal market demands for real property. As originally proposed in 1971, a land bank would serve to acquire parcels of property to be held for future strategic uses, such as public buildings, open greenspaces, or specific uses not accomplished by normal market conditions.[50] The underlying belief was that the interplay of government regulations and market conditions would not adequately meet public priorities. By creating a "bank" to own and control a fluctuating stock of real property assets, the government could both soften the adverse effects of market contractions and expansions and achieve targeted public goals.[51]

In the decades since they were first proposed, land banks have been created in five major urban areas in the United States (St. Louis, Cleveland, Louisville, Atlanta, and Flint) and in numerous smaller communities.[52] The primary focus of these land banks has been to acquire vacant, abandoned, and tax delinquent properties which, prior to the land bank acquisition, were a major detriment and liability to the surrounding properties and neighborhoods. By definition, these properties produce no tax revenues and only harm the larger community. In acquiring ownership and control of these properties, the land bank can immediately move to rehabilitate or demolish the offending structures and stabilize the neighborhood. With broad disposition authority, the land bank can also engage in strategic transfers to accomplish specified public purposes such as the development of affordable housing.

As a city confronted with weakening market demand and declining population prior to Katrina, New Orleans already confronted a surplus of residential housing and a large stock of vacant, abandoned, and tax adjudicated properties. The central recommendation of the National Vacant Properties Campaign was the creation of a land bank in New Orleans to acquire, control, and strategically convey these properties.[53]

What was true before Katrina became a necessity in its aftermath. The number of vacant and abandoned properties increased five-fold, and the population further declined by fifty percent. Two potential entities emerged, either of which could have served as a land bank. The Road Home Corporation, as the real estate owning affiliate of the LRA, could have acquired large numbers of parcels in exchange for

50    *See* Haar, *supra* note 2.

51    Frank S. Alexander, *Land Bank Strategies for Renewing Urban Land*, 14 J. Affordable Hous. & Comty. Dev. L. 140, 143–44 (2005).

52    Frank S. Alexander, Land Bank Authorities: A Guide for the Creation and Operation of Local Land Banks 5–7 (Local Initiatives Support Corp. 2005), *available at* http://www.lisc.org/content/publications/detail/793.

53    *See New Orleans Technical Assessment and Assistance Report*, *supra* note 3.

its assistance payments. However, the public preference to remain in New Orleans and rebuild and the governmental policy not to require transfers of ownership left the LRA and the Road Home Corporation as funding agencies rather than real estate managers.

The second possibility for a land bank in New Orleans is NORA. Mayor Nagin anticipated that NORA would become "the depository for swaths of wrecked residential property."[54] There are four potential sources of real property which could be acquired by NORA at little or no cost: (1) transfers of property acquired by the Road Home Corporation, (2) expropriations, (3) tax adjudicated properties, and (4) acquisition of properties as a result of city enforcement of public demolition liens and nuisance abatement liens. Additionally, if funds are available, NORA could acquire properties through direct market purchases.

The combination of homeowner expectations and governmental policies indicate thus far that the Road Home Corporation will not be a significant source of properties for NORA. Expropriations may be a viable source of the inventory, but this is contingent on both the availability of funds to pay compensation and achieving clarity through judicial rulings or supplemental legislation on the impact of Amendments #5 and #6 in 2006 to the Louisiana Constitution.

Tax adjudicated properties are the single strongest source of an inventory for NORA's land banking activities. To be effective, however, the inventory must have insurable and marketable title and new procedures must be made available through legislative amendments and local government operating policies. A major reform of the property tax enforcement system in Louisiana could significantly assist in the conversion of abandoned tax delinquent properties from liabilities into assets for the entire community.[55]

When a property owner ultimately elects to abandon his or her property even after receipt of disaster assistance, it becomes the responsibility of the local government to take action to demolish the improvements when appropriate in order to protect public health and safety. On February 1, 2007, the City Council of New Orleans amended its local ordinances to strengthen the ability of the City to demolish structures.[56] If the City of New Orleans expends funds to demolish structures pursuant to this ordinance, it can place a lien on the property for the amount of the expenditures and then enforce the "super-priority" status of that lien pursuant to state law, forcing a sale of the property to a third party or its direct acquisition by the City.[57]

---

54  Frank Donze, *Low-Profile Agency Gains Blight-Bust Powers: Unlikely Agency Key to Rebirth*, TIMES-PICAYUNE (NEW ORLEANS), Oct. 11, 2006, at 1.

55  Such a transformation is precisely what occurred with the enactment of a comprehensive tax foreclosure reform in Michigan and the subsequent enactment of the Michigan Land Bank Act. *See* ALEXANDER, LAND BANK AUTHORITIES, *supra* note 52, at 7.

56  New Orleans, La., Ordinance 22499 (Feb. 1, 2007) (adding Section 26-264 (redesignated as 26-263)).

57  LA. REV. STAT. ANN. §§ 13:2575(B)(2)(f), 13:2575(C) (2006).

## Conclusion

Land use planning presents the challenge of normative guiding with empirical anticipation. The interplay of market conditions and governmental regulations may be well intentioned, but rarely possesses the flexibility to adjust to sudden changes or unanticipated needs. A land bank authority is designed to moderate market demand and public needs by acquisition of excess supply when demand falls, or provision of supply for targeted purposes in the face of high demand and insufficient resources.

Louisiana, and most importantly the City of New Orleans, presented a strong case for the role of a land bank prior to Katrina, Rita, and Wilma. With these disasters, New Orleans needs all of the tools that are possible in order to engage in the land use planning appropriate for recovery and rebuilding. A land bank in New Orleans, taking control of properties with marketable and insurable title, would be the added dimension that is necessary.

# Chapter 4
# Place, Disasters, and Disability

Debra Lyn Bassett

## Introduction

Hurricanes Katrina and Rita cast a bright spotlight upon a number of important issues, including, among others, issues of race, issues of class, and issues regarding our nation's emergency preparedness. Still another issue highlighted by the hurricanes, but one that did not garner the same level of subsequent examination or discussion, was the issue of "place."

"Place" received some limited attention during the 2005 hurricane season, even if inadvertently, because place indeed mattered. Only particular places are susceptible to hurricanes generally, and only specific places suffered any impact from Hurricanes Katrina and Rita. Place was not interchangeable or irrelevant—some places were more geographically vulnerable than others.

"Place" matters in law and policy, but its significance is rarely acknowledged. The failure to recognize the significance of place in law and policy stems from assumptions that place is irrelevant, and results in unjustified generalities that have undermined the effectiveness of many laws and policies in their implementation. In empirical studies, researchers control for variables that might have an impact on the outcome. Place might, or might not, be one such variable; if place is not a controlled variable, the researcher has thereby indicated that she considers place irrelevant to the potential outcomes. The same is true in law and policy: when place is not specifically mentioned, that omission reflects a belief that place is irrelevant.

Law and policy tend to seek generalities. After all, we want laws and policies to have broad, societal applicability rather than narrow, individualized applicability. As in empirical studies, in some instances, place indeed may be irrelevant. But places are not interchangeable in the manner that some seem to suggest, nor are places a mere neutral backdrop. Place has more widespread relevance than currently tends to be recognized.

## The Urban Assumption

The degree to which we underplay and undermine the significance of place in law and policy is quite remarkable. Despite the perils of generalization, attempts to minimize differences and to find commonality tend to predominate.[1] Place inserts specificity and boundaries into discussions that are seeking generalities—and thus serves potentially to limit relevance and applicability. Not only are laws and policies typically viewed without regard to place, but current discussions of diasporas and globalization inherently undercut place with their emphasis on dispersion and consistent reach. A perhaps unintended consequence of heralding globalization is the homogenization of place, in which place is viewed as interchangeable, a mere neutral backdrop without independent significance.

To some degree, seeking universality and commonality is understandable and practical. After all, if too many variables are introduced, a formula, program, or approach becomes too case-specific to have any real utility. But there is also a danger that we may sometimes carry unexamined generalizations too far, resulting in unjustified assumptions of similarities that do not, in fact, exist. It is these unjustified assumptions of similarities without regard to place that form the focus of this chapter.

Ignoring place has benefits. In particular, ignoring place reduces the number of factors that must be taken into account, with a concomitant sense (even if that sense is false) of greater consistency and cohesion. Thus, ignoring place tends to promote contentions that seek unity, consistency, and sameness.

However, ignoring place carries perils as well. Ignoring place does not make it go away. When no distinctions are drawn, and all are treated as if place were consistent or irrelevant, the lack of distinction carries its own assumptions—assumptions drawn from majority or dominant perspectives. Just as is true of assumptions of maleness and whiteness absent other factors or indicators, similar assumptions adhere with respect to place.

One specific assumption with respect to place is the assumption of an urban location. Approximately eighty percent of the population of the United States lives in urban areas,[2] so an urban assumption will often be correct. But an urban

---

1    *See* Paul Schiff Berman, *Towards a Cosmopolitan Vision of Conflict of Laws: Redefining Governmental Interests in a Global Era*, 153 U. PA. L. REV. 1819, 1861 (2005).

[I]n order to create a set of universal legal norms that overrides local variation, one needs to presuppose a world citizenry devoid of both particularist ties and normative discussion about the relative importance of such ties. Thus, universalism can cut off debate about the nature of overlapping communities just as surely as territorialism or parochialism does.

2    STATE PROFILES: THE POPULATION AND ECONOMY OF EACH U.S. STATE 3 (Courtenay M. Slater & Martha G. Davis eds., 1st ed. 1999) ("About 80 percent of the U.S. population lived in metropolitan areas in 1997."). Although "urban" and "rural" are common terms, I (and many others) have repeatedly observed that the two terms fall on a continuum and elude clear definition. Debra Lyn Bassett, *Ruralism*, 88 IOWA L. REV. 273, 287–88 (2003) [hereinafter Bassett, *Ruralism*] ("The terms 'urban' and 'rural' have imprecise and potentially overlapping definitions . . . . [A] community's population, standing alone, will not sufficiently differentiate a 'rural' area from an 'urban' or 'suburban' one.").

assumption presumes, in the twenty percent of instances involving a non-urban setting, that a non-urban location makes no difference. Unquestionably, in some circumstances the urban versus non-urban distinction does not matter. For example, the premeditated killing of another without justification or excuse is a homicide, regardless of whether the killing occurred in an urban or non-urban area. But in other instances, assuming uniformity of place can lead to unjustified or erroneous conclusions.

I have previously written about urban—or "anti-rural"—bias,[3] and in those writings I have observed that urban bias in law and policy is wide-ranging.[4] Indeed, the urban assumption—urbanity as the assumed point of reference—is a fact of life in the United States.[5] Anecdotally, it takes little to note the prevalence of urban-related, as contrasted with rural-related, news stories. One commentator has suggested that due to media deadlines, journalists naturally and necessarily tend to select subjects that are nearby, and that news stations are located in urban population centers.[6] However, we need rely neither on anecdotal evidence nor on assumptions or suppositions. A 2002 study by the W.K. Kellogg Foundation undertook a systematic study of news coverage, finding both that there is relatively little media coverage of rural America and that the little coverage given tends to be negative.[7]

We saw this phenomenon in the context of Hurricane Katrina. Although the television networks and newspaper accounts reported extensively on the devastation wreaked by Hurricanes Katrina and Rita, place bore an unacknowledged impact on

---

3   *See* Debra Lyn Bassett, *The Rural Venue*, 57 ALA. L. REV. 939 (2006) [hereinafter Bassett, *Rural Venue*]; Debra Lyn Bassett, *Distancing Rural Poverty*, 13 GEO. J. ON POVERTY L. & POL'Y 3 (2006) [hereinafter Bassett, *Distancing Rural Poverty*]; Bassett, *Ruralism*, *supra* note 2; Debra Lyn Bassett, *The Hidden Bias in Diversity Jurisdiction*, 81 WASH. U. L.Q. 119 (2003); Debra Lyn Bassett, *The Politics of the Rural Vote*, 35 ARIZ. ST. L.J. 743 (2003) [hereinafter Bassett, *Rural Vote*].

4   *See, e.g.*, Bassett, *Ruralism*, *supra* note 2, at 323; *see id.* at 327 (noting urban bias "in a variety of . . . federal laws [and] policies . . . reach[ing] into a broad range of areas"); *see also* Katherine Porter, *Going Broke the Hard Way: The Economics of Rural Failure*, 2005 WIS. L. REV. 969, 972 (urging the "consider[ation of] rural perspectives in studies of various legal fields").

5   *See* KNOWING YOUR PLACE: RURAL IDENTITY AND CULTURAL HIERARCHY 3–4 (Barbara Ching & Gerald W. Creed eds., 1997) ("[T]he urban has come to be the assumed reference when terms are used that could in theory refer to both rural and urban subjects").

6   Barry C. Feld, *Race, Politics and Juvenile Justice: The Warren Court and the Conservative "Backlash,"* 87 MINN. L. REV. 1447, 1533 (2003).

7   W.K. Kellogg Found., *Perceptions of Rural America: Media Coverage* 32–33 (2003), *available at* http://www.wkkf.org/Pubs/FoodRur/MediaCoverage_00253_03795. pdf (noting that rural coverage "was notable for its absence," and that "on the rare occasions in which it appeared, it was frequently used in connection with records of criminal activity. A remarkable seventy-eight percent of discussions of rural life on television news dealt with crime").

these reports: the media's attention centered on urban areas, to the near-exclusion of rural areas. In particular, the plight of the hurricane victims who lived in the urban area of New Orleans received massive, ongoing coverage, whereas the plight of the hurricane victims who lived in the remote rural areas of Mississippi, Louisiana, and Alabama did not.

One tempting rationalization for the media focus on urban areas and urban events is the reality that urban areas and events typically involve larger numbers of people, and therefore may be justified as more newsworthy, more relevant, more credible, or as carrying more significance. But there is an undercurrent, or perhaps more accurately an underbelly, to this rationalization: an urban focus and urban emphasis amounts to an urban bias—according a greater value to urban areas and urban dwellers, and a lesser value to rural areas and rural dwellers.

Urban bias is also seen in American culture more generally. In addition to negative rural stereotyping in film, literature, and television specifically,[8] urban bias dictates trends, fashion, music, and more generally, simply what is seen as being desirable.[9] Indeed, many define "culture" in terms that, by definition, exclude rural areas. Defining "culture" as the existence within a geographical area of such amenities as a symphony, opera, ballet, museums, and live theater correspondingly defines those communities without those amenities as lacking culture. In describing American culture and looking to the characteristics or behavior typical of Americans, urban bias results in descriptions of urban culture.[10]

But urban bias has an impact beyond greater public visibility and trend-setting—urban bias has an economic impact as well. Two areas illustrating this economic impact are federal programs and poverty.

*Federal Programs and Services*

The urban assumption in the federal government begins at the beginning—with how "urban" and "rural" are defined. The Census Bureau provides a specific

---

8    *See* Bassett, *Ruralism, supra* note 2, at 292–99.

9    *Id.* at 314, n.184 ("[R]ural dwellers . . . unlike urban dwellers, are unlikely to be perceived as 'cool' or as trend-setters.").

10    *See* RALPH A. WEISHEIT ET AL., CRIME AND POLICING IN RURAL AND SMALL-TOWN AMERICA 2 (2d ed. 1999) ("[C]ontemporary American culture is considered not only homogenous, but an urban culture."); Craig A. Arnold, *Ignoring the Rural Underclass: The Biases of Federal Housing Policy*, 2 STAN. L. & POL'Y REV. 191, 195 (1990) (noting "an American cultural bias toward that which is urban. This bias is created by a pervasive belief in the rightness and inevitability of urbanization.").

definition for "urban."[11] However, the Census Bureau's definition of "rural" is simply what is left over—that which is not "urban" is remaindered as "rural."[12]

More disturbingly, the federal government's urban assumption results in urban-centricity such that the urban focus not only overshadows, but genuinely does not care about that which is rural. Urban-centricity translates into differential federal funding. According to the Consolidated Federal Funds Report for 2001, the federal government returned $6,131 on a per capita basis to urban areas, but $6,020 to rural areas—a $5.5 billion rural disadvantage annually.[13] The rural disadvantage also extends to community development and resources. Urban community development receives two to five times more federal funding, per capita, than rural community development.[14] In 2001, federal spending on rural, as contrasted with urban, community resources was $286 per person less—a $14.1 billion rural disadvantage.[15]

In discussing federal spending with respect to rural areas, typically the discussion eventually turns to farm subsidies, because farm subsidies are widely cast as the federal government's sop to rural areas. A 2001 study found—to no one's surprise—that most Americans associate "rural" with farming and agriculture.[16] Accordingly, farm subsidies could be a good method for addressing rural needs if it were not for one small problem: the vast majority of rural dwellers neither live on farms nor make their living by working on farms. According to a 2006 report

---

11   *See* U.S. Census Bureau, Census 2000 Urban and Rural Classification, *available at* http://www.census.gov/geo/www/ua/ua_2k.html (last visited Nov. 13, 2008) (providing a detailed definition of "urban").

12   *See id.*; *see also* JANET M. FITCHEN, ENDANGERED SPACES, ENDURING PLACES: CHANGE, IDENTITY, AND SURVIVAL IN RURAL AMERICA 246 (1991) ("The official definition assigned to rural America is a definition by exclusion: Essentially, that which is not metropolitan America is rural America."); WEISHEIT ET AL., *supra* note 10, at 183–84 ("A negative definition of rural defines it implicitly by the absence of certain conditions or community attributes that are viewed as distinctively urban. In these terms, rural is defined by default as not-urban—i.e., whatever remains after urban areas have been designated.") (emphasis omitted).

13   Nat'l Rural Network, *Why Rural Matters II: The Rural Impact of the Administration's FY07 Budget Proposal* 4 (2006), *available at* http://www.rupri.org/ruralPolicy/publications/2007budgetanalysis.pdf.

14   *Id.*

15   *Id.*

16   *See* W.K. Kellogg Found., *Perceptions of Rural America* 2–3 (2001), *available at* http://www.wkkf.org/pubs/FoodRur/pub2973.pdf ("[T]he overwhelming majority of people in our study—both rural and non-rural—believe agriculture is the dominant industry of rural America. When asked to name the main industries of rural America, nearly all respondents name agriculture, farming, or ranching.").

sponsored by The Carsey Institute at the University of New Hampshire, only 6.5 percent of the rural labor force is engaged in farming.[17]

The fact that more than ninety percent of rural dwellers are neither farm dwellers nor farm workers has been known for some time. In treating farm subsidies as meeting the needs of rural dwellers, lawmakers are relying not on facts, but on outdated rural stereotypes.[18] This overshadowing of rural issues by urban issues occurs in another economic area—that of poverty.

*Poverty*

Inner-city homelessness and poverty often predominate in discussions and images of poverty in the United States. Commentators have noted urban bias with respect to poverty both in the United States and in other countries.[19] As an initial matter, urban bias results in a focus on urban poverty rather than rural poverty.[20] Although urban poverty is certainly problematic and worthy of attention, the focus on urban poverty overshadows the reality that rates of poverty are consistently higher in rural areas—and have been every year since 1959.[21]

Place is the most important factor in determining the likelihood that someone will live in poverty. Rural dwellers are significantly more likely to be poor than non-rural dwellers.[22] Of all the counties with poverty rates above the national level,

---

17    Kenneth Johnson, *Demographic Trends in Rural and Small Town America, in* 1 REPORTS ON RURAL AMERICA 7 (U. of New Hampshire, Carsey Institute, Issue No. 1, 2006), *available at* http://www.carseyinstitute.unh.edu/documents/Demographics_complete_file. pdf.

18    *See id.*

19    *See generally* MICHAEL LIPTON, WHY POOR PEOPLE STAY POOR: URBAN BIAS IN WORLD DEVELOPMENT (1976) (discussing urban bias with respect to poverty worldwide).

20    *See* RURAL SOC. SOC'Y TASK FORCE ON PERSISTENT RURAL POVERTY, PERSISTENT POVERTY IN RURAL AMERICA 175 (1993) ("Considering the amount of attention devoted to the problem of urban poverty, it is perplexing that rural poverty seldom attracts much notice. Official poverty rates are consistently higher in rural areas, regardless of race."); Kenneth L. Deavers & Robert A. Hoppe, *The Rural Poor: The Past as Prologue, in* RURAL POLICIES FOR THE 1990s 85, 88 (Cornelia B. Flora & James A. Christenson eds., 1991) ("The American public generally perceives poverty as an urban problem. However, the incidence of poverty is actually higher in nonmetro areas.").

21    *See* U.S. Dep't of Agric., Econ. Res. Serv., *Rural Income, Poverty, and Welfare: Rural Poverty* (Nov. 10, 2004), *available at* http://www.ers.usda.gov/briefing/ IncomePovertyWelfare/ruralpoverty/ ("Nonmetro poverty has been higher than metro in every year since 1959."); *see also id.* (noting that in 2003, the urban poverty rate was 12.1 percent, while the rural poverty rate was 14.2 percent).

22    *See* David A. Cotter, *Addressing Person and Place to Alleviate Rural Poverty*, PERSPECTIVES ON POVERTY, POL'Y & PLACE (RUPRI Rural Poverty Res. Ctr.), Aug. 2003, at 9 (noting that this is the case "even after accounting for a considerable array of household and labor market variables"); Bruce Weber & Leif Jensen, *Poverty and Place: A Critical Review of Rural Poverty Literature* (RUPRI Rural Poverty Res. Ctr., Working Paper Series), June

approximately eighty-four percent are rural. Moreover, more than eighty rural counties have poverty rates of more than thirty percent. Twelve of those eighty counties have poverty rates above forty percent. In fact, counties with "extreme poverty rates" are disproportionately concentrated in rural areas.[23]

Poverty rates are highest in the most rural areas,[24] and rural areas have a disproportionately large portion of the poor.[25] Not only is the level of poverty striking in rural areas—of the 250 poorest counties in America, 244 are rural[26]—but poverty becomes more acute in more remote rural areas. Poverty and place have a direct and proportional relationship: the more rural the place, the higher the likelihood of poverty.[27]

Despite place's significant contribution to poverty, laws and policies aimed at ameliorating poverty have persisted in pursuing person-based, rather than place-based, approaches.[28] This failure to consider place in our laws and policies is not restricted to poverty, but is seen more generally.

---

2004, at 20 ("[T]here is something about living in a rural area that increases one's odds of being poor. This conclusion holds even when one controls for individual and household characteristics.").

23   HOUSING ASSISTANCE COUNCIL, TAKING STOCK: RURAL PEOPLE, POVERTY, AND HOUSING AT THE TURN OF THE 21ST CENTURY 20–21 (2002), *available at* http://ruralhome.org/pubs/hsganalysis/ts2000/index.htm; *see also* Rural Poverty Res. Ctr., *What are Persistent Poverty Counties?*, *available at* http://www.rprconline.org (explaining that "[p]ersistent [p]overty [c]ounties are those that have had poverty rates of 20% or higher in every decennial census between 1970 and 2000," and noting that eighty-eight percent—340 of the 386 persistent poverty counties—are rural).

24   *See* U.S. Dep't of Agric., Econ. Res. Serv., Rural Dev. Res. Report No. 100, *Rural Poverty at a Glance* 4 (2004).

25   *See* J. Dennis Murray & Peter A. Keller, *Psychology and Rural America: Current Status and Future Directions*, 46 AM. PSYCHOLOGIST 220, 222 (1991); Ann R. Tickamyer & Cynthia M. Duncan, *Poverty and Opportunity Structure in Rural America*, 16 ANN. REV. SOC. 67, 68 (1990).

26   ELIZABETH BEESON & MARTY STRANGE, WHY RURAL MATTERS: THE NEED FOR EVERY STATE TO TAKE ACTION ON RURAL EDUCATION 1–2 (2000), *available at* http://www.mrea-mt.org/rural_matters.html; *see also* OSHA GRAY DAVIDSON, BROKEN HEARTLAND: THE RISE OF AMERICA'S RURAL GHETTO 77 (1996) (noting that of the 150 worst "Hunger Counties" in the United States, ninety-seven percent are in rural areas).

27   *See* Kathleen K. Miller & Bruce A. Weber, *How Do Persistent Poverty Dynamics and Demographics Vary Across the Rural-Urban Continuum?*, MEASURING RURAL DIVERSITY, Jan. 2004, at 6, *available at* http://srdc.msstate.edu/measuring/series/miller_weber.pdf ("Poverty rates are highest in more remote rural counties and lowest in metro counties.").

28   *See* Bassett, *Distancing Rural Poverty*, *supra* note 3, at 27–28.
Policies and remedies concerning rural poverty typically are "person-based," targeting individuals or households and involving programs such as food stamps, Aid to Families with Dependent Children (AFDC), housing vouchers, training, and job counseling. . . . Yet these "person-based" programs, despite providing some benefit, have eradicated neither urban nor rural poverty. Particularly in light

## Laws, Policies, and the Impact of Place

The urban assumption has a pervasive influence on law and policy.[29] When lawmakers and policymakers approach law and legal issues from an exclusively urban perspective, this urban assumption necessarily infects the resulting proposals, programs, policies, and legislation.

As a general matter, the urban assumption is pernicious because it is unrecognized and unacknowledged, resulting in invalid generalizations. One example of an invalid generalization resulting from urban bias comes from the use of urban models in designing policies and programs. Because rural areas often are not considered separately—because the unique needs and characteristics of remote rural areas are not always considered—urban models are often employed in designing policies and programs, even when the intended beneficiaries of those policies and programs include rural dwellers. In designing policies that include the delivery of services, an urban focus or urban model might lead a policymaker to make the assumption that service recipients will effectively and efficiently receive their benefits, and administrative and distribution costs will be lower, by using a centralized location. This assumption, although widely true for urban areas, is largely untrue for rural areas, where smaller, more geographically dispersed populations, typically lacking any form of mass transit, require lengthy travel to get to so-called "centralized" locations.

The urban assumption adopts "economies of scale" as the primary form of distribution. However, the concept of "economies of scale" itself reflects urban bias. "Economies of scale," by definition, require more demand or larger numbers in order to achieve such economies. Such an approach, of course, works just fine in urban areas, but often is lacking in rural areas with few residents, especially when the rural area is both remote from other population centers and its population is widely dispersed.

More broadly, America has embraced economic models and rationales that tend to reward urban areas and tend to penalize rural areas. Such economic concepts as "economies of scale," "profitability," "cost effectiveness," "cost-benefit analyses," and "market efficiencies" create justifications for deregulation, privatization, and the promotion of business interests in both law and policy. But rural markets are unlikely to satisfy any of these economic-based concepts. Rural markets tend to

---

of the geographical and racial concentration of poverty in some areas, a second look is warranted at "place-based" policies and programs such as subsidies, business tax credits, and other tax incentives which target particular poor areas and neighborhoods.

*Id. See generally id.* at 26–31.

29    *See* David Freshwater, *Rural America at the Turn of the Century: One Analyst's Perspective*, 15 RURAL AM. 2, 3 (2000), *available at* http://www.ers.usda.gov/publications/ruralamerica/sep2000/sep2000c.pdf ("Congress, dominated by urban interests, focuses on urban issues and often ignores the effects of policies on rural areas.").

be remote, dispersed, and sparsely populated. A dispersed population is more expensive to serve than a concentrated one. Remote and sparsely populated communities often translate into higher transportation costs with concomitant decreases in profitability, cost effectiveness, and market efficiencies.

Moreover, an urban assumption overlooks a number of rural practical realities. Differing practical realities of place exist for urban versus rural areas, such that the everyday assumptions held by urban dwellers often are inapplicable to rural dwellers. In particular, there are different practical realities with respect to the availability of technology, communications, and transportation for urban and rural areas.

Although urban dwellers are accustomed to, and therefore assume, the ready availability of telephone service, Internet access, and transportation, these assumptions are often untrue for those who live in remote rural areas. In remote rural areas, if one cannot afford telephone service or if one's service is disrupted, a neighbor's telephone or pay phone may be several miles away, and cell phone service may not be available at all. In many remote rural areas, high-speed Internet access is unavailable,[30] and dial-up Internet access not only requires telephone service, but often is available only through a long-distance call.[31] Urban dwellers may assume ready access to television, but cable television is not available to all rural dwellers, and without cable, many rural homes are located too far from television stations to obtain any signal. Urban dwellers tend to assume that transportation is readily available. However, many rural dwellers own older, unreliable vehicles,[32] and unlike urban areas, back-up forms of transportation—such as taxicabs, subways, buses, or light rail—often do not exist. Indeed, forty

---

30  *See* MARK DRABENSTOTT & KATHARINE H. SHEAFF, EXPLORING POLICY OPTIONS FOR A NEW RURAL AMERICA: A CONFERENCE SUMMARY 3 (2001), *available at* http://www.kc.frb. org/PUBLICAT/Exploring/RC01DRAB.pdf ("Much of rural America still lacks high-speed Internet access"); *see also* Cheryl A. Tritt, PLI Order No. 6911, *Telecommunications Future*, 852 PLI/Pat 85, 91 (Dec. 2005) ("[T]he available data shows that rural areas are significantly less likely to receive broadband services than urban areas").

31  *See* TVA RURAL STUDIES, OTA FOLLOW-UP CONFERENCE REPORT: RURAL AMERICA AT THE CROSSROADS 4 (2001), *available at* http://www.rural.org/workshops/rural_telecom/ OTA_followup_report.pdf ("[L]ong-distance calls tend to account for a higher percentage of rural customers' calls since they must call outside of their local exchange more often than urban customers in order to reach a variety of businesses and services. The situation is exacerbated by the need to call long distance to gain access to advanced services like Internet, e-mail, or telephone support."); *see also id.* at 70 ("Internet access does not favor the remote user; urban users can obtain network services and Internet access with a local phone call, whereas rural users typically must pay a long-distance charge for the same access.").

32  *See Transportation Barriers to Employment of Low-Income People* (Univ. of Wis., Center for Community Econ. Dev.), 1998, at 1, *available at* http://www.aae.wisc.edu/pubs/ cenews/docs/ce258.txt (last visited May 9, 2006) (noting that "[e]ven when ownership occurs, there are many questions about vehicle reliability and function").

percent of all rural residents live in counties that have no public transportation.[33] Moreover, most urban areas have ready access to an airport, whereas nearly eighty-three percent of rural counties are beyond commuting distance to a major airport.[34]

The urban perspective assumes the availability of choices, whether in shopping, health care, education, employment, or housing. In many remote rural areas, there is no local shopping, there is no local doctor or hospital, there is no local school, there is no large employer, and there are no housing projects. Obtaining medical care, or even just shopping for groceries, may require traveling several miles or several hundred miles, with only one option then available. Moreover, the lack of market competition often results in higher prices.[35] Education may require a long

---

33    Thomas D. Rowley, *Rural Disabled Struggle for Independence*, RURAL MONITOR NEWSLETTER 1 (Fall 2003), *available at* http://www.raconline.org/newsletter/web/Fall03_vol10-2.html (last visited April 19, 2008). *See* Timothy Baldwin, *The Constitutional Right to Travel: Are Some Forms of Transportation More Equal than Others?*, 1 Nw. J. L. & Soc. Pol'y 213, 213 (2006) ("Few roads, particularly in suburban and rural communities, offer any form of public transportation."); Nina Glasgow, *Older Americans' Patterns of Driving and Using Other Transportation*, 15 RURAL AM. 26, 26 (2000), *available at* http://www.ers. usda.gov/publications/ruralamerica/sep2000/sep2000f.pdf ("[P]ublic transit and paratransit services (door-to-door transportation designed for older and disabled individuals who are unable to use public transit) are limited or lacking in many, especially rural, communities."); Eileen S. Stommes & Dennis M. Brown, *Transportation in Rural America: Issues for the 21st Century*, 16 RURAL AM. 2, 4 (2002), *available at* http://www.ers.usda.gov/publications/ ruralamerica/ra164/ra164b.pdf ("Rural public transit, the rural analogue to bus service in metro areas, is available in approximately half of the rural counties nationwide. Few are found in the most rural, isolated areas."); *see also* Am. Pub. Transp. Ass'n, Public Transportation: Wherever Life Takes You, *available at* http://www.publictransportation. org/reports/asp/mobility_rural.asp (last visited November 13, 2008) (noting that forty-one percent of rural community residents have no access to transit).

34    *See* Fred Gale & Dennis Brown, *How Important Is Airport Access for Rural Businesses?*, 15 RURAL AM. 16, 17 (2000), *available at* http://www.ers.usda.gov/ publications/ruralamerica/sep2000/sep2000e.pdf (last visited May 9, 2006) ("Over 1,900 nonmetro counties (of nearly 2,300 total) are not within easy commuting distance of a major airport."); *see also id.* at 16 (all "hub" airports—large, medium, and small—are located in metropolitan areas).

35    *See* Phil R. Kaufman, *Rural Poor Have Less Access to Supermarkets, Large Grocery Stores*, 13 RURAL DEV. PERSPECTIVES 19, 19 (1999), *available at* http://www. ers.usda.gov/publications/rdp/rdp1098/rdp1098c.pdf (noting that "more distant [rural] households may face significantly higher food prices to the extent that supermarkets and other large retail food outlets are not accessible to them").

bus ride to another community.[36] Even when some choice is available, the options tend to be much more limited in rural areas.[37]

Thus, the difference between urban and rural areas is more than merely population density and the geographical distance between them: place is not uniform and interchangeable, but instead carries potentially serious issues of access and availability.

When laws and policies omit any references to place, this omission permits the urban assumption to prevail. In some instances, an urban assumption does not matter because place truly is irrelevant. In other instances, however, laws and policies may carry unexamined generalizations too far, resulting in unjustified assumptions of similarities that do not, in fact, exist.

The urban assumption's impact on federal programs, poverty, and laws and policies, come together with particular force in the area of disability. The next part of this chapter discusses this intersection of place and disability generally, and then examines the additional issues raised in the context of disasters.

## Place, Disability, and Disasters

### *The Intersection of Place and Disability*

Nearly twenty percent of the U.S. population suffers from a disability, which includes impairments of a physical, mental, sensory, and cognitive nature.[38] Although the percentage of disabled individuals is relatively constant across

---

36    *See* Craig Howley, The Rural School Bus Ride in Five States: A Report to the Rural School and Community Trust, at i (2001), *available at* http://oak.cats.ohiou. edu/~howleyc/bus2.htm (last visited May 8, 2006) (finding that in eighty-five percent of the rural elementary schools studied, the one-way duration of school bus rides exceeded thirty minutes, and that in twenty-five percent of those rural schools, the one-way duration exceeded sixty minutes); *see also* Lorna Jimerson, Slow Motion: Traveling by School Bus in Consolidated Districts in West Virginia 7 (Rural Achool and Community Trust 2007), *available at* http://www.ruraledu.org (last visited March 19, 2007) (noting that due to school consolidations, 31.1 percent of students riding a school bus travel an hour or more *each way*).

37    The lack of options is seen even in shopping for groceries. *See* Lois Wright Morton & Troy C. Blanchard, *Starved for Access: Life in Rural America's Food Deserts*, Rural Realities, *available at* http://www.ruralsociology.org/pubs/RuralRealities/Issue4.html (last visited March 12, 2007) ("Some rural areas . . . are . . . 'food deserts'—areas with limited, if any, grocery stores . . . . Filling the void in some parts of rural America are convenience stores and gas stations, which charge a premium for a limited range of food choices, often with low nutritional value.").

38    Jeanne Argoff & Harilyn Rousso, *Hardest Hit and Least Protected*, Found. News & Commentary (2005), *available at* http://foundationnews.org/CME/article.cfm?ID=3489; *see also* Univ. of Mont. Rural Inst., *Rural Facts: Update on the Demography of Rural*

urban and rural areas,[39] the impact of a disability is exacerbated by poverty and place. "Access is the major issue for people with disabilities—access to health care, housing, transportation, education, and employment. Inaccessibility is oppression."[40] As discussed above, restrictions on the availability of technology, communications, and transportation increase vulnerability—as do lower levels of education and income. According to one report, "[p]eople with disabilities are more likely to be poor than any other minority group in the country,"[41] and, as discussed earlier, poverty bears a direct relationship to place.

---

*Disability Part One: Rural and Urban*, Apr. 2005, *available at* http://rtc.ruralinstitute.umt.edu/RuDis/RuDemography.htm.

> As does rural, 'disability' has many definitions. The 2000 U.S. Census classified a person as having a disability if any of the following conditions were true: 1. A person aged five or older reported a long-lasting sensory, physical, mental or self-care disability; 2. A person aged 16 or older reported difficulty going outside the home because of a physical, mental, or emotional condition lasting six months or more; or 3. A person aged 16 to 64 reported difficulty working at a job or business because of a physical, mental, or emotional condition lasting six months or more.

39   Univ. of Mont. Rural Inst., *supra* note 38 (reflecting disability percentages of 19.2 percent in urban areas and 19.9 percent in rural areas).

40   Brad Bernier & Linda Gonzales, Issues in Rural Independent Living 56, *available at* http://eric.ed.gov/ERICDocs/data/ericdocs2/content_storage_01/0000000b/80/24/92/4f.pdf.

41   Nat'l Council on Disability, *The Needs of People with Psychiatric Disabilities During and After Hurricanes Katrina and Rita: Position Paper and Recommendations*, July 7, 2006, *available at* http://www.ncd.gov/newsroom/publications/2006/peopleneeds.htm [hereinafter Nat'l Council on Disability, *Psychiatric Disabilities*]; see also Dan Atkins & Christie Guisti, *The Confluence of Poverty and Disability*, *available at* http://www.housingforall.org/rop0304%20poverty%20and%20disability.pdf (last visited Feb. 19, 2007).

> It is relatively simple to make the causal connection between disability and poverty. Individuals with disabilities are often excluded from the labor market. Fears of increased costs, inflexibility in considering necessary accommodations, and outright prejudice, all contributed to an artificially small job market for people with disabilities. Even when included, people with disabilities often work fewer hours and in lower-paying or lower-skilled positions.

Bernier & Gonzales, *supra* note 40, at 56 ("[M]ost people with disabilities are unemployed or impoverished"); Susan S. Lang, *Federal Policies Keep People with Disabilities in a "Poverty Trap," Say Cornell Experts in Urging Major Reforms*, Cornell Univ. News Serv., Aug. 31, 2005, *available at* http://www.news.cornell.edu/stories/Aug05/disability.poverty.ssl.html (last visited Feb. 19, 2007).

> Under federal rules, people with disabilities must be unemployed in order to receive benefits. But the support they receive isn't enough to keep them out of poverty. If they do work to supplement their income, they are penalized by losing benefits. Working-age Americans with disabilities are more than twice as likely to live in poverty than other Americans;

Although there are many types and forms of disability, many physical and psychological disabilities require medical oversight—which raises another problem of both access and availability for many remote rural areas. Rural areas often lack quality medical care—fewer than nine percent of the nation's physicians practice in rural areas, even though rural dwellers comprise more than twenty percent of America's population.[42] Rural areas simply lack the financial and community resources to recruit and retain adequate numbers of medical professionals.[43]

Due to the inadequate number of facilities and physicians, rural hospitals and practitioners have little choice but to focus on general medicine[44]—specialists are largely the province of urban areas because rural areas lack the financial incentives and the client base to support them. Those with mental disabilities face even greater problems: in 1999, eighty-seven percent of the designated Mental Health Professional Shortage Areas in the United States were rural.[45] The shortage of rural mental health professionals necessarily forces rural primary care physicians into serving mental health concerns.[46] Unfortunately, however, studies have concluded that "[p]rimary care physicians have a poor track record of detecting, accurately diagnosing, and appropriately treating or referring mental health and substance

---

*see also* Atkins & Guisti, *supra*, at 6 ("For those who are so disabled that competitive work is an impossibility, Social Security Disability Insurance and Supplemental Security Income are most often relied upon. However, federal benefits do not provide a living wage, making poverty an inevitability.").

42 *See* Patrick H. DeLeon, Mary Wakefield & Kristofer J. Hagglund, *The Behavioral Health Care Needs of Rural Communities in the 21st Century*, *in* RURAL BEHAVIORAL HEALTH CARE: AN INTERDISCIPLINARY GUIDE 23, 26 (B. Hudnall Stamm ed., 2003).

43 *See* Sue A. Kuba & Mary Beth Kenkel, *The Wellness of Women: Implications for the Rural Health Care Provider*, *in* PRACTICING PSYCHOLOGY IN RURAL SETTINGS: HOSPITAL PRIVILEGES AND COLLABORATIVE CARE 113, 123 (Jerry A. Morris ed., 1997) (noting the problems of "physician burnout and difficulties in retaining physicians in rural areas"); *see also* B. Hudnall Stamm et al., *Introduction*, *in* RURAL BEHAVIORAL HEALTH CARE: AN INTERDISCIPLINARY GUIDE 3, 8 (B. Hudnall Stamm ed., 2003) ("People living in rural and frontier areas need health care, but it can be difficult to recruit and retain professionals to provide that care.").

44 *See* James H. Bray, Michael F. Enright & John Rogers, *Collaboration with Primary Care Physicians*, *in* PRACTICING PSYCHOLOGY IN RURAL SETTINGS: HOSPITAL PRIVILEGES AND COLLABORATIVE CARE 55, 57 (Jerry A. Morris ed., 1997) (noting that "rural physicians . . . do not have ready access to specialists or colleagues to share responsibility for patient care").

45 *See* Larry Gamm, Sarah Stone & Stephanie Pittman, *Mental Health and Mental Disorders—A Rural Challenge*, *available at* http://www.srph.tamhsc.edu/centers/rhp2010/ 08Volume1mentalhealth.htm (last visited Feb. 18, 2007).

46 Bray et al., *supra* note 44, at 55 ("Particularly in rural areas, primary care physicians are usually the first medical professionals to encounter patients' behavioral health problems."); *see also* Univ. of Mont. Rural Inst., *supra* note 38 ("Given the shortage of rural mental health professionals, the primary-care doctor is often the main contact for mental health concerns").

abuse problems. . . . In fact, the recognition rate of mental disorders by primary care physicians in hospital settings has been surveyed at from 10% to 50% . . ..."[47]

> Unlike the urban centers with multiple hospitals in close proximity, specialized psychiatric hospitals and day treatment facilities available minutes away, and a broad array of doctors of psychology and psychiatry available, rural hospitals often must rely on collaboration between a handful of general physicians and one or two psychologists or a part-time consulting psychiatrist who lives in a remote urban center.[48]

The shortage of rural physicians and mental health professionals is exacerbated by geographical dispersion and transportation issues that hinder the ability of rural dwellers to get to medical care.[49] As one study observed, rural communities that are adjacent to an urban center benefit from lower mortality rates,[50] as contrasted with more remote, isolated rural communities.

Thus, the burdens carried by those who are disabled often are exacerbated by accompanying issues of poverty and place. Despite the preference in our laws and policies to avoid place-specific references, place often carries a significance that renders its omission a furtherance of urban bias, and a corresponding detriment to rural areas. In particular, and as relevant to this volume, place in fact puts some citizens at higher risks during natural disasters and hinders their ability to recover from such disasters.

## The Vulnerability of the Rural Disabled in Disasters

Natural disasters raise the specter of particularly disastrous consequences for the disabled. Whether in the context of hurricanes, tornadoes, earthquakes, wildfires, tsunamis, floods, avalanches, or other natural disasters, such disasters tend to implicate the necessity for flight and flexibility.[51] For the physically disabled, the ability to flee may be severely circumscribed by the availability of a handicapped-

---

47　Jerry A. Morris, *The Rural Psychologist in the Hospital Emergency Room, in* PRACTICING PSYCHOLOGY IN RURAL SETTINGS: HOSPITAL PRIVILEGES AND COLLABORATIVE CARE 81, 85 (Jerry A. Morris ed., 1997).

48　*Id.*

49　Bray et al., *supra* note 44, at 61 (noting that in rural communities, "people often have to travel great distances over difficult terrain to receive care").

50　Lois Wright Morton, *Spatial Patterns of Rural Mortality, in* CRITICAL ISSUES IN RURAL HEALTH 37, 40 (Nina Glasgow et al. eds., 2004).

51　*See* Nat'l Council on Disability, *Saving Lives: Including People with Disabilities in Emergency Planning*, Apr. 2005, *available at* http://www.ncd.gov/newsroom/publications/2005/saving_lives.htm (last visited Dec. 20. 2006) [hereinafter Nat'l Council on Disability, *Saving Lives*] ("Disaster preparedness and emergency response systems are typically designed for people without disabilities, for whom escape or rescue involves walking, running, driving, seeing, hearing, and quickly responding to directions").

accessible van—or by the availability of a sufficiently strong non-disabled person to carry the individual to the attic, to the storm cellar, or down the stairs of a high-rise building. For the mentally disabled, the ability to flee may be limited by comprehension issues, by fear of the outside world, or by outsiders' often irrational fear of the mentally ill. Lacking alternatives and financial resources, the disabled can easily become trapped in their homes. And even if the disabled obtain the assistance needed to physically escape from a disaster, their ongoing need for medical care, prescription medicine, or psychiatric treatment can present difficult issues.

As Hurricane Katrina powerfully illustrated, place carries profound significance both for disability law and for the disabled. Twenty-five percent of Katrina's evacuees were disabled[52]—a proportion that is itself twenty-five percent higher than the nineteen to twenty percent that we would expect.

> [T]he mounting evidence demonstrates that the hurricanes did not affect everyone in their path equally. People with disabilities, who often have the fewest resources and the greatest barriers to evacuation, were among the hardest hit. . . . [O]f the 61 percent of people who did not evacuate before Katrina hit, 38 percent said they were either physically unable to leave or had to care for someone who was physically unable to leave.[53]

The evacuation of disabled residents during Hurricane Katrina was hampered by the failure to include the disabled in disaster planning.[54] Despite a number of other disasters offering lessons to be learned—9/11 in New York, hurricane experiences in Florida, and earthquakes in California, among others—and despite the fact that the danger of flooding in New Orleans was well known, the same omissions in disaster planning with respect to the disabled occur over and over again.

> The same access mistakes appear to be made repeatedly in disaster management activities. Lessons learned after a disaster about reducing access barriers following disasters are not integrated into subsequent practice. Such barriers include access to physical plants, communications, and programs in recovery centers; other structures and buildings used in connection with disaster operations such as first aid stations, mass feeding areas, portable payphone stations, portable toilets, temporary housing; and shelters, which may present barriers to identification, access, management, training, and services.[55]

---

52  *See* Information on Disability for Empowerment, Advocacy and Support, *Katrina Disability Information*, Feb. 2007, *available at* http://katrinadisability.info (last visited Feb. 18, 2007).

53  Argoff & Rousso, *supra* note 38.

54  *See* Nat'l Council on Disability, *Psychiatric Disabilities, supra* note 41.

55  Nat'l Council on Disability, *Saving Lives, supra* note 51.

The inadequacies of disaster planning are particularly exacerbated in the context of psychiatric disabilities. There is a tendency to associate "disabled" with "wheelchair," such that many other forms of disability, including deafness, blindness, and psychiatric issues, receive even less attention in disaster planning. Hurricane Katrina provided some horrifying examples of discrimination, mismanagement, and lack of accountability against the mentally disabled, including emergency shelters that refused entry to the mentally disabled; group home residents who were lost by emergency officials; and mentally disabled evacuees who were institutionalized inappropriately.[56]

Individuals with psychiatric disabilities experienced discrimination both during Hurricane Katrina's evacuation efforts[57] as well as when they attempted to seek refuge in emergency shelters; many people died or unnecessarily suffered traumatic experiences.[58]

> First responders and emergency managers such as shelter operators often violated the civil rights requirements of the Americans with Disabilities Act and Section 504 of the Rehabilitation Act. As a result, people with disabilities did not have access to critical services and relief. Some of the most common forms of discrimination included: People with disabilities were segregated from the general population in some shelters while other shelters simply refused to let them enter. People with psychiatric disabilities were denied access to housing and other services because of erroneous fears and stereotypes of people with psychiatric disabilities.

> [D]isaster response plans often did not include protocols to evacuate people with psychiatric disabilities. During evacuations, emergency officials physically lost residents of group homes and psychiatric facilities, many of whom are still missing. Others have not or cannot return home because essential supports have not been restored or because the cost of living has increased too much. When people with psychiatric disabilities arrived at evacuation locations—ranging from state parks to churches—those locations often were not prepared to meet the medical and mental health needs of the evacuees with psychiatric disabilities.

---

56　Nat'l Council on Disability, *Psychiatric Disabilities*, *supra* note 41.
Some people with psychiatric disabilities were sent to state psychiatric institutions or jails when all they needed was a medication refill. A recurring theme was that people with psychiatric disabilities were placed in nursing homes and institutions, not because they required that level of care, but because there was nowhere else for them to go, or because they needed medications that the shelters did not have.
*See also id.* ("One Mississippi advocate reported that American Red Cross shelters were only opened in urban areas, not rural areas, in Mississippi.").

57　*See, e.g., id.* ("Evacuees with disabilities had a difficult time conveying the trauma caused by the unexpected arrival of uniformed officers who ordered them out of their homes and sometimes forcibly removed them.").

58　*Id.*

Many people with psychiatric disabilities never made it to evacuation shelters because they were inappropriately and involuntarily institutionalized. Some of these people still have not been discharged, despite evaluations that indicate they should be.[59]

The reality that most laws and policies do not address place was seen in another Katrina-specific example. The State of Louisiana's Hurricane Evacuation and Sheltering Plan, as it existed at the time of Hurricanes Katrina and Rita, noted some of the problems in evacuating New Orleans, but did not take note of the problems unique to evacuating rural areas, leaving both the acknowledgement of such issues and the planning to address such issues to the local parishes.[60] And, in a recurring theme, emergency shelters tend to be centrally located, which in rural areas necessarily means that shelters are geographically spread out and require a reliable means of transportation to get there.[61]

Even when the disabled were safely evacuated, other issues arose during recovery efforts that illustrate not just the risk, but the reality of forgetting the disabled in disaster planning and recovery. For example, despite the disproportionate impact of the hurricanes upon disabled individuals, it took a lawsuit to make the Federal Emergency Management Agency (FEMA) provide trailers that were accessible for those with a physical disability. The lawsuit, which settled in September 2006, required FEMA to provide trailers with accessibility features for those who are disabled, including ramps, wider doorways, and grab bars, as well as lower appliances, sinks, and cabinets.[62]

The repeated failure to include the disabled in discussions concerning disaster planning risks the health and the very lives of the disabled. The tension and fear created by a disaster situation rises exponentially for the disabled, who, depending on their particular disability, may have limitations regarding their mobility, comprehension, or coping abilities. These problems can be exacerbated in rural areas, where technology, communications, transportation, and health care are not always available to the same degree and in the same manner as in urban areas. Accessibility, availability, and options can be serious issues in rural areas—essentially handicapping rural areas at the outset, and thereby imposing an additional handicapping condition on disabled individuals living in such rural areas. These underlying issues of accessibility, availability, and options necessitate additional attention to "place" in terms of the disabled generally, and in the context of disaster planning specifically.

---

59   Nat'l Council on Disability, *Psychiatric Disabilities, supra* note 41.

60   Office of Emergency Preparedness, State of Louisiana, *Southeast La. Hurricane Evacuation and Sheltering Plan*, Jan. 2000, at II-1 to II-4.

61   *Id.* at VI-1.

62   *See* Brou v. FEMA, No. 06-0838 (E.D. La. 2006), *available at* http://www.fema.gov/pdf/library/brou_fema.pdf.

Unfortunately, disaster planning is not the only area in which place carries an impact. Place also plays a role in disaster recovery. Following the major hurricanes of 2005, low-income households generally, and rural households in particular, suffered disadvantages during the subsequent recovery efforts due to choices in laws and policies that disregard the impact of place. In the United States, private property insurance and individual savings are the primary financial resources for repairing and rebuilding. But full insurance coverage and financial reserves tend to be the province of those with strong financial resources, not those who are barely getting by.

Relying on an approach to recovery that is market- and insurance-driven disadvantages low-income and rural households—both homeowners and renters— because they are more likely to lack insurance, to have inadequate insurance, and to lack important insurance options, such as flood, hurricane, or earthquake coverage, full replacement value coverage, and coverage for temporary housing expenses.[63]

Of the 5.9 million people living in the counties declared eligible for individual hurricane assistance, 1.6 million of them—or twenty-seven percent—were in rural areas.[64] The median family income of the rural victims was about one-fourth lower and the poverty rate about one-third higher than for the urban victims.[65]

The American dream is home ownership. However, low-income families are often funneled into homes that are older, built in more vulnerable areas, constructed with lower quality materials or poorly built, and constructed under older, less stringent building codes, particularly in rural areas.[66] Mobile homes provide the opportunity for home ownership at a dramatically lower cost than traditional housing.[67] Most cities have restrictions regarding mobile homes, and

---

63   *See* Walter Gillis Peacock & Chris Girard, *Ethnic and Racial Inequalities in Hurricane Damage and Insurance Settlements*, *in* HURRICANE ANDREW: ETHNICITY, GENDER AND THE SOCIOLOGY OF DISASTERS 171, 180 (Walter Gillis Peacock et al. eds., 1997).

64   *See* Rural School & Cmty. Trust, *Hidden Rural Realities of Hurricane Katrina*, 8 RURAL POLICY MATTERS (The Rural School and Community Trust, No. 9) Sept. 2006, *available at* http://www.ruraledu.org/site/c.beJMIZOCIrH/b.2059003/apps/nl/content. asp?content_id=%7B50A94578-EBF2-4B5F-ACD7-DEB4C04C541B%7D&notoc=1 (last visited Feb. 20, 2007).

65   *Id.*

66   *See* R. Bolin & L. Stanford, *The Northridge Earthquake: Community-Based Approaches at Unmet Recovery Needs*, 22 DISASTERS 21, 38 (1998); Hous. Assistance Council, *supra* note 23.

67   *See* Lori Nitschke, *Manufactured Homes a Big Factor in Rural Homeownership in U.S.*, POPULATION REFERENCE BUREAU (2004), *available at* http://www.prb.org/Articles/2004/ ManufacturedHomesaBigFactorinRuralHomeownershipinUS.aspx ("[T]he median value of manufactured homes was $31,200, according to the latest census, compared with $119,600 for all owner-occupied homes"). *See generally* LANCE GEORGE & MILANA BARR, MOVING HOME: MANUFACTURED HOUSING IN RURAL AMERICA (Housing Assistance Council, 2005), *available at* http://www.knowledgeplex.org/showdoc.html?id=137748 (last visited Feb. 20,

rural areas tend to be more lenient. However, mobile homes create an additional vulnerability—mobile homes are less sturdy than traditional housing and more susceptible to extensive damage in natural disasters.[68] Rural residents in Hurricane Katrina's path were more than twice as likely as their urban counterparts to live in mobile homes.[69] Nearly a quarter of housing units in the rural disaster areas were mobile homes, compared with one-tenth of those in the urban disaster areas.[70]

Disadvantages to rural households persist into the legal system's bankruptcy provisions. Amendments in 2005 to the bankruptcy laws restrict access to bankruptcy as a method of discharging debt and starting fresh.[71] A recent study concluded that rural households filing for bankruptcy earn significantly lower incomes and have higher debt-to-income ratios than urban households filing for bankruptcy.[72] In addition to these financial disadvantages, the new bankruptcy laws require debtors to undergo credit counseling and complete a personal financial management course.[73] These new provisions are particularly burdensome for rural households—credit counseling agencies do not tend to exist in remote rural areas, and completing a personal financial management course is likely to require travel to a more urban area.[74]

Higher rates of poverty, as well as geographical isolation and dispersion and lack of public transportation, all render rural populations more vulnerable to natural disasters. The greater vulnerabilities for low income and rural households translate into an increased likelihood of insufficient insurance, inadequate insurance settlements, and less government assistance to repair and rebuild. When we factor in disability, we see still greater vulnerability.

---

2007) ("Mobile homes, manufactured homes, trailers—by whatever name, these units are an important part of rural America's housing landscape. . . . [W]ith less than one-quarter of the nation's homes, rural areas contain half of all U.S. manufactured homes.").

68   *See* Philip Rosenbloom, *Homeowners, and Tenants Too: Mobile Homeowners Face Unique, Yet Familiar, Challenges*, NAT'L HOUS. INST. (2000), *available at* http://www.nhi.org/online/issues/112/rosenbloom.html (last visited Feb. 20, 2007) ("One of the most well-known safety issues particular to mobile homes is their trouble resisting severe weather conditions, such as tornadoes, hurricanes, and flooding. A recent study by FEMA's Building Performance Assessment Team indicates that no mobile home can withstand even a medium-grade tornado.").

69   *See* Rogelio Saenz & Walter G. Peacock, *Rural People, Rural Places: The Hidden Costs of Hurricane Katrina*, RURAL REALITIES, *available at* http://www.ruralsociology.org/pubs/RuralRealities/Issue1.html (last visited March 12, 2007).

70   *Id.*

71   *See* BAPCPA Act of 2005, Pub. L. No. 109-8, 119 Stat. 23 (2005) (codified at 11 U.S.C. §§ 101–1502).

72   *See* Porter, *supra* note 4, at 998, 1001.

73   *See* BAPCPA, Pub. L. No. 109-8, §§ 105–106, 119 Stat. 36–37 (2006) (codified at 11 U.S.C. §§ 109(h)(1), 111(a)).

74   Porter, *supra* note 4, at 1023–24.

## Conclusion

Despite the desire for laws and policies with broad societal applicability, the failure to account for "place" can create false generalities. Urban assumptions regarding technology, communication, and transportation—as well as accessibility, availability, and options more generally—are largely untrue for rural areas, especially remote rural areas. In particular, place puts rural dwellers, and especially disabled rural dwellers, at higher risks during natural disasters and hinders their recovery. As was seen during Hurricanes Katrina and Rita, the failure to include the special considerations of the rural and the disabled in disaster planning has the potential for life-threatening consequences.

## Acknowledgements

Many thanks to Robin Paul Malloy for his invitation to participate in the 2006 Property, Citizenship, and Social Entrepreneurism Workshop, and to the workshop participants for their helpful comments. I also presented this paper as part of the Faculty Enrichment Series at the University of Florida College of Law and would like to thank the UF faculty for their helpful comments and suggestions.

# Chapter 5

# Natural Disasters and Persons with Disabilities

Janet E. Lord, Michael E. Waterstone, and Michael Ashley Stein

## Introduction

On January 3, 2006, the *Washington Post* ridiculed United States efforts towards ensuring disability-inclusiveness in its development schemes as an example of foreign aid run amok on senseless expenditures.[1] It accused Congress of having parodied "its own mania for control" by mandating that American-financed construction in the developing world comply with United States disability law. The editorial asserted that in consequence of this policy "remote clinics in Afghanistan have wheelchair ramps" despite the fact "that there are no wheelchairs in the vicinity."[2] Putting aside the editorial's legal, social, and factual inaccuracies,[3] it is striking that an otherwise esteemed publication reached such an inapposite conclusion regarding the place of disability in the context of development. Only three months earlier, disdain for disability integration had contributed to many avoidable tragedies in the wake of Hurricanes Katrina and Rita.[4]

Emergency situations arising from natural disasters invariably cause human suffering. It is the responsibility of domestic governments and international humanitarian assistance organizations to minimize this anguish to the greatest extent possible, especially for vulnerable populations. Almost by definition, advance planning is crucial. Yet all too often governments, humanitarian assistance agencies, and other policy makers fail to adopt a disability perspective in natural disaster humanitarian crisis situations. With distressing frequency, the disability experience is either neglected completely or lost when cast among other vulnerable groups. Below, we examine these failures in several contexts, and make suggestions for more integrated and disability-appropriate advance planning. We

---

1 Editorial, *Reforming Foreign Assistance*, WASH. POST., Jan. 3, 2006, at A16.

2 *Id.*

3 Letter from Lex Frieden, then-Chairperson of the National Council on Disability, to Fred Hiatt, Editorial Page Editor, THE WASHINGTON POST (Jan. 27, 2006), *available at* http://www.ncd.gov/newsroom/correspondence/2006/hiatt_01-27-06.htm. In an open letter, Frieden noted several errors in the editorial.

4 *See* Michael E. Waterstone & Michael Ashley Stein, *Emergency Preparedness and People with Disabilities*, 30 MENTAL & PHYSICAL DISABILITY L. REP. 338 (2006).

introduce the problem through the lens of United States domestic policy during Hurricanes Katrina and Rita, and then globalize the problem by examining the role of disability and humanitarian assistance programming in the developing world.

Our assertion in this chapter is straightforward: considering the disability experience and including persons with disabilities when planning disaster relief in the first instance minimizes human harm and reduces (re)development costs in the future.

### Hurricanes Katrina and Rita: Failures of Governmental Natural Disaster Planning

Historically, federal-level disaster preparedness has not adequately acknowledged the circumstances of persons with disabilities. On July 24, 2004, President Bush issued an Executive Order entitled "Individuals with Disabilities in Emergency Preparedness." This Order unambiguously required administrative agencies to support the safety and security of individuals with disabilities in situations involving disasters, including floods and hurricanes.[5] Nevertheless, the National Response Plan—issued by the Department of Homeland Security in December 2004 as an "all-discipline, all-hazards plan that establishes a single comprehensive framework for the management of domestic incidents"—nowhere mentions disabled persons.[6]

In July 2005, a year after the Executive Order, the Interagency Coordinating Council (ICC), which is comprised of senior leadership from twenty-three federal departments and agencies, issued an interagency report discussing the vulnerabilities and challenges facing the fifty-four million Americans with disabilities in time of disaster.[7] The report recognized that disaster mitigation, preparedness, response, and recovery planning efforts overlooked people with disabilities. Although it attempted the first steps of establishing a concerted interagency approach to deal with these complex issues, the report was operating in the shadow of overwhelming historic neglect.

Sadly, the various federal administrative agencies charged with disaster preparedness—primarily, though not exclusively, the Department of Homeland Security, the Federal Emergency Management Agency (FEMA), and the Department of Health and Human Services—and the larger effort of federal disaster relief coordination, failed in their obligations to provide for the needs of persons with disabilities during Hurricanes Katrina and Rita. Temporary shelters

---

5  Exec. Order No. 13,347, 69 Fed. Reg. 44,573 (July 22, 2004).

6  U.S. Dep't of Homeland Security, National Response Plan iii (2004), *available at* http://www.dhs.gov/xlibrary/assets/NRPbaseplan.pdf.

7  U.S. Dep't of Homeland Security Office for Civil Rights and Civil Liberties, Individuals with Disabilities in Emergency Preparedness (2005), *available at* http://www.dhs.gov/xlibrary/assets/CRCL_IWDEP_AnnualReport_2005.pdf.

lacked accessible entrances and restrooms; people with disabilities were separated from their families, who often provide them support; and evacuees were displaced without assistive technologies.[8] The mainstream relief entities were severely challenged in finding medical necessities, including wheelchairs and medication; obtaining Braille and captioned information; and securing personal assistance services.[9] The National Organization on Disability reported that less than thirty percent of shelters had access to American Sign Language interpreters; eighty percent lacked TTYs; sixty percent did not have televisions with open caption capability; and only fifty-six percent had areas where oral announcements were posted.[10]

People with disabilities had no centralized source of disability-related information, and relief workers had not been trained to assist them.[11] Worse, many shelters turned away disability specialists and their offered assistance. For example, disability organizations in Louisiana had difficulty securing permission to enter shelters so as to identify the needs of evacuees with disabilities, and to provide them with service referrals.[12] Disability trained professionals in the Gulf Coast areas have reported impending crises, as Red Cross shelters are being closed without plans for accessible housing alternatives.[13]

Although litigation under existing civil rights statutes is one way of improving the government's disaster readiness for people with disabilities,[14] these preparations ultimately demand a better integrated and implemented policy approach throughout the federal government. Among the lessons learned from Hurricanes Katrina and Rita is that the needs of the disabled population must be both recognized and integrated into future federal policy planning. Policymakers can only properly

---

8   Lex Frieden, *Involve People with Disabilities in Relief Plans: Let's Learn from Our Mistakes Before the Next Disaster Strikes*, CLARION-LEDGER, Jan. 7, 2006.

9   *Id.*

10   *See also* The Henry J. Kaiser Family Foundation, The Washington Post/Kaiser Family Foundation/Harvard University Survey of Hurricane Katrina Evacuees, *available at* http://www.kff.org/newsmedia/washpost.cfm (last visited Nov. 13, 2008) (detailing that twenty-two percent of polled Astrodome evacuees were physically unable to leave, and twenty-three percent were caring for someone who was physically unable to leave).

11   *See* Frieden, *supra* note 8.

12   *Id.*

13   *Id. See also* Jennifer Medina, *Storm and Crisis: Voices from the Storm: Stuck in a Shelter, and Left Asking "Why?,"* N.Y. TIMES (Oct. 5, 2005), at A25; Mary Jimenez, *Bossier Civic Center Closes Special Needs Shelter*, SHREVEPORT TIMES (Oct. 7, 2005), at 1A.

14   *See* Brou v. FEMA, No. 06-0838 (E.D. La. Filed Feb. 16, 2006) (class of persons with disabilities bringing suit against FEMA under the Section 504 of the Rehabilitation Act, the Fair Housing Amendments Act, and the Stafford Act, seeking injunctive relief requiring FEMA to provide accessible trailers and develop accessible information systems). A settlement, which was reached on September 26, 2006, requiring FEMA to provide accessible housing to the plaintiffs and some others, may be found at http://www.fema. gov/pdf/library/brou_fema.pdf.

target priorities and develop appropriate responses if they first acknowledge the life experience and concerns of persons with disabilities.

There are signs from within the federal government that expertise on issues impacting the disability community will gain a stronger foothold in disaster planning. After Hurricanes Katrina and Rita, President Bush ordered the Department of Homeland Security to conduct a review, in cooperation with local counterparts, of emergency planning in every major city. In a September 23, 2005 memo, Secretary Michael Chertoff ordered that this review include rigorous examination of plans for persons with disabilities. The ICC issued preliminary statements on lessons learned from Hurricanes Katrina and Rita and disaster preparedness,[15] with the formal report scheduled for July 2006 release.[16]

The Department of Justice also released a new technical assistance document that sets forth "action steps" in five areas: planning, notification, evacuation, sheltering, and returning home.[17] These steps include soliciting and incorporating input from people with different types of disabilities; ensuring that evacuation plans enable disabled persons to safely evacuate or be evacuated by others; making certain that temporary shelters are accessible; developing site-specific instructions for shelter staff and volunteers to address disability-related concerns; providing that persons who use service animals are not separated from them when sheltering; making sure that a reasonable number of shelters have back-up generators for life-saving medical devices and a way to keep medications such as insulin refrigerated; having available accessible communication for individuals who are hard of hearing, blind, and visually impaired; and identifying temporary accessible housing that can be used if persons with disabilities cannot immediately return home.[18]

At the same time, Bills failed in both the House and Senate that would have required, among other things, that a disability coordinator be appointed within the Department of Homeland Security to coordinate and effectively implement all federal government disability disaster preparedness policies.[19] Although not the only choice that could improve policy planning in this area, such a coordinator could have been a useful tool to integrate an otherwise chaotic approach to federal disability policy. The appointment of a Disability Coordinator is still possible due

---

15    The ICC's plans are set forth in a PowerPoint entitled *Interagency Coordinating Council on Emergency Preparedness and Individuals with Disabilities: Hurricane Katrina Lessons Learned, Proposed Approach* (Feb. 15, 2006), and in a brief article entitled *The Impact of Hurricanes Katrina and Rita on People with Disabilities: What Lessons Should We Learn?* (Mar. 2006) (unpublished documents, on file with authors).

16    It has not been released as of this writing in April 2007.

17    DISABILITY RIGHTS SECTION, CIVIL RIGHTS DIVISION, U.S. DEPARTMENT OF JUSTICE, AN ADA GUIDE FOR LOCAL GOVERNMENTS: MAKING COMMUNITY EMERGENCY PREPAREDNESS AND RESPONSE PROGRAMS ACCESSIBLE TO PEOPLE WITH DISABILITIES (last update Aug. 5, 2006), *available at* http://www.ada.gov/emerprepguidescrn.pdf.

18    *Id.*

19    S. 2124, 109th Cong. § 1 (2005); H.R. 4704, 109th Cong. § 2 (2006).

to a mandate included in a Homeland Security Appropriations bill that was signed by President Bush, but as of this writing that position has not been filled.[20]

## Disability and Humanitarian Assistance Programming in the Developing World

Hurricanes Katrina and Rita poignantly demonstrated the inadequacy of United States disaster preparedness for meeting the needs of persons with disabilities. But this problem is international in scope. Recent humanitarian emergencies abroad—both natural disasters and crises resulting from armed conflict—have revealed the failure of large-scale assistance operations conducted by international agencies to respond appropriately to the needs of disabled beneficiaries. Indeed, the responses of the humanitarian community to successive disasters during 2005 resulted in a crisis of accountability when numerous studies, including a United Nations commissioned review of overall humanitarian responses and the Tsunami Evaluation Coalition report, found that transparency, communication and accountability to affected populations was notably lacking in relief efforts.[21] Below, we examine these failures, and show that, as in the case of the United States domestic policy, there is a lack of proactive thinking and integration of the life experiences of persons with disabilities in international humanitarian action.

### *Disability and Natural Disaster: Asian Tsunami*

The experience of tsunami relief efforts in Asia disclosed a number of challenges related to the readiness of large-scale relief operations implemented by humanitarian assistance organizations to respond effectively to the needs of people with disabilities. Initial reports suggest that these organizations were largely unprepared and ill-equipped to address even the most basic needs of people with disabilities in the provision of shelter, food, water, and health care services.

For example, the Center for International Rehabilitation (CIR) conducted an assessment of humanitarian assistance in tsunami affected regions of India, Thailand, and Indonesia.[22] The report found that the majority of temporary

---

20    *See* National Council on Disability Public Consultation, *Homeland Security, Emergency Preparedness, Disaster Relief and Recovery* (May 31, 2007), *available at* http://www.ncd.gov/newsroom/publications/2007/ncd_consultant_05-31-07.htm.

21    John Cosgrave, Synthesis Report: Expanded Summary: Joint Evaluation of the International Response to the Indian Ocean Tsunami (Tsunami Evaluation Commission 2007), *available at* http://www.tsunami-evaluation.org/NR/rdonlyres/2E8A3262-0320-4656-BC81-EE0B46B54CAA/0/SynthRep.pdf.

22    International Disability Rights Monitor, *Disability and Tsunami Relief Efforts in India, Indonesia and Thailand* (2005), *available at* http://www.ideanet.org/cir/uploads/File/TsunamiReport.pdf.

shelters were not accessible to people with physical disabilities. The Indonesian government, for example, requested the International Organization for Migration to construct eleven thousand semi-permanent homes and shelters for the tsunami-affected population.[23] The design could house up to seven people or be adapted for use as a medical clinic or school. Nevertheless, these structures (including their latrines) were inaccessible to people with physical disabilities.[24] Also in Indonesia, food distribution systems relied heavily on an internal displacement camp system that was inaccessible.[25] Among the many health challenges throughout affected areas, there was a major shortage of assistive devices. Most serious was the lack of mental health or counseling services for disaster affected populations. Where mental health services were available, they tended to be inaccessible because of a lack of transportation options, or where physically attainable, their focus was limited to addressing shelter needs.[26]

Initial assessment of reconstruction efforts in tsunami-affected areas suggests that rebuilding damaged and destroyed infrastructure is proceeding without regard for disability-related issues, many of which could be addressed at little or no cost if integrated into the planning process of reconstruction. According to CIR, the majority of post-tsunami reconstruction simply does not take accessibility into account. One of the major conclusions of the report is that this absence of disability-related standards is largely due to the exclusion of disabled persons from planning consultations.

*International Standards*

International legal standards—both obligations set forth in international treaties[27] as well as principles enshrined in customary international law[28]—underscore the obligation to provide protection and assistance to affected populations in time of

---

23    *Id.* at 48–49.

24    *Id.* Similarly, in India temporary shelters were barrier-free, but latrines were located far away from the shelters, thereby compromising access. *Id.* at 24.

25    *Id.* at 48.

26    *Id.* at 7.

27    The Third and Fourth Geneva Conventions recognize special respect and protection to be accorded to persons with disabilities in the context of evacuation and the treatment of persons deprived of their liberty. *See* Geneva Convention Relative to the Treatment of Prisoners of War, Aug. 12, 1949, 6 U.S.T. 3316, 75 U.N.T.S. 135 (Third Geneva Convention), Articles 16, 30, 44–45, 49, and 110; Geneva Convention Relative to the Protection of Civilian Persons in Time of War, Aug. 12, 1949, 6 U.S.T. 3516, 75 U.N.T.S. 287 (Fourth Geneva Convention), Articles 16–17, 21–22, 27, 85, 119, and 127. The Fourth Geneva Convention, Article 16(1), also provides that such persons "shall be the object of particular protection and respect."

28    Thus, Rule 138 of the ICRC Customary International Humanitarian Law commentary provides that elderly, persons with disabilities and infirm people affected by armed conflict are entitled to special respect and protection as a rule of international

humanitarian crisis, including persons with disabilities. While recognition that persons with disabilities are a particularly at-risk population in emergency crises is reflected in many international instruments, it has rarely given rise to specific policies and practices or effective field-level interventions that seek to ensure that the needs of disabled people are addressed.

Many international humanitarian assistance organizations (including United Nations specialized agencies and large private voluntary organizations) do characterize their work variously as protection-oriented, "rights-based," and, in particular, addressing the needs of the most vulnerable. The United Nations High Commissioner for Refugees, for example, embraces the rights of refugees within an international protection framework, underlining the reality that refugees, by definition, do not enjoy the protection of their home countries. Its mandate is to provide international protection and promote durable solutions to their problems.[29] Nonetheless, it has no disability-specific policy. Similarly, the premier Danish Refugee Council (DRC) has as its mandate the "[p]rotection and promotion of durable solutions to refugee and displacement problems, on the basis of humanitarian principles and human rights" and draws on numerous international standards and guidelines to inform its approach.[30] The DRC likewise has no disability policy per se, rather, it embraces an approach that is aimed at capturing the most vulnerable in need of assistance. As such, the implicit claim is that the needs of all—including affected people with disabilities—are addressed in humanitarian and relief programming at all stages.

The Sphere Project's Humanitarian Charter and Minimum Standards in Disaster Response, an effort to develop an operational framework for accountability in disaster response, does specifically acknowledge their applicability to disabled persons.[31] Nonetheless, the Charter provides little to no guidance on how the needs of persons with disabilities may be accommodated in the sector-specific indicators for water, food security, shelter and health.[32] Typically, programmatic policies and guidelines rarely do more than identify disability in a laundry list of socially differentiated groups requiring protection. References to disability-specific information in indicators and guidance notes are scant.[33]

---

humanitarian law. Jean-Marie Henckaerts & Louise Doswald-Beck, 1 CUSTOMARY INTERNATIONAL HUMANITARIAN LAW 489 (Cambridge U. Press 2005).

29   *See* http://www.unhcr.org/protect.html.

30   The mandate was approved by the Executive Committee of the Danish Refugee Council in 2004 and is restated in its May 2005 DRC Comprehensive Framework for Assistance (unpublished documents, on file with authors).

31   The Sphere Project, *Humanitarian Charter and Minimum Standards in Disaster Response* (2004), *available at* http://www.sphereproject.org.

32   *Id.* at Introduction: Chapter 4, Minimum Standards in Water Supply, Sanitation, and Hygiene Promotion.

33   *Id.* at Appendix 1, Health Services Assessment Checklist.

In recent years, humanitarian organizations have responded to growing criticism that they are failing to meet the specific needs of affected populations by developing common codes and accountability initiatives.[34] One such response was the drafting of the Code of Conduct for the International Red Cross and Red Crescent Movement and NGOs in Disaster Relief (Code).[35] The Code underscores the principles driving humanitarian assistance efforts, including the mandate to "alleviate human suffering amongst those least able to withstand the stress caused by disaster."[36] The provision of aid is to be provided on the basis of non-discrimination, that is, "regardless of the race, creed or nationality of the recipients and without adverse distinction of any kind."[37] Aid, where possible, is to be based on a thorough assessment of the needs of disaster victims and the local capacities already in place to meet those needs. The Code, therefore, embraces an approach that is highly relevant to persons with disabilities insofar as they are a severely at-risk population in humanitarian crises. Also of note is the explicit embrace of the principle of beneficiary participation in humanitarian assistance.[38] The Code thus provides a point of departure for ensuring the rights of persons with disabilities are in fact protected in the context of humanitarian action.

While the foregoing are all important efforts, deepening responsibility will require building the capacity of agency personnel, including accountability staff, to discern the varying needs of beneficiaries and assess in a meaningful way the

---

34   The commitment to beneficiary accountability is reflected in various other initiatives to make humanitarian assistance organizations more accountable to those they serve. Thus, the Humanitarian Accountability Partnership was founded in 2003 as an effort to improve the accountability of humanitarian action to intended beneficiaries through self-regulatory initiatives and compliance verification. Humanitarian Accountability Partnership (HAP), *The Humanitarian Accountability Report 2005* (2005), *available at* http://www. hapinternational.org. Other similar initiatives which are responsive to the crisis of quality and accountability in humanitarian action include ALNAP, Compas Qualité, and People in Aid. For a brief overview of the development of accountability initiatives within the humanitarian assistance community, *see* HAP at 7–13.

35   Code of Conduct for the International Red Cross and Red Crescent Movement and NGOs in Disaster Relief (1995), *available at* http://www.icrc.org/Web/Eng/siteeng0.nsf/ html/57JMNB. The Code of Conduct was prepared jointly by the International Federation of Red Cross and Red Crescent Societies and the International Committee of the Red Cross and was sponsored by the following relief organizations: Caritas Internationalis, Catholic Relief Services, The International Federation of Red Cross and Red Crescent Societies, International Save the Children Alliance, Lutheran World Federation, Oxfam, The World Council of Churches, the International Committee of the Red Cross.

36   *Id.* Principle 1.

37   *Id.* Principle 2.

38   The Code states that "[w]ays shall be found to involve programme beneficiaries in the management of relief aid" and further provides that "disaster response assistance should never be imposed upon the beneficiaries" and "[e]ffective relief and lasting rehabilitation can best be achieved where the intended beneficiaries are involved in the design, management and implementation of the assistance programme." *Id.* Principle 7.

extent to which the specific requirements of vulnerable populations are being reached and served. Moreover, effective processes will have to be put in place to ensure that stakeholder consultations can effectively impact operations in the field.

A recent initiative funded by the United States Agency for International Development (USAID) seeks to address the integration of disability issues into the programming of large humanitarian assistance organizations. This builds on USAID's incremental efforts to integrate a disability dimension in its foreign assistance programming.[39] Oregon-based Mobility International USA,[40] a disability and development organization specializing in education exchange programming and women's leadership, is responsible for implementing the three-year project which aims to support members of InterAction, the coalition of some one hundred and sixty humanitarian organizations working on disaster relief refugee-assistance and sustainable development worldwide. The project aims to increase participation by people with disabilities, especially women and girls with disabilities, in InterAction member agencies as volunteers, trainers, field staff, policy makers, administrators and beneficiaries. It also seeks to improve implementation of the Disability Amendments to the InterAction Private Voluntary Organizations Standards[41] in organizational governance, management, and programs. The amended Standards provide, among other things, that members " develop a written policy that affirms its commitment to the inclusion of people with disabilities in organizational structures and in staff and board composition" and further provides that the disability policy "should be fully integrated into an organization's plans and operations, in a manner consistent with its mission and the constituency it serves."[42] The organizations with whom Mobility International has partnered include American Friends Service Committee,[43] Church World

---

39   *See* U.S. AGENCY FOR INTERNATIONAL DEVELOPMENT, USAID DISABILITY POLICY PAPER (1997), *available at* http://pdf.dec.org/pdf_docs/PDABQ631.pdf. *See also* U.S. Agency for International Development, *USAID Disability Policy – Assistance* (2004), *available at* http://www.usaid.gov/about_usaid/disability; U.S. Agency for International Development, USAID Acquisition and Assistance Disability Policy Directive (2004), *available at* http://www.usaid.gov/about_usaid/disability/; U.S. AGENCY FOR INTERNATIONAL DEVELOPMENT, USAID ACQUISITION AND ASSISTANCE POLICY DIRECTIVE (DISABILITY POLICY ON NEW CONSTRUCTION) (2005), *available at* http://www.usaid.gov/about_usaid/disability/.

40   *See* http://www.miusa.org/.

41   InterAction PVO Standards, Disability Amendments, Sections 2.6.3; 6.4.3; 6.4.3.1; 7.4; 7.6; 7.9.15, *available at* http://www.interaction.org/pvostandards/index.html.

42   *Id.*, at Section 2.0 (Governance).

43   *See* http://www.afsc.org/. In 1996, the American Friends Service Committee introduced Implementing Affirmative Action Principles in Program in order to build upon its historic commitment to incorporate affirmative action into its work. The plan calls for involving and integrating people into the organization from four target area groups including: third world people; women; people with disabilities; and gay, lesbian, and bisexual people. *See* http://www.afsc.org/jobs/aaprinci.htm.

Service,[44] Holt International Children's Services,[45] Mercy Corps International,[46] and Trickle Up Program.[47]

As the failures in the Asian tsunami experiences make clear, this type of planning is desperately needed. Current approaches claiming to be "rights-based" and which articulate a framework within which the needs of "vulnerable populations" are prioritized and accommodated must account for how such interests are being addressed at all stages of assistance programming. In the absence of disability-specific guidelines, opportunities are being missed to effectively and appropriately provide accommodations. Worse, such shortcomings in acute crises lead almost inevitably to long-term development failures and additionally missed chances to promote inclusion in reconstruction efforts. Disability-specific guidelines and standards set the stage for responsible and human rights-compliant programming later on when vulnerable populations take part in development and (re)construction processes. The interests of persons with disabilities are critically affected in decision-making processes across the development spectrum. Vague frameworks, which purport to address the vulnerability of all population groups, may indeed do more harm than good insofar as they create the sense that "something is being done." In sum, humanitarian assistance in international natural disaster contexts is failing the needs of persons with disabilities.

**Conclusion and Recommendations**

While specific issues concerning disability in governmental planning and humanitarian assistance, and the development process more broadly, have been under-examined, they have nonetheless emerged as an issue worthy of consideration. It remains the case, however, that governments and humanitarian assistance organizations are generally working on the assumption that the mere mention of the disabled as one among an array of vulnerable groups in need of protection will lead to results on the ground. This superficial approach has not addressed the needs of persons with disabilities, nor has it provided the specific and detailed type of guidance required. Subsuming disability under the rubric of vulnerable groups at particular risk and in need of protection may also serve to reinforce outmoded conceptions of people with disability as objects to be acted upon, thereby perpetuating medical models of disability. Persons with disabilities and their representative organizations must be recognized as resources essential to the development process and, in particular, as agents in the building of inclusive societies in which rights flourish.

---

44    *See* http://www.churchworldservice.org.
45    *See* http://www.holtintl.org.
46    *See* http://www.mercycorps.org.
47    *See* http://www.trickleup.org.

There are, nonetheless, some hopeful signs of change. On the American domestic front, policy makers seem to be growing more attuned to the needs and insights of the disability community. Time will tell, however, if and how the political process allows needed policy changes to be met. Similarly, it remains to be seen if government officials will capitalize on rebuilding opportunities to create a more inclusive and accessible environment. On the international front, positive steps are also being taken. A handful of development agencies have committed themselves to disability-inclusive schemes, and global standards are being drafted to provide direction to less informed actors. As with the situation with the United States, it is still unclear how effective these initial efforts will be or how widely adopted.

Looking forward, the emergence of an international disability rights framework should form the foundation for more thoughtful, disability-specific planning in the humanitarian assistance realm.[48] Notably, the recently adopted United Nations Convention on the Rights of Persons with Disabilities[49] contains specific obligations that require the holistic integration of disability into domestic laws and policies,[50] international assistance and cooperation,[51] and most trenchantly, protection of disabled persons in situations involving humanitarian emergencies.[52] Such measures are to be taken in accordance with the obligations that States Parties

---

48    The World Health Organization has, in recent years, devoted more specific attention to the impact of disasters on disability in terms of their disproportionate affect on persons with disabilities and their creation of individuals in need of rehabilitation services. *See, e.g.*, DEP'T OF INJURIES AND VIOLENCE PREVENTION, WORLD HEALTH ORGANIZATION, DISASTERS, DISABILITY, AND REHABILITATION (2005), *available at* http://www.who.int/violence_injury_ prevention/other_injury/disaster_disability2.pdf.

49    Convention on the Rights of Persons with Disabilities, G.A. Res. 61/106, U.N. Doc. A/RES/61/106 (Dec. 13, 2006), *available at* http://www.un.org/esa/socdev/enable/ rights/convtexte.htm [hereinafter UN Disability Convention]. The treaty was adopted by general consensus at the United Nations on December 13, 2006, and opened for signatures by States Parties on March 30, 2007. It will enter into force following the deposit of the 20th instrument of ratification. Updated information about the Convention can be found at the United Nations Enable website, *available at* http://www.un.org/esa/socdev/enable/ index.html.

50    *See* UN Disability Convention, *supra* note 49, at art. 4 (States Parties must "adopt all appropriate legislative, administrative and other measures" and "take into account the protection and promotion of the human rights of persons with disabilities in all policies and programmes").

51    *See id.* at art. 32 (States Parties "recognize the importance of international cooperation and its promotion, in support of . . . ensuring that international cooperation, including international development programmes, is inclusive of and accessible to persons with disabilities.").

52    *See id.* at art. 11 (States Parties are required to take "all necessary measures to ensure the protection and safety of persons with disabilities in situations of risk, including situations of armed conflict, humanitarian emergencies and the occurrence of natural disasters.").

have in respect of the rights of persons with disabilities under both international humanitarian law and international human rights law. While existing policies and guidelines pertaining to vulnerable populations in humanitarian emergencies purport to apply to a wide range of groups, including persons with disabilities, they fail in their application to guide interventions in the field.

Lessons learned from on-going efforts to integrate gender into humanitarian assistance operations show that progress can indeed be made, but that specific guidance, as opposed to empty invocations of "mainstreaming" is required.[53] Gender and development approaches have had some success utilizing analysis tools and analytical frameworks designed to help integrate gender issues into development and relief operations.[54] At the same time, the gender integration experience shows the futility of expecting mainstreaming to occur in a knowledge vacuum.[55] Instead, it is essential to create gender competence among staff members within and across existing structures such that all development programs are gender-inclusive. Ultimately, responsibility for gender integration resides not only in gender-specific units, but also across the institution.

Drawing preliminary lessons from the gender and development experience, it is important to recognize that disability is not an issue that can be casually tacked onto existing humanitarian assistance and development models, nor can it be added merely as an extra or, more commonly (and pejoratively) "special" component in the government planning process. Disability-specific planning paves the way for responsible development programming over the long term including meeting the Millennium Development Goals. These and other initiatives to enhance the accessibility of humanitarian and development programming to persons with disabilities must be supported by specific guidelines for implementing policy and field staff training at all phases and across all sectors.

**Acknowledgement**

Brief update: The UN Disability Convention discussed on page 81, went into force on May, 3, 2008.

---

53 Julie Mertus demonstrates the progress made in addressing gender issues in humanitarian assistance organizations that had adopted and fully operationalized gender policies and the shortcomings in those that had not yet integrated a gender specific component into their work. *See* JULIE A. MERTUS, WAR'S OFFENSIVE ON WOMEN (2000).

54 For a comprehensive treatment of gender analysis frameworks, see CANDIDA MARCH, INES SMYTH & MAITRAYEE MUKHOPADHYAY, A GUIDE TO GENDER ANALYSIS FRAMEWORKS (1999). *See also* MARY B. ANDERSON & PETER J. WOODROW, RISING FROM THE ASHES: DEVELOPMENT STRATEGIES IN TIMES OF DISASTER (1998).

55 The Oxfam Gender Training Manual similarly discloses the benefits of gender-specific training in the framework of humanitarian assistance operations. SUZANNE WILLIAMS, THE OXFAM GENDER TRAINING MANUAL (1994).

# Chapter 6

# Insurance and the Flood

Aviva Abramovsky

A truism of life is not just that bad things happen to good people, but that bad things happen to *all* people. Much of our life is spent weighing options and making choices that seem best able to provide us with a measure of stability, opportunity, and the chance of happiness. At its most fundamental, this process can be termed "risk management." Risk management, therefore, is inherent in all human endeavors. It is an aspect of individual self-determination, family planning, and social functioning. The appropriateness and extent of risk management and mitigation processes by government, be they regarding terror, fire, or flood, may be among the most pressing political questions of our time.

That risks abound is uniformly agreed. Yet, the form of risk abatement and the propriety of loss compensation by government never ceases to be politically divisive. Captured within this debate over governmental purpose lies a relatively simple two-part question: which risks rise to the level of social responsibility and does that responsibility require societal cost sharing to prevent or mitigate the cost of harm? The question becomes more politically divisive when issues of property are concerned. Is the loss of a home a societal responsibility? If loss of a single home expands to loss of an entire community does it *then become* a societal responsibility? And, most divisive of all, if the opportunity existed for individual loss mitigation through purchase of insurance, has it ceased to be a societal responsibility for those inappropriately insured?

It is unquestioned that the government engages in many and various forms of risk management. All systems of law and regulation exist, in one manner or another, to apportion risk. The regulation of financial markets, the existence of workers compensation, and the availability of bankruptcy protection are forms of risk management. Disaster management might actually be seen as one of the oldest and longest standing responsibilities of government. Given the simple unpredictability and arbitrariness of natural disasters, with their inevitably great impact on large populations, government planning and action is a critical and necessary element of public planning. Catastrophes can be mitigated, but they cannot be avoided entirely, they are part of the definitional nature of disaster.

While it seems that the roster of horrors facing the American people is ever increasing, simple flooding is the most common, and frequently the most destructive, of the natural disasters. Floods occur in nearly every geographic area of the United States and, by their nature, often affect areas of large population. The enormous impact on both lives and property has long been recognized by both the government and the private insurance industry. For over a century, these two sectors have been negotiating their various assumption of risk for such losses. As a result of litigation arising from Hurricanes Katrina and Rita, the apportionment of responsibility solely to the federal government is in the process of being formally and finally acknowledged by the courts.

Flood risk is a unique hazard. Early on, the insurance industry recognized that accepting risk of flood loss was an unattractive business proposition and has been striving to exit covering that risk with finality. Exclusions of flood, or the industry's more general term "water," have been appearing in homeowners' policies for decades. As a result, and recognizing the grave societal impact of having such a pervasive risk uninsurable in the private market, the United States government took the unusual move of entering the insurance market as an insurance provider. For over twenty-five years the government has been underwriting losses from flood and providing such coverage through separate flood insurance policies. The relationship between flood insurance and private homeowner's insurance, however, has been one fraught with a certain amount of uncertainty. Despite homeowners' insurance policies' explicit exclusion of loss from flood, there has long been some confusion as to their liability for flood damage arising from a storm. Understandably, for the novitiate reading their homeowner's policy, the distinction between "driven rain" and "storm surge" is not intuitively clear. Likewise, there have long been disputes as to the apportionment of responsibility in the event of what's termed the "concurrent cause" scenario where loss to the home occurs from two causes, one covered and one excluded. The sheer amount of case law and insurance scholarship on these various points validates this confusion and supports the necessity for some final clarity on the issue.

There appears to be some prospect for the Katrina and Rita litigations to finally make these determinations. The political context in which this litigation has emerged is emotionally charged. Families have experienced the loss of loved ones, homeowners have experienced the loss of everything or nearly everything of material value including their homes, and business-owners have lost their place of business. It is no surprise then that politics have become intermingled in the restoration process. Moreover, fundamentally, the allocation of financial responsibility in the wake of disaster inherently becomes political in its reduction. A loss must be borne by one of three basic funding sources: the victim, the government, or the insurance industry. In the end, how society structures and allocates responsibility in the event of disaster largely and fundamentally characterizes a political decision on the role of government in catastrophe planning. For many Americans, the result of the Katrina litigations seems to strongly suggest that homeowners and individuals must show extraordinary care in making their insurance decisions.

Much of the litigation that has been occurring has involved not claims involving flood insurance as provided by the National Flood Insurance Program (NFIP), but homeowner policies which contain a flood exclusion provision. For many, the distinction between the two insuring systems is unclear and the implications of the insurance industry having, with near universality, pushed the risk of loss from flood to the public sphere are murky indeed. However, as discussed below, the history and administration of the flood insurance system is relevant to many aspects of the homeowner's insurance industry and particularly relevant to the little discussed overarching issue of the government's appropriate responsibility in the event of a mass disaster to those without other sources of recovery.

## Katrina and the Flood: A Disaster of Expectations

It has been over two years since the Gulf Coast was devastated by a series of hurricanes causing the most severe and most costly flood damage in the nation's history. "Failure" might be the word most appropriately linked to this greatest of recent national disasters: failure of the levees, failure of structures, failure of communication networks, and perhaps most devastatingly, failure of expectations. That hurricanes and flooding caused great havoc was not unexpected, but the delay and continuing denial of certain forms of relief most definitely was.

Among the most surprising failures of expectations occurred in the realm of homeowner's insurance. Rarely has an insurance product been the focus of such enormous expectation with such a great divergence in understanding. Among the many vivid events witnessed during and in the wake of Katrina, some of the most poignant images coming from the Gulf Coast in the weeks following the disaster included messages homeowners spray-painted on the side of their homes. Messages included pleas of desperation written by homeowners to their own privately acquired insurance carriers. Spray-painted signs like "God Help Us and State Farm Also" were broadcast and reproduced by television stations, newspapers, and websites.[1] People's responses to their insurance carriers and their frustrations with a system taken mostly for granted became a story in and of itself.

In its essence, insurance is easily comprehensible. Despite the voluminous pages of print that epitomize the common standard-form homeowner's insurance policy, at its heart, insurance offers a simple promise—pay your premiums and we will take part of your risk away. This concept, of protection in time of need, is marketed and sold with simple but evocative themes common to the industry. Themes like protection, reliability and community abound in industry advertising. Who isn't familiar with the "Good Hands" of Allstate or that "Like a Good Neighbor, State Farm is There"? Yet, the actual extent of what was excluded by standard-form homeowners' policies surprised hundreds of thousands of homeowners.

---

1   That sign was highlighted by the British Broadcasting Corporation (BBC) for both domestic and international viewing. See news.bbc.co.uk.

## Insurance Confusion: A Story in Three Parts

Insurance is confusing. Most people, when queried, would likely admit that they are not a hundred percent certain of what all the various forms of insurance they own actually cover. The fact that millions of people continue to pay billions of dollars for a product that they do not entirely understand remains one of the stranger, identifiably irrational, insurance market phenomena. Actual policyholders, however, are not alone in their confusion regarding coverage afforded under their various policies. They are joined in good company with large numbers of claims adjusters, legislators, and the courts.

The Gulf Coast losses were almost perfectly arranged to create homeowner confusion in the wake of a flooding disaster, particularly since the flood occurred as a result of the passage of a hurricane causing massive community devastation. This confusion can be broadly broken down into three separate problems. First, there exists the problem of the actual extent of coverage available under the policy. Given that these policies are standard and nearly universal in their coverage of private homes, the fact that so much uncertainty clings to their efficacy is odd. This uncertainty is understandable, however, given the disparity of court interpretation of the documents. Second, the flood scenario triggers another level of confusion as a result of separate flood-specific homeowners' policies being available through the government. The interplay between the two policies is particularly confusing and rife with counterintuitive claims handling. This confusion is primarily a result of the National Flood Insurance Program's reliance on private insurance claims handlers to manage the flood claim *alongside* the private insurance claim. Given the differing financial liability for claims handler's employers, there exists a structural incentive for the claims handler to find the cause of a loss "flood" rather than "wind." Third, there is an overarching confusion as to the government's role and responsibilities, generally, in the post-disaster scenario. A lack of cohesive policy and seemingly counterproductive divisions of assistance programs understandably proves confusing to disaster victims. Given the fact that the National Flood Insurance Program and disaster relief and assistance are both administered by the Federal Emergency Management Agency (FEMA), the failure of that agency to have a cohesive policy overseeing the interplay of its programs is understandably confusing to all.

## Homeowner's Insurance: Am I Covered?

Even the term "coverage" evokes images of protection. Like the Travelers Insurance Company red umbrella, the concept of "coverage" is linked to images promising protection from the proverbial storm. This promise, however, is *a limited* promise; the demarcation of this limitation being the subject of furious debate and continuing, ongoing litigation with the operative law for determining those limits being the law of contracts. Contracts law theory has always been a slightly uncomfortable fit as the operating canon of insurance law. While an insurance policy is certainly a legally enforceable agreement, the disproportionate effect on one party for what could amount to a reasonable good faith mistake has led to some unusual rulings in coverage situations. For instance, the original trial court interpretation of the term "flood" in the *In Re Katrina Canal Breaches Consolidated Litigation* was deemed ambiguous; with flood being construed as reapplying only to naturally occurring phenomenon, rather than what occurred as a result of the breakdown of the levees. While the United States Court of Appeals for the Fifth Circuit has recently overruled that decision and determined "flood" to unambiguously cover the levee breaches, the mere fact that the lower court disagreed gives credence to the argument that insurance policy interpretation is considerably more unclear post-loss than it appears when originally reading a policy.

Those familiar with the Katrina story are aware that much of the coverage debate has circled around the definitions of loss from "wind" versus loss from "water." The technical and legal theory for determining causation, however, can in and of itself seem a bit obscure. In Katrina-affected areas, damage to property clearly involved *both* wind and rain. As such, the common problem of determining the legal duty of the insurance company where there has been concurrent causation— one covered and one excluded—requires the court to interpret how the policy clauses dealing with concurrence should be interpreted. In doing so, the court reviews the various jurisdictional rules on how the "proximate cause" of the loss should be identified when two causes are entwined in the fact pattern which led to the damage. Arguably, this obscurity and the definitional challenge of separating the two concepts when the property is damaged as a result of hurricanes, could well be responsible for some of the policyholder's misconceptions about coverage in the Gulf region. Again, the fact that the courts have been forced to interpret many of these clauses, particularly the anti-concurrent causation clauses, for the first time in their jurisdictions, suggests that policyholder misconceptions may well have been justified, if not entirely prudent.

*Rules of Coverage*

Initially, the scope of insurance coverage available for any specific loss is determined by looking to the policy itself. The insurance policy is the memorialization of the agreement between the parties and its terms are to be given legal effect. The courts' analyses of homeowners' insurance policies affected by Katrina have been undertaken in an identical manner to the interpretation of policy provisions disputed in any coverage litigation. Since homeowners' policies are generally standard-form, court decisions on policy language in any given homeowner's case will likely determine availability of coverage for all similarly situated homeowners.

The point of departure in coverage analysis is first to determine the basic contractual structure used by the insurance company in defining the extent of risk the policy transfers from the homeowner to the insurer. As the United States Court of Appeals for the Fifth Circuit identified when interpreting a

Mississippi homeowner's policy, regionally "almost all homeowners' policies" are "'comprehensive' or 'all-risk'" policies under which "all damage to dwellings or personal property not otherwise excluded is covered."[2] This simple insuring phrase is itself the source of much confusion. A translation of that statement could better be articulated as stating that the insurance company agrees to cover all damage to the home, except such damage as it does not. Moreover, this language of exclusion is written so as to delineate exclusion from coverage in terms of what "caused" the damage. For this reason, identical property damage to a wall or a roof could be covered or not depending on what "caused" that damage. When the "cause" of damage is not among the list of those "causes" specifically excluded, coverage exists. If, however, the cause of the damage is amongst the list of exclusions, coverage is denied.

In the regular course of things, determinations as to availability of coverage are made by a "claims handler" who surveys any alleged loss. Given the laundry list of excluded causes, the term "all-risks" or "comprehensive" coverage seems to be quite the misnomer. In fact, many have argued that it is this strange structure of insuring promises which create much of the confused coverage expectations of a policyholder. Other than serving as a successful marketing technique, such drafting practice does offer the policyholder one distinct legal advantage. By constructing the contract in such a manner, it becomes the insurer's burden to prove that the cause of the loss was, in fact, excluded. Hence the relevance of a "wind" rather than "water" determination is made apparent.

For the purposes of homeowner's coverage, however, it has long been understood that the nature of storms requires three different policy interpretations in order to fully determine liability. These are the policy provisions concerning (1) wind, (2) water, and (3) the concurrent action of wind *and* water.

Wind need not be explicitly mentioned *as* covered, because so long as it is not excluded, such cause of loss would come within the "comprehensive" grant of coverage originally made. To exclude floods, however, inclusion of language making that cause of loss specifically *excluded* would have to be articulated within the policy. Generally, the policy exclusion of floods is found within the broader policy language excluding "water." The common water exclusion is found in the policy under the title "Property Exclusions." Found within this policy section is the phrase excluding "water or damage caused by water borne material," along with the definitional statement that "[w]ater and water-borne material *means*: . . . flood, surface water, waves, tidal waves, [or] overflow of a body of water."

The primary grounds for a coverage dispute, therefore, revolve around two central inquiries. First, does the excluding clause unambiguously define that which it attempted to exclude. The second inquiry being, whether such unambiguously excluded loss provision affects coverage for damages that occurred concurrent with a covered cause of loss. The initial question of whether the insurance policy is ambiguous is a matter of law. To make this determination, extrinsic evidence is

---

2    Leonard v. Nationwide Mut. Ins. Co., 499 F.3d 419, 424 (5th Cir. 2007).

generally inadmissible. With the Fifth Circuit's reversal of *In Re Katrina Canal Breaches Consolidated Litigation*[3] as well as the Fifth Circuit's affirmation of *Leonard*,[4] the term flood has been found unambiguous as a matter of law. As such, further analysis of possible interpretation of the clause is precluded. Moreover, the *Leonard* Court further determined the plaintiffs' losses to have been "clearly" caused by flood and, hence, excluded from coverage, finding "The Leonards' neighborhood had suffered a seventeen-foot storm surge, causing the entire ground floor of their residence to become inundated under five feet of water blown ashore from the Mississippi Sound."[5] By such a determination, the exclusion stands for those plaintiffs as a matter of law.

Still, the mere fact that an exclusion is found unambiguous and applicable would not necessarily vitiate all coverage to the extent that the damage was also caused by a covered peril in the absence of other language in the policy. That text is frequently described as the "anti-concurrent causation clause," despite the fact that it is merely a few sentences in the introductory language of the excluded perils list. The text of a standard-form anti-concurrent causation clause, found within the introductory language of the Policy Exclusion section, states:

> We do not cover loss to any property resulting directly or indirectly from any of the following. Such a loss is excluded *even if* another peril or event contributed concurrently or in any sequence to cause the loss.

Once the courts determined that the term "water" unambiguously excludes flood, it was still necessary to determine whether the above language was itself unambiguous. In *Leonard*, the Fifth Circuit, when interpreting this language, held that "[t]he plain language of the policy leaves the [district] court no interpretive leeway to conclude that recovery can be obtained for wind damage that 'occurred concurrently or in sequence with the excluded water damage.'"[6] Thus, by virtue of the anti-concurrent causation clause, "[t]he only species of damage covered under the [homeowner's] policy is damage *exclusively* caused by wind."[7] Disregarding plaintiffs' argument that such interpretation made the policy illusory for the purpose of most hurricane coverage in coastal areas, in the absence of legislation or specifically articulated public policy to the contrary, the court reiterated that only such reading of the anti-concurrent causation clause could stand.

---

3   Vanderbrook v. Unitrin Preferred Ins. Co. (In re Katrina Canal Breaches Consol. Liti.), 495 F.3d 191 (5th Cir. 2007), *overruling* In re Katrina Canal Breaches Consol. Liti. v. Encompass Ins. Co., 466 F. Supp. 2d 729 (E.D. La. 2006).

4   Leonard, 499 F.3d at, *aff'g* Leonard v. Nationwide Mut. Ins. Co., 438 F. Supp. 2d 684 (S.D. Miss. 2006).

5   *Id.* at 426.

6   *Id.* at 430.

7   *Id.*

The recent Fifth Circuit rulings make clear that flood insurance has never been more necessary. Until these decisions made the effect of the anti-concurrent causation clause expressly clear, there had long been some understanding that the private homeowner's insurance market would bear the costs of at least a portion of the damage—that caused by wind—even if that hurricane caused some concurrent flood damage. For the fifty-two percent of the population living in coastal areas, the Katrina litigation has clarified much concerning the scope of insurance coverage available in the private market. Should other states likewise agree that the anti-concurrent causation clause is unambiguous, coverage for both direct flood losses and coverage for wind damage occurring synergistically with flood damage is effectively no longer available on the private market. This second element, of relief for wind claims which occur in any sequence with flood, creates somewhat of a new problem for disaster planners such as the federal National Flood Insurance Program, the government's answer to private insurers' exit from the direct flood loss market forty years ago. The NFIP does not offer any coverage for loss from wind. Hence, in Mississippi at least, neither private nor public insurance is currently available for concurrent or sequential wind loss involving flooding.

## Government As Risk Manager and Government As Insurer

Floods are the most common and destructive natural disaster in the United States. According to NFIP statistics, ninety percent of all natural disasters in the United States involve flooding and, as such, the insurance industry's ability to exclude coverage for flood losses, particularly in cases of concurrent causation, is especially relevant to the insurance industry. Likewise, the fact that floods are so common and so economically devastating, particularly to homeowners, has resulted in homeowner's insurance availability becoming a governmental concern.

Traditionally, the conception of government provision of a flood insurance market is not linked to the concept of property protection alone. Rather, the National Flood Insurance Program was devised with the intent of offering to compliant municipalities a benefit to their constituents if they were compliant with federal attempts at flood planning and loss mitigation techniques. Hence, in areas not compliant with NFIP or otherwise suspended from the program, homeowner's flood insurance is not available. Still, such homeowners are not without recourse to some FEMA benefits in the event that their homes are damaged or they are displaced as a result of a declared disaster event. As discussed below, however, relief available solely through FEMA differs in certain critical respects from that available through the NFIP.

Provision of flood insurance as a federal program, however, has changed a portion of the discussion regarding insuring responsibilities as part of disaster relief responsibilities. A sense of political *schadenfreude* has permeated some of the discourse concerning disaster relief for those homeowners without flood insurance, with certain political elements concerned about encouraging the moral hazard of uninsured homeownership. Beyond doubt, however, the NFIP program itself is not without moral hazards within its own administrative procedure.

Particularly grave and provocative is the appropriateness of mingling a public disaster mitigation tool with private insurance industry interests and profits. To call the government's National Flood Insurance Program a purely public affair is a misnomer. Over ninety-six percent of government flood insurance policies are sold through private insurance companies and the process of handling the claims is undertaken by those companies' employees. Among some of the many problems recognized by such a program is the inherent conflict of interest facing those claims handlers when forced to make a determination after a storm as to whether the loss was caused by flood—a governmental liability—or caused by wind, their employer's liability. Other grave concerns, present in all too many instances of private "outsourcing" of government responsibility, is the lack, as recognized by the Government Accounting Office, of cost accountability and supervision.

Strangely, however, the remarkable conflict of interest inherent to the claims handling process of ninety-six percent of all flood insurance has received relatively little media attention. It has, however, received quite a bit of Congressional attention. Representative Gene Taylor (D. Miss.) had the misfortune to suffer the total loss of his own home, along with Trent Lott (R. Miss.).[8] Taylor has testified and run several congressional inquiries, based on others describing the current administration of the NFIP a "raid on the . . . [T]reasury."[9] Thus, while the NFIP is a good beginning for property loss mitigation, as described later in this chapter, it suffers from some serious operational difficulties in its current form. To criticize a government agency, however, it is first necessary to understand it.

### The Development of the NFIP: A History of Disaster

The history of flood insurance is indelibly linked to the history of catastrophic hurricanes in the United States. In fact, it was in response to Hurricane Carol hitting the New England coast in 1954 and Hurricane Hazel damaging North Carolina in 1955, that flood insurance first became commercially unavailable to large numbers of homeowners except at prohibitive rates supplied only by Lloyd's of London. These two hurricanes resulted in the call for government action in the flood insurance market, which would later evolve into our current NFIP.

---

8   Joe Hohns, *Sen. Lott's Home Destroyed by Katrina*, CNN, Sept. 4, 2005, http://www.cnn.com/2005/POLITICS/08/30/katrina.lott/.

9   The Gavel, http://www.speaker.gov/blog/?p=476 (last visited Nov. 2, 2007), *citing* Rebecca Mowbray, *Procedural Changes Speeded Insurance Payouts, But May Have Allowed Abuses*, Times-Picayune (New Orleans), June 11, 2007, http://blog.nola.com/times-picayune/2007/06/procedural_changes_speeded_ins.html.

In 1956, Congress enacted its first Flood Insurance Act, setting the underpinnings and certainly calcifying much of the scope and ideology for a new public plan that would attempt to mitigate the public's reliance solely on disaster relief in the event of a loss from this most common of natural disasters. The 1956 Act provided the availability of flood insurance directly from the federal government. It also began the first iteration of legislative attempts to induce localities to take steps towards mitigation of flood risks by providing a "restriction of the program, after an initial period of operation, to localities which adopted floodplain zoning." However, one year after its creation and without selling a single policy, the Federal Flood Indemnity Administration—the governing administrative agency for the program—"ceased operation when Congress not only failed to appropriate necessary subsidy funds to finance the insurance program but declined to appropriate operating funds for the agency."[10]

Over the next decade, little of note occurred towards the resolution of the continuing flood insurance quandary, other than continued study. In 1968, study complete, Congress enacted a new National Flood Insurance Act. This legislation again required land use plans, but in this iteration, designated a voluntary group of insurance companies as "responsible for the dissemination of information to the public, the distribution, sale and processing of all polices, and the adjustment of all claims."[11] Included in the Act were provisions allowing for subsidies of flood insurance premiums, in the attempt to ensure their affordability.

In the summer of 1969, shortly after the enactment of the 1968 Act, Hurricane Camille made its historic landfall. Causing massive devastation of the Gulf Coast region, Camille would be the Hurricane that all later storms, including Katrina, would be measured against. Camille also revealed that the federal program had, as yet, resulted in little increased coverage for flood losses. Emergency provisions quickly followed providing for, among other measures, an expanded definition of flood to include mudslide and the expansion of coverage to small businesses' commercial properties.

While the emergency provisions enacted as a response to Camille extended the number of properties insured under the program, the 1972 landfall of Hurricane Agnes and serious flooding in South Dakota revealed that awareness of the program was simply insufficient. Moreover, a strange counter-incentive to community certification of eligibility arose as a result of rather draconian forfeiture provisions included in the program. The program required that those who were eligible for

---

10    David A. Grossman, *Flood Insurance: Can a Feasible Program Be Created?*, 34 LAND ECON. 352 (1958), *available at* JSTOR, http://links.jstor.org/sici?sici=0023-7639%2 8195811%2934%3A4%3C352%3AFICAFP%3E2.0.CO%3B2-7 (listed as Vol. 34, No. 4, 352, 352 (Nov., 1958)).

11    Dan R. Anderson, *The National Flood Insurance Program—Problems and Potential*, 41 J. RISK & INS. 579, 582, *available at* JSTOR, http://links.jstor.org/sici?sici=0022-4367 %28197412%2941%3A4%3C579%3ATNFIPP%3E2.0.CO%3B2-F (listed as Vol. 41, No. 4, 579, 582 (Dec., 1974)).

flood insurance for more than one year above a threshold income level, but did not make use of it, would be denied disaster relief for the amount insurance would have covered in the event of a flood. The reality on the ground after Agnes revealed that communities were simply unwilling to seek the eligibility designation for fear of being held responsible for the loss of disaster benefits to the uninsured among them.

Insurance is a strange commodity. Despite the incredible publicity surrounding the Camille and Agnes disasters, property owners were not seeking coverage in sufficient numbers to actually offer serious community mitigation in the event of major flooding, nor were the numbers nearly sufficient to allow the federal Flood Insurance Agency to receive sufficient premiums to seriously offset losses to the public coffers from prudent premium gathering. Interestingly, there was still no movement to simply *force* property owners to acquire flood insurance; nor, conversely, was any serious discussion of simply *guaranteeing* a primary level of flood insurance to the American public undertaken. Instead, programs seeking to increase awareness of the product were initiated, and as one scholar noted, "various measures to assist, encourage, and even pressure communities in gaining eligibility were adopted and proposed."[12]

By 1973, Congress recognized that more stringent inducements were necessary. In that year, the Flood Disaster Protection Act was enacted mandating flood insurance for buildings within flood zones as a prerequisite to communities receiving certain federal aid, federal disaster relief, and loans from banks insured by the federal government. Not surprisingly, in response to this legislation, participation in the program jumped from 100,000 policies before Agnes to two million by 1979. That same year, the flood insurance program, along with the Flood Insurance Agency itself, was moved under the administration of FEMA.

While evidence from Katrina reflects the fact that flood insurance coverage is still far from pervasive in many risk laden areas, by 1986 sufficient quantities of flood insurance premiums were being collected to make the agency largely self-funding By 2004, the program covered nearly five million policyholders, though much of this increase was likely linked to the increasingly pervasive requirement of mortgage lenders to require the purchase of flood insurance on properties within designated flood zones and a concomitant rise in the pervasiveness of mortgages in the housing market. From the mid-1980s, the National Flood Insurance Program remained mostly solvent and successfully operated as a separate self-funding sub-agency of FEMA.

## Katrina, Rita, and NFIP Losses

The magnitude and cost to the NFIP for Hurricanes Katrina and Rita is staggeringly out of proportion to its prior loss history. As a result of those storms, the agency

---

12   *Id*. at 592.

received more than 224,000 claims.[13] "For both Hurricanes Katrina and Rita, FEMA estimates that it has paid approximately $16.2 billion in claims, with average payments of over $95,000 and $47,000, respectively."[14] In order to put these catastrophic costs of events in perspective, according to a recent GAO report, that $16 billion figure in claims for flood damage as a result of Hurricane Katrina constitutes significantly more than "the $14.6 billion it had paid for the cumulative total of all flood events from 1968 until Hurricane Katrina occurred."[15] The NFIP estimates that these numbers encompass approximately ninety-nine percent of all flood claims received.[16]

Such enormous dollar values and the continued pervasiveness of property damage from flood requires that the flood insurance program analyze not only its availability and saturation in high-risk areas, but also the National Flood Insurance Program's role in rate setting in repetitive loss areas. In recent years, even prior to the dramatic losses evidenced in Katrina, Congress has begun to turn its attention to mitigating the repetitive loss problem affecting certain properties and areas. In 2004, it enacted the National Flood Insurance Reform Act, which along with increasing maximum coverage amounts, implemented the Community Rating System and established grants for mitigation projects. That legislative action came too late to allow the NFIP program to remain solvent.

In years where losses are heavy, and in order to ensure that the NFIP remains solvent, FEMA has statutory authority to borrow funds from the U.S. Treasury.[17] In the past there have been occasions where the NFIP has borrowed money from the U.S. Treasury because it did not have enough money to cover the claims. The NFIP, however, was able to repay the money borrowed. Unfortunately, Hurricane Katrina caused so much property damage and devastated such a large area that the NFIP did not have enough money to cover all of the claims filed. As a result of this unforeseen and unprecedented disaster, the NFIP borrowed billions of dollars from the Treasury. FEMA's borrowing authority was increased by Congress from $1.5 billion to $20.8 billion after Hurricane Katrina, and as of May 2007, FEMA's debt to the Treasury was $17.5 billion.[18] It is almost certain that this amount will not be paid back in full. The NFIP's current premium income is approximately

---

13    Letter from Peter R. Orszag, Cong. Budget Office, to Hon. John M. Spratt, Chairman, H. Budget Comm., The Federal Government's Spending and Tax Actions in Response to the 2005 Gulf Coast Hurricanes 7 (Aug. 1, 2007).

14    U.S. Gov't Accountability Office, Publ'n No. GAO-07-991T, National Flood Insurance Program: Preliminary Views on FEMA's Ability to Ensure Accurate Payments on Hurricane-Damaged Properties 6 (2007).

15    U.S. Gov't Accountability Office, Publ'n No. GAO-07-1078, National Flood Insurance Program: FEMA's Management and Oversight of Payments for Insurance Company Services Should be Improved 1 (2007).

16    U.S. Gov't Accountability Office, *supra* note 14, at 5.

17    U.S. Gov't Accountability Office, *supra* note 15, at 9, *citing* 42 U.S.C. § 4016.

18    Letter from Peter R. Orszag to Hon. John M. Spratt, *supra* note 13, at 8.

$2 billion per year.[19] With a debt of $17.5 billion, and only $2 billion coming in through premiums paid by policyholders, the Treasury department will most likely never be repaid the money owed. This is certainly to be the case if another Katrina-like catastrophe were to strike in the near future.

The process of Katrina flood litigations has also sparked some new and dramatic changes to the scope of the NFIP's mission. On September 28, 2007, the House passed H.R. 920, the Multi Peril Insurance Act of 2007. Sponsored by Representative Taylor, the Act would make available multi-peril coverage for damage resulting from windstorms or floods by the NFIP. Such extension of coverage available from the National Flood Insurance Program would be a dramatic expansion of coverage available from the government. While it would considerably resolve the wind–water issue in the event of future hurricanes, such dramatic expansion of a government insurance program would likely find little support from President George W. Bush. Despite the provision's clear popularity in the Gulf states, it is unclear if the Act could obtain a veto proof majority.

## Operation of the National Flood Insurance Program: A Confusion of Interests

The NFIP is managed by the Mitigation Division of the Federal Emergency Management Agency (FEMA), a part of the United States Department of Homeland Security (DHS). Under this program, buildings are covered up to $250,000 and personal property is covered up to $100,000.[20] Flood Insurance is available in those areas which the National Flood Insurance Program approves.

According to the GAO, as of May 2007, more than 20,300 American communities participated in the NFIP.[21] As part of their participation, these communities adopt and agree to enforce state and community floodplain management regulations to reduce future flood damage.[22] In exchange for these actions, the NFIP makes federally backed flood insurance available to homeowners and other property owners in these communities. Moreover, as is well known, the NFIP requires that homeowners with mortgages from federally regulated lenders on property in communities identified to be in special high-risk flood hazard areas purchase flood insurance on their property for at least the outstanding mortgage amount. The NFIP also offers homeowners optional, lower-cost coverage to protect homes in areas of low to moderate risk.

---

19   U.S. Gov't Accountability Office, Publ'n No. GAO-07-1079T, Gulf Coast Rebuilding: Observations on Federal Financial Implications 14 (2007).

20   FEMA, National Flood Insurance Program Summary of Coverage, 1, http://www.fema.gov/pdf/nfip/summary_cov.pdf (last visited Nov. 13, 2008).

21   U.S. Gov't Accountability Office, *supra* note 15, at 8.

22   *Id.*

The fact that the NFIP is a governmental program is somewhat misleading. While the government maintained complete and exclusive control over coverage and claim denial from 1977 until 1983, and the government continues to bear the complete financial risk in the event of losses, its exclusive role in the actual operation and claims handling of losses from flood have dramatically decreased since that year with the creation of the WYO or "Write Your Own" Program. In essence, the WYO program allows participating insurance companies to issue flood policies in the company's name. For instance, a policyholder could buy flood insurance from Allstate, a WYO partner with FEMA. The policyholder would then receive his flood policy with the name "Allstate" at the top of the policy, even though the actual product, flood insurance, is actually only available from and through FEMA and the NFIP. Regardless of the name on the policy, the ultimate liability remains with the federal government alone.

Despite the seeming inconsequence of choosing a WYO policy from a private insurer as your medium for the acquisition of flood insurance, given the uniformity of terms authorized by FEMA, a WYO policy is different from an exclusively NFIP issued policy in many pertinent respects. By contracting with a WYO insurance partner in the flood insurance program, the WYO company, rather than a government officer, adjusts the actual flood claim as well as settles and pays all claims arising from the flood policies. This payment is then reimbursed to the WYO insurer by the NFIP. In exchange for their sales and claims servicing, the WYO insurance company partner is compensated in a variety of ways. According to the GAO, compensation for sales activity are as follows:

> For selling and servicing NFIP policies, FEMA pays WYO insurance companies
> (1) a flat 15 percent of premiums for agent commissions; (2) a percentage for
> operating expenses, which historically also averages about 15 percent, based
> on industry averages for other lines of insurance; and (3) bonuses of up to 2
> percent of their total annual premium revenues for increasing the number of
> NFIP policies they sell.[23]

Furthermore, the WYO insurance company partner is compensated for its claims handling and operating costs:

> After flood losses, FEMA pays WYO insurance companies for adjusting and
> processing policyholders' claims according to (1) an adjustment fee schedule
> used by the insurance industry for other types of insurance claims and (2)
> an allowance of 3.3 percent of each claim settlement amount to pay for their
> processing expenses. The WYO insurance companies collect their operating
> costs from FEMA based on these methodologies. Any portion of the premium

---

23    *Id.* at 4.

revenues retained by the WYO insurance companies that are not used to cover expenses may be retained as profit.[24]

As a result of the opportunity for lucrative compensation for their sales and claims handling, the proportion of WYO policies to total flood insurance policies sold have increased dramatically. For example, in 1986, WYO insurance companies administered nearly 1 million of a little over 2 million policies in force. By February 2007, WYO insurance companies moved from having administered about fifty percent of the policies in force at that time to nearly ninety-six percent of the about 5.4 million policies now in force.

Undoubtedly the financial incentives provided to the WYO insurers to market and sell flood policies accounts for at least some portion of the expansion of property owners choosing the coverage. However, some immediate concerns regarding this system of compensation become immediately apparent. Among them is the fact that the compensation for expenses does not require the submission of any evidence of the actual costs incurred. The WYO expense reimbursement system, of course, is hence strikingly dissimilar to the detailed reporting necessary in submissions to FEMA by disaster victims who seek reimbursement for emergency losses. The disparity is quite stark. For example, claims handling expenses are paid at a flat rate of 3.3 percent of the claims settlement amount. This flat rate has been in place and unchanged for over twenty-five years. Claims handling and processing expenses are deemed to include costs such as setting up operations in the affected areas and getting to the homeowners. However, there can be no assurance that the 3.3 percent figure accurately reflects the company's costs incurred since, "FEMA does not consider actual expenses incurred by the companies for their services to the NFIP and does not collect actual expense data from the WYO insurance companies."[25] Moreover, 3.3 percent for claims processing is not an inconsiderable sum. It translates to $3,300 per $100,000 granted by the company in settlement under the flood policy. For a company like State Farm with many multiple billions of dollars in coverage, such a processing fee alone could account for over $3 million, likely a far greater sum than the company could realistically be expected to have spent processing those claims.

Moreover, the percentage payment for claims handling may, in part, be responsible for the seemingly great disparity on the amount of dollars paid out by insurers under private homeowner's insurance compared to payments made according to flood insurance policies. For example, Congressman Gene Taylor has shown that payments by private insurers in three Mississippi coastal counties average approximately $22,000 while payments made under NFIP policies averaged $142,000.[26] The insurance industry claims that this is due to the fact

---

24  *Id.* at 4–5. *See also* 42 U.S.C. § 4017.

25  *Id.* at 5.

26  Anita Lee, *U.S. Rep. Gene Taylor Sees Fraud In Insurer Denials; He Suspects NFIP, Taxpayers Are Being Cheated*, Sun Herald (Biloxi, MS), Oct. 24, 2006, *available at*

that the NFIP covers flood damage, while private homeowner's insurance does not. Congressman Taylor, however, pointed to the conflict of interest inherent in a situation where the same company claims handler would have to decide whether a loss should be covered by the company's private policy, with his company's assets responsible for the loss, or find coverage under the NFIP policy where the government would be responsible for the full amount of the loss. When further including the 3.3 percent processing fee acquired by the company on every dollar settled on the policyholder arising from the flood policy, the incentive to find flood as the cause would influence any reasonable person.

The existence of this conflict has not been lost on NFIP insiders. In his testimony before the United States Senate Committee on Banking, Housing, and Urban Affairs, J. Robert Hunter, former Administrator of the NFIP and current Director of Insurance for the Consumer Federation of America, testified that he had long been aware of the conflicts of interests inherent to the NFIP system. That their dual role as adjusters for both the private and public policies affects their decision-making process had forced Mr Hunter to dismiss certain insurance companies from the NFIP program. In that instance, prior to the development of the WYO payment incentives, insurance companies were denying claims under flood policies in fear that a grant of coverage under certain provisions of the flood policy would require them to grant claims falling under similar policy language in the private policies. Likewise he questioned how an identical claims handler could operate without a conflict of interest when adjusting a homeowner's policy compared to the flood policy given the opposing fiscal incentives of the two systems.

## After the Hurricane Comes the Introspection: A Confusion of Policy

This chapter began with a relatively simple two-fold question: which risks rise to the level of social responsibility and does that responsibility require societal cost sharing to prevent or mitigate the cost of harm? Our discussion of the answer in terms of flood damaged homes required a look at the two "insurances" potentially available as a source of risk transfer away from direct government relief work. There is a conception that proper disaster recovery planning should include policy support of insurance acquisition. It is this idea, among other reasons, that is given in support of the government's presence as insurer in the flood market at all. Yet, there has been an absolute failure to legislate a cohesive public policy that would actually allow for the government, homeowners, and insurers to accurately form a reliable understanding of their various rights and responsibilities in the wake of a flood disaster.

Among the issues already addressed is the absence of federal legislation formalizing the demarcation of private insurance responsibility and flood insurance responsibility in the event of a classic concurrent hurricane loss. This

---

http://www.SunHerald.com (search archives for "Taylor Sees Fraud In Insurer Denials").

issue is critical, particularly as it concerns the correct valuation of homeowner's insurance for the policy purchaser. The complete denial of a claim, as a result of concurrent causation, severely limits the value of the policy in ways beyond simple recovery for the property damage. All homeowners' policies include a "loss of use" provision that provides a certain amount of money for monthly living expenses, including rent, if the home is damaged so severely that it cannot be occupied. This provision is not available from NFIP flood insurance and it is among the costs to be considered when planning holistic recovery schemes. Without loss of use insurance monies, the vast majority of displaced people have no other recourse than FEMA emergency aid for living space and rent. This issue is partially responsible for the difference in the insurance stories of Katrina and those of New Yorkers after 9/11. In New York, the majority of displaced homeowners were able to offset their loss of access to their homes with insurance proceeds. Hence, no stories of FEMA trailers on Wall Street.

Similarly, when discussing the cost of revising or expanding the NFIP program or even in the policy debate over the appropriateness of the Fifth Circuit's interpretations of the anti-concurrent causation clause, it is important to recognize the potential societal and dollar cost to government as a result of housing relocation and assistance. Disaster relief is very expensive and it behooves policy planners to consider all the ancillary costs of disaster relief and recovery when planning its insurance public policy.

For example, Congress appropriated $45.3 billion for FEMA's Disaster Relief Fund as a result of the Gulf Coast Hurricanes in 2005—Katrina, Rita, and Wilma.[27] As of July 2007, $34.6 billion from the Disaster Relief Fund had been allocated toward relief for victims of Katrina, with $25.3 billion of that amount having been expended.[28] At the same time, $4.2 billion was allocated for victims of Rita with $3 billion of that amount having been expended.[29] Much of those costs accrued as a result of there being insufficient housing costs coverage available to those displaced by the storm.

Hurricane Katrina displaced approximately 1 million people: "Hurricane Katrina was also the most expensive disaster in history, devastating far more residential property and completely destroying or making uninhabitable an estimated 300,000 homes."[30] Under the National Response Plan (NRP), issued by the Department of Homeland Security (DHS) in 2004, FEMA was the agency primarily responsible for housing as well as human services in the event of a disaster.

There are three types of individual disaster assistance available from FEMA: (1) Housing Needs; (2) Other than Housing Needs; and (3) Additional Services. Housing needs can encompass temporary housing, repair, replacement, or permanent

---

27  Letter from Peter R. Orszag to Hon. John M. Smith, *supra* note 13, at Table 1.
28  *Id.* at Table 2.
29  *Id.* at Table 2.
30  U.S. Gov't Accountability Office, Publ'n No. GAO-07-88, Disaster Assistance: Better Planning Needed for Housing Victims of Catastrophic Disasters 9 (2007).

housing construction.[31] In order to qualify for "Housing Needs" assistance, there are five separate criteria that an individual must meet. These include: (1) your losses are in an area the President has declared to be a disaster; (2) you have filed for insurance benefits and either the damage to your property is not covered by your insurance policy or the settlement you received is insufficient to cover your losses; (3) you or someone you live with must be a citizen of the United States, a non-citizen national, or a qualified alien; (4) the home at issue is where "you usually live" and it is also "where you were living at the time of the disaster"; and (5) either you are unable to live in your home now, you cannot get to your home due to the disaster, or repairs are required on your home due to the disaster.[32] There are several criteria that if met will result in your disqualification from receiving this sort of assistance: (1) you have other, adequate rent-free housing available; (2) the home was a secondary or vacation residence; (3) the expenses resulted only from leaving your home as a precaution and you were able to return to your home immediately after the incident; (4) you refused assistance from your insurance provider(s); (5) your only losses are business losses or items not covered by this program; (6) the home is in a designated flood hazard area and your community is not participating in the National Flood Insurance Program, (you may still be able to qualify for rental assistance or "Other than Housing" assistance).[33]

FEMA's public assistance grants have provided more than $8.3 billion to communities affected by Hurricane Katrina and Rita.[34] For Hurricane Rita, FEMA provided $935.7 million for rental assistance, temporary lodging, and housing repairs, and another $198.8 million was provided to cover loss of personal property, medical costs, and other serious disaster-related expenses not covered by insurance.[35] This aid was given through either the public assistance programs or through the individual assistance program.

Hence, over $9 billion was spent on housing related costs. Granted, these figures include the costs of housing assistance for a number of people who were likely not homeowners. However, the fact that over 220,000 flood insurance claims were made in an area where approximately 300,000 homes were destroyed suggests that housing relocation costs also be considered in the reform rubric of the NFIP. There is a clear public policy in favor of encouraging insurance planning as part of proper disaster planning. It makes little sense to restrict the opportunity

---

31    FEMA, Disaster Assistance Available from FEMA, http://www.fema.gov/assistance/process/assistance.shtm#0 (last visited Nov. 13, 2008).

32    FEMA, Do I Qualify for "Housing Needs" Assistance?, http://www.fema.gov/assistance/process/qualify_housing.shtm (last visited Nov. 13, 2008).

33    *Id.*

34    Press Release, FEMA, 2 Years Later: Federal Funds for Gulf Coast Recovery Exceed $8.3 Billion (Aug. 24, 2007), *available at* http://www.fema.gov/news/newsrelease.fema?id=39209.

35    Press Release, FEMA, FEMA Assistance for Hurricane Rita recovery tops $2 billion (Sept. 24, 2007), *available at* http://www.fema.gov/news/newsrelease/fema?id=40949.

to purchase coverage, even subsidized, government provided coverage, when the *absence* of such coverage simply makes a different part of the same agency responsible for providing that housing. Therefore, an expansion of the NFIP to include housing costs and loss of use seems reasonable.

Arguably, the NFIP may not be capable of staying completely solvent in the event of another similar mass disaster, especially if dramatic expansion of the perils covered is undertaken. As a matter of disaster planning, however, the captured efficiencies of a holistic flood damage plan may equal out the losses accrued in its pure "insurance" context. Granted, there is the persistent problem of conflict of interest and likely inflated administration costs endemic to the WYO flood insurance system. Likewise, however, FEMA's disaster relief itself has not exactly been without its criticisms of inefficiency, fraud, and insider dealings. The use of an expanded NFIP may prove the superior option for the actual *provision* of loss mitigation funds.

**Conclusion**

There is little doubt that hurricanes Katrina, Rita, and Wilma have caused untold misery in the affected areas. There is also little doubt that poor comprehensive insurance planning—public and private—added to the misery. Mitigation of the misery from the storms was and is an ongoing societal responsibility. While insurance plays an important role in that mitigation, it can never completely alleviate the full effects of that social responsibility. Insurance programs, however, particularly those already subsidized by the government, can be nearly infinitely flexible in their manner of risk-sharing and the scope of their coverage. There is nothing preventing the NFIP from being completely reconstituted so as to allow states or municipalities to simply buy block coverage for all homeowners in designated risk areas, with the method of premium apportionment to those areas left up to those municipalities to determine.

If the events of 2005 on the Gulf Coast exhibit anything, it is that the system in place lacks cohesion, efficiency, and imagination. Hurricane disasters *will* happen; it cannot be in the best interest of any citizen for the government to continually respond to them on an ad hoc basis. No area of government deserves greater focus than its disaster response policy. No political question of our time can be more important than articulating that policy. Failure to address these issues simply will result in continued uncertainty and the consistent waste of large amounts of money. That is in the best interest of no one.

Additionally, unless flood insurance becomes mandatory and universally available to all homeowners, the government must come to terms with its responsibility to those communities where the rebuilding will be slowed as a result of the absence of sufficient assets. In assembling a disaster mitigation and rebuilding policy, without universality, it becomes incumbent on either the courts or government to determine an equitable solution for homeowners who had been operating under a common and not entirely unreasonable, though unilateral, mistake as to the protections afforded them with only a homeowner's policy. If coverage cannot be found for such people through the private homeowner's insurance for which they had been paying premiums, and, in fact, it is determined as a matter of law to be unavailable to such homeowners operating under such a good-faith mistake, as a matter of disaster policy it would not be too unreasonable for the government to provide flood coverage ex post, with a reasonable offset for the premiums the homeowner would have paid had he contracted with the government for flood coverage. It seems rather odd, as a matter of disaster policy, to relegate the mistaken homeowner to a situation without any government insurance relief as a result of their not having formally contracted with that particular government agency.

Chapter 7

# Participation and Disintermediation in a Risk Society

Robert J. Rhee

Humanity has always lived in the shadow of catastrophic risk. The common definition of catastrophe is "a momentous tragic event ranging from extreme misfortune to utter overthrow or ruin."[1] A catastrophe connotes a large, broadly distributed loss. Frequency of event and severity of loss are inversely correlated. Severe losses are infrequent, but they may still be within the range of expectation. Highly destructive terrorist attacks, hurricanes, and earthquakes are certainly foreseeable. Most catastrophes are also localized events. Despite great misfortune, they do not significantly affect the broader society, economy, or even the insurance industry. But there is a category of catastrophes that surpasses ordinary expectations. An extreme catastrophe (mega-catastrophe) is an event so severe that the exogenous shock ripples out from the immediate locus of loss to the greater society. These events test the traditional network of compensation and insurance schemes.

The problem is one of distributing risk and loss. Important questions are raised. Who should bear the risk? How should compensation be conceived? What should be the mechanism for risk distribution? The answers depend, in large part, on the number of participants in the distribution scheme and the cost associated with risk spreading.[2] In extreme catastrophes, the major participants are victims, insurers, and government.[3] The availability of private insurance is limited by the capital held and the extent of contractual risk transfer. When capital cannot support

---

1    WEBSTER'S NINTH NEW COLLEGIATE DICTIONARY 214 (1983). The insurance definition is a loss of $25 million or more. *See* ISO, *PCS Catastrophe Serial Numbers*, http://www.iso.com/products/2800/prod2802.html (definition by ISO, a leading insurance information and services firm). *See generally* ERIK BANKS, CATASTROPHIC RISK: ANALYSIS AND MANAGEMENT (2005).

2    *See* KENNETH S. ABRAHAM, DISTRIBUTING RISK: INSURANCE, LEGAL THEORY, AND PUBLIC POLICY 14–31 (1986).

3    This does not include charity, which is not an insignificant participant in the delivery of compensation. In the broader scheme, charity typically constitutes a fraction of the compensation provided. For example, in the case of 9/11, victims received on average $3.1 million, with sixty-nine percent coming from the September 11th Victim Compensation Fund, twenty-three percent from insurance, and eight percent from charity. LLOYD DIXON & RACHEL KAGANOFF STERN, COMPENSATION FOR LOSSES FROM THE 9/11 ATTACKS xxiii (RAND 2004).

the risk or when insurance penetration is insufficient, government compensation fills the void and provides disaster relief, either through ex ante insurance or ex post compensation. Without public relief, the residual risk bearer is always the victim.

In most cases of loss or accident, the mix of cost internalization and compensation through the network of traditional insurance, tort action, government relief, social and familial institutions works fairly well. This scheme, however, is stressed when losses become extreme: cost internalization may be deemed too much for a large class of victims; traditional insurance may not have sufficient capacity to absorb the loss; the tort system may be too slow and costly and may increase the secondary costs of dislocation; ordinary government services, social and familial institutions may become overwhelmed. The standard model of compensation was tested by two of the most devastating catastrophes to strike the United States in modern history—9/11 and Hurricane Katrina. These catastrophes raise important questions about the adequacy of participation in a risk society and the role of the government. Is there a right mix of risk spreading among participants? Is there an efficient matching of those exposed to risk with those who are willing to bear the cost? What are the costs of risk spreading? Poorly managed risk can not only amplify the consequences of catastrophes, but can also cause derivative manmade catastrophes.[4] Thus, these questions touch not only economic choices, but their moral consequences as well.

The problem of insurance and risk distribution is both a private activity and a public function.[5] In specific areas, such as flooding and terrorism, the government provides insurance and compensation.[6] A public role is necessary because, it is believed, private insurance alone cannot bear the risk of extreme loss. The collection of tax revenue is broad and indiscriminant as to one's risk exposure and appetite to bear it, and the distribution of public funds in times of catastrophe is subject to a complex mix of perceived need, sympathy, and politics that is neither entirely consistent nor predictable. The democratization of risk distribution is a prominent aspect of catastrophic risk and loss management.

This chapter explores the limitations of the private and public risk distribution and compensation schemes. The experiences of 9/11 and Katrina provide the context

---

4   *See* Robert J. Rhee, *Catastrophic Risk and Governance After Hurricane Katrina: A Postscript to Terrorism Risk in a Post-9/11 Economy*, 38 Ariz. St. L.J. 581, 593–602 (2006).

5   *See generally* Insurance, Government, and Social Policy (Spencer L. Kimball & Herbert S. Denenberg eds., 1969).

6   *See generally* National Flood Insurance Act of 1968, Pub. L. No. 90-448, 82 Stat. 572 (2000); Terrorism Risk Insurance Act of 2002, Pub. L. No. 107-297, § 101(a)-(b), 116 Stat. 2322, 2322–23 (2002); Terrorism Risk Insurance Extension Act of 2005, Pub. L. No. 109-144, 119 Stat. 2660 (2005); Terrorism Risk Insurance Program Reauthorization Act of 2007, Pub. L. No. 110-160, 121 Stat. 1839 (2007).

for the discussion of this theme. This chapter argues that traditional insurance and government compensation are often inadequate, and that an alternative mechanism of private risk distribution is needed. An alternative scheme may mean the disintermediation of the traditional insurance and government functions, and a move towards more direct market transactions between those who are exposed to risk and those participants who are willing to bear it. Disintermediation may better spread risk, reduce the secondary cost of dislocation, and incentivize proper mitigation measures. The result would not only be more efficient from an economic point of view, but also be more just and fair.

## Era of Mega-Catastrophes

Throughout much of human history, catastrophes have been blamed on bad luck or the distemper of gods. But catastrophes are not simply a matter of fortune's winds. Human choices play a significant role in the causality and consequence of catastrophes. The most obvious example of a frequently recurring manmade catastrophe is war. Beyond this, society lives and builds in the path of hurricanes, on coastlines and geological faults. Whereas the ancients lacked the knowledge to understand the risk around them,[7] modern society has a deep appreciation of the dangers associated with many of its activities.

In the twilight of the twentieth century, the frequency and severity of catastrophes surged. In 1992, Hurricane Andrew struck the Florida coast and caused insured losses of approximately $21 billion.[8] At the time, it was the largest loss from a single event in insurance history. In the same year, the Irish Republic Army bombed central London and caused $671 million in insurance losses, foreshadowing a more virulent form of terrorism.[9] In 1994, the Northridge earthquake inflicted insured losses of approximately $17 billion,[10] and $43 billion in economic losses.[11] In 1995, the Kobe earthquake caused $147 billion in economic losses,[12] at the time

---

7   The intellectual understanding of risk is a relatively modern science. *See* PETER L. BERNSTEIN, AGAINST THE GODS: THE REMARKABLE STORY OF RISK (1996).

8   Auriela Zanetti et al., *Natural Catastrophes and Man-Made Disasters in 2003, in* SIGMA 2004, at 38, tbl.10 (Swiss Re, Sigma No. 1/2004, 2004) [hereinafter Sigma No. 1/2004] (giving data indexed to 2003 value; property damage and business interruption loss).

9   TERRORISM AND INSURANCE 3 (Swiss Re 1993).

10   Sigma No. 1/2004, *supra* note 8.

11   DAN L. CRIPPEN, A CBO STUDY: FEDERAL REINSURANCE FOR DISASTERS 9–10 (Cong. Budget Office 2002).

12   DAVI M. D'AGOSTINO, CATASTROPHE INSURANCE RISKS: THE ROLE OF RISK-LINKED SECURITIES AND FACTORS AFFECTING THEIR USE, GENERAL ACCOUNTING OFFICE (GAO) No. 02-941, at 12, fig. 2 (2002).

perhaps the most costly natural catastrophe in modern history.[13] Since insurance penetration in Kobe was shallow, only $4 billion was insured loss.[14]

The unprecedented catastrophes of the 1990s portended a new century of mega-catastrophes. On September 11, 2001, the terrorist attacks caused about $80 billion in direct economic loss,[15] of which about $36 billion was insured.[16] The event was the largest insurance loss from a single event. On December 26, 2004, the Asian tsunami killed approximately 280,000, becoming one of the deadliest natural catastrophes in the modern era. On August 29, 2005, Katrina inflicted about $200 billion in damages and 1,700 deaths.[17] Currently, insurance litigation is working through the legal system, but the private insurance loss (not including insurance loss from the National Flood Insurance Program) is estimated to be over $40 billion, which would surpass that of 9/11.[18] Both 9/11 and Katrina were one in one hundred year events. The 1906 San Francisco earthquake and fire is the closest comparable to Katrina because of the scale of destruction to a major American city, and 9/11 because of the impact on the insurance industry from a single event.[19]

What has accounted for this destructive surge? Bad luck cannot be discounted. It was bad luck that Katrina was a direct blow to New Orleans rather than a glancing one, and that the intelligence and law enforcement agencies failed to foil the terrorist plot. But bad luck is simply a matter of timing, just as the "Big One" will eventually strike the West Coast. A part of the answer is that catastrophes are more severe because tropical storms have become more frequent and severe. Also, severity of catastrophe is a function of value at risk. In this regard, economic asset values have increased. There is a continuing concentration of population

---

13    Saul Levmore & Kyle D. Logue, *Insuring Against Terrorism—and Crime*, 102 MICH. L. REV. 268, 270 (2003).

14    D'AGOSTINO, *supra* note 12.

15    U.S. GEN. ACCOUNTING OFFICE, CATASTROPHIC INSURANCE RISKS: STATUS OF EFFORTS TO SECURITIZE NATURAL CATASTROPHE AND TERRORISM RISK 1 (2003).

16    CONGRESSIONAL BUDGET OFFICE, CONGRESS OF THE UNITED STATES, PUBL'N No. 2940, FEDERAL REINSURANCE FOR TERRORISM RISKS: ISSUES IN REAUTHORIZATION 1 (2007) [hereinafter CBO Report].

17    Rawle King, *National Flood Insurance Program: Treasury Borrowing in the Aftermath of Hurricane Katrina*, CONG. RES. SERV., June 6, 2006, at 2.

18    *See* Patricia L. Guinn, *Hurricane Katrina: Analysis of the Impact on the Insurance Industry* 3 (Towers Perrin 2005). Insurance claims could result in a loss as high as $60 billion. *See* Spencer M. Taylor, *Insuring Against the Natural Catastrophe After Katrina*, 20 NAT. RESOURCES & ENV'T 26, 26 (2006); *Katrina Damage Estimate Hits $125B*, USA TODAY, *available at* http://www.usatoday.com/money/economy/2005-09-09-katrina-damage_x.htm (last visited Apr. 1, 2008).

19    *See* Robert J. Rhee, *Terrorism Risk in a Post-9/11 Economy: The Convergence of Capital Markets, Insurance, and Government Action*, 37 ARIZ. ST. L.J. 435, 443 n.32 (2005).

and economic assets in large urban and coastal areas.[20] And, after a century of catastrophic wars and the apocalyptic possibilities of the Cold War, the lesson learned is that human life and welfare are most precious. There is more value at risk, making the same catastrophe more severe.

Human hands can not only unleash enormous catastrophes such as the worst case scenarios of global warming or nuclear detonation, but they can amplify the consequences of natural risks. Even when causality cannot be influenced, human choices can magnify or mitigate the destructive pulses of fortune.[21] Consider the fact that natural disasters with the greatest fatalities tend to be in less developed countries whose political economy may be incapable of adequately mitigating risk.[22] While the occurrence of a natural catastrophe may be fortuitous, risk spreading and mitigation are uniquely human activities.

Katrina provides a good case study. The hurricane was an independent event, but the catastrophe occurred as a result of the consequences of a long chain of human decisions. Since the earliest settlement in New Orleans, residents knew that the land mass was subject to flooding. In 1965, Congress authorized the construction of the levee system.[23] The government could have built the levees to withstand a category 5 hurricane. But ultimately, the system was built to withstand a storm approximately equivalent to a fast-moving category 3 hurricane.[24] It was believed that such a storm strikes coastal Louisiana once every 200 years.[25] With the clarity of hindsight and the realization of global warming, this estimate has proven to be erroneous. Since the 1970s, the frequency of category 4 and 5 hurricanes and the destructiveness of tropical storms have doubled.[26] This experience suggests that the original probability estimate was wrong. Of course this is hindsight bias, and the point is not that the original assumption was wrong since no one can predict weather patterns forty years into the future. Rather, no allowance was made for the possibility of error. The one in two hundred year assessment reflected the best guess probability, suggesting that the government accepted the risk that, in any given year, the city had a 0.5 percent chance of a catastrophic breach. In light of the difficulty of long-term weather prediction, the possibility of error, and the magnitude of harm from error, the decision to set the engineering standard

---

20    Christopher M. Lewis & Kevin C. Murdock, *Alternative Means of Redistributing Catastrophic Risk in a National Risk-Management System, in* THE FINANCING OF CATASTROPHIC RISK 52 (Kenneth A. Froot ed., 1999).

21    *See generally* THE SOCIAL AMPLIFICATION OF RISK (Nick Pidgeon et al. eds., 2003).

22    Rhee, *Terrorism Risk, supra* note 19, at 532 tbl.4 & n.450.

23    Pub. L. No. 89-298, § 204, 79 Stat. 1073 (1965).

24    U.S. GOV'T ACCOUNTABILITY OFFICE, PUBL'N NO. GAO-06-322T, HURRICANE PROTECTION: STATUTORY AND REGULATORY FRAMEWORK FOR LEVEE MAINTENANCE AND EMERGENCY RESPONSE FOR THE LAKE PONTCHARTRAIN PROJECT 4 (2005).

25    *Id.*

26    HARVARD MEDICAL SCHOOL, THE CENTER FOR HEALTH AND THE GLOBAL ENVIRONMENT, CLIMATE CHANGE FUTURES: HEALTH, ECOLOGICAL AND ECONOMIC DIMENSIONS 4 (Paul R. Epstein & Evan Mills eds., 2005).

at this level was fatally shortsighted. Katrina need not have killed thousands of Americans; it need not have destroyed billions of dollars of assets; it need not have flooded a major American city. Arguably, the "original sin" (so to speak) dates back to the decision to settle in a flood prone land, but recent government decisions on risk management dating back to 1965 are the most direct proximate cause of the mega-catastrophe. Katrina, the hurricane, was a natural event, but Katrina, the catastrophe, was certainly manmade.

Katrina illustrates the paradox of modern society. The understanding of risk in the modern era has rapidly developed: the geological and meteorological dynamics that trigger natural catastrophes, the laws of probability and risk, the underwriting of fortuitous risk, and the risk of markets and political economy. Advances in technology, awareness of risks, regulation and tort law, and greater sensitivity to loss have reduced many of the ordinary risks of living life in a complex world: transportation and consumer products are safer, healthcare is better, diseases have been neutralized, and workplace accidents are less frequent. Despite these advances, the frequency and severity of catastrophes have increased. Technology promotes welfare, but also harbors potentially dangerous risks. Industrialization provides cheap goods, but pollutes the environment. Nuclear power provides cleaner energy, but also poses a source of accidents or abuse. Genetically modified foods and nanotechnology better our lives, but may also pose hidden dangers. More innovations, yet unheard of or presently fantastical in concept, will rapidly follow as the growth of technology is geometric. Greater complexity begets greater means of breakdown.[27] Mega-catastrophic terrorism is real. Global warming, debatable only a few years ago, is a generally accepted phenomenon though the degree of adverse consequences in the future is uncertain. Rapid increase in human population stresses biodiversity. Population and economic assets continue to concentrate in mega-cities, many of which are in the path of natural catastrophes and prey to terrorism. The possibility of a technological mishap cannot be discounted. No one can foretell whether any of these risks will manifest into future mega-catastrophes.[28] It is also doubtful whether these risks are somehow quantifiable for the purposes of the all ubiquitous cost-benefit analysis.[29]

---

27    In addition to natural disasters and special manmade disasters like terrorism, we have also begun to see economic catastrophes arising from ordinary activities. For example, the 2001 power failures in California caused a productivity loss of $21.8 billion, income loss of $4.5 billion, and 135,000 jobs; and the power failure that blacked out the northeast United States on August 14, 2003 caused a $75–$100 million loss from food spoilage alone. CHRISTIAN BRAUNER, THE RISK LANDSCAPE OF THE FUTURE 15 (Swiss Re 2004).

28    *See* RICHARD A. POSNER, CATASTROPHE: RISK AND RESPONSE 21–91 (2004) (discussing various scenarios in which mega-catastrophes can occur).

29    *See* Rhee, *Catastrophic Risk and Governance, supra* note 4, at 585 n.27; *but see* POSNER, *supra* note 28, at 167–70 (calculating the value of human civilization at $600 trillion to conduct a cost-benefit analysis in catastrophe prevention program).

Ultimately, Katrina and 9/11 may well be once-in-a-lifetime disasters, iconic in stature and thus unique in the annals of history. This is the sanguine perspective. A more realistic view is that Katrina and 9/11 are harbingers of a new era of mega-catastrophes. Although all the factors of causality and consequence are not subject to control, the task at hand is to properly manage risk. The goals are three: mitigate risk, which entails the deterrence of costly behavior; spread risk so that the secondary costs of economic dislocation are reduced; and minimize the transaction cost of risk spreading and compensation delivery.[30]

## Sources of Compensation

### *Tort System*

In times of mega-catastrophes, compensation through the tort system is infeasible and undesirable. It is true that mass torts, typically arising from the occurrence of a large single accident or the release of a defective product into the marketplace, are frequently litigated. Despite the limitations of litigation, primarily the time delay and the costs of resolution,[31] the tort system adequately administers most disputes arising from accidents. Tort law works best when there is a clear transaction between the parties, blameworthiness is within the realm of reasonable debate, causation is clear, and credit risk is low. Although there are delays in compensation and high transaction costs relative to insurance or an ex post compensation fund, these costs constitute the price of accessing the civil dispute resolution system. Mass torts may raise public policy considerations, such as concerns for public safety and financial distress to industry, but they are in essence private disputes of right and wrong to be resolved among the parties.

In the case of a mega-catastrophe, these considerations typically do not hold. The concepts of fault and liability lose much of their plausibility. By definition, extreme catastrophes are highly unlikely events. They may be foreseeable just as an asteroid strike or a global pandemic are foreseeable, but such foresight may

---

30  *See* Guido Calabresi, The Costs of Accidents: A Legal and Economic Analysis (1970).

31  Much criticism has been levied against the cost of the litigation system. The cost, however, is not equally assumed. During the litigation process, each party discounts the value of a lawsuit based on the perceived risk and their economic bargaining positions. *See* Robert J. Rhee, *A Price Theory of Legal Bargaining: An Inquiry into the Selection of Settlement and Litigation Under Uncertainty*, 56 Emory L.J. 619 (2006); Robert J. Rhee, *The Effect of Risk on Legal Valuation*, 78 U. Colo. L. Rev. 193 (2007). This process results in a systematic discount of tort claims during the dispute resolution process. *See* Robert J. Rhee, *Tort Arbitrage*, 60 Fla. L. Rev. 125 (2008). Thus, the civil litigation system assures that the plaintiff internalizes some of the cost of accident.

not suffice for liability. Often, catastrophes are simply a matter of bad luck, and perfection of precaution against all perils has never been the standard of care in the fault system.[32] Even with a plausible case for liability, most private defendants would be judgment proof. It is a limitation of tort law that as damage assessment against a defendant reaches a threshold, the well of remedy begins to run dry, either because of the limited resources of the defendant or because the law refuses to impose liability that may cripple a socially necessary asset.[33] The extreme form of this problem is terrorism by stateless organizations. In the case of a judgment proof defendant, victims must find an alternative source of blame and deep pockets, which ironically may make a case for liability less plausible. From the perspective of a mass class of victims, the most credit-worthy defendant is a public entity. Federal and state governments, however, may have vigorous defenses, making compensation highly uncertain.

In most extreme catastrophes, the identity of the wrongdoer and the question of negligence are often speculative. Consider the case of 9/11. There would have been no recourse against the terrorists. Victims would have had to look to other defendants—perhaps the airlines, the landlords, and the government—but obviously the question of negligence would have been far from clear, resulting in complexity and uncertainty that would have required years of litigation.[34] Questions of duty, breach of care, and causation would have been substantial. Consider also the case of Katrina. The hurricane was a chance event, but the government's negligence in managing the crisis caused substantial injuries.[35] Any claim of negligence, however, would face substantial constitutional, statutory, and common law tort barriers to recovery.[36] Compensation through the tort system is highly uncertain, unpredictable, and costly, and the tort system is typically the

---

32   *See* Adams v. Bullock, 227 N.Y. 208, 210 (1919) (Cardozo) ("We think that ordinary caution did not involve forethought of this extraordinary peril."). While strict liability may be applicable in industrial accidents, it is difficult to see how the doctrine would apply in most other cases of catastrophe.

33   *See, e.g.*, Strauss v. Belle Realty Co., 482 N.E.2d 34 (N.Y. 1985) (precluding tort liability against utility for negligent blackout); H.R. Moch Co. v. Rensselaer Water Co., 159 N.E. 896 (N.Y. 1928) (precluding tort liability against water company for the failure to provide water during fire).

34   Most tort actions were waived through voluntary participation in the September 11 Victim Compensation Fund, which required waivers of tort actions. Air Transportation Safety and System Stabilization Act, 49 U.S.C. § 40101 (2003). In the end, 2879 claims out of 2976 deaths, about ninety-seven percent, were made under the fund. DIXON & STERN, *supra* note 3, at 24–25.

35   *See generally* U.S. HOUSE OF REPRESENTATIVES, A FAILURE OF INITIATIVE: FINAL REP. OF THE SELECT BIPARTISAN COMM. TO INVESTIGATE THE PREPARATION FOR AND RESPONSE TO HURRICANE KATRINA, H.R. Rep. No. 109-377 (2006); DOUGLAS BRINKLEY, THE GREAT DELUGE: HURRICANE KATRINA, NEW ORLEANS, AND THE MISSISSIPPI GULF COAST (2006).

36   *See, e.g.*, Federal Tort Claims Act, 28 U.S.C. § 2680 (2006).

least efficient means of compensation.[37] The uncertainty and delay may exacerbate economic dislocation and increase secondary cost. In sum, the tort system is not ideal when liability is potentially remote, source of remedy is limited, and social cost of delay is high.[38]

*Private Insurance*

Without the tort system, the old triumvirate of insurance, victim, and government bears the brunt of the losses. The availability of private insurance is subject to several limitations. It is, of course, a creature of contract, and thus an ex ante agreement is a predicate to compensation. The voluntary nature of contract influences the demand side of the insurance equation. Insurance penetration may be too shallow to provide adequate compensation. Homeowner's policies routinely exclude flood and earthquake insurance, and coverage for these hazards must be bought separately. Even in the area of life and health insurance, demand is not universal. Insurance penetration is a function of wealth as, outside of mandatory coverage, insurance is a discretionary spending item. The experience of 9/11 showed that a compensation fund was deemed necessary to substantially augment life insurance, even for a large segment of the victims who worked in the lucrative field of financial services;[39] the experience of Katrina showed that the penetration of flood insurance was not pervasive, even for a city whose land mass was below sea level. Moreover, the impact of a catastrophe is not shared equally. In times of crisis, the class of people most affected is the poor because they tend to be underinsured. The experience of the Asian tsunami tragically illustrates this disparate effect: the disaster was one of the worst natural catastrophes in history, and yet the insurance losses were rather minimal in relation to the scale of the calamity.[40]

On the supply side, the capital supporting the property and casualty market is limited.[41] The insurance industry can bear up to the region of $100 billion loss from a single event without a systemic failure.[42] Coverage for large scale

---

37    *See* Rhee, *Terrorism Risk*, *supra* note 19, at 440.

38    *See* MARSHALL S. SHAPO, COMPENSATION FOR VICTIMS OF TERRORISM 44–88 (2005) (discussing the problematic issues related to tort actions).

39    *See* DIXON & STERN, *supra* note 3.

40    *See* Rhee, *Catastrophic Risk and Governance*, *supra* note 4, at 590.

41    *See* AM. ACAD. OF ACTUARIES, PUBLIC POLICY MONOGRAPH, P/C TERRORISM INSURANCE COVERAGE: WHERE DO WE GO POST-TERRORISM RISK INSURANCE ACT? 12 (2004) ("The U.S. P/C industry's surplus stood at $347 billion at year-end 2003."); R. GLENN HUBBARD & BRUCE DEAL, THE ECONOMIC EFFECTS OF FEDERAL PARTICIPATION IN TERRORISM RISK 34 (2004) (noting that $199 billion of $347 billion of surplus in the U.S. P/C sector was devoted to commercial lines).

42    See J. David Cummins, Neil Doherty & Anita Lo, *Can Insurers Pay for the "Big One": Measuring the Capacity of the Insurance Market to Respond to Catastrophic Losses*, 26 J. BANKING & FIN. 557 (2002) (concluding that the insurance industry could fund a $100

catastrophes such as terrorism, earthquake, flooding, and hurricanes are limited in the private insurance market, and such coverage is frequently supplemented by government funds. In its current configuration, the private market has difficulty with underwriting extreme risks.[43] The reasons are complex, but they can be summarized as follows: catastrophic risk is difficult to model and thus insurers incorporate an appropriate risk premium into the price; American tax laws are unfavorable to the accumulation of an adequate reserve against an infrequent extreme event; and the small possibility of a large event requires an insurer to hold sufficient capital to protect against insolvency in any given year, and the capital held must generate a sufficient investment return such that capital costs drive premiums towards economic infeasibility.[44]

Lastly, the pricing of insurance is most cost efficient when the risk is characterized by high frequency of event and low severity of loss, such as automobile accidents and ordinary liability insurance. When the risk is low frequency and high severity, the typical profile of a catastrophe, or when other factors militate against insurability, such as flooding and nuclear accident, traditional insurance is often unavailable or expensive. The unpredictability of the aggregate risk pool requires a large risk premium that is commensurate with the capital that must be held to ensure solvency, and this risk premium may result in economic infeasibility of premiums, which would further drive down the demand for insurance.

Collectively, these economic dynamics and financial limitations suggest that traditional insurance leaves large gaps in the provision of compensation in times of extraordinary loss. It is only a partial solution to the problem.

*Public Insurance*

Private insurance and the tort system are limited, and victims cannot internalize the entirety of the loss without injustice and substantial secondary costs. Accordingly, government compensation is important. It can be delivered through an ex ante subsidized insurance program, such as the Terrorism Risk Insurance Act of 2002 (TRIA) and the National Flood Insurance Act of 1968, or through an ex post compensation scheme, such as the September 11 Victim Compensation Fund. Although government must always be involved in times of national or regional crisis, public distribution of risk and loss has been problematic in both ex ante and ex post programs.

---

billion loss event, but that such a loss would result in significant disruptions to the insurance market). Given that the industry holds more capital than it did in 2001, this threshold is probably higher now.

43   *See* Paul R. Kleindorfer & Howard C. Kunreuther, *Challenges Facing the Insurance Industry in Managing Catastrophic Risks, in* THE FINANCING OF CATASTROPHIC RISK, *supra* note 20, at 149–94.

44   *See* Rhee, *Terrorism Risk, supra* note 19, at 464–78.

Consider first public insurance programs. These programs are not influenced by ordinary market dynamics. One result is that public insurance tends to crowd out private insurance or anesthetize market developments.[45] TRIA is a good example. It is a temporary cost-sharing program that provides the insurance industry a federal backstop for extreme losses from terrorism. It was enacted with two stated purposes: to address "market disruptions and ensure the continued widespread availability and affordability" of insurance, and to "allow for a transitional period for the private markets to stabilize, resume pricing of such insurance, and build capacity to absorb any future losses."[46] Because the program was envisioned as a temporary price stabilization measure, it was enacted with a legislative life of three years. In the three years of the program, the insurance market stabilized; insurers raised more capital to replace the capital lost from the attacks; terrorism risk insurance became widely available with stabilized premiums and an increasing competitive market; and the general economy recovered from the initial shock.[47] These are good developments, but it is questionable whether TRIA influenced them in any meaningful way.[48] Worse, the TRIA has done more harm than good. The major problem is that "there has been little development or movement among insurers or reinsurers toward developing a private-sector mechanism that could provide capacity, without government involvement, to absorb losses from terrorist events."[49] Instead, the insurance industry's view of a permanent solution appears to be "a long-term, public-private partnership,"[50] meaning a long-term extension of a federal cost-sharing program. Thus far, the industry lobby has been successful. Despite price and economic stability, the government extended TRIA for another two years at the end of 2005, and then another seven years at the end of 2007.[51] Government insurance has created an expectation of corporate welfare, which anesthetizes the need for a private insurance solution.[52]

---

45  *See id.* at 491.

46  TRIA § 101(b).

47  *See* U.S. TREASURY DEP'T, BOARD OF GOVERNORS OF THE FED. RESERVE, SECURITIES AND EXCHANGE COMM'N & COMMODITY FUTURES TRADING COMM'N, TERRORISM RISK INSURANCE: REPORT OF THE PRESIDENT'S WORKING GROUP ON FINANCIAL MARKETS (2006). The conclusions of this report were predicted by scholars. *See, e.g.*, Rhee, *Terrorism Risk*, *supra* note 19, at 480 ("With that said, betting against a powerful insurance lobby is always a perilous venture.").

48  *See* Rhee, *Terrorism Risk*, *supra* note 19, at 458–59; Rhee, *Catastrophic Risk and Governance*, *supra* note 4, at 601.

49  U.S. GEN. ACCOUNTING OFFICE, PUBL'N NO. GAO-04-307, TERRORISM INSURANCE: IMPLEMENTATION OF THE TERRORISM RISK INSURANCE ACT OF 2002 28 (2004).

50  *Ensuring Economic Security in the Face of Terrorism: A Public-Private Partnership*, AM. INS. ASS'N ADVOCATE, Mar. 3, 2005, at 3.

51  *See supra* note 6.

52  *See* James G. Bohn & Brian J. Hall, *The Moral Hazard of Insuring the Insurers*, in THE FINANCING OF CATASTROPHIC RISK, *supra note* 20, at 363–83.

The 2007 long-term extension of TRIA is a sign that the temporary federal backstop may well be on its way to becoming a permanent public insurance fixture, though that clearly was not the government's original intent.[53] The government has extended TRIA despite the Congressional Budget Office's recent warning that:

1. abundance of evidence suggests that "Commercial policyholders as a group are not taking significant steps to avoid or mitigate terrorism risks associated with their existing properties";
2. federal insurance subsidy provides a disincentive to insurers "to make their premiums sensitive to their policyholders' risk of incurring losses from an act of terrorism"; and
3. "efforts to mitigate risk could increase in the absence of subsidized insurance."[54]

At best, we can conclude, as the CBO does, that federal insurance "does not lower the total costs of terrorism risk but rather shifts more of the burden from commercial property owners and their tenants to taxpayers."[55] The program is corporate welfare. More realistically, we can conclude that subsidized terrorism insurance "will tend to distort market incentives and may increase the costs of the economy over a long period."[56] In tangible terms, the existence of cheap, subsidized insurance may mean, for example, that the real estate developer constructs a tall glass office tower that is susceptible to a truck bomb as opposed to a concrete building with reinforced steel, or a corporation chooses to locate its assets in a highly dense environment such as New York City as opposed to the less prestigious or convenient New Jersey suburbs. In the case of terrorism risk, the government ultimately does more harm than good and the person most harmed is the American public, which ends up paying the cost of corporate welfare. Most will make this payment in the form of taxpayer dollars, but an unfortunate few may at some point in the future as a matter of probability pay in the form of additional lost lives and limbs.

In addition to creating bad incentives, government insurance programs are also susceptible to bad management. A single department within an agency typically manages an insurance program. "These micro-agencies, subject only to bureaucratic oversight, cannot compete with the private market, which is subject to the collective forces of supply and demand, innovation and strategy, and incentives and disincentives."[57] The National Flood Insurance Program (NFIP)

---

53   The goal of the insurance and business lobbies is to make permanent a federal cost-sharing program. *See* Rhee, *Catastrophic Risk and Governance, supra* note 4, at 600; Rhee, *Terrorism Risk, supra* note 19, at 491.

54   CBO Report, *supra* note 16, at 20, 21, 26.

55   *Id.* at 10.

56   Rhee, *Terrorism Risk, supra* note 19, at 491.

57   *Id.* at 492.

is a good example. The problem begins with underwriting. Flooding constitutes ninety percent of all natural disasters in the United States.[58] Like a nuclear accident, flooding is such a highly correlative risk that private insurers exclude coverage, leaving property owners three choices: internalize the loss, eliminate the risk by vacating or selling the property, or take mitigation measures.[59] In 1968, Congress changed this dynamic when it enacted NFIP. Flood insurance has proven to be a poorly executed, bad idea.[60] The problem starts with subsidization: "The program, by design, is not actuarially sound because Congress authorized subsidized insurance rates to be made available for policies covering some properties to encourage communities to join the program."[61] Premiums represent about thirty-five to forty percent of the actuarial risk, resulting in a program that is not financially independent and that largely subsidizes actual risk.[62] This is not surprising as public insurance programs have tended to be ex ante disaster relief cloaked in insurance terms.[63]

The cost-benefit analysis is not encouraging. The government saves one dollar in ex post disaster relief for every three dollars of flood insurance claims paid.[64] Why sustain an ex ante insurance program when an ex post compensation plan is available? The government's answer is that through its risk management and mitigation efforts, the program saves about $1 billion in flood damage each year.[65] But this figure is misleading because it is unknown whether the projected losses would have occurred without the program. Losses are influenced by the existence of subsidized flood insurance; without it, economic forces and rational incentives would have driven out many owners of high risk properties. A true cost-benefit analysis can be done only if these factors are decoupled. Thus, some of the claimed "savings" must surely be costs in disguise.

---

58   U.S. Gov't Accountability Office, Publ'n No. GAO-06-119, Federal Emergency Management Agency: Improvements Needed to Enhance Oversight and Management of the National Flood Insurance Program 1 (2005) [hereinafter Improvements Needed in NFIP].

59   *See* Adam F. Scales, *A Nation of Policyholders: Governmental and Market Failure in Flood Insurance*, 26 Miss. C. L. Rev. 3 (2007) (discussing the failure of public and private flood insurance from the perspective of insurance law).

60   *See* Rhee, *Terrorism Risk, supra* note 19, at 492–93 & nn.288–90.

61   U.S. Gov't Accountability Office, Publ'n No. GAO-06-174T, Federal Emergency Management Agency: Challenges Facing the National Flood Insurance Program 5 (2005) [hereinafter Challenges Facing the NFIP].

62   *Id.* at 4.

63   *See* Rhee, *Catastrophic Risk and Governance, supra* note 4, at 611 ("the flood insurance program is really a welfare distribution scheme cloaked in insurance terms"); Rhee, *Terrorism Risk, supra* note 19, at 493 (government insurance programs typically are wealth distribution schemes "under an insurance guise").

64   Challenges Facing the NFIP, *supra* note 61, at 2.

65   *Id.*

Underwriting aside, the management of the program has been problematic. Only about forty employees and 170 contractors in the Federal Emergency Management Agency manage the entire flood insurance program.[66] The program has 4.6 million policyholders in about 20,000 communities, and it has paid about $14.6 billion in claims as of August 2005.[67] Hurricanes Katrina and Rita added another $15 to $25 billion in claims.[68] Obviously, the program is vast and the financials suggest that the entire program could constitute a major business component of a publicly traded insurance company. Absent substantially more resources, the program cannot be effectively managed. The agency outsources the day-to-day management responsibilities to the private sector. About ninety-five percent of in-force policies are written by private insurance agents representing about ninety-five private insurance companies that issue policies and adjust claims.[69] These insurers, called "write-your-own companies," receive about a third of the premium income and remit the remainder to the government.[70] They also receive about 3.3 percent of the incurred losses as compensation for claims adjustment services.[71] Thus, private insurers, which bear no underwritten risk, profit more from the program if they issue more policies and incur more losses.

As one would expect, the program suffers from adverse selection problems. Repetitive loss properties, which account for only one percent of insured properties, comprise twenty-five to thirty percent of claims.[72] Repetitive loss is indicative of adverse selection, and the root cause is grounded in a policy requiring only high risk properties to obtain insurance.[73] FEMA is charged with assuring a minimum level of quality control in the program, but the oversight of private insurers has been problematic.[74] The agency's quality control methods have been found to lack "statistical validity," meaning that in conducting its insurance function, the agency does not have the information needed "to have reasonable assurance that program objectives are being achieved."[75] Thus, the process of information acquisition and analysis—the most vital function of a well-run insurance company—is unreliable, suggesting that the government agency is a rather poor assessor of risk.

If the problem with government insurance is just a matter of wealth transfer, the issue is simply a policy question on the appropriate use of public funds. One can argue that public funds should be used precisely to protect people who have been

---

    66   IMPROVEMENTS NEEDED IN NFIP, *supra* note 57, at 15.
    67   *Id.*, *supra* note 57, at 2.
    68   U.S. GOV'T ACCOUNTABILITY OFFICE, PUBL'N NO. GAO-06-183T, FEDERAL EMERGENCY MANAGEMENT AGENCY: OVERSIGHT AND MANAGEMENT OF THE NATIONAL FLOOD INSURANCE PROGRAM 2 (2005).
    69   IMPROVEMENTS NEEDED IN NFIP, *supra* note 58, at 13.
    70   *Id.*
    71   *Id.*
    72   *Id.* at 6.
    73   42 U.S.C. §§ 4012(b), 4012a(a), 4013(b)(2) (2000).
    74   *See* IMPROVEMENTS NEEDED IN NFIP, *supra* note 57, at 22.
    75   *Id.* at 28.

subject to a tragedy. But the calculus is not so simple. By creating moral hazards and bad incentive, government programs may amplify risk. Consider this curious fact: although the mortality rate from natural catastrophes has been declining in the twentieth century, deaths from floods have actually increased in the latter half of the twentieth century (even before Katrina).[76] Katrina is consistent with this deadly trend. The increased death toll coincides with substantial efforts by the government to manage flood risk, which includes NFIP and the New Orleans levee construction project. The suggestion is not that there is direct causation between increased deaths and government action, but putting more people in the path of floods, even when the risks are said to be mitigated, must be an influencing factor.[77] These dynamics have disparate effects along socioeconomic divisions. Because the poor have little economic choice in habitation, they bear the brunt of the costs associated with the destructive cycle of habitation, flooding, and rehabitation.[78] The intended risk mitigation has not come to pass; quite the opposite, the government flood program has incentivized the habitation and building in hazardous areas, putting more lives and assets at risk and raising the cost of ex post disaster assistance.

*Public Compensation*

Bad incentives are also created by ex post government compensation schemes. The problem of a moral hazard and the "Samaritan's Dilemma" is well known.[79] When there is a history of public compensation in response to a catastrophe, the precedent sets rational expectation. This expectation changes behavior—people may assume more risk than they would ordinarily take, not purchase insurance, or otherwise not mitigate risks as they would if they had to internalize the loss. Consider the case of 9/11. The government provided substantial compensation to victims. Individual victims were not the only beneficiaries of public funds. Businesses, large and small, too received substantial financial assistance, including protection from tort liability. Collectively, these benefits have set expectations and influenced risk-taking behavior. This has been confirmed by a congressionally mandated report, which concluded that the purchase of terrorism insurance has

---

76  *See* TED STEINBERG, ACTS OF GOD: THE UNNATURAL HISTORY OF NATURAL DISASTER IN AMERICA 73–74 (2000).

77  *Id.* at 97 ("[F]ederal flood insurance encouraged people to rebuild where they were destined to meet ruin again and again, a fact borne out by . . . repetitive claims.").

78  *See id.* at 105 (stating that flood insurance has "subsidized the poor in a place where real estate capitalism had forced them to live—on the margins, in the cheapest, riskiest and most flood-prone land").

79  James M. Buchanan, *The Samaritan's Dilemma*, *in* ALTRUISM, MORALITY, AND ECONOMIC THEORY (Edmund S. Phelps ed., 1975). *See* Saul Levmore, *Coalitions and Quakes: Disaster Relief and Its Prevention*, 3 U. CHI. L. SCHOOL ROUNDTABLE 1, 20 (1996) ("As already suggested, individuals might purchase less insurance the more they expect widespread losses and then relief.").

remained low due in part to the expectation that the government would bail out hard hit businesses.[80]

In addition to the moral hazard problem, the provision and amount of government relief are difficult to predict. Government action is often subject to a mix of political motivations, public sentiment, and the perceived need for economic stabilization, which may or may not be accurate.[81] This is illustrated by a comparison of 9/11 and Katrina. In the case of 9/11 victims, the September 11th Victim Compensation Fund was established within a matter of days. The fund paid out on average $2.08 million per claim, and a total payout of about $5.13 billion.[82] The scale of this scheme is unprecedented. The Katrina victims, however, received no comparable benefit. The reason for the difference in treatment is a complex brew.[83] In the case of 9/11, there were viable tort actions against the airlines, and a political compromise to shield the industry may have motivated the creation of the fund. The terrorist attack was a war-like incursion into American soil, and patriotism and broad sympathy for the national sacrifice influenced the political decision. On the other hand, despite the gross negligence of the government in handling the crisis, Katrina was a natural event, and thus sympathy for the victims did not encompass the notion that the victims were sacrificed in the course of some larger geopolitical struggle. No private industry is at systemic risk from tort liability, and tort recourse against the government would be extremely difficult. Lastly, the socioeconomic statuses of the victims are different. Many of the 9/11 victims worked on Wall Street, arguably one of the most important American industries, and were by and large in the upper stratum of American society. Katrina victims, on the other hand, were largely the poor, as is the case in most flooding deaths. The disparities in socioeconomic status and political clout and the resulting political action cannot be discounted. Thus, both 9/11 and Katrina killed thousands of victims, and yet the approaches to ex post compensation are markedly different.

Government compensation is problematic because politics is at its core. The perception of catastrophe is relative. For the victim, the scale and nature of the catastrophe matters not. For society, they matter in triggering the collective sense of sympathy and social obligation. For government, they matter for reasons of politics and economics. The shifting sands of public compensation raise the

---

80    "Take-up [of terrorism insurance] could also be affected by expectations that the Federal government would provide Federal disaster assistance following a [catastrophic chemical, nuclear, biological, radiological] event." REPORT OF THE PRESIDENT'S WORKING GROUP, *supra* note 47, at 79 n.242, (citing Rhee, *Terrorism Risk*, *supra* note 19).

81    Levmore identifies several factors in the calculus of public compensation: a well organized interest group, geographic concentration of victims, general public's ability to identify with the victims, moral hazard considerations, and the level of insurance coverage. Levmore, *supra* note 79, at 3–8, 18.

82    DIXON & STERN, *supra* note 3, at 25.

83    See Anthony J. Sebok, *The Response to the Disaster in New Orleans: Will There Be a Compensation Program Similar to the 9/11 Victims' Fund?* (Sept. 5, 2005), *available at* http://writ.news.findlaw.com/sebok/20050905.html.

issue of arbitrariness and fairness. Why should compensation be subject to the perception and sentiment of the collective whole? Why should compensation be subject to political calculation? For victims, at least, there is not a satisfactory answer to these questions other than it is the nature of the political process, which is not always rational or efficient.

Government compensation as a form of political action can be good or bad or both. It is difficult to be more precise than this generic, perhaps trite, statement for the assessment of the quality of the action is situational and each disaster may pose unique challenges. Furthermore, it is difficult to expect a purely principled approach to political action when its essence is one of collective compromise subject to the sometimes unpredictable interactions of various interest groups and conflicting principles. There is always the danger of unintended consequences, and relief cannot always be expected in times of crisis. In spite of these concerns, it is inappropriate to categorically reject ex post government action for the use of public funds must be a vital component of compensation in times of national crisis. To argue against this process is impractical and, one could argue, ignores the democratic process inherent in the distribution of wealth. Thus, there should always be a government option to intervene.

## Participation and Disintermediation

An effective risk distribution scheme requires two predicates. First is broad participation, and the second is minimization of cost. With respect to the first predicate, the participation of private insurance and government suggests that the risk is widely distributed to shareholders and taxpayers. The insurance industry is large in absolute dollar value, constituting approximately eight percent of the global gross domestic product.[84] Nevertheless, the amount of capital supporting catastrophic loss is limited in comparison to the potential loss. A loss of $100 billion, for example, would greatly stress the entire system, and yet a single event surpassing such a benchmark is easily foreseeable.

Traditional insurance is not only limited in scale, but surprisingly limited in scope. In addition to the burden of catastrophic fortuitous risk, individuals and families also bear most long-term economic risks.[85] Economic risks such as devaluation of one's home and profession, major risks in daily life, are not insurable in the market today.[86] Fortuitous risk is only a small segment of the potential

---

84    Ulrike Birkmaier & Camille Codoni, *World Insurance in 2003: Insurance Industry on the Road to Recovery*, in SIGMA 2004, at 33 (Swiss Re, Sigma No. 3/2004, 2004) (insurance premium volume was about $3 trillion, constituting eight percent of the global GDP, $470 per capita).

85    ROBERT J. SHILLER, THE NEW FINANCIAL ORDER: RISK IN THE 21ST CENTURY 7 (2003).

86    *Id.* at 4–5.

risk, and only a fraction of our wealth, those being interests in corporations, are commoditized and traded.[87] The participatory limitation of traditional insurance has prompted Robert Shiller to propose a radical reconfiguration of the financial and insurance markets wherein information markets are developed and new products quantify and package various economics risks to be traded and spread among a global risk pool. Although Shiller addressed only economic risks, the concern over the limitation of participation applies equally to catastrophic risk as well.

In contrast to the insurance market, the tax base is far broader in terms of participation. The scale and scope of participation are limited only by the tax base and public borrowing. Whenever there is public compensation, the public shares the financial burden of catastrophes. In this sense, the risk and cost are broadly distributed through the political mechanism, which is the default intermediary for the distribution of funds. As catastrophes become more frequent and severe, one would expect that private insurance, at least in its traditional form, would retreat and that government compensation, supported by broad political participation, would fill the void, absent some fundamental reconfiguration of the private insurance market or government's role in the management of catastrophic risk.

The second predicate requires that transaction cost be minimized. Cost has multiple facets. There is, of course, the cost of executing the risk transfer, which, in the case of the traditional insurance policy, is the expense and profit of the insurer. Because capital is limited, the resulting risk premium often makes catastrophic insurance coverage expensive or economically infeasible. This is a cost of financing. Additionally, there is the cost incurred from the failure to mitigate or avoid risk. A major concern here is the problem of freeriders and the resulting expectation of bailout. A risk pool works well if all participants are susceptible to varying degree to the same risk; thus, each participant agrees to underwrite the risk of others in consideration for the same. If, however, one is not susceptible to the same risk but made to pay, he subsidizes the cost of the risk. The freerider problem is apparent in the area of catastrophic risk. The most obvious risks of extreme catastrophes—earthquakes, hurricanes, and terrorism—are not evenly distributed or commonly shared. Large segments of the society are simply not exposed to one or more of these risks.[88] Thus, the Samaritan's Dilemma and government induced distortions in behavior towards risk mitigation and avoidance are problematic.

---

87    *Id.* at 8.

88    It is a popular conception that terrorism can strike at any time, any place, but in actuality the risk to some is trivially small. The average Kansan need not fear terrorists so much as the negligent driver or a tornado. Indeed, the belief that catastrophic terrorism is unpredictable, a popular mantra of many, is not really correct. In the past several decades, catastrophic terrorism has repeatedly struck three targets, resulting in catastrophic losses: the airlines, London, and New York. *See* Rhee, *Terrorism Risk*, *supra* note 19, at 470–71. Terrorists tend to attack areas of high population or asset density, and when they do not the attacks do not constitute a problem of catastrophic insurance losses. Thus, the policy

In the ideal world, private parties would contract to distribute risk among themselves, leaving the allocation of cost to the discipline of market pricing. In a smoothly operating market with adequate supply of capital, moral hazards are minimized and parties are properly incentivized to efficiently mitigate risk. This ideal is advanced if the number of participants in the private sector is increased, thus increasing capacity, and if the cost of transfer is reduced, thus allowing greater participation. Both the private market and the government can play vital roles in expanding the capital base that would allow more effective distribution of risk. Obviously, the problem is complex and there are many plausible strategies. The discussion here is limited to alternative risk transfer, disintermediation of risk agency, and catastrophe tax policy.

As a result of the surge in catastrophes, the insurance and financial markets have developed alternatives to traditional risk management techniques as a way to expand insurance capacity and make the pricing of catastrophic risk more efficient. The alternative risk transfer (ART) market integrates the insurance and financial markets to provide capital market based solutions.[89] The market allows capital market participants to directly participate in the underlying risk. The most significant ART product is insurance securitization, which is in essence a collateralized reinsurance obligation in the form of a structured note.[90] Instead of executing a standard treaty with a reinsurer, the insurer cedes all or a portion of the premium to a special purpose reinsurance vehicle (SPRV). The SPRV then issues a bond, which covers any liabilities from the reinsurance agreement. The bond proceeds are deposited into a collateral trust, and its assets serve as a guarantee for the SPRV's reinsurance obligation. The bond investor's return is measured as a spread over the risk-free rate, and the ceded premium funds this spread. Thus, in an insurance securitization, the bond market becomes the reinsurer of the underlying risk.

There is growing interest in catastrophic bonds ("Cat bonds"). The reasons are several: hardening prices in the reinsurance market; a demand for fully collateralized protection to minimize counterparty credit risk; growing interest by hedge funds devoted to alternative investments; the need for additional capital; and the need of institutional investors to diversify their portfolios. In an era of

---

question is whether those who are most at risk of catastrophic terrorism should internalize as much of the cost, or whether subsidization serves a legitimate policy consideration.

89  *See generally* Erik Banks, Alternative Risk Transfer: Integrating Risk Management Through Insurance, Reinsurance and the Capital Markets (2004). In addition to securitization, other products are contingent capital agreements and insurance derivatives. Contingent capital structures are contractual agreements to provide capital in the event of a predetermined loss. Insurance derivatives are instruments that are linked to a fortuitous, catastrophic event. *Id.*

90  The transaction structure is similar to traditional securitization, but with some important differences. *See* Tamar Frankel & Joseph W. LaPlume, *Securitizing Insurance Risk*, 19 Ann. Rev. Banking L. 203, 205 (2000).

global warming and more volatile weather patterns, securitization may take a broader role in spreading risk. Moreover, in a 2005 law review article, I suggested that Cat bonds can be used to securitize terrorism risk as a market alternative to public insurance.[91] Recently, in a August 2007 report, the Congressional Budget Office suggested the same.[92]

Thus far, Cat bonds constitute a fraction of the available capital.[93] Since their inception in the mid-1990s, they were slow to develop. The reinsurance market was in a soft price cycle for much of the 1990s and thus traditional reinsurance was cheaper than securitization. The cyclical nature of reinsurance alone does not explain the slow growth. The stunted growth is also attributable to regulatory problems: uncertainties of the accounting treatment of SPRVs and regulatory framework, the lack of a "pass through" tax treatment, and an underdeveloped information market on natural catastrophes that limit the size of the investment community.[94] These limitations have driven the Cat bond market offshore, where the regulatory burden is minimal, favorable tax treatment is given, and a pool of sophisticated investors are willing to undertake catastrophe risk for superior returns. For insurance securitization to grow, these regulatory uncertainties and tax policy impediments must be removed.[95]

The thrust of the ART market is to expand the number of participants in the distribution of risk. By doing this, the market increases the supply of insurance. Securitization disintermediates the insurer and directly connects policyholder to capital provider.[96] No longer is the risk transfer from policyholder to insurer and reinsurer; instead, risk is directly transferred to capital providers. Importantly, the participants in the ART market, like insurance companies, are sophisticated institutions only. Cat bonds are privately placed, not publicly issued. The risk is perceived to be so exotic that only institutional investors have a sophistication to undertake it. Thus, the market is limited.

---

91　See Rhee, *Terrorism Risk, supra* note 19.

92　CBO Report, *supra* note 16, at Appendix: Catastrophe Bonds and Other Risk – Transfer Mechanisms.

93　*See* U.S. Gen. Accounting Office, Catastrophic Insurance Risks: Status of Efforts to Securitize Natural Catastrophe and Terrorism Risk 14 (2003) ("[O]utstanding catastrophe bonds accounted for only 2.5% to 3.0% of worldwide catastrophe reinsurance coverage."); Rainer Helfenstein & Thomas Holzheu, *Securitization—New Opportunities for Insurers and Investors*, in Sigma 2006, at 24 (Swiss Re, Sigma No. 7/2006, 2006) (total outstanding volume of Cat bonds is about $23 billion).

94　*See* Rhee, *Terrorism Risk, supra* note 19, at 500–505.

95　*See id.* at 511–22.

96　The disintermediation is not complete for insurers are still required to originate the policies and service them. Moreover, most bonds are underwritten on a nonindemnity basis, meaning that liability is triggered by an agreed upon index rather than the actual loss. The risk of a spread between actual loss and liability is the basis risk. Thus, the primary insurer and reinsurer may still be exposed to basis risk. *See* Rhee, *Terrorism Risk, supra* note 19, at 503.

The concept of disintermediation in the private insurance market also raises the possibility of its application to the public sector. The government is the agent through which the public participates in catastrophic risk distribution. Like the way an insurer allocates the capital of its shareholders, the government allocates public funds. Unlike an insurer, however, it is a poor assessor of risk and its actions sometimes create more costs than benefits. It is not subject to market forces, and has less incentive to develop information necessary to assess risk and to properly distribute it. Similar to the process of securitization, a scheme that disintermediates the government should be a part of the public debate. The goal would be to devise a scheme that would allow individuals to invest capital directly in insurable assets within some form of a public framework.

Why does catastrophic risk distribution require the insurer or the government as intermediaries? The simple answer is that both are aggregators of capital. The insurance industry is justified by efficiently aggregating capital and thereby diversifying risk. This is consistent with the prevailing theory of the firm, which says that the firm reduces the transaction cost associated with conducting business.[97] The theory holds in most complex enterprises. Where transaction costs can be reduced further, the market has found ways to exploit efficiencies. The economic rationale of securitization is that it provides a lower cost of funding for the underlying transaction generating the securitized asset than a firm's cost of capital.[98] In other words, the bond investor requires less return on capital than the investor in the firm that would otherwise originate and hold the securitized asset. Thus, securitization exists because the aggregation of capital in the firm to fund the underlying activity is less efficient than a direct transaction with capital providers.

Likewise, the government is the intermediary only because it is the default aggregator of public capital and thus has a monopoly on the distribution of public funds. Public insurance and compensation programs are costly to taxpayers and impose secondary costs arising from the distortions they impart on the market and individual behavior. The ideal public risk distribution scheme would entail not only broader participation, but also more direct participation in the risk pool. Direct participation would assume more attributes of market transactions. Those exposed to catastrophic risk, which is to say a large segment of the population, pay a premium to transfer the risk to the pool, and thus the compensation scheme becomes more like private insurance and less like ex post public compensation.

What would public disintermediation look like? Speculation is required, of course, since no such scheme exists. The following is the sketches of one possible structure. With the help of the insurance industry, insurable assets subject to catastrophic risk are aggregated into diversified pools of assets. As a simple example, consider a pool of residential homes or commercial real estate from different parts of the country. The important concept here is diversification of

---

97   *See* Ronald H. Coase, *The Nature of the Firm*, 4 ECONOMICA 386 (1937).
98   *See* Rhee, *Terrorism Risk, supra* note 19, at 497–98 & n.307.

assets at risk in various identifiable mixes so that no single event can inflict a highly correlative loss on a limited number of risk bearers. Reinsurance achieves some diversification, but the insurance industry would underwrite the assets with the view of transferring a substantial quantity of risk to a public bond market. Participating insurers and reinsurers, however, would be required to retain a portion of the risk to avoid moral hazard problems. Individual and institutional investors may invest in the bonds, similar to an investment in Treasury bonds, subject to limitations of investment amount and credit quality of the bonds for individuals. Even with broader participation on the demand side of capital, there may still be an insufficient supply of capital, creating a large spread between market price and actuarial risk. Any shortfall in yield to investors can be made up with public funds added as a "sweetener." These sweeteners can be in the form of a tax exemption or a direct contribution to investment return. Thus, a hybrid public-private risk market is created.[99]

The power of the purse is the power to change behavior. If the above process results in more affordable insurance, it is possible to incentivize people to participate through the tax system. Thus far, there has not been a concerted effort to combine tax policy and catastrophe management into a scheme to distribute, manage, and mitigate risk. The most basic tax policy is based on the principle that income is taxed, and not risk exposure. The tax system, however, can be used to collect revenue based on projected costs of compensation per region and recoupment of monies spent. The concern here is one of fairness and efficiency. The allocation of public funds to provide compensation such as flood insurance or losses from terrorism is disproportionate. A better matching of source and use of funds is not only fairer, but also reduces the problem of subsidization. The suggestion is not individualized assessment as is the case in taxation of individual income, but rather a more specific assessment that may be characterized by geography or risk profile.

Tax policy can also be used to provide credits to those who have sufficient insurance or penalties for those who do not. A more benign perspective is that tax policy can incentivize investment. The primary example that comes to mind is the mortgage interest deduction. Home ownership is deemed a good thing, and likewise protection of the home from fortuitous risk is a good investment (indeed a condition of mortgage lenders is the purchase of homeowner insurance). In this regard, there are two basic questions: Is there a sufficient supply of economically feasible insurance? If so, are those exposed to catastrophic risk adequately participating? Tax policy can affect the answers to both questions. If there is an

---

99   I do not believe that the liquidity crisis of the second half of 2007 caused by mortgage-backed securities and credit derivatives undermines the arguments here. This crisis was caused by a systemic failure of the mortgage and financial industries to properly price risk. As a result, the markets have and will continue to undergo a painful repricing of risk. Indeed, the reaction of the market to past abuses and laxity confirms that markets in the long term work to correct badly priced assets and risks.

adequate supply—a prerequisite for moving away from ad hoc compensation and towards private insurance—tax policy can be more than a means of collecting revenue based on income. The tax system can be an effective tool in promoting risk distributive behavior through a system of insurance credits and penalties.

The concept of disintermediation, both in the private market and public finance, has the potential to change the risk landscape. The private market has been forced to innovate as a result of the trend towards more frequent and severe catastrophes and the stress placed on the traditional insurance system. These same forces are also placing a strain on the public compensation system. What would be the outcome if a category 5 hurricane hits Miami and a magnitude 8.0 earthquake strikes San Francisco, resulting in economic losses of half a trillion dollars in the same year? How will the government handle such a calamity? One would expect massive infusion of public funds to compensate victims and to rebuild the cities. This action would be appropriate and just, but if the vast majority of victims had been underinsured for flooding and earthquake one would surely question whether a more effective and just system could have delivered compensation. In the ideal world, those who are exposed to catastrophic risk ought to have paid into a risk pool an amount commensurate with the risk. This assumes that insurance was available and affordable, and the predicates are broad participation and reduced transaction cost. Such a reconfigured insurance system, based on a hybrid public-private infrastructure, would instill the proper incentives and avoid the freerider and expectation problems. Thus, the question of fairness and efficiency in public compensation and private insurance are inextricably linked.

## Conclusion

One would be hardly alone in predicting that catastrophes in the future will be more frequent and severe. With the experience of the 1990s and the first decade of the new century, the insurance industry has already accepted this premise as an operating condition. Increasing volatility of human and economic losses will continue to strain the current compensation schemes. A more effective participation in a risk society is needed. Two important conditions are the need to increase the pool of participants and to decrease the cost of participation. The financial and insurance markets have adapted to rapid changes in the risk landscape and have invented alternative risk transfer techniques to deal with the special problems. These techniques are relatively new, constituting a small but growing part of the market. Regulations and tax policies can be reformed to further facilitate the growth. It would be naïve to believe that capital markets, and private markets in general, work perfectly. My observation here is the conventional viewpoint that, despite their limitations, private risk markets are more efficient in reducing costs, which suggests the possibility of a better and fairer scheme in sum.

The government's role in catastrophe management should not stop at simply compensation. Policy should work from the principle that distortions in incentives should be limited. This calls for a reexamination of the approaches to ex ante and ex post compensation. In the long term, the government can explore ways to facilitate a disintermediation of the insurer and the government. The suggestion is not that they are or should be made superfluous. Far from it, they are vital to the overall scheme of risk mitigation and distribution. Rather, the suggestion is the modest proposition that every member of society can and should be an active participant in a risk pool, and that more direct participation would reduce the cost of risk transfer. This is the promise of disintermediation. In the private market, it has been realized by the tremendous growth of the asset securitization market, of which the growing market for insurance securitization is just a tiny fraction. In the arena of public finance, the government still remains the default aggregator of capital. The goal, then, is to construct a scheme that allows these market-based transactions to occur within the public-private framework of government and insurance.

## Acknowledgements

I thank Robin Paul Malloy for the invitation to participate in the Third Annual Property, Citizenship, and Social Entrepreneurism Workshop, hosted by Syracuse University. This chapter draws from my previous works on terrorism and catastrophic risks. *See infra* notes 4, 19. Substantial portions of the discussion here have been rewritten to fit the theme of this book project. Current events continue to unfold at the time of writing. It is important to distinguish financial instruments from their abuse. Also, excepting events like pandemics, most natural catastrophes, even the severest kinds like Hurricanes Andrew and Katrina, are expected to be regional, unlike the national housing market collapse that precipitated the current financial crisis.

# Chapter 8

# Small Business Recovery from a Natural Disaster: Lessons from Katrina

Rodney C. Runyan and Patricia Huddleston

## Introduction

The short-and medium-term effects of Hurricane Katrina have been chronicled in thousands of media accounts since its occurrence on August 28, 2005. Three months following the hurricane, we conducted interviews with local officials and small business owners in the Gulf Coast. The results of these interviews are part of a published study on small business and crisis,[1] but can be summarized briefly as two findings. First, the small business owners in the study did not plan for any disaster, including Katrina. Second, they were having great difficulty recovering from the hurricane. Yet, three months after the storm seemed to be too short a time to assess the actual recovery of small businesses affected by the storm. Destruction in some of the towns near New Orleans was nearly total (e.g., Biloxi, Waveland, and Bay St. Louis, MS), with buildings being leveled or having completely disappeared. Other towns had seemingly untouched buildings (e.g., Pascagoula, MS), where businesses still suffered almost complete loss of inventory, equipment, and records due to the flooding from the storm's thirty-four foot surge. A hurricane's storm surge is the water that is pushed toward the shore by the force of the storm winds.[2]

Due to this extraordinary level of devastation, it may have been unreasonable to expect a large number of small businesses to have recovered within three short months. We found that almost none of the small businesses in the downtown areas of these communities were operating three months later. Many of the small business owners interviewed in the first phase of the study[3] pointed to two key deterrents to their recovery: the Small Business Administration (SBA) and

---

1   Rodney C. Runyan, *Small Business in the Face of Crisis: Identifying Barriers to Recovery from a Natural Disaster*, 14 J. CONTINGENCIES & CRISIS MGMT. 12, (2006) [hereinafter *Small Business*].

2   National Hurricane Center, Hurricane Preparedness, http://www.nhc.noaa.gov/ HAW2/english/storm_surge.shtml (last visited Feb. 7, 2006).

3   *Small Business, supra* note 1.

the Federal Emergency Management Agency (FEMA). Specifically, problems accessing available capital were caused by the (perceived) daunting process of the SBA application. FEMA was cited as exacerbating the shortage of workers in the area by providing "too much" financial assistance to persons displaced by the storm, and "poaching" workers from local construction firms.[4]

Therefore, we went back to the same region and same towns in June of 2006. This was a full nine months after the disaster. The assumptions which we made were that most small business owners would, by that time, have obtained financing to rebuild or replenish their inventories and that FEMA assistance to local workers would have ended (thus removing the disincentive to work, cited as a problem in the first phase). These assumptions helped to form the questions which would be investigated during interviews with local officials and small business owners.

In the current study, we will briefly review the literature on crisis and small business. Following that will be an overview of the findings from the original study (Phase One).[5] The methods of Phases One and Two will be presented, followed by the results of Phase Two. A discussion of the results and implications will conclude the paper.

**Theoretical Crisis Framework**

The study of crises has provided a large body of literature reported in a diversity of scholarly outlets.[6] Though the variety of crisis studies has caused the refinement of a clear definition of crisis to be difficult, researchers have identified some common characteristics. Events that are considered to be crises in nature are usually characterized by high consequence, low probability, ambiguity, and decision-making time pressure.[7] Crises usually involve a large number of stakeholders,[8] thus increasing the consequences of a crisis beyond just a single business or organization. The probability of any particular crisis occurring is low, thus when one occurs, it is likely to be a surprise to an

---

4   *Id.*

5   For an in-depth discussion of both the literature and original findings, please see *Small Business*, *supra* note 1.

6   Joanne E. Hale, Ronald E. Dulek & David P. Hale, *Crisis Response Communication Challenges: Building Theory from Qualitative Data*, 42 J. Bus. Com. 112 (2005) [hereinafter Hale et al.]; Dominic Elliott, Kim Harris & Steve Baron, *Crisis Management and Services Marketing*, 19 J. Services Marketing 336 (2005) [hereinafter *Crisis Management*].

7   Alice Hills, *Seduced by Recovery: The Consequences of Misunderstanding Disaster*, 6 J. Contingencies & Crisis Mgmt 162 (1998); Christine M. Pearson & Judith A. Clair, *Reframing Crisis Management*, 23 Acad. Mgmt. Rev. 59 (1998).

8   Dominic Elliott & Martina McGuinness, *Public Inquiries: Panacea or Placebo?*, 10 J. Contingencies & Crisis Mgmt. 14 (2002).

organization.[9] The unlikely nature of the crisis may also cause organizations to have little understanding of the cause and effects of the crisis,[10] rendering the decision-making difficult due to ambiguous stimuli. Finally, the fact that an event is labeled a crisis infers a certain level of urgency,[11] thus putting pressure on decision-makers to act sooner rather than later. This may mean decisions are made without all available information.

The study of organizations and crises, and how organizations handle those events, is commonly referred to as "crisis management."[12] Crisis management is seen as having three distinct phases through which organizations pass: crisis prevention, response, and recovery.[13] The prevention phase of crisis management includes the concepts of mitigation and planning.[14] The response phase is deemed extremely important by some researchers,[15] as it is the point where decisions may save lives or lessen the negative effects of the crisis. Recovery is seen as the phase where organizations seek to minimize the impact of the crisis[16] and get back to pre-crisis levels.[17] This stage is entered into when the risk of additional direct damage has subsided.[18] It can also be the stage at which organizations begin to look for a scapegoat who can be blamed for the crisis itself.[19]

## Small Business and Crisis

A small business is defined by the SBA as one that is independently owned and operated, but is not dominant in its field of operation. Small businesses are characterized by several attributes which set them apart from larger businesses. Small businesses typically have revenue that is considerably less than comparable units within a large corporation, and employ fewer than 100 workers. There were

---

9　Charles F. Hermann, *Some Consequences of Crises Which Limit the Viability of Organizations*, 8 ADMIN. SCI. Q. 61 (1963).

10　Jane Dutton, *The Processing of Crisis and Non-Crisis Strategic Issues*, 23 J. MGMT. STUD. 501 (1988); Enrico L. Quarantelli, *Disaster Crisis Management: A Summary of Research Findings*, 25 J. MGMT. STUD. 373 (1988).

11　Quarantelli, *supra* note 10.

12　Hale et al., *supra* note 6.

13　Hills, *supra* note 7; Denis Smith, *Beyond Contingency Planning: Towards a Model of Crisis Management*, 4 INDUS. CRISIS Q. 263 (1990) [hereinafter *Beyond Contingency Planning*]; *Crisis Management*, *supra* note 6.

14　STEVEN FINK, CRISIS MANAGEMENT: PLANNING FOR THE INEVITABLE (1986).

15　*Crisis Management*, *supra* note 6.

16　*Id.*

17　Denis Smith, *Business (Not) as Usual: Crisis Management, Service Recovery and the Vulnerability of Organizations*, 19 J. SERVICES MARKETING 309 (2005).

18　Hale et al., *supra* note 6.

19　*Crisis Management*, *supra* note 6.

more than twenty-two million small businesses in the United States in 2004, accounting for approximately fifty percent of the U.S. GDP.[20]

In the crisis literature, much attention is given to planning for crises as a key to positive outcomes.[21] In other words, the success of an organization's response to crisis will depend to a certain extent on the type of planning with which it engaged before a crisis.[22] Yet, little work on crisis and small businesses appears in the extant literature; there is even less dealing with formal crisis planning by small businesses. The small body of research which does exist shows that there is little formal planning engaged in by small businesses.[23] The consensus of most studies is that the majority of small businesses do not engage in formal planning.

Small business is still very important to the economic vitality of cities, states, and the country.[24] Downtowns in small-and medium-sized cities are very important to a community's identity and sense of vitality.[25] These downtowns normally contain mostly service- and retail-oriented businesses.[26] These tend to have fewer financial resources and less access to capital.[27]

## Methodology

In Phase One, data were gathered through face-to-face interviews with small business owners and local business support agents (e.g., Chamber of Commerce; Economic Development Office; etc.) from several communities in the U.S. Gulf Coast within three months following Hurricane Katrina in the fall of 2005. That study provided an exceptional chance to gather small business data soon after a major disaster. Since little extant literature exists which describes studies in the

---

20  KATHERINE KOBE, SMALL BUSINESS ADMINISTRATION, THE SMALL BUSINESS SHARE OF GDP: 1998–2004, http://www.sba.gov/advo/research/rs299tot.pdf (last visited July 10, 2007).

21  FINK, *supra* note 14; Quarantelli, *supra* note 10; *Beyond Contingency Planning*, *supra* note 13; *Crisis Management*, *supra* note 6; Hale et al., *supra* note 6.

22  Pearson, *supra* note 7.

23  Stephen C. Perry, *The Relationship Between Written Business Plans and the Failure of Small Businesses in the U.S.*, 39 INT'L J. RETAIL & DISTRIBUTION MGMT. 201 (2000).

24  D. Keith Robbins, Louis J. Pantuosco, Darrell F. Parker & Barbara K. Fuller, *An Empirical Assessment of the Contribution of Small Business Employment to U.S. State Economic Performance*, 15 SMALL BUS. ECON. 293 (2001).

25  Rodney C. Runyan & Patricia Huddleston, *Getting Customers Downtown: The Role of Branding in Achieving Success for Central Business Districts*, 15 J. PRODUCT & BRAND MGMT. 48 (2006).

26  Clifford Guy & Mary Duckett, *Small Retailers in an Inner City Community: A Case Study of Adamsdown, Cardiff*, 31 INT'L J. RETAIL & DISTRIBUTION MGMT. 401, 401 (2003).

27  BRUCE A. KIRCHHOFF, ENTREPRENEURSHIP AND DYNAMIC CAPITALISM: THE ECONOMIES OF BUSINESS FIRM FORMATION AND GROWTH 9 (1994).

area of small businesses and disaster, a qualitative research design was employed. The use of qualitative data to gain understanding of under-researched phenomena is often called for by researchers.[28]

## Participant Selection[29]

In brief, we identified affected communities using the Weather.com and the National Mainstreet Organization's websites. Following the identification of such communities, we developed a contact list through the local Chamber of Commerce. Each local Chamber helped us to build a list of respondents to interview.[30] In Phase Two, we contacted several of the original participants to conduct follow-up interviews.

## Interview Method

A semi-structured interview format was utilized, with a question guide used to provide a level of continuity between interviews. The number of persons interviewed in Phase One totaled seventeen, with two focus group sessions and three individual interviews. Each interview session lasted approximately ninety minutes. Interviews were conducted within a downtown business office or meeting room in each of the towns. In Phase Two, we interviewed at least one participant from Phase One. Where possible, we interviewed a person who had general knowledge of the local business community. This included one economic development director, one local bank president, and one Mainstreet Director. Each of these stakeholders interacts with small business owners on a daily basis as part of his (or her) job duties and is thus able to provide feedback on the small businesses as a whole in his town. As with Phase One, we also toured the affected areas to view first-hand the general condition of businesses in each town. This allowed us to make an assessment of the state in which the town was, from a neutral viewpoint.

---

28    DAVID SILVERMAN, INTERPRETING QUALITATIVE DATA: METHODS FOR ANALYZING TALK, TEXT AND INTERACTION (1993); John O. Summers, *Guidelines for Conducting Research and Publishing in Marketing: From Conceptualization Through the Review Process*, 29 J. ACAD. MARKETING SCI. 405 (2001).

29    For a detailed description of the sampling procedure, please refer to *Small Business*, *supra* note 1.

30    For demographic profiles of each town, see Table 8.1.

## Table 8.1 Community Characteristics

| Characteristic | Biloxi | Covington | Hammond | Pascagoula | Picayune |
|---|---|---|---|---|---|
| Total Population | 50,115 | 8,483 | 17,639 | 26,200 | 10,535 |
| **Sex:** | | | | | |
| Female | 24,807 (49.5%) | 4,542 (51.1%) | 9,630 (54.6%) | 12,984 (49.6%) | 5,762 (54.7%) |
| Male | 25,308 (50.5%) | 3,941 (48.9%) | 8,009 (45.4%) | 13,216 (50.4%) | 4,773 (45.3%) |
| **Race:** | | | | | |
| White | 35,782 (71.4%) | 6,875 (81.0%) | 9,455 (53.5%) | 17,387 (66.4%) | 6,665 (63.3%) |
| Black | 9,521 (19.0%) | 1,794 (21.1%) | 8,156 (46.2%) | 7,503 (28.6%) | 3,859 (36.6%) |
| Other | 1,804 (3.6%) | 142 (1.7%) | 209 (1.2%) | 1,009 (3.8%) | 118 (1.1%) |
| **Educational Attainment:** | | | | | |
| High School Graduate (includes equivalency) | 8,240 (16.4%) | 1,325 (15.6%) | 2,155 (12.2%) | 5,033 (19.2%) | 676 (6.4%) |
| Bachelor's Degree | 3,719 (7.4%) | 1,046 12.3%) | 1,383 (7.8%) | 1,601 (6.1%) | 666 (6.3%) |
| Graduate or Professional Degree | 2,233 (4.5%) | 717 (8.4%) | 981 (5.6%) | 906 (3.5%) | 373 (3.5%) |
| **Industry:** | | | | | |
| Agriculture, forestry, fishing and hunting, and mining | 262 | 71 | 99 | 168 | 103 |
| Manufacturing | 1,253 | 169 | 494 | 2,487 | 534 |
| Retail trade | 2,586 | 477 | 1,171 | 1,163 | 459 |
| Educational, health, and social services | 3,735 | 909 | 1,993 | 1,899 | 954 |
| Arts, entertainment, recreation, accommodation, and food services | 5,156 | 456 | 1,029 | 822 | 336 |
| **Class of Worker:** | | | | | |
| Self-employed workers in own, not incorporated business | 1,134 | 374 | 292 | 544 | 281 |

## Results

*Phase One*

Based on the extant crisis literature, a crisis event will be characterized by low probability, ambiguity, high consequence, and decision-making time pressure.[31] The phases which an organization goes through in a crisis are: prevention, response, and recovery.[32] Qualitative analyses were conducted to determine if the small businesses in the Phase One portion of the study fit these two theoretical frames.[33] We briefly note those findings here to provide a clear frame for the current study's findings. From the interviews in Phase One, we were able to address each of these characteristics as they applied to the small business owners who participated. We include a few quotes from respondents as they apply to each construct, to elucidate the findings.

*Low Probability*   A crisis often results from a surprise to an organization.[34] Interviews provided generally the same response: the residents and business owners did not expect the type of devastation that occurred. One comment included, "I don't think that anybody thought it was going to be the devastating storm that it was, that I remember", and another, "I usually board up my windows. I have been through the ritual many times. That is what I did for many hurricanes."

Most business owners went through their normal pre-storm routine of boarding up windows and doors, moving computers on top of desks, and closing early. But a very small number (perhaps one or two out of hundreds) actually removed inventory from their buildings, and none reported moving equipment.

*Ambiguity*   Most small business owners in the Gulf Region had never seen a storm leave devastation such as that of Katrina. This meant that few considered the cause and effect relationships that occurred. Ambiguity revealed from Phase One came from several different sources, including the inability to assess damage and lack of clear-cut methods to finance recovery. One interviewee mentioned, "[I]t wasn't that because of the flooding they couldn't get to their business . . . but rather because they evacuated the city. . . . They couldn't get back because of gas, traffic, or bridges being out."

Lack of financing options available also impeded affected business owners. Small business owners are decision-makers; they usually have no one to answer to except themselves. Yet, following Katrina, most of these small business owners were faced with a situation that prevented them from making decisions effectively.

---

31   Pearson, *supra* note 7.
32   Hale et al., *supra* note 6.
33   For detailed and in-depth results of Phase One, please refer to *Small Business*, *supra* note 1.
34   Hermann, *supra* note 9.

The process to acquire the needed capital is one which is overwhelming to many very small businesses, especially when dealing with the SBA. According to the study's informants, there was only one small business which had applied for and obtained an SBA loan three months after Katrina.

*High Consequence*    Charles Martin argued that crises may be dependent on firm size.[35] For example, cash flow impediment would constitute a crisis for a small firm as many small businesses are dangerously reliant upon cash flow for day-to-day operational capital. Thus, a major crisis such as Katrina will interrupt cash flow for lengths of time which are devastating to such businesses. For these business owners and others like them, the negative consequences of decisions such as these include financial ruin if revenues do not cover both current and old debt. One interviewee noted, "I had a cash flow problem the first month because we couldn't get out mail [for invoicing]," while another said "[T]he first ten days to two weeks it was so dead in terms of business [and we] were really worried whether [we] were going to make it through in terms of cash flow."

*Decision-Making Time Pressures*    Crises infer a level of urgency in decision-making.[36] Katrina caused business owners to go through a succession of decisions, with each one requiring a small amount of time to ponder. Many of these decisions were made without all available information that is normally needed for decisions of such enormity. For example, would the customers who remained have the economic capability to purchase goods and services from the businesses? One interviewee said, "We reopened within two weeks of the storm, but had little business. We were very worried that we would not make it long enough to wait for customers to return."

*Prevention*    Preventing a natural disaster is beyond the means of humans. But preventing many of the crises which result from such disasters is not impossible. Several of the informants spoke of Hurricane Camille (1969) as the storm by which many locals measured storms, as it was extremely destructive. But it was revealed that business owners who had been through Camille reacted no differently than those to whom Katrina was a new phenomenon. Thus, even if previous experience might have mitigated effects of the storm, that experience was not utilized.

*Response*    In the response phase of crisis management, organizations shift their resources to reducing the harm to their business.[37] The Gulf Coast communities in this study were mostly beyond any ability to minimize damage to their businesses in terms of inventory and equipment. One interviewee noted that "I don't think all

---

35    Charles L. Martin, *Blending Services and Crises: A Few Questions and Observations*, 19 J. SERVICES MARKETING 346 (2005).

36    Quarantelli, *supra* note 10.

37    Hale et al., *supra* note 6.

the U-hauls in the world getting down and getting inventory out would have done anything." But some business owners' responses made the difference between a long period of being closed and taking advantage of being one of the few open businesses. Business owners who responded quickly and decisively were able to capture large amounts of the revenues in the months immediately following Katrina. An interviewee acknowledged that "Our business is up almost 100% over last year at this time. The only problem that I have is finding enough employees."

*Recovery* The crisis literature describes the recovery phase as the stage at which organizations attempt to "learn" from the crisis.[38] Possibly due to the business type of the respondents (i.e., small and independent), there was little, if any, discussion of learning from Katrina and its aftermath. We posed this question to all of our informants: to date, what has been the chief obstacle to recovery? Several different answers were given, with one persistent theme from every group: the lack of access to capital, cash flow, communication, and employees which all tied directly and indirectly to FEMA and the SBA. One interviewee noted that "working capital is one of the things . . . when you've been out of business for two and a half months you can't pay inventory, you can't pay to fix your place . . . ." Another said, "We were still required to put in a three year tax return [for SBA loans] . . . most of that stuff all got washed away."

Hindrances attributed to FEMA focused mostly on the amount of money and assistance that were being provided to residents displaced by Katrina. Interviewees felt certain that FEMA money was serving as a disincentive to work, while jobs went unfilled. No one begrudged assistance for those who had been displaced by the storm. But all of the respondents were hoping for FEMA to set and maintain a deadline for ending all non-housing allowances. One comment was, "We have workforce issues too . . . and it's just so frustrating because the Red Cross money and the FEMA money . . . there's [sic] funds everywhere . . . everybody's [businesses] needs help. Until that money runs out they don't see the long term . . . they don't seem to see the urgency of going back to work."

The SBA difficulties were different. Several of the interviewees maintained that few of their fellow business owners had ever taken out any type of business loan, themselves included. This meant that the process of applying for an SBA loan was daunting on two levels: the lengthy and (perceived) intrusive application, and the idea that they (the business owner) would be taking on a large debt to finance operations or repairs. Since many of these small business owners fund their operations from weekly cash flow, it is understandable that most do not have the ability to survive even a few weeks without revenue. And yet most of the businesses in two of the five towns had been closed for nearly three months.

---

38    Hale et al., *supra* note 6; *Crisis Management*, *supra* note 6.

*Phase Two*

Having determined that the situation faced by small business owners during and immediately following Katrina did indeed meet the criteria of a crisis, and having covered the concepts of prevention, response, and recovery, it seemed that further investigation was needed. The findings from Phase One made it clear that a natural disaster affecting a large number of small business owners in a town is a significant crisis for both the business owner and all stakeholders in the community. One of the goals of Phase One was to examine the recovery process for the small businesses following Katrina. In the hardest hit areas, there had been very little actual recovery three months later. In June of 2006, we returned to the Gulf Coast to interview several of the original respondents. The key research question was: how far along are the small businesses in the recovery phase nine months after Katrina? What we found was quite disheartening. Recovery ranged from none to complete recovery, with some small business owners nearing or surpassing pre-Katrina levels. But this situation was not much different from what we found in Phase One. Six months later, only a few businesses which were closed in November of 2005 were now open again.

There were two extremes, which can be illustrated in describing two towns which are in close proximity to each other. These two towns are Waveland and Biloxi, MS. Both were virtually wiped off the map by Katrina, with many buildings and homes completely destroyed. Three months after Katrina, both towns were in similar condition, with every building in their downtown areas sustaining very high levels of damage or complete destruction, and only a few businesses in operation. In both cases, the businesses which were in operation were several blocks inland from the shoreline. But the extent to which the two towns were recovering was very different six months later.

*Waveland*   Driving into Waveland, one saw little evidence of the devastation wrought by Katrina. Just off the highway, near the street which takes one toward the Gulf and the downtown shopping district, is a two-story building. The building houses a furniture and antique dealer, who moved into the building just weeks before Katrina. The building was far enough inland that it sustained only minor flood damage. The owner was fortunate that much of the inventory had yet to be delivered to the store. Now nine months after the storm, the owner is doing tremendous business. Who were his clientele? Wealthy residents along the Gulf who were replacing and refurnishing homes which were severely damaged in Katrina. Being many blocks from the Gulf and a stroke of luck in not having filled his store with inventory before Katrina, he was now the beneficiary of the hundreds of people who needed furniture for their homes.

Along the same road, almost a mile to the south (toward the Gulf), signs of the storm began to emerge. FEMA trailers were there and piles of rubble began to multiply as one approached the old-town shopping district. Up ahead, the Gulf of Mexico was visible, and what looked like a few damaged buildings. But suddenly it seems like you have driven right up to the edge of the beach. There is no road, no sidewalk, and only one partially intact building. According to two people walking by, we were standing on what used to be Beach Blvd., which ran along the Gulf. To the left and the right are remnants of small shops and cafes. Nine months after Katrina, in the Waveland central business district, there were no signs of rebuilding old buildings, nor were there any new buildings replacing the old ones. A Google search for Waveland turns up a website titled "Waveland to Wasteland."[39] It is filled with pictures and postings from residents, detailing both the devastation and the seeming indifference paid to it by state and federal governments.

*Biloxi*   Biloxi suffered horrific damage from Katrina, with nearly its entire downtown destroyed. Driving through the town three months following the hurricane, one found huge three-story casino barges hundreds of feet inland. These had been picked up by the storm surge, and unceremoniously deposited on top of homes and businesses. Hotels, restaurants, and gas stations on the shoreline were gone, leaving little more than the cement slabs upon which they used to sit. The main employers in Biloxi were the ten casinos which were anchored in the water (to meet the state law of not being land-based). Of those ten, two were completely destroyed, while the remaining eight sustained some levels of damage. Little more than clean-up projects were being undertaken at that time, with construction crews removing debris by the semi-truck load every day.

Interviewees during Phase One included local government officials as well as small business owners. The government officials seemed to be most concerned that the casino operators might not rebuild and leave Biloxi, thus taking with them jobs and tax revenue. However, this is not what happened. By June of 2006, it was clear that the key players in the casino operations were not only going to stay in Biloxi, but would likely invest and expand their operations. Several of the operators invested millions of dollars immediately in renovating their existing casinos on the water.

The state of Mississippi reached a compromise with Biloxi and the casino operators to allow on-land casinos on a restricted strip of land in downtown Biloxi. The casinos would have to be within an 800-foot section near the shoreline, in an area originally zoned for casino activities such as connected restaurants and hotels. This compromise paved the way for the casino companies to invest collectively in excess of $1 billion. An additional incentive for this building boom is a new tax incentive from the federal government. The credit applies to non-gambling

---

39   Waveland to Wasteland, http://www.femaforgotwaveland.com (last visited July 14, 2007).

facilities which open along the Gulf Coast before the end of 2008. Although the casinos will not qualify for a tax credit, all of the restaurants, hotels, and retail businesses which support casinos will qualify.

Thus, nine months following Katrina, we find two communities which had experienced similar damage, but were now going in opposite directions. The first, Waveland, seems to have little value to the state in terms of tax revenues. Large corporations see few opportunities there. The second, Biloxi, because of its attractiveness to the gaming industry, represents potential for significant tax revenues for both the state and local governments. Additionally, large casino operators like Harrah's, MGM Mirage, and others see the potential to aggregate and create a gambling center in the southeast. Because of the near total destruction of the downtown area, and the cost to rebuild faced by small business owners, the large casino operators were able to buy large sections of land on which to build new operations. This would likely have been much more difficult prior to Katrina, as much of the land would have to have been purchased individually. Thus, it seems that luck and opportunistic behavior contributed greatly to the enhanced recovery of this town.

*Barriers*    Barriers to recovery identified by many of the business stakeholders related to disincentives to work and lack of access to capital.[40] We asked several of the respondents from the original study if these impediments had been removed or ameliorated in the six months since. The disincentive to work created by housing, food, and other allowances provided by FEMA still existed. FEMA extended these through August of 2006, even though they had already been extended several times. Businesses in the Gulf Coast area were still experiencing worker shortages, despite the fact that wages offered were well above the norm. One interviewee stated that he was leaving his job managing a local non-profit to work for a grocery store chain in the New Orleans area. The chain was paying a starting wage of over $12 per hour, with a signing bonus and promise of overtime wages for the foreseeable future.

The SBA situation seemed to be less problematic than had been reported by most in the three months following Katrina. Several small business owners in each of the original study's communities had applied and been approved for SBA loans. Some had yet to receive the funds, but the loan was approved nonetheless. In most cases, the business owners had availed themselves of assistance in filling out the SBA paper work. This type of assistance is often offered by local economic development offices as well as many Chambers of Commerce. However, most small business owners viewed the SBA application process as overwhelming. Out of the hundreds of small businesses affected by Katrina, nine months after this disaster, only a very small percentage actually received government funding to help recovery.

---

40   *Small Business*, *supra* note 1.

## Lessons Learned

The second phase of the study reported here deals with only a few of the original research questions. We sought to discover whether the key barriers to economic recovery for the small businesses in the Gulf Coast post-Katrina still remained nine months after the storm. We found that for the most part, those barriers continued to remain in place. It is controversial to call for a reduction in financial assistance to those displaced from their homes or jobs due to disasters. During the 2006 Symposium on Katrina sponsored by the Center on Property, Citizenship and Social Entrepreneurship, this topic was discussed by several of the participants. The question arose regarding victims of such disasters. Two answers emerged from this discussion. First, perhaps the trauma of losing one's home and job might actually prevent someone from working for a period of time. Second, maybe many of the people receiving FEMA assistance were hoping to return to their jobs imminently, and saw no need to apply for and work on a temporary basis. This is a question which should be addressed in future studies: does FEMA assistance following a disaster actually impede recovery? If so, how and to what extent?

The argument that the SBA impedes recovery is perhaps much easier to make. The SBA is a huge government bureaucracy, requiring the completion of copious amounts of forms, papers, and documentation to qualify for loans. This is certainly not a major impediment to start-up businesses, nor to those who are seeking capital for expansion. In both cases, time is not necessarily of the essence and a month or two delay will not make or break the business. However, when a small business has been put completely out of operation, the owner and employees will probably not see a paycheck until the business is back up and running again. Thus, time is of the utmost importance. It is in this type of situation that the SBA seems to have failed miserably, but it is the very situation faced following a natural disaster of a large magnitude.

Anecdotal evidence points to the SBA learning from the aftermath of Katrina. One of the interviewees in Phase Two reported that some local business owners were facing less bureaucracy problems with the SBA. It still took a relatively long period of time to obtain a loan, but the SBA was providing more "hands-on" assistance for small business owners. From our study, we can make another recommendation that the SBA should consider: drastically streamline the process following disasters such as this. The SBA could work in a more cooperative way with local banks and economic development offices to provide immediate short-term financial assistance to small business owners. This could come in the form of a "bridge" loan to get the owner through the first month or so when there are no revenues. Local stakeholders such as bankers and Chamber Directors have a direct, working knowledge of local businesses. Therefore, they are well positioned to assist with loan decisions based on company viability. Time being of the essence to the small business owner, the time-consuming and tedious paperwork process could be completed in the weeks which follow.

The likelihood of a major disaster such as Katrina occurring again seems to be quite high. Thus, it is incumbent upon local and state officials to communicate these problems and shortcomings to the federal government. Small business owners are truly the backbone of the U.S. economy, and need the type of support that will help them survive and recover from disasters such as Katrina.

## Acknowledgements

This research was funded by the University of South Carolina-College of Hospitality, Retail, and Sport Management's Research Support Initiative.

# Chapter 9
# Legislation and Criminalization Impacting Renters Displaced by Katrina

Olympia Duhart and Eloisa C. Rodriguez-Dod

## Introduction

The pictures, they say, are worth a thousand words.

Even today, more than two years after Hurricane Katrina laid waste to the Gulf Region,[1] it is hard, if not impossible, for many people to return home. The powerful storm decimated parts of Mississippi, Alabama, and Louisiana.[2] It also displaced a record number of men, women, and children. Some estimates are as high as 800,000.[3]

But while governmental agencies, volunteer efforts, and charities have rushed to rebuild the homes of those displaced by the storm, a huge number of Hurricane Katrina victims have been left with little or no assistance. Beyond the camera lens and often overlooked in the vivid portrayals of hurricane damage are renters, who

---

1 The hurricane made landfall in Louisiana on August 29, 2005. Elisabeth Bumiller, *In New Orleans, Bush Speaks with Optimism but Sees Little of Ruin*, N.Y. TIMES, Jan. 13, 2006, at A12.

2 DOUGLAS BRINKLEY, THE GREAT DELUGE 159 (2006). "The entire Gulf Coast region from Southeast Louisiana to Alabama, was declared a federal disaster area . . . ." *Id.*

3 About 1.5 million people were directly affected by Hurricane Katrina, and more than 800,000 people were forced to live outside of their homes. Dep't of Homeland Sec., *Hurricane Katrina: What Government Is Doing*, http://www.dhs.gov/xprepresp/programs/gc_1157649340100.shtm (last visited May 11, 2007) [hereinafter *What Government Is Doing*].

comprise almost half of those displaced by Hurricane Katrina.[4] Renters are often last in line for government benefits and other assistance.[5]

Moreover, the hostility to renter's rights that continues to pervade the community after Katrina has created additional obstacles for low-income renters attempting to resettle in the area.[6] Further, even one-time homeowners have been forced to turn to rental housing[7] as the long, slow recovery assistance process works its way through the region.

The difficulties facing renters in the New Orleans region after the storm are emblematic of the difficulties confronting many "evacuees" who are forced to find temporary housing following a disaster.[8] The hurdles facing renters in the region are varied and extensive. Among the obstacles for renters in the New Orleans region are the scarcity of land on the south shore of Lake Ponchartrain,[9]

---

4    In New Orleans, fifty-five percent of the housing units affected were rental units. NAT'L LOW INCOME HOUS. COAL., PRELIMINARY ESTIMATE 9-22-05, HURRICANE KATRINA'S IMPACT ON LOW INCOME HOUSING UNITS ESTIMATED 302,000 UNITS LOST OR DAMAGED, 71% LOW INCOME (2005), http://nlihc.org/doc/05-02.pdf (last visited May 11, 2007). Forty-seven percent of the housing units in the entire Katrina-affected area were rental units. *Id.* By some estimates, almost 84,000 rental units were destroyed or heavily damaged by Katrina and the ensuing flood. Susan Saulny & Gary Rivlin, *Little Aid Coming to Displaced New Orleans Renters; Homeowners Are Seeing Lion's Share of Post-Katrina Help*, N.Y. TIMES, Sept. 17, 2006; *see also* overview of, The Small Rental Property Program, at 1 (Dec. 4, 2007), *available at* http://www.road2la.org/rental/overview.htm (stating that nearly 82,000 rental housing units received major damage or severe damage during Hurricanes Katrina and Rita).

5    David Hammer, *Relief Far off for La. Rental Owners*, TIMES-PICAYUNE (NEW ORLEANS), Jan. 4, 2007.

6    *See* People's Hurricane Relief Fund and Oversight Coalition, Tenants Rights Working Group, www.peopleshurricane.org (last visited May 9, 2007). The group targets local and federal officials to meet a list of tenant demands to protect the rights of renters impacted by Hurricane Katrina. *Id.*

7    Eric Dash & David Leonhardt, *Invasion of Reluctant Renters; So Many Evacuees and, Luckily, So Many Apartments in Cities of Refuge*, N.Y. TIMES, Sept. 16, 2005, at C1. Immediately following the storm, federal officials estimated that between 400,000 to one million people from the Gulf Region scattered across the nation in search of housing, "perhaps the country's largest single migration since the Civil War." *Id.* In New Orleans, scores of homeowners were forced to find temporary housing within the state while they waited for their houses to be repaired, or for the flooding to abate. *Id.*

8    The staggering increase in disasters and catastrophes worldwide has led to a burgeoning transient population. Warren Friedman, *Denial of Housing to Renters Because of Criminal Background* 1 (Nov. 8, 2006) (unpublished comment, on file with author).

9    BUREAU OF GOVERNMENTAL RESEARCH, THE ROAD HOME RENTAL HOUSING PROGRAM: CONSEQUENCES FOR NEW ORLEANS, 11 (2006), *available at* http://www.bgr.org/Consequences_ for_N.O._091506.pdf (last visited May 11, 2007) [hereinafter THE ROAD HOME]. The City of New Orleans is located on subsiding swampland on the delta of the Mississippi River. *See* U.S. HOUSE OF REPRESENTATIVES, SELECT BIPARTISAN COMM. TO INVESTIGATE THE PREPARATION

increases in labor and material costs for repairs,[10] higher insurance,[11] infrastructure uncertainty,[12] rental property inflation,[13] poverty,[14] construction problems,[15] zoning restrictions,[16] and criminalization.[17] Some of these problems can serve as a "snapshot" of sorts for the obstacles for renters who must find housing following a temporary, unforeseen displacement.

## Restrictions on Renters: Hits and Misses

In the field of legislation concerning rental properties, there have been some near hits and misses. Remarkably, some local lawmakers erected barriers, rather than relief, for the already embattled renters. For example, one particularly egregious example of a legislative impediment to the return of renters is St. Bernard's Parish Code #670-09-06. Passed by the St. Bernard Parish Council in September 2006, the local ordinance placed a rental restriction on single family residences that prohibited landlords from renting to anyone other than blood relatives.[18]

---

FOR AND RESPONSE TO HURRICANE KATRINA, 109TH CONG., A FAILURE OF INITIATIVE 51 (Comm. Print 2006), *available at* http://www.katrina.house.gov/full_katrina_report.htm (last visited May 11, 2007) [hereinafter A FAILURE OF INITIATIVE]. The City's average elevation is six feet below sea level. *Id.*

10    THE ROAD HOME, *supra* note 9, at 11.

11    HUD APPROVES $4.2 B FOR LOUISIANA'S "ROAD HOME" REBUILDING PROGRAM, USA TODAY, July 11, 2006.

12    THE ROAD HOME, *supra* note 9, at 12.

13    *Renters in New Orleans See Prices Rise 39 Percent*, N.Y. TIMES, Sept. 17, 2006 [hereinafter *Renters See Prices Rise 39 Percent*]. "It is not uncommon for apartments in the French Quarter to rent at rates three times higher than before Katrina." Darryl Lorenzo Wellington, *New Orleans: A Right to Return?*, DISSENT, Fall 2006, http://www. dissentmagazine.org.article/?article=695&print=1 (last visited Apr. 3, 2007).

14    Long before Katrina, poverty was a serious problem in New Orleans. *Child Poverty in States Hit by Hurricane Katrina*, CHILD POVERTY IN 21ST CENTURY AM. (Nat'l Center for Children in Poverty, New York, N.Y.), Sept. 2005, at 1, 2; *see also* Nicholas Seidule, *A Fly in the Soup Bowl: Using the State-Created Danger Doctrine to Find Liability Against the State of Louisiana for the Katrina Disaster*, 5–10 (unpublished manuscript, on file with The Nova Law Review).

15    THE ROAD HOME, *supra* note 9, at 12.

16    *See* discussion *infra* "Restrictions on Renters: Hits and Misses" and accompanying notes.

17    *See* discussion *infra* "Crime and Punishment—A Landlord's Way" and accompanying notes. Furthermore, the term "criminalization" in this chapter is being used in a slightly different connotation than its dictionary meaning. It is being used expansively to refer to the criminal characterization of people who have either not gone through the justice system, or who are saddled with ancient, minor infractions.

18    St. Bernard Parish, La., Ordinance 670-09-06 (March 7, 2006). The legislation did create an exception with Council approval. *Id.* In March 2006, the Parish originally

The ordinance stated:

> No person or entity shall rent, lease, loan, or otherwise allow occupancy or use
> of any single family residence located in an R-1 zone by any person or group of
> persons, other than a family member(s) related by blood within the first, second
> or third direct ascending or descending generation(s), without first obtaining a
> Permissive Use Permit from the St. Bernard Parish Council.[19]

The ordinance carried strict penalties. Violators were to be found guilty of a misdemeanor and subject to a fine "of not less than $50.00 and not more than $250.00 per day for each day of an un-permitted rental, lease, or occupancy of each property in violation" of the ordinance.[20]

The parish of St. Bernard also reserved the right to pursue civil remedies in the District Court of the parish against any person who allowed use of any property in violation of the ordinance, or anyone who occupied or used any property in violation of the ordinance.[21] The St. Bernard Parish Council asserted that the ordinance was needed to "maintain the integrity and stability of established neighborhoods as centers of family values and activities. . . ."[22]

In its short, unhappy life, the ordinance quickly prompted a lawsuit grounded in challenges based on the Fair Housing Act of 1968,[23] 42 U.S.C. §§ 1981, 1982 and 1983, and the Equal Protection Clause of the Fourteenth Amendment to the United States Constitution.[24] The plaintiff, the Greater New Orleans Fair Housing Action

---

approved an ordinance that placed a moratorium on single-family homes becoming rental properties "until such time as the post Katrina real estate market in St. Bernard Parish stabilizes." St. Bernard Parish, La., Ordinance 670-09-06 (Sept. 19, 2006). The Ordinance under discussion here concerns a narrow exception to the original moratorium.

19    *Id.*

20    *Id.* Each day of unpermitted occupancy of each property constituted a separate offense subject to a separate fine. *Id.*

21    *Id.*

22    *Id.* The ordinance was adopted by vote on September 19, 2006. *Id.* Five members of the council voted in favor of the ordinance; two members (including the chairman) voted against the ordinance. *Id.* Within one month, by its October 3, 2006 council meeting, the Parish was requesting a District Attorney opinion on the ordinance. *See* Official Proceedings of the Council of the Parish of St. Bernard, State of Louisiana, taken at a regular meeting held on, Oct. 3, 2006, at 1, *available at* http://www.sbpg.net/10-3-06minutes.doc.

23    *See* 42 U.S.C. § 3604(a) (2006). "The Fair Housing Act makes it unlawful to discriminate against any person in the terms, conditions, or privileges of sale or rental of a dwelling, or in the provision of services or facilities in connection therewith, on the basis of race, color, religion, sex, familial status, national origin, or handicap." *Discrimination in Sale or Rental Terms and Services*, 15 AM. JUR. 2D CIVIL RIGHTS § 392 (2007).

24    The Equal Protection Clause states: "No State shall make or enforce any law which shall abridge the privileges or immunities of citizens of the United States; nor shall any State deprive any person of life, liberty or property, without due process of law; *nor*

Center, Inc. ("GNOFHAC"), sought injunctive relief, declaratory judgment, and remedial relief.[25]

The basis for the civil rights complaint was rooted in the demographic composition of St. Bernard Parish, a community that sits a few miles east of downtown New Orleans.[26] St. Bernard Parish is overwhelmingly white.[27] Specifically, St. Bernard's population of 67,000 prior to Hurricane Katrina was nearly ninety percent white.[28] Among homeowners in the parish, there is a greater gulf between the black and white residents. White residents own ninety-three percent of all owner-occupied units in the parish.[29] Finally, minorities in the parish are disproportionately reliant on rental properties in the region: Nearly one in two black households in St. Bernard rented before the storm, and one in three Hispanic households in the parish rented before the storm.[30] By contrast, only one in four

---

*deny to any person within its jurisdiction the equal protection of the law*." U.S. CONST. amend. XIV, § 1 (emphasis added).

25    Greater New Orleans Fair Hous. Action Ctr., Inc. v. St. Bernard Parish, No. 2:06-CV-07185 (E.D. La. filed Oct. 3, 2006). The Greater New Orleans Fair Housing Action Center ("GNOFHAC") argued that the council's enactment of the ordinances constituted "a practice and policy of housing discrimination on the basis of race and national origin." *Id.* It asserted that its injuries included interference with the organization's efforts to promote equal housing opportunity for its constituents, the depletion of resources needed to counter unlawful housing practices, and interference with the constituent's enjoyment of the benefit of living in an integrated community. *Id.* The GNOFHAC argued that the Fair Housing Act is violated "even when seemingly neutral zoning policies have a discriminatory effect on a particular protected class and cause harm to a community through the perpetuation of segregation." *See* News Release, Greater New Orleans Fair Hous. Action Ctr., Fair Housing Center Files Suit Against St. Bernard Parish; Announces New Conference Regarding Lawsuit, *available at* www.gnofairhousing.org (last visited May 11, 2007).

26    Louisiana Plans, Long-Term Recovery Planning, St. Bernard Parish, http://www.louisianaspeaks-parishplans.org/IndParishHomepage.cfm?EntID=13 (last visited May 14, 2007). St. Bernard Parish is located between the Mississippi River and Lake Borgne. *Id.* The Parish covers 465 square miles in land area. *Id.*

27    Billy Sothern, *A Question of Blood*, THE NATION, Mar. 27, 2007, *available at* http://www.thenation.com/doc/20070409/sothern.

28    According to pre-Katrina statistics from the U.S. Census Bureau, the 2000 Full-count Characteristics of St. Bernard Parish showed that the demographic breakdown was 84.3 percent white, 7.6 percent black, and 5.1 percent Hispanic. Greater New Orleans Community Data Center, St. Bernard Parish: People & Household Characteristics tbl. 2, *available at* http://www.gnocdc.org/st_bernard/people.html (last visited May 14, 2007).

29    According to one report, "whites own virtually all single-family homes in the parish (ninety-three percent according to 2000 census data)." Press Release, Lawyer's Committee for Civil Rights Under Law, St. Bernard Parish Agrees to Halt Discriminatory Zoning Rule (Nov. 13, 2006), *available at* http://www.lawyerscommittee.org/2005website/publications/press/press111306.html (last visited May 14, 2007).

30    Michelle Chen, *Housing Watchdogs Call Post-Katrina Ordinance*, THE NEW STANDARD, Oct. 6, 2006, *available at* http://newstandardnews.net/content/index.cfm/

white households in St. Bernard rented before the storm.[31] The displacement caused by Hurricane Katrina in nearby New Orleans also boosted the minority population in need of rental housing.[32]

In their suit, the challengers argued that the ordinances passed by the parish had the intent and effect of denying rental housing availability for minorities.[33] The ordinance effectively restricted the bulk of the single-family home rentals in the parish to whites. The challengers contended that the zoning restrictions operated as a pretext to discriminate against minorities in the housing market.[34] Interestingly, a member of the St. Bernard Parish Council who had voted against the ordinance also asserted in a local newspaper column that it was intended to keep blacks from moving to the parish.[35]

Courts have long recognized de facto racial discrimination of legislation by examining the discriminatory intent and impact of such laws.[36] Disparate impact is measured by the discriminatory effect a challenged legislation will have on a protected class.[37] Discriminatory intent examines the purpose for which the challenged legislation was enacted.[38] Not only did the St. Bernard Parish ordinance disproportionately limit the rental access of minorities, but the stated reason for the ordinance was to preserve the "integrity" of the community, which was predominantly white.

Not surprisingly, the ordinance was met with a barrage of media criticism and community complaints from both civic and watchdog groups.[39] Because Katrina

---

items/3731.

31  *Id.*

32  "African Americans were more likely to be flooded, more likely to be displaced, less likely to be able to return . . . ." Gary Younge, *New Orleans Forsaken*, THE NATION, Aug. 31, 2006, at 3, *available at* http://www.thenation.com/doc/20060918/younge (last visited May 14, 2007).

33  Greater New Orleans Fair Hous. Action Ctr., Inc. v. St. Bernard Parish, No. 2:06-CV-07185 (E.D. La. filed Oct. 3, 2006).

34  *Id.*

35  A journalist characterized Council President Lynn Dean as "eccentric, outspoken and white—like the rest of the members [of the council]." Sothern, *supra* note 27. Dean discussed the ignoble motives of the ordinance in his column in the *St. Bernard Parish Voice. Id.*

36  *See* Yick Wo v. Hopkins, 118 U.S. 356 (1886). In *Yick Wo*, the United States Supreme Court reversed a Chinese challenger's conviction under a facially neutral San Francisco ordinance as a violation of equal protection. *Id.*

37  *See* Palmer v. Thompson, 403 U.S. 217 (1971). The Court found no evidence in the record to show that the challenged state action affected "blacks differently from whites." *Id.* at 225.

38  *See* Washington v. Davis, 426 U.S. 229 (1976) (holding that purposeful discrimination must be proven to establish an equal protection violation).

39  *See, e.g.*, News Release, Greater New Orleans Fair Hous. Action Ctr., Fair Housing Centers File Suit Against St. Bernard Parish; Announces New Conference Regarding Lawsuit (Oct. 3, 2006), www.gnofairhousing.org.

had effectively decimated St. Bernard Parish, the need for affordable housing in the area was paramount. In addition, critics say the ordinance was a thinly veiled pretext for discriminating against blacks.[40]

Council members from St. Bernard Parish defended the ordinance as an effort to maintain owner-occupied houses and keep out speculators.[41] The council members said their concern was that speculators would buy low-cost damaged homes, make minimal repairs, and then rent them out, "which could depress home values in traditionally owner-occupied homes."[42]

In a subsequent incarnation, the legislation re-emerged as Ordinance #697-12-06.[43] In its more diluted form, the new ordinance on the zoning restrictions regarding the rental of single-family residences removed the consanguinity restriction and instead imposed a Permissive Use Permit requirement for anyone who wished to rent, lease, loan, or otherwise allow occupancy of any single family residence in an identified zone.[44]

This newer ordinance retains the criminal sanctions,[45] as well as the civil penalties,[46] that could be imposed for violations. The ordinance also exempts single family residences that were rental properties before the enactment of the ordinance.[47]

Another prospective piece of legislation which would have actually served the rights of renters trying to relocate after the storm never obtained the requisite

---

40    "This racist ordinance needs to be declared unconstitutional and the leaders closely monitored until they repent or resign." Sothern, *supra* note 27 (quoting Letter to the Editor, Times-Picayune (New Orleans), Oct. 1, 2006).

41    Steve Cannizaro, *St. Bernard Parish Government, Parish Council Proposing Major Changes to Rental Property Ordinance*, Dec. 7, 2006, *available at* http://www.sbpg. net/dec0506f.html (last visited Dec. 7, 2006).

42    *Id.*

43    The St. Bernard Parish amended the ordinance at its council meeting on Dec. 19, 2006. St. Bernard Parish, La., Ordinance 697-12-06 (Dec. 19, 2006); *see also* Official Proceedings of the Council of the Parish of St. Bernard, State of Louisiana, taken at a regular meeting held on Dec. 19, 2006, *available at* http: //www.sbpg.net/12-19-06minutes. doc.

44    St. Bernard Parish, La., Ordinance 697-12-06 (2006). The Permissive Use Permit requirement also requires that landlords make a prior application to the St. Bernard Parish Planning Commission for "review, evaluation and recommendation concerning the matter." *Id.*

45    The violation of the ordinance constitutes a misdemeanor, and is subject to a fine of not less than $50 a day and not more than $250 for each day of unpermitted rental, lease, or occupancy. *Id.*

46    Civil penalties for tenants and landlords who violated the ordinance were not less than $100 a day for each day of unpermitted occupancy, as well as administrative costs, court costs, and attorney fees for investigation and prosecution of the civil matter. *Id.*

47    *Id.* The council member who proposed the original legislation said the changes demonstrated the parish's intent to protect property values by maintaining owner-occupied neighborhoods rather than discrimination. Cannizaro, *supra* note 41, at 1.

support to transform into law. The Elimination of Barriers for Katrina Victims Act, H.R. 4213, would have provided a mechanism for people with criminal backgrounds to avail themselves of government assistance.[48] Generally, the blanket exclusion in place for people with criminal backgrounds operated to deny affordable housing access for those with a prior criminal record.[49] While landlords are vested with inherent authority to deny tenancy to those with criminal backgrounds, the application of this practice to Katrina evacuees proved especially problematic.[50]

First, the use of the criminal background records for Katrina evacuees are riddled with problems. Some evacuees have criminal records for ancient, minor infractions.[51] Others have inaccurate records, which attach criminal records to the wrong renters.[52] Further, the notorious time delays caused by Katrina have all but stalled the criminal justice system in New Orleans.[53] The result is that many people charged with crimes were left in a criminal justice limbo that excluded them from rentals because of their arrests, but did not grant them a speedy resolution to the criminal charges.[54] Unfortunately, the Elimination of Barriers for Katrina Act died for lack of support.[55]

---

48    Elimination of Barriers for Katrina Victims Act, H.R. 4213, 109th Cong. (2005–2006). The proposed legislation would have suspended temporarily the application of laws that would have denied federal benefits and entitlements to victims of Hurricane Katrina or Hurricane Rita who would have been rendered ineligible because of convictions for certain drug crimes. *Id.*

49    *See* discussion *infra* "Crime and Punishment—A Landlord's Way" and accompanying notes.

50    Kirsten D. Levingston, *Denying Housing to Those with Criminal Records Will Perpetuate Cycles of Crime*, Christian Sci. Monitor, Mar. 8, 2006, at 9.

51    *Id.* Those with outdated criminal backgrounds argue that the criminal backgrounds are unrepresentative of the lives they live today. *Id.* Further, the criminal background exclusion has a long reach, even impacting the family members of those convicted of crimes. One mother of three from New Orleans reported that her entire family was unable to obtain housing in Texas because her husband had served time for possession of crack cocaine. *Id.*

52    The privatization of criminal background records has led many to question the veracity of backgrounds. *Id.*

53    Leslie Eaton, *Judge Steps in for Poor Inmates Without Justice Since Hurricane*, N.Y. Times, May 23, 2006, at A1.

54    *Id.*

55    Elimination of Barriers for Katrina Victims Act, H.R. 4213, 109th Cong. (2005), *available at* http://www.govtrack.us/congress/billtext.xpd?bill=h109-4213.

## Crime and Punishment: A Landlord's Way

Rental housing problems can exact a demanding toll on criminals and alleged criminals. Individuals with past arrest or conviction records, and particularly those who have served jail time, generally find it more difficult than others to integrate into society—they cannot readily secure jobs or affordable housing.[56] This failure to obtain affordable housing generally leads to homelessness[57] and may eventually lead to recidivism.[58]

Although some convicts may be able to live with their families, others are not so fortunate.[59] These individuals typically must resort to public housing.[60] Under federal regulations currently in place, state public housing authorities may require criminal background checks of prospective and current tenants.[61] Consequently, in a majority of states, the public housing authorities consider a person's criminal background, including an arrest that did not lead to conviction, in making individualized determinations as to an applicant's eligibility for public housing.[62] In addition, three states immediately reject any applicant who has a criminal record.[63] These federal regulations allow the public housing authority not only to deny housing to the alleged criminal, but may also deny housing to the criminal's family if the criminal were to live with the family.[64]

This problem regarding the lack of housing for persons with criminal records is of particular concern in New Orleans after Hurricane Katrina due to various factors. The crime rate in New Orleans was incredibly high prior to the hurricane; thus, a disproportionately large number of individuals could or would have been denied public housing.[65] However, both public and private rental housing was

---

56   Levingston, *supra* note 50, at 1. *See also* CORRINE CAREY, HUMAN RIGHTS WATCH, NO SECOND CHANCE: PEOPLE WITH CRIMINAL RECORDS DENIED ACCESS TO PUBLIC HOUSING 16 (2004); PAUL SAMUELS & DEBBIE MUKAMAL, LEGAL ACTION CENTER, AFTER PRISON: ROADBLOCKS TO REENTRY: A REPORT ON STATE LEGAL BARRIERS FACING PEOPLE WITH CRIMINAL RECORDS (Legal Action Center 2004) 10, 16, *available at* http://www.lac.org/lac/upload/lacreport/LAC_PrintReport.pdf (last visited Apr. 11, 2007).

57   *See, e.g.*, Levingston, *supra* note 50; CAREY, *supra* note 56, at 16.

58   *See* CAREY, *supra* note 56, at 43. "[S]uccessful reentry into society is much more difficult for people who have been arrested or convicted of crimes." SAMUELS & MUKAMAL, *supra* note 56, at 8.

59   CAREY, *supra* note 56, at 16.

60   *Id.*

61   24 C.F.R. § 960.203(c)(2), (3) (2006); 24 C.F.R. §§ 5.901-5.903 (2006).

62   *See* SAMUELS & MUKAMAL, *supra* note 56, at 8, 16.

63   *Id.* at 16.

64   CAREY, *supra* note 56, at 21 n.51.

65   *See* ACORN, REBUILDING AFTER HURRICANE KATRINA: ACORN PLANNING PRINCIPLES, 16, *available at* http:// www.acorn.org/fileadmin/KatrinaRelief/report/Planning_Principles. pdf (last visited Apr. 11, 2007).

already scarce before the hurricane,[66] and, obviously, worsened thereafter.[67] In addition, after Hurricane Katrina, the criminal system radically disintegrated. There were increased incidents of arrests, many of which were for misdemeanors.[68] Nonetheless, these arrests have created criminal records for those particular individuals. And to make matters worse, many pending criminal cases were brought to a standstill due to the hurricane's physical destruction of court files and evidence.[69] This great number of unresolved cases has added to the number of criminals and alleged criminals that cannot readily find public housing. As public housing is not feasible for these individuals, they must turn to more costly private rentals in an attempt to find a place to live.[70]

A private landlord is generally free to choose to whom he or she rents real property. The only limitations generally imposed are found under the Fair Housing Act (FHA).[71] The FHA makes it unlawful for a landlord "[t]o refuse to . . . rent . . . or otherwise make unavailable or deny, a dwelling to any person because of race, color, religion, sex, familial status, or national origin."[72] Additionally, a landlord may not "discriminate in the . . . rental, or . . . otherwise make unavailable or deny, a dwelling to any . . . renter because of a handicap" of the renter or anyone

---

66    See Deon Roberts, *Real Estate Expert: N.O. Population Will Recover Slowly*, New Orleans City Bus., Feb. 1, 2006; Marcia Johnson, *Addressing Housing Needs in the Post Katrina Gulf Coast*, 31 T. Marshall L. Rev. 327, 328 (2006).

67    *See* Michelle Chen, *New Orleans' Displaced Struggle for Housing, Jobs, Neighborhoods*, The New Standard, Oct. 21, 2005, *available at* http://newstandardnews.net/content/index.cfm/items/2514 (last visited Apr. 15, 2007); Gwen Filosa & Michelle Hunter, *Rental Quandary: Scarce Units, Costly Repairs and Surging Rents Hit Tenants and Landlords Hard*, Times-Picayune (New Orleans), Dec. 12, 2005, at 1.

68    *See* Levingston, *supra* note 56.

69    *See generally* Christopher Drew, *In New Orleans, Rust in the Wheels of Justice*, N.Y. Times, Nov. 21, 2006, at A1.

70    Thus, this discussion will focus on the concerns associated with rentals by private landlords to those with arrest or conviction records, with a look at the crisis which has unfolded in New Orleans. For a more complete discussion of public housing issues, *see generally* James C. Smith, *Disaster Planning and Public Housing* (Paper on file with the author and will appear as a chapter in a forthcoming book on affordable housing to be published as vol. 3 in the Law, Property, and Society series from Ashgate Publishing, Robin Paul Malloy, editor, 2009); *see also* Carey, *supra* note 56.

71    42 U.S.C. § 3604. This is the only limitation for landlords that do not participate in public housing programs, such as Section 8. As stated earlier in this chapter, some state and local governments have enacted more restrictive statutes and ordinances limiting a landlord's right to freely rent to prospective tenants. Much of this legislation has been subject to challenge. Most recently, the City of Hazleton, Pennsylvania was sued in federal court over its enactment of an ordinance prohibiting private landlords from renting to illegal immigrants. Lozano v. City of Hazleton, No. 3:06-cv-1586 (M.D. Pa. filed Aug. 15, 2006). The resolution of the case was still pending as of the date of publication of this book.

72    42 U.S.C. § 3604(a) (2006).

who will reside with or is associated with the renter.[73] Thus, as long as a private landlord does not discriminate against one of these protected classes, the landlord may, in his or her discretion, freely implement any selection criteria in renting to prospective tenants.

No known law exists preventing a landlord from conducting a criminal background check before renting to a prospective tenant. Only one state requires a landlord to conduct criminal background checks, but only under limited circumstances.[74] Private landlords in Arkansas may be ordered to perform a criminal background check of a prospective tenant if a municipality's criminal nuisance abatement board declares the premises to be a public nuisance.[75] Thus, the implementation of criminal background checks is mostly the prerogative of a private landlord. Given the shortage of housing after Hurricane Katrina's destruction of New Orleans, and given that criminal background checks are already an impediment to securing public housing, a private landlord's implementation of a criminal background check for prospective tenants in New Orleans compounds an already existing housing crisis for those with arrest records.[76]

These criminal background checks serve no purpose to private landlords other than permitting them to have some basis on which to exclude prospective tenants from renting the premises.[77] Under the common law, landlords are generally not liable to tenants for crimes committed against them by other tenants.[78] However, liability may attach if the landlord: 1) had actual or constructive knowledge that would make the tenant's conduct reasonably foreseeable and the landlord did not take reasonable precautions;[79] 2) had a special relationship with the perpetrator or

---

73   *Id.* § 3604(f).

74   ARK. CODE ANN. § 14-54-1705 (2006).

75   *Id.*

76   As it is, many private landlords have been using consumer credit checks when screening prospective tenants. This too serves as a deterrent to criminals, particularly those who have served a sentence, in obtaining affordable rental housing as their crimes generally affect their credit status. *See* CAREY, *supra* note 56, at 32 n.104. Credit checks generally require an applicant's consent. 15 U.S.C. § 1681(b); *see also* FLA. STAT. § 501.005 (2006) (consumer may request a "security freeze" prohibiting release of consumer report information without consumer's consent). However, in Florida, a consumer may not freeze information in the consumer report if it concerns and is used solely for tenant screening. *Id.* § 501.005(12)(j).

77   *See* CAREY, *supra* note 56, at 19, 21. "Exclusions based on criminal records are usually justified in terms of promoting the safety of . . . tenants." *Id.*

78   *See generally* Deborah J. La Fetra, *A Moving Target: Property Owners' Duty to Prevent Criminal Acts on the Premises*, 28 WHITTIER L. REV. 409, 439 (2006).

79   *See, e.g.*, T.W. v. Regal Trace, Ltd., 908 So. 2d 499, 506 (Fla. Dist. Ct. App. 2005) (landlord had duty to warn tenants of alleged sexual assault committed by one tenant on another minor tenant); Thompson v. Tuggle, 183 S.W.3d 611 (Mo. Ct. App. 2006) (landlord did not breach duty where it had no knowledge that tenant owned gun); Western Invs., Inc. v. Urena, 162 S.W.3d 547, 549 (Tex. 2005) (question of fact as to whether landlord's

victim;[80] or 3) assumed an implied or express obligation to provide security to the tenant and breached that obligation[81]—the latter two reflect the state of the law in Louisiana.[82]

In the Louisiana case of *Smith v. Howard*, a tenant shot and killed another tenant, whom she believed to be a burglar outside her window.[83] The victim's estate sued both the tenant and the landlord.[84] The complaint alleged that the landlord caused the victim's death by failing to

> (1) evict [the other tenant] after her neighbors reported to the [landlord] that she was a threat to their safety and to the safety of visitors; (2) maintain a proper screening program so as to avoid renting to tenants with a history of violent propensities; (3) maintain policies requiring tenants to state whether they have any dangerous weapons; (4) have a program for following up reports of violent conduct by tenants against other tenants or visitors; (5) insure the safety and security of guests; and (6) warn tenants and guests on the premises of the dangers posed by the tenant.[85]

The appellate court affirmed the trial court's dismissal of the complaint.[86] The court relied on the well-settled law that, unless a special relationship exists, there is no duty to control the actions of a third person and prevent him from causing harm to someone else.[87] The court further noted that landlords do not have a special relationship with those who live on their premises, and, accordingly, owe no such duty to a tenant.[88] Therefore, because landlords will suffer no liability, criminal

---

knowledge of other crimes in the area rendered tenant's assault by another tenant reasonably foreseeable by landlord); Johnson v. Slocum Realty Corp., 595 N.Y.S.2d 244, 245 (N.Y. App. Div. 1993) (landlord has duty to protect tenants from "foreseeable criminal intrusions").

80   *See, e.g.*, Foxworth v. Hous. Auth. of Jefferson Parish, 590 So. 2d 1347, 1348–49 (La. Ct. App. 1991) (landlord has no duty to control actions of tenants unless some special relationship, such as lease provision requiring protective services, exists); N.W. and D.W. v. Anderson, 478 N.W.2d 542, 543 (Minn. Ct. App. 1991) (landlord has no duty to warn tenants unless landlord has "special relationship to either the [tenant] whose conduct needs to be controlled or to the foreseeable victim of that conduct").

81   *See, e.g.*, *Foxworth*, 590 So. 2d at 1348 (landlord has no duty to provide security unless landlord assumed the obligation); Holley v. Mt. Zion Terrace Apartments, Inc., 382 So. 2d 98 (Fla. Dist. Ct. App. 1980) (part of rent dedicated expressly for security creates question as to landlord's contractual liability to provide such protection).

82   *See* Smith v. Howard, 489 So. 2d 1037, 1038 (La. Ct. App. 1986); *Foxworth*, 590 So. 2d at 1348; Terrell v. Wallace, 747 So. 2d 748 (La. Ct. App. 1999).

83   *Howard*, 489 So. 2d at 1038.

84   *Id.* at 1037–38.

85   *Id.* at 1038.

86   *Id.*

87   *Howard*, 489 So. 2d at 1038.

88   *Id.*

background checks create unnecessary impediments to some prospective tenants who are in dire need of affordable rental housing.

The incidents of arrest in the United States disproportionally impact people of color.[89] In New Orleans, the rate of arrest of black men increased after Katrina.[90] Using arrest and conviction records as a basis to deny private rentals may lead to unjust and catastrophic results. Arrests have included offenses that range from small infractions to felonies.[91] Minor infractions may include crimes such as "taking items from hardware stores and convenience stores and 'disturbing the peace.'"[92] Currently, a private landlord may readily investigate an applicant's criminal background, and many are doing just that.[93] Unlike consumer credit checks that require the person's consent due to privacy concerns,[94] a defendant's consent is not required to obtain a copy of the defendant's criminal record.[95] In many instances, arrest and conviction records are easily available on the Internet; however, the results of such a search may be inaccurate or may lead to incorrect or misleading conclusions. Although a majority of states allow defendants to seal or expunge records of arrests that did not lead to conviction,[96] thirty-three states prohibit the sealing or expungement of any conviction records and seventeen states allow only some conviction records, such as first-time offenses, to be sealed or expunged.[97] Criminal records in twenty-eight states are available on the Internet,[98] in addition to records available at the courthouse. In Louisiana, records of convictions, whether old or minor, are available for review.[99] In addition, the state makes accessible records of defendants on parole.[100] Louisiana does, however, permit the sealing of

---

89   *See generally* U.S. Dep't of Justice, Bureau of Justice Statistics, Profile of Jail Inmates (2002), *available at* http://www.ojp.usdoj.gov/bjs/pub/pdf/pji02.pdf (last visited Apr. 15, 2007); U.S. Dep't of Justice, Bureau of Statistics, *Blacks Were Almost Three Times More Likely than Hispanics and Five Times More Likely than Whites to Be in Jail*, http://www.ojp.usdoj.gov/bjs/glance/jailrair.htm (last visited Apr. 15, 2007).

90   *See* George Ploss, *America's Real "Prisoner's Dilemma,"* U. Wire, Mar. 27, 2007.

91   *See* Levingston, *supra* note 50.

92   *Missing Stories from Katrina Coverage: Survivors Locked up in Makeshift Jail*, The Praxis Project, Sept. 6, 2005, 3, *available at* http://www.thepraxisproject.org/tools/YMC_katrina.doc (last visited Apr. 11, 2007).

93   Carey, *supra* note 56, at 19.

94   *See supra* note 76 and accompanying text.

95   Samuels & Mukamal, *supra* note 56, at 15.

96   *Id.*

97   *Id.*

98   *Id.*

99   *Id.* at http://www.lac.org/lac/upload/reportcards/19_Image_Louisiana.pdf (last visited Apr. 11, 2007).

100   *Id.*; *see also* La. Dep't of Public Safety and Corrections, *Parole Board Dockets*, http://www.corrections.state.la.us/Offices/paroleboard/paroledockets.htm (last visited Apr. 11, 2007).

some arrest records if the arrest did not lead to conviction and, at least, some arrest records are shielded from the public eye.[101] Nonetheless, there is no prohibition on using these records as a basis for denial of rental housing. But what happened to "innocent until proven guilty"? Is a minor or old conviction really a credible and reasonable basis on which to deny housing?

Louisiana should consider enacting a law, similar to a bill proposed in Illinois,[102] that would limit a private landlord's ability to deny housing based on any arrest or conviction records. In January 2005, Illinois Representative Chapin Rose introduced a house bill, amending its Landlord and Tenant Act, that would permit a private landlord to perform criminal background checks on prospective tenants; however, the original version of the bill noted that a "landlord may refuse to lease the property . . . if the criminal background check of the person contains any *felony convictions* or indicates that the person is a *registered sex offender.*"[103] Consequently, only those actually convicted of committing certain egregious crimes would be susceptible to being denied a private rental.

Some may argue that a reason for conducting a criminal background check is to circumvent the FHA, and serve as a pretext to discrimination.[104] The proposed Illinois bill, both in its original and amended versions, includes a proviso that "[t]he landlord may not use the criminal background check to discriminate against a protected class."[105] Thus, the bill recognized the dangers concomitant with permitting a landlord to employ a criminal record as a basis for refusing to rent to a tenant.

---

101    *See* LA. REV. STAT. ANN. § 44:9 (2006); *see also* SAMUELS & MUKAMAL, *supra* note 56, at http://www.lac.org/lac/upload/reportcards/19_Image_Louisiana.pdf (last visited Apr. 11, 2007).

102    *See* H.B. 0367, 94th Gen. Assem. (Ill. 2005), *available at* http://www.ilga.gov/legislation/BillStatus.asp?DocNum=367&GAID=8&DocTypeID=HB&LegId=14619&SessionID=50&GA=94 (last visited Apr. 11, 2007) [hereinafter Illinois Bill].

103    *Id.* (emphasis added). The bill was later amended in February 2005 to permit the landlord to refuse to rent to a prospective tenant if:

(i) the individual's tenancy would constitute a direct threat to the health or safety of other individuals or the individual's tenancy would result in substantial physical damage to the property of others; or (ii) the individual has been convicted by any court of competent jurisdiction of the illegal manufacture or distribution of a controlled substance as defined in the federal Controlled Substances Act or the Illinois Controlled Substances Act.

*Id.* Unfortunately, this amendment would seemingly permit a landlord to interpret an arrest or conviction record and determine that renting to such individual could create a threat under subsection (i). This proposed bill is still pending, and the legislative session ended *sine die. Id.*

104    *See, e.g.*, Eliza Hirst, *The Housing Crisis for Victims of Domestic Violence: Disparate Impact Claims and Other Housing Protection for Victims of Domestic Violence*, 10 GEO. J. ON POVERTY L. & POL'Y 131, 133 (2003).

105    Illinois Bill, *supra* note 102.

**Conclusion**

More than two years after Katrina left her mark on the Gulf Coast, renters are left with few options to resettle in their former communities. Funding programs set aside to benefit renters are few and far between. While landlords who own from one to four rental units can tap into $869 million in public funding,[106] such programs pale in comparison to the $7.5 billion devoted to owners of damaged homes.[107]

In January 2007, The Road Home launched a Small Rental Property program, which was designed to provide incentives to rebuild affordable rental housing.[108] Even though there may be proposed tax incentives to lure developers back into the area, such solutions may address long-term needs, but do little to meet the immediate need for affordable rental communities. Not only are renters priced out of communities, but minority renters are also increasingly faced with bias in the market.[109]

Moreover, various attempts at enacting legislation have exacerbated the problem by limiting access to rentals. Other curative measures—such as the proposed federal legislation to eliminate barriers—have simply been abandoned. The tension created by the landlord's ability to deny housing to renters with criminal backgrounds highlights competing policy concerns in the region. On one hand, there is the need to protect the safety of the residents of rental property by properly screening out criminals. On the other hand is the need to provide affordable housing access to those with a prior criminal record.

As the rebuilding process continues in the Gulf Region, the difficulties for renters presented by legislation and criminalization demonstrate that there is a need to focus the lens on these issues which impact renters. The obstacles raised by Katrina, the flood, and the ensuing housing difficulties have a pronounced negative impact on minority communities. A snapshot of the housing crisis for renters displaced by Hurricane Katrina serves as a powerful reminder for other communities suddenly forced to rebuild.

---

106   Hammer, *supra* note 5, at 1. The program will be managed by the federal Department of Housing and Urban Development, the state Office of Community Development and ICF International. *Id*; *see also* THE ROAD HOME, *supra* note 9, at 5.

107   Hammer, *supra* note 5, at 1.

108   *See* Press Release, The Road Home, Rental Property Owners Encouraged to Apply to "The Road Home" Small Rental Property Program (Jan. 29, 2007), *available at* http://www.road2la.org/news_releases/rental_launch_012907.htm. The Small Rental Property Program provides incentives, such as no interest forgivable loans, to property owners to rent their small-scale rental properties to low- and moderate-income tenants at affordable rates. The Road Home, *Overview of Small Rental Property Program*, http://www.road2la.org/rental/overview.htm (last visited May 14, 2007).

109   A recent study revealed that black residents "encountered discrimination nearly six times out of ten when apartment hunting in the New Orleans area post-Katrina. . . ." Gwen Filosa, *Bias Found in Rental Market*, TIMES-PICAYUNE (New Orleans), Apr. 25, 2007, *available at* http://www.nola.com/topnews/2007/04/bias-found-in-rental-market.html.

## Acknowledgements

Olympia Duhart thanks Nicholas Seidule for his excellent work on this chapter.

Eloisa C. Rodriguez-Dod expresses her gratitude to Warren Friedman for his assistance and contribution.

# Chapter 10
# Navigating the Topography of Inequality Post-Disaster: A Proposal for Remedying Past Geographic Segregation During Rebuilding

Michèle Alexandre[1]

In January 2007, a number of students from the University of Baltimore's Hurricane Student Network and I spent a week in New Orleans in an attempt to contribute a pebble to the massive task of reconstructing and rebuilding New Orleans. During one of my "gutting"[2] assignments with the People's Organizing Committee,[3] I was assigned to help clean, gut, and restore a public housing unit. As a group of us went through the household's contents, encountering numerous rats and other harmful parasites, my first instinct was to throw away all of the contents of the house.

I was in the process of implementing this agenda when I met the owner of the housing unit. She was a small, frail woman who could have been my mother. As she watched me place her clothes and her other belongings in a "throw away" pile, her eyes began to water. Finally, she stopped me and told me: "This [is] all I have. I had to leave everything when the storm came and I have been away from my home for a year and a half. Please, let's look to see if we can salvage anything." At that moment, I was forced to step out of my efficiency-motivated mindset and had to

---

1    Thanks to Robin Paul Malloy and the Center on Property, Citizenship, and Social Entrepreneurism (PCSE) at Syracuse University College of Law for organizing the November 2006 PCSE Workshop. Thanks also to all the participants of the November 2006 PSCE Workshop for their comments and feedback.

2    "Gutting" involved stripping the damaged houses of everything, including sheetrock, leaving only their foundational structures. It was the first step in the process of rebuilding the flood-damaged homes.

3    The People's Organizing Committee is a subset of the New Orleans Survivor Council which works with displaced residents around the nation in order to help them move back to New Orleans. Among various tasks, they help restore destroyed/damaged homes and public housing units as well as help provide information to New Orleanians as to how displaced and returning New Orleanians can best advocate for their interest during the rebuilding process. *See* http://www.peoplesorganizing.org.

remind myself that for Ms. Jackson,[4] this was not a regular spring cleaning. For her, this was a last attempt at salvaging any remnant of her life pre-Hurricane Katrina. Ms. Jackson, like many others, did not want her pre-Katrina life to be discarded as no longer useful or relevant. In January 2007, thousands of displaced New Orleanians were still living in FEMA trailers across the nation.[5] Not much has changed as we recently marked the third anniversary of the devastating storm.[6]

Three years after Hurricane Katrina devastated New Orleans, the city is still far from restored.[7] As the rebuilding process raises questions regarding funding and adequate governmental diligence, it should cause us to consider the practical ramifications of labeling a city a "disaster city."[8] In other words, once it becomes clear that a city is disaster prone, who should bear the cost of remedying the harm caused by particular disasters as well as preventing future disasters?[9] Should taxes be levied against individuals living in non-disaster areas in order to protect those living in disaster-prone cities?[10]

The answers to these questions lie in the historical background of the particular city.[11] The historical reasons why individuals are forced to live in vulnerable regions should dictate whether or not the burden of rebuilding and of protecting that region should be shared by all or only by those affected.[12] Throughout the course of our

---

4    For the sake of privacy and out of respect, I have used fictitious names.

5    FEMA is an acronym for Federal Emergency Management Agency. *See* FEMA, *Katrina and Rita Breakdown of Manufactured Housing Units as of 8/14/07, available at* http://www.fema.gov/txt/hazard/hurricane/2005katrina/gulf_manufactured_housing_by_ type.rtf. According to FEMA, over 34,000 private citizens still lived in manufactured housing in August 2007. *Id.*

6    *See* Gordon Russell, *On Their Own: In The Absence Of Clear Direction, New Orleanians Are Rebuilding A Patchwork City*, Times-Picayune (New Orleans), August 27, 2006, at 1 (Hurricane Katrina's second anniversary was on August 29, 2007).

7    *See* Neela Banerjee, *In New Orleans, Rebuilding With Faith*, N.Y. Times, October 26, 2007, at 16 (discussing the "patchy" efforts toward restoring New Orleans that has missed a large part of poorer neighborhoods, and the faith-based organizations that have stepped in to provide assistance).

8    *See* Robert J. Rhee, *Catastrophic Risk And Governance After Hurricane Katrina: A Postscript to Terrorism Risk In A Post-9/11 Economy*, 38 Ariz. St. L.J. 581, 597–98 (2006) (discussing the costs of developing a disaster prone area and identifying insurers, the government, victims, or a combination of the three as the candidates for bearing the inherent costs of such development).

9    *See id.*

10    *Id.*

11    *See generally* Andrene Smith, *Different World: Financial Determinants of Well-Being in New Orleans in Black and White*, 14 Geo. J. Poverty L. & Pol'y 179 (2007) (discussing the historical "systematic devastation" that existed in New Orleans long before Katrina, and its effect on the present state of poor New Orleans residents since Katrina).

12    *Id.*

history, people have had various motivations for settling in a region.[13] The search for gold and wealthier pastures, for example, greatly motivated the settlement of the western part of the United States.[14] The desire to escape Jim Crow laws in the South also explains the heavy migration of African Americans to cities such as Chicago and New York.[15] Furthermore, post-Emancipation, former enslaved Africans were forced to settle in less desirable and dangerous parts of cities as a result of occupational and residential segregation.[16] Reported statistics on postwar Pittsburgh, for example, revealed that:

> on the eve of the war, over half of the Black population was concentrated in 3 out of 27 wards . . . The extent of residential segregation from whites varied by ethnic groups. Blacks were least segregated from Rumanians and most segregated from Czechoslovakians. It appears then that the ghetto of Pittsburgh was not a product of the migration of blacks from the South during World War I. Instead black concentrations had existed before the war, and the increase during the war had little measurable effect on the pre-established residential pattern.[17]

This pattern of residential segregation is one that was duplicated across the nation. Along with residential segregation, occupational segregation impacted African Americans' ability to overcome geographic and occupational restrictions. For example, studies of post-World War I Pittsburgh showed that "the war only had a small measurable effect in reducing occupational segregation between black men and white men . . . and had no effect in reducing occupational segregation between white and black women.[18]"

In light of these facts, can we really afford to disregard the past when allocating burdens and responsibilities in the area of disaster prevention and/or post-disaster restoration? No, we cannot. New Orleans's past helps explain the current housing

---

13   *See* Claude de Ville de Goyet & André Griekspoor, *Natural Disasters, The Best Friend of Poverty*, 14 GEO. J. POVERTY L. & POL'Y 61, 66–67 (2007) (discussing that the decision to live in disaster-prone areas is typically based on some need and not necessarily made with knowledge of the risk involved). Goyet and Griekspoor note as an example that some families tend to feel that the risk of disaster in the future is worth living in an area in which they can meet their economic needs. *Id.*

14   Judith L. Maute, *Response: The Value of Legal Archaeology*, 2000 UTAH L. REV. 223, 237.

15   Mary L. Dudziak, *The Court and Social Context in Civil Rights History*, 72 U. CHI. L. REV. 429, 445 (2005) (book review).

16   Phyllis Craig-Taylor, *To Be Free: Liberty, Citizenship, Property, and Race*, 14 HARV. BLACKLETTER L.J. 45, 58–61 (1998).

17   Joe T. Darden, *The Effect of World War I on Black Occupational and Residential Segregation: The Case of Pittsburgh*, 18 J. OF BLACK ST. 297, 308 (1988).

18   *Id.* at 307.

distribution in the city of New Orleans.[19] When one visits New Orleans and witnesses the great discrepancy and inequality existing in the housing distribution throughout the city, one cannot help but marvel at the fact that such topographical

---

19   *See* THE BROOKINGS INST. METRO. POL'Y PROGRAM, NEW ORLEANS AFTER THE STORM: LESSONS FROM THE PAST, A PLAN FOR THE FUTURE 20 (2005), *available at* http://www. brookings.edu/metro/pubs/20051012_NewOrleans.pdf:

. . . how Hurricane Katrina affected particular New Orleanians and their neighborhoods depended intimately on where they lived, and that owed heavily to the metropolitan area's troubling social, economic, and land-use trends in recent decades.

The region's sharp racial and income disparities across geography and topography placed blacks and poor people disproportionately in the flood zone. The region's unbalanced patterns of sprawl and concentrated poverty reinforced that pattern and placed thousands of suburbanites in harm's way along the lakefront corridor . . .

To that extent, the disastrous impact of Hurricane Katrina in 2005 was not inevitable. It represented instead a malign intersection of weather and water with a man-made social and racial topography that had been created over decades.

What happened to greater New Orleans when Katrina struck had a lot to do with what was happening there before the disaster—that is plain. But there remains another link in the chain: What was happening before Katrina owes at least in part to government policies, including federal ones.

Granted, how the disaster played out also reflected the accidents of history, as well as the influence of state and local policy decisions. Most obviously, the city founders' placement of their "inevitable city" in an "impossible" water-logged setting, as Peirce Lewis describes it, determined much of what transpired. Likewise, the legacy of Jim Crow-era municipal ordinances and later deed covenants also mattered, as those codes helped to systematically exclude blacks from better-drained white communities, determining much of the area's pre-Katrina social geography.

Yet for all that, the federal hand in New Orleans' development has been extraordinary, significantly influencing (in partnership with state and local decision-making) how the metropolitan area grew and Katrina's impact. Most notably, the federal influence on regional housing policy—in conjunction with state and local choices—clearly exacerbated racial and ethnic disparities in New Orleans. Likewise, the federal roles in building highways and providing flood protection—again in partnership with state and local transportation departments, land-use regimes, and levee boards— promoted unsustainable growth patterns that accentuated divisions and placed more New Orleanians in harm's way.

*Id.*

inequalities exactly mirror the real social and racial inequalities that have plagued New Orleans for the past two centuries.[20]

In this chapter, I argue that New Orleans' history of geographic segregation mandates that the burden of restoring the city be shared by all United States citizens. One useful method for implementing this nationwide burden sharing would be to levy a uniform one to two percent tax based on individuals' income. This uniform tax would be minimal and would be consistent with other taxes raised for the public good, such as the security taxes levied on air travel post September 11, 2001. The funds accumulated from levying the taxes can be used to address some of the financial needs of individuals in disaster stricken areas. This proposal is consistent with the theory of burden-sharing based on ability to pay,[21] which is sometimes used to allocate proportional responsibility among diverse and differently situated individuals. In the international realm, this principle has sometimes been applied in the face of a need "for nations to share in joint and sometimes costly projects for the common good."[22] Consistent with this practice, the burden-sharing based on ability to pay "rests on equal sacrifice notions . . . and implies either proportional or progressive tax schedules."[23] Comprehensive disaster insurance[24] is one of the solutions that have been advanced to alleviate financial needs in times of disaster. This solution, however, because it shifts the burden of remedying the financial woes caused by disaster onto the disaster stricken individuals, does not fully achieve equity. In shifting the burden of providing remedies to the would-be-harmed individuals, the comprehensive disaster insurance proposal does not account for the role that residential and occupational segregation have had on individuals' choice of geographic residence. This burden should be shared as a way of holding the other cities and states accountable for their silent ratification of these types of geographic segregation. Furthermore, this model of burden-sharing should not be limited to the restoration of New Orleans. It should be implemented in all instances where we can demonstrate that certain groups have historically been pushed out of geographically safe and desirable regions of the United States and have been forced to live in precarious and dangerous areas. This chapter is divided into three parts. In the first, I investigate the ways in which cities have been geographically segregated and continue to be so today through various land-use related municipal decisions. In the second, I consider how geographical

---

20    *See* Daniel A. Farber, *Disaster Law and Inequality*, 25 Law & Ineq. 297, 320 (2007) (stating: "Social disadvantage can kill in very obvious ways during a disaster" and noting President Bush's statement that "the poverty of so many in the region 'has roots in a history of racial discrimination'").

21    Irvin B. Kravis & Michael W.S. Davenport, *The Political Arithmetic of International Burden Sharing*, 71 J. Pol. Econ. 309, 313–14 (1963).

22    *Id.*

23    *Id.* at 313–314 n.14.

24    Howard Kunreuther, *The Case for Comprehensive Disaster Insurance*, 11 J. L. & Econ. 133 (1968).

segregation has contributed to causing disproportionate harm in New Orleans. In the third, I argue that remedying New Orleans' geographical segregation should be one of the primordial goals of the rebuilding efforts and I enunciate a standard that can be used to determine whether rectifying geographical segregation should play a role in disaster prevention as well as in post-disaster rebuilding plans.

## Geographic Segregation and its Manifestation Across the United States

The term "geographic segregation" refers to the ways in which land use regulations and/or public housing distribution plans are often used by local officials, city developers, and federal agencies to create disparate neighborhoods between white residents and residents of color.[25] These disparate neighborhoods are often mostly white neighborhoods versus neighborhoods of color, with white neighborhoods having disproportionately more beneficial access to resources than the non-white neighborhoods.[26]

---

25    *See* J. Peter Byrne & Michael Diamond, *Affordable Housing, Land Tenure, and Urban Policy: The Matrix Revealed*, 34 FORDHAM URB. L.J. 527, 561 (2007) (discussing the effect of the practice of wealthy communities transferring their obligations to provide low income housing to more needy communities; this practice among others promotes geographic segregation).

> Historically, many American suburbs and urban neighborhoods have sought to exclude low-income housing and residents to the extent feasible. Popular fears about reduced property values, increased crime, and higher taxes, combined with racial prejudice, have sometimes fueled zoning and other siting policies that relegate most low-income people to enclaves of poverty within older suburbs or the central city.

*Id.* at 563.

26    *See* Keith N. Hylton & Vincent D. Rougeau, *Lending Discrimination: Economic Theory, Econometric Evidence, and the Community Reinvestment Act*, 85 GEO. L.J. 237, 246 (1996) (describing how racial desegregation also influences the disparate treatment received from lending institutions by inner city non-whites and suburban whites):

> The cause of this inconsistency is that geographic racial segregation and the "credit imbalance" go hand-in-hand. The areas in which banks are failing to serve the credit needs of the community happen to be inner cities inhabited by relatively poor minority groups. If the entire minority population of the United States were dispersed so that its density in each area matched that of the country as a whole, the problem of geographical imbalance in credit allocation probably would not be controversial. Likewise, if the entire poor white population of the country were concentrated in inner cities, there would have been no perception of unfairness in banks lending largely to suburban homebuyers and businesses. It likely would have been determined that the decisions were economically motivated.

*Id.*

Examples of the existence of geographically segregated areas include the 8-Mile Road in Detroit, Michigan[27] and Montgomery, Alabama.[28]

When attempting to distribute burdens and responsibilities in reconstruction of disaster cities, it is important to understand that the economically disadvantaged members of those communities will be affected adversely in disproportion to members belonging to the higher economic echelons.[29] Most economically

---

27    *See* Khaled Ali Beydoun, *Without Color of Law: The Losing Race Against Color Blindness in Michigan*, 12 Mich. J. Race & L. 465, 479–480 (2007), stating:

Detroit's degree of hyper-segregation ranks it among the worst in the country, if not the worst, and Michigan's aggregate racial segregation is quite dire. Michigan's racial polarization exists on various plateaus, but what is most striking is the geographical separation that nearly mirrors the racial segregation. Detroit's spatial and geographic segregation is perhaps its most well-known characteristic today. The oft-celebrated 8-Mile road, which separates Black from White and rich from poor, has effectively succeeded the Motown sound and "The Motor City" as Detroit's lasting image, particularly with the continuing spiral of the automobile industry. . .

Metropolitan Detroit's various neighborhoods and suburbs are sharply homogenous, with individual racial groups virtually monopolizing entire sections. Oakland County's extremely affluent suburbs are predominantly White, while the ethnic enclaves of Detroit house tightly concentrated communities of color. Therefore, although metropolitan Detroit and Michigan statistically appear to be quite racially and ethnically diverse, coexistence and meaningful inter-community interaction is effectively non-existent. In addition, cross-cultural literacy is minimal at best. Naturally harkening the repercussions of the racial powder-keg that was Detroit during the late 1960's race rebellions, the racial demography that ensued is not only a living relic of that chapter of Detroit's recent history, but also an ever present testament of the robust racial tension and racist spirit that continued after the rebellions. . .

*Id.*

28    *See* Robert D. Bullard, *Addressing Urban Transportation Equity in the United States*, 31 Fordham Urb. L.J. 1183, 1192, (2004) (discussing how the dismantling of public transportation in Montgomery contributed to further isolations of poor people of color while highway projects benefiting rich, mostly white property owners increased):

[T]he city dismantled its public bus system—which served mostly blacks and poor people. The cuts were made at the same time that federal tax dollars boosted the construction of the region's extensive suburban highways. The changes in Montgomery took place amid growing racial geographic segregation and tension between white and black members of the city council. The city described its actions "publicly as fiscally necessary, even as Montgomery received large federal transportation subsidies to fund renovation of non-transit improvements."

*Id.*

29    *See* William P. Quigley, *Obstacle to Opportunity: Housing That Working and Poor People Can Afford in New Orleans Since Katrina*, 42 Wake Forest L. Rev. 393, 414–18 (2007) (discussing the massive displacement and inability to participate in reconstruction of the poor affected by disaster). Quigley also notes that more affluent homeowners have

disadvantaged individuals are consistently found in areas with high concentration of public housing or in dilapidated segments of urban enclaves.[30] Consequently, individuals and entities that benefit from the amelioration of suburban sprawl often reside in predominantly white and/or economically affluent neighborhoods.[31] These benefits are conferred at the neglect of the poor neighborhoods.[32]

Geographic exclusion remains an ongoing problem in the United States.[33] More affluent neighborhoods are guaranteed to attract businesses, individuals, and governmental officials willing to contribute their resources to these neighborhoods.[34] In turn, the cycle of prosperity continues as residents and governmental officials eventually reap particular benefits, either by means of increased property values, thriving businesses or by increasing the re-electability of particular officials.[35] Members of those advantaged communities, as well as city and federal officials, should, at the very least, be asked to contribute in higher taxes and mandatory

---

at least the ability to assert their property rights, while the poor have no such rights and rising property values make it nearly impossible for those displaced to return. *Id.* The author suggests that in areas such as post-Katrina New Orleans, the result is a "much smaller, older, whiter, and more affluent city." *Id.* at 416.

30    See Martha Mahoney, *Law and Racial Geography: Public Housing and the Economy in New Orleans*, 42 STAN. L. REV. 1251, 1256–57 (1990) stating:

It is necessary to peel back the usual distinctions and assumptions about what is public and private action in housing and urban development. Some activities, such as funding housing programs and determining tenant eligibility, were clearly areas of federal governmental responsibility. More interesting, however, are questions regarding the impact of governmental policy on the private market, and the ways in which this shaped urban development and the nature of public housing. How did different levels of governmental decision-making mask responsibility for policies and their implementation? What was the impact of the legal rules—for example, the fundamental legality of discrimination in both housing and employment— underlying development? When we think of segregation as a legal regime imposed actively by the state (not merely through an accretion of market exchanges), we tend to focus only on the South. However, the segregatory processes of housing finance and suburban development were national in scope and, at the inception of the public housing program, projects were officially planned and constructed on a segregated basis as far north as New Jersey and Pennsylvania.

*Id.*

31    Smith, *supra* note 11, at 186–88.

32    *Id.*

33    *See, e.g.* Mahoney, *supra* note 30.

34    M. Paige Ammons, Book Note, *Private Governance for All: A Desirable Outcome or a Cause for Concern?* 9 N.Y.U. J. LEGIS. & PUB. POL'Y 503, 514 (2005) (reviewing ROBERT H. NELSON, PRIVATE NEIGHBORHOODS AND THE TRANSFORMATION OF LOCAL GOVERNMENT (2005)) (stating ". . . increased property values and tax base can improve schools and services and attract 'desirable' businesses").

35    Mahoney, *supra* note 30, at 1256–57 (describing the effect of governmental housing policies on economically disadvantaged individuals).

contributions when disadvantaged communities' economic vulnerability cause them to be adversely impacted.[36] Furthermore, the fact that our nation has turned a blind eye to geographic segregation for the past few decades mandates that advantaged communities around the nation assume some proportional economic responsibilities in the rebuilding processes of damaged neighborhoods.[37] In these contexts, the blame should not be placed on the vulnerable residents of these damaged regions.[38] Rather, economically advantaged individuals should be called to question their historic acquiescence to alienating federal policies[39] and be asked to contribute to the amelioration of the distressed neighborhoods.

## Geographic Segregation in New Orleans

New Orleans is a city with a mixed[40] historical legacy.[41] Its culture has been influenced by French,[42] Spanish colonizers,[43] German inhabitants,[44] its original

---

36    *See* Robert M. Finley, *Fixing a Hole Where the Rain Gets in: The Case for a National Homeowner's Insurance Plan*, 14 GEO. J. POVERTY L. & POL'Y 155, 173 (2007) (posing various means to provide for the poor during and in the wake of a disaster: "The catastrophe in New Orleans proved that the failures of government and society to sufficiently address the needs of those at the bottom cannot continue").

37    *See* Sherrie Armstrong Tomlinson, Note, *No New Orleanians Left Behind: An Examination of the Disparate Impact of Hurricane Katrina on Minorities*, 38 CONN. L. REV. 1153, 1178–80 (2006) (noting that the government failed to adequately respond to the needs of the disadvantaged after Hurricane Katrina and discussing the widespread desire to provide some form of post-disaster relief for affected residents). Tomlinson focused particularly on Congressional efforts to establish a "Victim Restoration Fund" similar to that established for victims of 9/11. *Id.*

38    *See id.* at 1186–88, stating:

[The] displacement [of evacuees] . . . will create economic consequences for their new locales as large numbers of evacuees compete with local residents for housing and for employment . . .

Congress can help send the message that African-American citizens must not be disadvantaged and neglected to such a degree again.

*Id.*

39    *See generally* CHARLES ABRAMS, FORBIDDEN NEIGHBORS 205–06 (1955).

40    *See* LYLE SAXON, FABULOUS NEW ORLEANS 73–91, 92–98, 134–47, 160–65 (1952).

41    Donnald McNabb & Louis E. "Lee" Madère, Jr., *A History of New Orleans*, http://www.madere.com/history.html.

42    Barbara L. Bernier, *The Praxis of Church and State in the (Under) development of Women's Religion from France to the New World*, 7 WM. & MARY J. WOMEN & L. 659, 683–84 (2001).

43    *Id.* at 684.

44    *See generally*, http://www.gatewayno.com/history/louisiana.html. *See also* EDWIN A. DAVIS AND RALEIGH A. SUAREZ, LOUISIANA: PELICAN STATE (5th ed. 1985); C.C. LOCKWOOD,

Native American inhabitants, African Americans, as well as Caribbean immigrants.[45] Its geographical location, however, is one of the most unique aspects of New Orleans.[46] It is located on the Mississippi River and is surrounded by water.[47] Although New Orleans' location is very attractive,

> the actual site is miserable, swampy land located in a dangerous, hostile environment, where the Mississippi debouches into the Gulf.[48] The site's problems are numerous.[49] The older and main parts of New Orleans rest on the natural levees of the Mississippi, about fifteen feet above sea level, with the firmest, most solid soil being silt.[50] Most of the modern city is at or below sea level, with the Mississippi usually flowing past the city at a height of ten to fifteen feet above sea level, flooding at twenty feet.[51]

Due to its location and the bowl-like shape of New Orleans, the areas of the city that are geographically safer locations are the ones located on the city's natural levees.[52] Before Hurricane Katrina, many commentators had issued warnings about the city's precarious location.[53] Unfortunately, the events of August 2005 proved those warnings to be fully justified.

---

DISCOVERING LOUISIANA (1986); MILTON B. NEWTON, ATLAS OF LOUISIANA (1972).

45    *Id.*

46    *See* Marva Jo Wyatt, *Ports, Politicians and the Public Trust: The Los Angeles Port Funds Controversy Comes Face to Face with Federal Law*, 9 U.S.F. MAR. L.J. 357, 375–76 (1997) (noting that New Orleans has a unique geographic "location at the gateway of the nation's most significant inland waterway, the Mississippi River").

47    City-data.com, *New Orleans: Geography and Climate*, http://www.city-data.com/us-cities/The-South/New-Orleans-Geography-and-Climate.html.

48    Marcia Johnson, *Addressing Housing Needs in The Post Katrina Gulf Coast*, 31 T. MARSHALL L. REV. 327, 334 (2006), stating:

[f]rom its beginning, New Orleans was a city developing in an area of marshes and swamps that challenged the imagination of builders, architects and engineers alike. The geological problems became exacerbated by the growth of the city in the wake of federal and local government policies that encouraged development in these areas.

*Id.*

49    *See id.*

50    McNabb & Madère, *supra* note 41.

51    *Id.*

52    Robert G. Dean, *New Orleans and The Wetlands of Central Louisiana*, 36 THE BRIDGE 35, 39 (2006) (noting that the best safety system for New Orleans is one that mimics the natural levee system).

53    *See* McNabb & Madère, *supra* note 41, stating:

. . . However, despite all the dangers and hazards of the site, the city was built and has flourished. Since the situation was so excellent, the site has been altered by man to "make do," although not all problems have been banished by twentieth century technology, as witness occasional flooding, hurricanes, and sinking foundations.

*Id.*

The geographical layout of New Orleans proved to be instrumental to the disproportionate levels of damage Hurricane Katrina caused in various parts of New Orleans.[54] Areas located on New Orleans' natural levees, for example, experienced much less damage and have been able to recover more quickly than areas of New Orleans located below sea level, like the lower Ninth Ward.[55] This pattern seems also to correlate with the disproportionate race/class effects that resulted from Hurricane Katrina.[56] Poor and black individuals were left stranded while more affluent and predominantly white individuals were either able to escape New Orleans before the storm or suffered little damage.[57]

History plays a great role in shaping the character and quality of individuals', cities', regions' and countries' lives.[58] If one traces back the historical roots of a region, for example, one can find out why its regions are constantly in debt or why its neighborhoods appear segregated. New Orleans' modern geographic segregation dates back to decades of implementation of nefarious public housing policies.[59] These public housing policies, combined with societal discrimination

---

54  *See* B.E. Aguirre, *Dialectics of Vulnerability and Resilience*, 14 Geo. J. on Poverty L. & Pol'y 39, 52–53 (2007), stating "[t]he historical patterns of urban growth in New Orleans segregated minorities to land areas prone to flooding, such as the Ninth Ward and Mid City. These were also areas of concentrated poverty . . . . Katrina-impacted geographical areas were disproportionately occupied by poor, minority, and African-American populations").

55  *See* The Brookings Inst., *supra* note 19, at 21:
the first major way federal policy exacerbated how the storm affected New Orleans is through its low-income housing policies. Over 60 years, these policies catered to the very poor by concentrating many of them in special enclaves that in New Orleans lay almost exclusively in the lower-lying, more flood-vulnerable sections of the city.
*Id.*

56  *See id.* at 2, "Before the storm, metropolitan New Orleans was a racially divided, low-wage metropolis built on a marsh in hurricane country. Consequently, to replicate such a place more or less as it was now that the storm is over would be not just short-sided and wasteful, but wrong."

57  B.E. Aguirre, *supra* note 54 at 52–53.

58  *See* Mahoney, *supra* note 30 at 1256, stating:
We can only formulate sound policy and create remedies for past wrongs if we understand the crucial forces at work. The key to our findings will be how we conceptualize the inquiry: What we see will depend on the lens through which we look. If we look only at the housing projects themselves, their construction and administration, we will see only government policy. But we also need to see what has happened to the projects—who fills them, why people live there, what other possibilities existed. Housing and employment discrimination, facilitated by both state and private actors, along with a host of development decisions played a role in the evolution of the projects.

59  Smith, *supra* note 11, at 185–87.

against blacks, led to an increase in the number of applicants to housing projects.[60] The housing projects which started as mixed white and black neighborhoods became gradually all black as whites fled to other more desirable housing.[61]

In addition, as New Orleans was forced to desegregate after the Civil Rights Movement, Public Housing officials drastically reduced the number of resources available to tenants.[62] These reductions occurred after the Civil Rights Movement even in formerly all-white, coveted housing projects.[63] For example, the maintenance crew of the Parkchester apartments, an all-white veterans federally funded housing project in the 1950s, was cut from one hundred to twenty-five and even later to ten, according to tenants.[64] Parkchester remained all white and fully staffed until desegregation was implemented pursuant to the Civil Rights Movement.[65] The Parkchester example not only demonstrates the ways in which governmental housing policies negatively impact poor tenants, but it also shows the benefit that those same disparaging policies conferred on white/economically privileged citizens.

### Rebuilding of New Orleans: A Potential Model for Remedying Past Geographic Segregation and for Enunciating a Standard for Requiring the Levying of a Contributory Tax

In rebuilding New Orleans, the task of apportioning responsibility is one that has already proved quite controversial.[66] Over the past three years, the blame has periodically shifted back and forth from local officials to the federal government.[67] A determination, however, of citizen's social responsibility to the rebuilding of New Orleans is equally as important as the allocation of governmental

---

60   *Id.*

61   *See* Mahoney, *supra* note 30, at 1280, stating:
Gradual turnover, not rapid white flight, desegregated the projects. Whites stopped moving in but continued moving out at rates similar to the rates at which they had moved before. Apartment turnover increased the percentage of black families in each project over a period of three to four years . . . Ironically, by the time blacks began to move in, the existing industrial base had diminished rapidly. The port soon modernized to handle containerized cargo, requiring far fewer employees than before. Jobs were available for whites, but not blacks, in the suburbs.

62   Stacy E. Seicshnaydre, *The More Things Change, the More They Stay the Same: In Search of a Just Public Housing Policy Post-Katrina*, 81 Tul. L. Rev. 1263, 1271–72 (2007).

63   Mahoney, *supra* note 30, at 1280.

64   *Id.* at 1281.

65   *Id.*

66   John K. Warren, *Restoring Responsibility and Accountability in Disaster Relief*, 31 Wm. & Mary Envtl. L. & Pol'y Rev. 893, 912–16 (2007).

67   *Id.*

responsibility. In addressing New Orleans' rebuilding conundrum, the focus on the interaction of private citizens' social responsibility toward each other has been lacking.[68] While the charitable donations provided by the rest of the country to New Orleans were good steps, additional steps are necessary in order to determine citizens' responsibility to those affected by disasters.[69] Such determination should take these efforts out of what is usually considered a philanthropic choice to a moral and social imperative that can help generate additional funds for rebuilding projects. In addition, creating a social imperative for the rest of the country to contribute to rebuilding will create a sense of interconnectedness between those affected by the disaster and the rest of the country. It will help align the privileged and the underprivileged to a common goal: rebuilding a thriving community. The levying of the proposed taxes should be accompanied by concrete marketing and informative campaigns designed to explain the reasons for the contributory tax. Post-Hurricane Katrina, there exists within the nation a raised consciousness about the vulnerability of individuals in disaster-prone areas. The marketing campaigns should make the most of this new awareness. The marketing campaigns combined with this raised consciousness may serve to diminish any resentment that the proposed tax might illicit.

In rebuilding and rehabilitating damaged cities, remedying past geographic segregation[70] ought to be one of the primordial goals. If not clearly stated, cities run the risk of reproducing the same segregatory policies that existed pre-disaster.[71] Once the goal is formulated, the various modes of past segregation ought to be identified as well as the steps that need to be taken to eradicate them. Identifying

---

68   Rob Wilcox, Note, *Housing in Post-Katrina New Orleans: Legal Rights and Recourses for Displaced African-American Residents*, 2 Nw. J.L. & Soc. Pol'y 105, 108–09 (2007) (discussing the move of New Orleans' local government toward a plan that partners with the citizenry to develop long-term goals).

69   *See id.*

70   Spencer Overton, *Race, Privilege and Campaign Finance*, 79 N.C.L. Rev. 1541, 1547 (2001). Examples of past geographic segregation include the following:
[T]he Federal Housing Administration (FHA), formed in 1934, promoted a model racially restrictive covenant that whites could use to maintain neighborhood "stability," thereby explicitly promoting segregated home ownership among whites, and discouraging home ownership among non-whites. Federally subsidized mortgages often required that owners incorporate into their deeds racially restrictive covenants, and builders adopted the covenants to ensure that their property qualified for federal insurance. After perpetuating this segregation, the federal government, concerned more about race than any other demographic trend, "consistently gave black neighborhoods the lowest rating for purposes of distributing federally subsidized mortgages." Private lenders often followed the federal system in making loan decisions.
*Id.*

71   *See* Seicshnaydre, *supra* note 62, at 1268, noting that segregatory practices that were common in the past have resurfaced in post-Katrina New Orleans.

the segregatory policies and the steps to prevent duplicating them will force implementers to consciously distribute resources in a fairer fashion than they have done in the past.[72] Identifying past geographic segregatory policies gives notice of a zero-segregation tolerance to the implementers and holds them accountable for disregarding citizens' concerns. The above proposals should, of course, be combined with equitable models of urban redevelopment[73] that are geared toward eradicating residential segregation. When attempting to restore disaster stricken areas, deliberate preventive policies and tactics must be implemented so as to prevent the duplication of the prior system of residential segregation.

Past geographic segregation should be remedied by levying a contributory rebuilding tax on complicit communities as well as requiring contributions from state and federal governmental agencies.[74] The underlying justification for the contributory rebuilding tax is that the policies and actions that facilitated the geographic exclusion of the less privileged transferred benefits to the privileged.[75] Affluent neighborhoods benefit from an increased number of businesses, from allocation of greater funding to public facilities, and increased property values at the expense of the financially disadvantaged, which are generally excluded from these negotiations.[76] The standard for determining tax-based contributions for past geographic segregation should be: 1) proof of the existence of policies pre-disaster that promoted economic and racial disparities between neighborhoods;[77] 2) showing that these policies caused alleged economic and racial disparities and conferred various benefits on specific neighborhoods or certain groups of individuals;[78] and 3) a demonstration of the types of harm that resulted from the existence of such

---

72    *See id.* at 1266, acknowledging the power that the government has to effect a change in discriminatory policies that result in segregation: "segregation in public housing. . . is not the result of random, free-market decision making by public housing consumers, but rather is a vestige of government-sponsored policies and practices reinforced by discrimination in the private market."

73    Michèle Alexandre, *Love Don't Live Here Anymore: Economic Incentives for More Equitable Models of Urban Redevelopment*, 35 B.C. Envtl. Aff. L. Rev. 1 (2008).

74    Kenneth T. Jackson, Crabgrass Frontier: The Suburbanization of the United States 190–218 (1985).

75    Carol Necole Brown & Serena M. Williams, *The Houses That Eminent Domain and Housing Tax Credits Built: Imagining a Better New Orleans*, 34 Fordham Urb. L.J. 689, 718–19 (2007).

76    *Id.*

77    Overton, *supra* note 70. at 1545, stating:
Governmental entities have long used racial identity to define and allocate property rights. Official government action in the form of proclamations, statutes, and court decisions took land from Native Americans based on their racial and cultural identity, and reallocated this property to white private actors. The law contemplated and enforced the appropriation of labor from African Americans through slavery, which primarily benefited white private actors.

78    Brown & Williams, *supra* note 75, at 719.

disparities.[79] Discriminatory impact, not intent, should be sufficient to establish patterns of geographic segregation. Once levied, the tax collected can help fund the rebuilding efforts of the particular disaster city. Such taxes will also ensure that affluent, as well as less affluent individuals become invested in rebuilding healthy neighborhoods. This feeling would encourage privileged residents, who formerly might have been indifferent to poorer neighborhoods, to scrutinize the implementation of housing distribution policies, in order to avoid a recurrence or a raise in the contributory tax.[80]

## Conclusion

Advocating for a levy of additional taxes is admittedly never popular. The proportional and minimal aspects of the proposed contributory tax have the potential of making it more palatable to skeptics. Under the contributory tax model, all individuals would only be taxed a small percentage of their income in times of disaster and only when it is determined that geographic segregation played a crucial one in the choice of residence. In addition, the momentum created by Hurricane Katrina's ravages makes it a ripe time for implementing this proposal. The sharing of responsibility based on ability to pay is a model of proportional responsibility that has been implemented at times in the international area in order to reach as equitable an arrangement among disparate nations.[81]

In this context, distributing proportional responsibility among all ensures that we all become invested in providing adequate remedies for those stricken by disasters. The fact that the proposed contributing tax will be nationally levied, and is likely to be minimal, might make it more acceptable. In addition, the momentum created by the recent disasters has created a ripe environment for attempting such proposals. This requirement will also ensure that contributing citizens would be motivated to place adequate political pressure on governmental officials to use the money levied for its intended use.

---

79   *Id.* at 710–11.

80   Overton, *supra* note 70, at 1546, 1557, stating that ". . . a number of other government policies have promoted racial disparities in property distribution . . ."

81   *See generally* Kravis & Davenport, *supra* note 21.

Chapter 11

# How the New Federalism
# Failed Katrina Victims*

Erin Ryan

## I. Introduction: Toward a System of Checks *and* Balance

In perhaps the most famous rhetorical gesture of the New Federalism,[1] Chief
Justice Rehnquist opined that "[*t*]*he Constitution requires a distinction between*

---

    \*   This chapter contribution is excerpted from: *Federalism and the Tug of War Within:
Seeking Checks and Balance in the Interjurisdictional Gray Area* 66 MD. L. REV. 503
(2007). These excerpts are used with permission of the *Maryland Law Review*. While not
indicated in the text here, these excerpts omit significant portions of the original article at
the end of Parts I and II, after the third paragraph of Part II, and at the end of Part III, where
this chapter concludes. Section numbers and note numbers have been changed from the
original article to reflect their current arrangement in this chapter. See the original article
for the complete discussion. Erin Ryan retains the right to use any and all parts of this work
in the future without further permission from Ashgate Publishing.

    1   In the standard litany of the New Federalism decisions, the Court addressed: (1) the
extent of the federal commerce power, *see, e.g.*, United States v. Morrison, 529 U.S. 598,
627 (2000) (invalidating a section of the Violence Against Women Act of 1994 (VAWA));
United States v. Lopez, 514 U.S. 549, 551 (1995) (overturning the Gun-Free School Zones
Act of 1990 as beyond the scope of commerce power); *but see* Gonzales v. Raich, 545 U.S.
1, 32–33 (2005) (affirming federal authority to proscribe intrastate production and use of
medical marijuana despite contrary state law); (2) the extent of Congress' power under the
post-Civil War Amendments, *see, e.g.*, Bd. of Trs. v. Garrett, 531 U.S. 356, 374 (2001)
(finding that the pecuniary remedy in the Americans with Disabilities Act of 1990 (ADA)
did not satisfy the requirements of congruence and proportionality, which are needed to
establish a valid exercise of Congressional power under the Fourteenth Amendment);
*Morrison*, 529 U.S. at 627 (refusing to sustain a section of the VAWA under Section
Five of the Fourteenth Amendment); Kimel v. Fla. Bd. of Regents, 528 U.S. 62, 82–83
(2000) (concluding that the Age Discrimination in Employment Act of 1967 (ADEA) is
"not 'appropriate legislation' under Section Five of the Fourteenth Amendment"), City of
Boerne v. Flores, 521 U.S. 507, 536 (1997) (finding that the Religious Freedom Restoration
Act of 1993 (RFRA) exceeded Congress' authority under Section Five of the Fourteenth
Amendment); (3) the extent of Congress' ability to command state executive branch and
legislative activity, *see, e.g.*, Printz v. United States, 521 U.S. 898, 935 (1997) (holding
that Congress may not compel state and local law enforcement to implement a federal
regulatory program); New York v. United States, 505 U.S. 144, 161 (1992) (holding that

*what is truly national and what is truly local.*"[2] And yet, even conceding the value of the federalism principles thereby implied, we have yet to seriously reckon with the question that hangs after the rhetorical satiety dissipates: *What about everything in between?* The question makes a simple point about a complex body of jurisprudence—the Supreme Court's controversial "New Federalism" decisions—which, in essence, is that the New Federalism breeds controversy precisely because it imposes an overly simple theoretical model on a complex area of law. Just as such critical legal fields as environmental, public health, and national security law have begun to embrace the need for greater interconnectivity in the management of regulatory problems that span multiple jurisdictions, the New Federalism decisions chart a course toward greater jurisdictional separation—setting the stage for the kind of conflict and confusion that characterized the failed response to Hurricane Katrina. This chapter argues that American federalism can ably weather this storm, but it will require that we (1) recognize the interjurisdictional zone that so complicates the project; (2) better understand the tensions between underlying federalism values there exacerbated; and (3) articulate an administrable means of mediating between them so as to best realize the ultimate objectives of our constitutional design.

This the New Federalism fails to do, as have preceding interpretive movements that espoused similar ideals until they too were overcome by competing federalism concerns for which their theories could not account. In this most recent round, the Court's reasoning has proceeded from a model of state–federal relations based on a severe construction of dual sovereignty, the constitutional principle by which regulatory authority is allocated between the independently-functioning federal and state governments. Under this strict-separationist model, state and federal governments are idealized as operating in mutually exclusive spheres of jurisdiction, without overlap. Regulatory matters are styled as properly local or national concerns, state and federal authority is segregated accordingly, and the Tenth Amendment polices the supposed bright-line boundary between them. The distinguishing characteristics of the New Federalism decisions are premised on this ideal, which stands in contrast to much of the existing map of American government (so characterized by areas of concurrent or interlocking state and

---

the Tenth Amendment forbids Congress from "commandeering" state legislative action under a federal regulatory program); *but see* Reno v. Condon, 528 U.S. 141, 151 (2000) (finding that a federal law regulating state action did not commandeer state legislative and administrative process); and (4) the extent of state sovereign immunity, *see, e.g.*, Alden v. Maine, 527 U.S. 706, 712 (1999) (limiting Congress' power to authorize suits against state governments in state courts); Seminole Tribe v. Florida, 517 U.S. 44, 47 (1996) (limiting Congress' power to authorize suits against state governments in federal courts). For further discussion, see Erin Ryan, *Federalism and the Tug of War Within: Seeking Checks and Balance in the Interjurisdictional Gray Area*, 66 MD. L. REV. 503, pt. III.A., at 539–54 (2007) [hereinafter *Tug of War*].

    2   *Morrison*, 529 U.S. at 617–18 (emphasis added).

federal jurisdiction that its dual sovereignty has been likened to the intertwining layers of a marble cake[3]). Nevertheless, the New Federalism's approach has altered the American federalism discourse, changing the way we think about the allocation of state and federal authority in modern regulatory endeavors.

Although they have attracted intense academic attention, these changes are hardly esoteric matters of interest only to judges and law professors. For better or worse (and in different respects, probably both), they would alter the way that Congress approaches lawmaking,[4] and the way that the Executive approaches administration.[5] At least in the latter case, the answer may well be "for worse" because, by many accounts, the ideals associated with the New Federalism's project of better differentiating state from national authority may have contributed to the delayed federal response to the devastating aftermath of Hurricane Katrina in New Orleans. News reports indicate that, as pressure mounted on the White House to assume responsibility for key tasks not performed at the local level, the federal response was paralyzed as senior advisors stalled in debate over the federalism implications of providing the needed assistance.[6] This chapter takes the Katrina aftermath as a primary example of how the New Federalism's ideological

---

3    MORTON GRODZINS, THE AMERICAN SYSTEM 8, 60–153 (Daniel J. Elazar ed., 1966).

4    Whether the lines of influence primarily run from the Court's decisions to Congressional legislation or vice versa is a chicken-and-egg problem over which much ink has been spilled. Still, when state actions or statutes are invalidated by the Supreme Court, Congress often seeks to repair the infirmity with conforming legislation. *See, e.g.*, Military Commissions Act of 2006, Pub. L. No. 109-366, 120 Stat. 2600 (2006) (authorizing the President to prosecute enemy combatants in military tribunals in direct response to *Hamdan v. Rumsfeld*, 126 S. Ct. 2749 (2006), which invalidated the practice for lack of Congressional authorization). The Court's federalism jurisprudence appears similarly motivating, as suggested by the care with which the 1994 Congress crafted the "federal interest" provision of the VAWA (albeit unsuccessfully, see *Morrison*, 529 U.S. at 613–14), presumably in response to the anticipated critique in *Lopez* of the Gun-Free School Zones Act of 1990 for failure to assert a constitutionally valid federal interest. (After a multiplicity of amendments, the VAWA was passed by the House and Senate in late August and signed into law on September 13, 1994, Pub. L. No. 103-322, 108 Stat. 1796 (1994), before *Lopez* was decided in April 1995, but after the relevant briefing had been submitted on June 2, 1994 (Brief for the United States, 1994 WL 242541), July 19, 1994 (Brief for Respondent, 1994 WL 396915), and August 17, 1994 (Reply Brief for the United States, 1994 WL 449691).) *But see Boerne*, 521 U.S. at 536 (invalidating Congress' attempt to reverse the effect of a prior Supreme Court decision with the Religious Freedom Restoration Act of 1993). Although it is difficult to assert a definitive causal direction in the dialectic between legislative and judicial decision-making, the New Federalism's ideals seek to impact decision-making at both levels, and have been embraced by decision-makers at both levels. *See Tug of War, supra* note 1, at 539–54.

5    *See Tug of War, supra* note 1, at 522–39 (discussing the role of federalism considerations in the federal response to Hurricane Katrina).

6    *See id.*, at 522–39. Interestingly, the public castigation that the federal government received for its failed Katrina response suggests that the New Federalism has *not* changed

trajectory[7] can obstruct interjurisdictional problem-solving by confusing, rather than clarifying, the proper roles of national and local regulatory authorities. But the Katrina aftermath is only the most mediagenic example of confusion spawned by the New Federalism's intolerance for interjurisdictional complexity. Similar confusion has arisen in other like contexts, ranging from environmental to antiterrorism programs, resulting in uncertain policymaking efforts and New Federalism-inspired legal challenges to regulatory partnerships that link state and federal actors in related spheres of authority.[8]

Challenging the strict-separationist premise that all regulatory issues *can* be clearly characterized as matters of either local or national jurisdiction, this chapter suggests that some regulatory targets are better understood within a separate, interjurisdictional sphere that legitimately implicates both local and national responsibility. As defined here, an "interjurisdictional regulatory problem"[9] is one whose meaningful resolution demands action from both state and federal regulatory authorities, either because neither has all of the jurisdiction necessary to address the problem as a legal matter,[10] or because the problem so implicates both local and national expertise that the same is true as a factual matter.[11] Because assigning responsibility for management of such a problem to the exclusive attention of either the local or national government is an ultimately arbitrary endeavor,[12] the better criteria for federalism consideration is whether regulation

---

the way that large sectors of the public think about the respective roles of state and federal government.

7    The strict-separation ideal extrapolated from the New Federalism decisions exceeds their doctrinal impact at present, and we continue to operate from within a predominantly cooperative federalism system. *See id.*, at 637–42. Nevertheless, it has already infiltrated the regulatory mindset of policymakers. *See id.*, at 522–39. As such, the strict-separationist trajectory of New Federalism warrants scrutiny now, before its culmination further complicates our ongoing navigation of good governance.

8    *See, e.g., id.*, at 577–80.

9    In recognition that not every public quandary ranks among the "regulatory problems" with which we are here concerned, I note that for the purposes of this piece, "regulatory problems" are those associated with the classic targets anticipated by administrative law—such as market failures, negative externalities, and other collective action problems reasonably susceptible to efficient resolution by government activity. *See id.*, at 567–96.

10    An example of this type of de jure interjurisdictional regulatory problem is the regulation of stormwater pollution. *See id.*, at 572–80.

11    Examples of such de facto interjurisdictional regulatory problems include the regulation of air pollution and domestic efforts to combat terrorist attacks from abroad. *See id.*, at 580–84.

12    Establishing precise boundaries around the category of interjurisdictional regulatory problems invites disagreement, ranging from dispute over whether a given problem truly implicates both local and national concern to dispute over whether the given problem is truly amenable to a regulatory solution. I leave such legitimate arguments aside for the purpose of this piece, which introduces an interjurisdictional conceptual framework to the federalism discourse through a sample of problems that meet the criteria in a relatively

within this interjurisdictional "gray area" ultimately advances or detracts from the full panoply of federalism values that underscore Tenth Amendment dual sovereignty. But the New Federalism approach vindicates some of these values to the exclusion of others, thus threatening the ability of state and federal government to cope with complex problems in adherence to a strict-separationist vision that misses the full federalism target.

Interjurisdictional problems pose special difficulty for federalism because their circumstances exacerbate inherent tension between the underlying values of American federalism, principally the promotion of government accountability, the checks and balances that dual sovereignty affords against tyranny, and the socially desirable benefits associated with the protection of local autonomy (including regional diversity, regulatory efficiency, and innovation yielded by interjurisdictional competition). Each value represents an underlying principle of good government that we ask federalism to help us realize, and each is claimed in support of the need for judicially enforceable federalism constraints.[13] But in addition to these more familiar values, the federalism premise of as-localized-as-possible governance (or "subsidiarity") incorporates an often overlooked problem-solving value. Directing that public decision-making take place at the most local level *possible* implies the most local level with *capacity*—or the most local level of government that may actually be able to solve the problem. Tensions exist between the satisfaction of each of these values in any given model of federalism, but a central federalism tension is located between the anti-tyranny "check-and-balance" value and the underappreciated "problem-solving" value.[14]

Indeed, the historic progression of the various models of federalism that informed Supreme Court interpretation over the twentieth century reflects a pendulum-like attempt to achieve the proper balance between underlying federalism values, each model perhaps overcompensating for the excesses of its predecessor.[15] After the Great Depression crippled the capacity of state and local governments to cope with unprecedented levels of social and economic despair, the Supreme Court adopted a model of federalism that exalted the problem-solving value at the expense of the check-and-balance value to approve pragmatic New Deal legislative programs that expanded federal jurisdiction into traditionally local arenas. Cooperative federalism, the predominant model of federalism since World War II, recovers some of the balance through a partnership-based approach to regulation in areas

---

uncontroversial manner. They are uncontroversial because they address matters that have remained targets of regulatory response over time, and because most would agree that they implicate the obligation or expertise of both a local and a national actor. As discussed in Part IV of *Tug of War*, these include a variety of environmental and land use problems, natural disaster management issues, public health crises, and counterterrorism and national security matters. *See id.*, at 567–96.

13   *See id.*, at 596–629.

14   *See id.*, at 620–28.

15   *See id.*, at 629–43.

of interjurisdictional overlap, allowing state and federal governments to take responsibility for interlocking components of a collaborative regulatory program. However, cooperative federalism has also been criticized as an overly pragmatic model that insufficiently protects anti-tyranny values.[16] Responding to concerns that cooperative federalism is, at best, undertheorized (and at worst, more coercive than collaborative), the New Federalism reestablishes the supremacy of the check-and-balance value over all others in an effort to bolster the line between state and federal authority against pressures (some perhaps political, others genuinely interjurisdictional) that would blur the boundary.

Demanding attention from both a national and local actor, interjurisdictional problems do blur that boundary, pitting concerns about tyranny and needs for pragmatism against one another. But it is arguably the tension between federalism's check-and-balance and problem-solving values that has made our system such a robust form of government—enabling it to adjust for changing demographics, technologies, and expectations without losing its essential character. A model of federalism that engages these tensions is a model that can endure. But the New Federalism's focus on preserving bright-line boundaries above all else renders it unable to effectively mediate the competition between federalism values, contributing to a governmental ethos that obstructs even desirable regulatory activity in the interjurisdictional gray area (such as federal initiative that might have been taken in the aftermath of Hurricane Katrina). Taken to its extreme, the New Federalism model can lead to jurisdictional gridlock, posing obstacles to novel approaches to interjurisdictional regulatory partnerships[17] and discouraging efficient responses to some of society's most pressing problems.[18]

In this ironic respect, the New Federalism simply does what New Deal federalism did in the opposite direction—shortchanging the problem-solving value in the name of the check-and-balance value, which it mistakes for federalism generally. In so doing, the New Federalism lays too proprietary a claim to the essence of American federalism itself—implying that faithfulness to the Constitution requires its approach and *only* its approach, when federalism is really a more variegated institution. Exploration of how different models of American federalism have variously prioritized different values over time reveals

---

16    *See id.*, at 637–42.

17    For example, the innovative state–federal partnership created by the Clean Water Act's Phase II Stormwater Rule, though negotiated with the participation of the states over a ten-year period, was challenged fiercely (though unsuccessfully) on Tenth Amendment grounds. *See* Envtl. Def. Ctr., Inc. v. EPA, 344 F.3d 832, 843–45 (9th Cir. 2003); National Pollutant Discharge Elimination System—Regulations for Revision of the Water Pollution Control Program Addressing Storm Water Discharges, 64 Fed. Reg. 68,722, 68,724, 68,743 (Dec. 8, 1999); *see also Tug of War*, *supra* note 1, at 577–80.

18    For example, federalism-related concerns may have frustrated a more efficient regulatory response during the aftermath of Hurricane Katrina. *See Tug of War*, *supra* note 1, at 522–39.

New Federalism's approach as merely one alternative among many, each true to constitutional design in its unique vindication of the fundamental federalism values. Like so many other constitutional concepts, then, federalism ultimately invites interpretive choices.[19] As such, we should invest in the jurisprudential development of a federalism model that more explicitly (and capably) balances all competing values than have New Deal federalism, cooperative federalism, and New Federalism, enabling a structure of governance that best realizes the demands we make upon our political institutions.

---

19  Of course, some argue that the only valid interpretation is that of the original architects of the Constitution, and that anything else reflects "judicial activism," or inappropriate judicial aggrandizement. *See, e.g.*, Raoul Berger, Government by Judiciary 283–84, 363–70 (1997); Antonin Scalia, A Matter of Interpretation: Federal Courts and the Law 46 (1997); Robert H. Bork, *The Constitution, Original Intent, and Economic Rights*, 23 San Diego L. Rev. 823, 824–25 (1986); Edwin Meese III, *Toward a Jurisprudence of Original Intent*, 11 Harv. J.L. & Pub. Pol'y 5, 7 (1988); William H. Rehnquist, *The Notion of a Living Constitution*, 54 Tex. L. Rev. 693, 698 (1976); Antonin Scalia, *Originalism: The Lesser Evil*, 57 U. Cin. L. Rev. 849 (1989). If textual directives prove problematic over time (for example, the original Constitution's tacit approval of slavery or dated plans for federal taxation), the appropriate response is not to engage in interpretive "subterfuge" but to correct the defect by formal amendment (for example, the Thirteenth and Sixteenth Amendments, respectively). U.S. Const. amend. XIII, XVI. *See* William Van Alstyne, *Interpreting* This *Constitution: The Unhelpful Contributions of Special Theories of Judicial Review*, 35 U. Fla. L. Rev. 209 (1983).

Scholars from opposing schools of thought argue that all constitutional interpretive choices—including "originalist" interpretations—are equally subject to the hermeneutic biases of the interpreter by virtue of the pockets of ambiguity inherently embedded within written texts. *See, e.g.*, Reva B. Siegel, *She the People: The Nineteenth Amendment, Sex Equality, Federalism, and the Family*, 115 Harv. L. Rev. 947, 1032–34 (2002) (asserting that incorporation of historical understanding into modern constitutional interpretation is an "irreducibly normative" endeavor); Peter J. Smith, *Sources of Federalism: An Empirical Analysis of the Court's Quest for Original Meaning*, 52 UCLA L. Rev. 217, 287 (2004) (reviewing the "vast body of primary historical materials . . . that support a spectrum of constitutional meaning" and the accordingly futile project of constraining judicial interpretation with originalist principles); *see also* Stephen R. Munzer & James W. Nickel, *Does the Constitution Mean What It Always Meant?*, 77 Colum. L. Rev. 1029, 1032–33 (1977); Robert Post, *Theories of Constitutional Interpretation*, in Representations 13 (1990). Although none dispute the proper recourse to amendment for correcting clearly defective textual provisions, they argue that some degree of interpretive lawmaking is a necessary part of the judicial function in applying vague constitutional commands to new controversies. *See, e.g.*, Laurence H. Tribe, Comment, *in* Scalia, A Matter of Interpretation, *supra*, at 68–72 (discussing the problem of choosing the correct "level of abstraction" at which constitutional clauses should be construed). This chapter proceeds from the latter assumption in finding deliberate interpretive space in the model of dual sovereignty implied by the Constitution, most directly in the text of the Tenth Amendment.

There is, of course, a wide range of views on what those demands should rightly be. Some advocate for ambitious regulatory problem-solving,[20] others for a government that limits itself to as little interference with private activity as possible.[21] Some, chafing against New Federalism excess, have suggested that American federalism is itself an anachronistic artifact of earlier times, which may as well fade into the same obscurity to which the distinction between law and equity has retired.[22] But the suggestion is as unlikely as it would be unwise.[23] In the United States, the real issue is not *whether* federalism, but *what kind* of federalism best serves the hopes and needs that we hang on the continued vitality of our system of government. My first proposition is thus positivist but value-neutral: regardless of our competing views on what constitutes good government, we should recognize that the interpretive model of federalism we embrace is linked with this determination, as different blends of the foundational federalism values will foster distinctive characteristics in governance.

Acknowledging that reasonable minds will disagree on the characteristics of ideal government, I nevertheless take a normative stance in my criticism of the New Federalism ideals, making this chapter's second proposition less value-neutral. In critiquing strict-separationist dual sovereignty's failure to account for the interjurisdictional gray area, I proceed from the assumption that good government should address those market failures, negative externalities, and other collective action problems that individuals are ill-equipped to resolve on their own

---

20    *E.g.*, RICHARD J. LAZARUS, THE MAKING OF ENVIRONMENTAL LAW (2004) (endorsing regulatory approach to many environmental problems).

21    *E.g.*, MURRAY N. ROTHBARD, FOR A NEW LIBERTY: THE LIBERTARIAN MANIFESTO (rev. ed. 1978).

22    For example, Edward Rubin has observed that

[f]ederalism is indeed worth discussing; it is a basic, truly fundamental question of political organization. Fortunately, the United States has not needed to confront this question, as a matter of practical politics, for nearly a century. That is what makes it so much fun to talk about. Like a healthy person talking about medical care, a congenitally thin person talking about dieting, or a rich person talking about money problems, we can lavish exuberant attention on the subject without any sense of urgency or danger. . . . [T]here is also an intrinsic pleasure in talking about how much one has of something that one does not need, and that other people desperately require. Edward L. Rubin, *The Fundamentality and Irrelevance of Federalism*, 13 GA. ST. U. L. REV. 1009, 1010 (1997).

23    *See* Vicki C. Jackson, *Federalism and the Uses and Limits of Law:* Printz *and Principle?*, 111 HARV. L. REV. 2180, 2213–23 (1998) (arguing in favor of American federalism's continued vitality despite cogent criticism of the New Federalism approach in the Tenth Amendment context); *cf.* Edward L. Rubin & Malcolm Feeley, *Federalism: Some Notes on a National Neurosis*, 41 UCLA L. REV. 903, 951 (1994) (conceding, despite skepticism, that the states serve beneficial roles as mechanisms of decentralization and that American federalism might retain value for reasons of historical and cultural identity).

and that so threaten public welfare as to warrant a regulatory response[24] despite the libertarian-highlighted risks that inherently attend the exercise of governmental authority.[25] As we face interjurisdictional problems that meet these criteria, we deserve a model of federalism that anticipates the competition between federalism values that will arise in the interjurisdictional gray area so invisible to New Federalism.

## II. The Stakes: How the New Federalism Failed Katrina Victims

*A. Which Federalism?*

Roughly defined, federalism refers to a system of government in which power is divided between a central authority and regional political sub-units, each with authority to directly regulate its citizens. Federal governments worldwide display a variety of structural choices by which this design is accomplished, but domestic federalism is well-defined in the concurrent sovereign authority of the central United States government and the fifty states, commonly referred to as "dual sovereignty."[26] Americans are citizens of both the United States and the individual states in which they reside, and subject to the respective laws of each. The Constitution enumerates those powers under which the federal government is authorized to make law (e.g., the commerce power, the spending power, and the

---

24    The most basic examples include the provision of common defense, the policing of border-crossing harms, and the facilitation of efficiency in commerce. *See supra* note 9; *Tug of War*, *supra* note 1, pt. IV.A., at 567–84.

25    *E.g.*, ROTHBARD, *supra* note 21, at 45–69 (outlining the dangers of state power accumulation for private property rights and personal freedoms).

26    *See, e.g.*, Douglas Laycock, *Protecting Liberty in a Federal System: The US Experience*, *in* PATTERNS OF REGIONALISM AND FEDERALISM: LESSONS FOR THE UK 119, 119 (Jörg Fedtke & Basil S. Markesinis eds., 2006) ("Every federalism responds to a unique history, and thus every federalism is different from every other."). For example, the European Union, Canada, India, and Switzerland are all federalism-based polities whose federations exhibit unique characteristics. The American dual sovereignty principle is well illustrated in *Collector v. Day*, in which the Supreme Court stated that:

> The general government, and the States, although both exist within the same territorial limits, are separate and distinct sovereignties, acting separately and independently of each other, within their respective spheres. The former in its appropriate sphere is supreme; but the States within the limits of their powers not granted, or, in the language of the tenth amendment, "reserved," are as independent of the general government as that government within its sphere is independent of the States. 78 U.S. (11 Wall.) 113, 124 (1870).

war power),[27] and the states may regulate in any area not preempted by legitimate federal law.[28]

Yet the fact that Americans are citizens of two separate sovereigns does not resolve the precise contours of the relationship between the two. Constitutional analysis sometimes reveals pockets of textual ambiguity that must be resolved by application of some interpretive federalism theory—a model that describes how the given federal system should work.[29] Accordingly, there is more to the variety among models of federalism than the specific array of regional sub-units around a centrality. Even within a single structural polity, conceptual variation may exist in construing the details of the relationship between sovereigns and the framework of federalism designed to protect it. This has been aptly demonstrated in the United States by the Supreme Court's ongoing experimentation with federalism constraints, in pursuit of its evolving vision of the dual sovereignty that is mandated but incompletely described by the Constitution.

American dual sovereignty is implied in various constitutional provisions that refer to the separate states,[30] but it is most encapsulated as a constitutional directive in the Tenth Amendment's affirmation that "[t]he powers not delegated to the United States by the Constitution, nor prohibited by it to the States, are reserved to the States respectively, or to the people."[31] This statement establishes that the Constitution (1) delegates some powers to the federal government, (2) prohibits some to the states, and (3) reserves powers that fit in neither of these two sets to the states (or perhaps the people). Standing alone, the Tenth Amendment's only unique contribution is to suggest that there are at least some unspecified powers that belong wholly to the states. But it does not specify what these are; we can only parse them out by negative inference to other constitutional provisions that specifically delegate federal authority or proscribe state action. It further (and unremarkably) affirms that the Constitution delegates some authority to the federal government, and, read together with the inherently vague Supremacy Clause,[32] suggests that at least some of this authority may be wielded

---

27   U.S. Const. art. I, § 8.

28   U.S. Const. amend. X.

29   *See supra* note 19.

30   *E.g.*, U.S. Const. art. IV, § 4 ("The United States shall guarantee to every State in this Union a Republican Form of Government . . . .").

31   U.S. Const. amend. X.

32   U.S. Const. art. VI, cl. 2 ("This Constitution, and the Laws of the United States which shall be made in Pursuance thereof; and all Treaties made, or which shall be made, under the Authority of the United States shall be the supreme Law of the Land; and the Judges in every State shall be bound thereby, any Thing in the Constitution or Laws of any State to the Contrary notwithstanding."). The Supremacy Clause tells us that federal law is "supreme," but from there to field preemption nevertheless requires an interpretive leap.

exclusively at the federal level, preempting contrary state law. However, neither the Tenth Amendment nor the Supremacy Clause nor any other provision in the Constitution decisively resolves whether there may also be regulatory spaces in which both the states and the federal government may operate (if they have not been withdrawn from either's commission by express constitutional limitation or purposeful preemption). Drawing the conclusion that such overlapping regulatory space exists requires an interpretive leap, but so does the extrapolation of wholly mutually exclusive spheres of authority.[33] Either conclusion demands application of some exogenous theory about what American federalism means, or what, in essence, federalism is *for*. That we have relied on one theory or another to resolve the matter (in ways that may eventually come to seem obvious if only by virtue of their repetition) does not negate the role of federalism theory in getting us to that point.

What, then, is federalism "for"? Ultimately, polities turn to federalism to promote a set of governance values that they hope federalism will yield. Foremost among them are the preservation of individual liberties through checks and balances on accountable sovereign power[34] and the promotion of diversity and competition associated with local autonomy,[35] both tempered with a healthy regard for the role of government as the superintendent of regional collective action problems.[36] Nevertheless, these values are suspended in a network of tension with one another. Preserving local autonomy can conflict with the protection of individual liberty. Centralized resolution of collective action problems can undermine checks and balances. In protecting its preferred vision of dual sovereignty, each interpretive approach advances the fundamental federalism values in some way, but the tension between them means that emphasizing one value may result in the de-emphasis of another.[37] In deciding which values take precedence under what circumstances, we

---

33   *See Tug of War*, *supra* note 1, text accompanying notes 153–59; *see also* Jackson, *supra* note 23, at 2191 (noting that the Constitution's assumption that states would continue to exist "does not tell us whether states can be required to help carry out federal law").

34   *See, e.g.*, *New York*, 505 U.S. at 181 ("[T]he Constitution divides authority between federal and state governments for the protection of individuals. . . . [F]ederalism secures to citizens the liberties that derive from the diffusion of sovereign power." (internal quotation marks omitted)).

35   *See, e.g.*, Gregory v. Ashcroft, 501 U.S. 452, 458 (1991) (noting that federalism "increases opportunity for citizen involvement in democratic processes; it allows for more innovation and experimentation in government; and it makes government more responsive by putting the States in competition for a mobile citizenry").

36   *See Tug of War*, *supra* note 1, at 596–629.

37   *See id.*, at 596–643.

choose, consciously or not, among different models of federalism that then inform our lawmaking and adjudication.[38]

In the United States, political discourse has tended more and more to treat the ideals of the diffusion of sovereign power and the pragmatic concerns of problem-solving as a federalism thesis and antithesis—principles in opposition to one another, rather than complementary elements of the overall federalism project. Regardless, a federalism model that subordinates pragmatic concerns to the maintenance of formalist boundaries between the reservoirs of state and federal power is clearly a legitimate political choice. Despite much of the rhetoric attending the New Federalism, however, it is not the *only* interpretive possibility, nor the only model true to the principles enshrined in the Constitution.[39] The same principles support a variety of other models, many of which have been experimented with over the course of our nation's history.[40] Each serves a slightly different understanding of the dual sovereignty relationship, promises a slightly different construction of governmental priorities, and thereby leads to slightly different substantive ends.

For interpreters of the American Constitution, then, the relevant choice is not one between federalism and non-federalism, but of *which federalism*—which model of federalism best promotes the kind of governance that we seek. These are, of course, the real stakes at hand. And so it could certainly be that, in the end, most Americans want exactly the kind of government promoted by the New Federalism model, although popular reaction to the Katrina disaster raises serious questions about such a proposition.[41] Ultimately, I argue that the New Federalism model is not the best available choice, given the concerns raised here about its ability to contend with the interjurisdictional problems that confront all levels of government. Either way, however, we should at least recognize the true nature of

---

38   One might fairly ask, "[w]ho is the 'we' of whom you speak?" James Boyd White, *Law as Language: Reading Law and Reading Literature*, 60 TEX. L. REV. 415, 442 (1982) (internal quotation marks omitted); *see id.* at 442–43 ("In place of the constituted 'we,' that it is the achievement of our past to have given us, we are offered an unconstituted 'we,' or a 'we' constituted on the pages of law journals."). As aforementioned, this chapter argues that American federalism, as set forth in the text and structure of the Constitution, invites interpretive choices by judges, legislators, and policymakers. *See supra* note 19 and accompanying text. The subject thus warrants consideration by all participants in the legal community, though it is ultimately the job of the Supreme Court to provide definitive interpretive guidance to the rest (as the chapter recommends).

39   See generally David J. Barron, *Fighting Federalism with Federalism: If It's Not Just a Battle Between Federalists and Nationalists, What Is It?*, 74 FORDHAM L. REV. 2081 (2006) (discussing how different Supreme Court justices have implicitly invoked different models of federalism in justifying their analyses).

40   *See Tug of War, supra* note 1, at 629–43.

41   *See id.*, at 522–39 (discussing the relationship between federal restraint during the Katrina aftermath and New Federalism ideals); *infra* note 92 (detailing public disapproval of federal restraint during the relief effort).

the choice as one among alternatives—and make that choice with attention to the stakes involved. After all, this is not merely the stuff of political grandstanding and academic navel-gazing; the costs of our choices about federalism are very much extracted at the level of everyday lives (in the most tragic of cases, many at a time).

For this reason, our discussion proceeds to a consideration of the stakes of the federalism debate, illustrating the kinds of governmental decision-making that take place in the shadow of the model of federalism that we choose. The catastrophic aftermath of Hurricane Katrina in New Orleans provides such a scenario, one that called for governmental response from the most local to the most national level, requiring regulatory decision-makers to contend with questions about how federalism principles should dictate their interaction. Surely, the spectacularly failed response owes much to the unprecedented demands of the circumstances (and perhaps to more ordinary problems of incompetence) that have nothing to do with federalism. And yet, the additional overlay of federalism issues helped further derail what might otherwise have been a more effective response, thanks to uncertainty among state and federal actors about their respective roles. This uncertainty appears to have stemmed from a set of beliefs about the proper exercise of state and federal authority coincident with the strict-separationist philosophy of the New Federalism revival.

## B. Federalism and Katrina

Of all that was striking during the national tragedy of the Hurricane Katrina aftermath, a few things stood out: the shameful images of abject poverty within the United States,[42] the inspiring heroism of individuals who rose to the occasion, the staggering force of nature's fury, and the stunning failure of the most powerful nation on earth to respond effectively to the foreseeable effects of a predicted storm. But if we shouldn't have been surprised by the poverty, heroism, or storm surge, the latter failure was hard to fathom—and by many accounts, proceeded from unprecedented confusion among federal, state, and local responders regarding the allocation of their roles and responsibilities, and how to proceed in the face of this uncertainty.[43]

---

42 Equally shameful were the lingering dynamics of racial unfairness apparent in these images of abject poverty. *See, e.g.*, Representative John Lewis, *"This is a National Disgrace,"* NEWSWEEK, Sept. 12, 2005, at 52 ("It's so glaring that the great majority of people crying out for help are poor, they're black. There's a whole segment of society that's being left behind.").

43 *See, e.g.*, Joe Whitley et al., *Homeland Security After Hurricane Katrina: Where Do We Go from Here?*, 20 NAT. RESOURCES & ENV'T 3 (2006) (describing the failures of state and federal coordination during the Katrina response).

*1. "Operating System Crash" by the National Response Plan*    According to eyewitness accounts and primary documents cataloging the relevant events,[44] the response to Katrina was characterized by failures in coordinated command and communications between local, state, federal, and volunteer responders, as authorities struggled to determine what the federalism directives in applicable federal laws mandated regarding whom should be responsible for which parts of the response. Revised after the 9/11 attacks and issued in 2004, the new National Response Plan (NRP) recognizes that saving lives and protecting the health of the public are top priorities of incident management.[45] However, the NRP also demarcates that, in emergency situations, states will be responsible for the implementation of police powers traditionally within their purview (such as local law enforcement, fire protection, and delivery of food and shelter), and the federal government will act in a supportive capacity, responding to specific requests by state authorities for assistance.[46]

Although the Federal Emergency Management Agency's (FEMA) seeming paralysis in the face of the post-Katrina crisis may suggest incompetent leadership,[47] it is also attributable to a federalism-related "operating system crash" under the NRP, which faltered just as software does when unable to parse unanticipated inputs. According to the NRP's federalism directive, federal authorities could not act preemptively, lest they tread in the protected realm of state sovereign authority.[48] However, state authorities were unable to make the specific requests for assistance anticipated under the NRP. Local infrastructure was so damaged by the storm that communications were down,[49] and state and local authorities were apparently so overwhelmed themselves that they did not know what to ask

---

44    For a compilation of documents collected by congressional investigators, including a conference call transcript between state and federal authorities before Katrina struck New Orleans, *see* Eric Lipton, *Key Documents Regarding the Government Response to Katrina*, N.Y. TIMES, http://www.nytimes.com/ref/national/nationalspecial/10katrina-docs.html (last visited Mar. 15, 2007).

45    U.S. DEP'T OF HOMELAND SEC., NATIONAL RESPONSE PLAN 6 (2004) [hereinafter NRP]. For an excellent review of the federal statutory framework dictating federal involvement in disaster response, *see* DANIEL A. FARBER & JIM CHEN, DISASTERS AND THE LAW: KATRINA AND BEYOND 24–56 (2006).

46    NRP, *supra* note 45, at 8, 15.

47    In particular, former FEMA Director Michael Brown did not fare well in media accounts of his performance. *See, e.g.*, Paul Krugman, Op-Ed., *The Effectiveness Thing*, N.Y. TIMES, Feb. 6, 2006, at A23 (characterizing Brown's performance as "ludicrous"); *see also* Evan Thomas et al., *How Bush Blew It*, NEWSWEEK, Sept. 19, 2005, at 30, 38 (questioning Brown's credentials for appointment as head of FEMA).

48    *See* NRP, *supra* note 45, at 9.

49    The *New York Times* described the crippling effect on the National Guard:
The morning Hurricane Katrina thundered ashore, Louisiana National Guard commanders thought they were prepared to save their state. But when 15-foot floodwaters swept into their headquarters, cut their communications and disabled their high-water trucks, they had their hands full just saving themselves.

for.[50] It may also be that state authorities were simply unprepared or incompetent to play the role anticipated of them by the NRP.[51] But as former FEMA Director Michael Brown would later testify before Congress in defense of his agency's decision-making: "The role of the federal government in emergency management is generally that of coordinator and supporter. . . . [a role] fully supported by the basic concept of federalism, recognizing that the sovereign states have primary responsibility for emergency preparedness and response in their jurisdictions."[52] Thus, as Katrina bore down on the Gulf Coast, these departures from the NRP's script left regulatory responders struggling to decipher, in essence, which parts of the response effort were the proper purview of the state, and which the proper purview of the federal government.[53]

---

For a crucial 24 hours after landfall on Aug. 29, Guard officers said, they were preoccupied with protecting their nerve center from the waves topping the windows at Jackson Barracks and rescuing soldiers who could not swim. The next morning, they had to evacuate their entire headquarters force of 375 guardsmen by boat and helicopter to the Superdome.

It was an inauspicious start to the National Guard's hurricane response, which fell so short that it has set off a national debate about whether in the future the Pentagon should take charge immediately after catastrophes.

Scott Shane & Thom Shanker, *When Storm Hit, National Guard Was Deluged Too*, N.Y. TIMES, Sept. 28, 2005, at A1.

50   WHITE HOUSE, THE FEDERAL RESPONSE TO HURRICANE KATRINA: LESSONS LEARNED 42 (2006), *available at* http://www.whitehouse.gov/reports/katrina-lessons-learned.pdf. According to the White House's own report:

An important limiting factor of the Federal response . . . is that the Federal response is predicated on an incident being handled at the lowest jurisdictional level possible. A base assumption to this approach is that, even in cases where State and local governments are overwhelmed, they would maintain the necessary incident command structure to direct Federal assets to where they are most needed. In the case of Katrina, the local government had been destroyed and the State government was incapacitated, and thus the Federal government had to take on the additional roles of performing incident command and other functions it would normally rely upon the State and local governments to provide.

*Id.*

51   Michael Brown told Congress that his "biggest mistake was not recognizing, by Saturday [August 27, 2005], that Louisiana was dysfunctional." *Hurricane Katrina: The Role of the Federal Emergency Management Agency: Hearing Before the H. Select Bipartisan Comm. to Investigate the Preparation for and Response to Hurricane Katrina,* 109th Cong. 12 (2005) [hereinafter *September 27 Katrina Hearing*] (testimony of Michael Brown, former Director, FEMA).

52   *September 27 Katrina Hearing, supra* note 51, at 3–4 (statement of Michael Brown, former Director, FEMA), *available at* http://katrina.house.gov/hearings/09_27_05/brown092705.pdf [hereinafter Brown Statement].

53   *See* Eric Lipton et al., *Storm and Crisis: Breakdowns Marked Path from Hurricane to Anarchy*, N.Y. TIMES, Sept. 11, 2005, § 1 [hereinafter Lipton et al., *Breakdowns*] (noting

Global security specialist Joseph Whitley, former general counsel at the U.S. Department of Homeland Security, made the following observations following the response to Katrina:

> During the first few hours and days after landfall, we saw breakdowns in communication within and among every level of government: between federal, state and local officials; and, perhaps most critically, between government and the citizens of the affected areas. We saw an inability to establish with any certainty what was actually happening and to deploy the appropriate resources to deal with each situation. Many citizens in the Gulf Coast region and elsewhere in the United States may have lost confidence in the government's ability to respond to a catastrophic event.[54]

Whitley suggests that coordination failures stemmed partly from inconsistencies between the two primary sources of procedural guidance for state and federal cooperation during emergencies—the Robert T. Stafford Disaster Relief and Emergency Assistance Act (the Stafford Act)[55] and the NRP—and partly from the tensions inherent in catastrophic disaster management, due to the respect heeded by federal and state actors for the principles of federalism.[56]

---

that dozens of interviews with officials showed that "the crisis in New Orleans deepened because of a virtual standoff between hesitant federal officials and besieged authorities in Louisiana"); Eric Lipton et al., *Storm and Crisis: Political Issues Snarled Plans for Troop Aid*, N.Y. TIMES, Sept. 9, 2005, at A1 [hereinafter Lipton et al., *Political Issues*] ("Interviews with officials in Washington and Louisiana show that as the situation grew worse, they were wrangling with questions of federal/state authority . . . ."); Thomas et al., *supra* note 47, at 40 (reporting that as of September 2, "[a] debate over 'federalizing' the National Guard had been rattling in Washington for the previous three days").

54    Whitley et al., *supra* note 43, at 3. Whitley, a current member of Alston & Bird LLP's Global Security & Enforcement Practice Team, further observed:

From top to bottom, Katrina exposed some of our vulnerabilities as a nation. State and local governments must continue to address communication issues that were identified as crucial after the attacks of September 11, 2001. They must provide trained professional staff to manage response efforts. Continued and expanded coordinated training of federal, state, and local government officials is an absolute must. For emergency management lawyers, it is absolutely essential that we share "best practices" and coordinate our educational and training efforts so that government and the private sector at all levels better understands [sic] each other's needs and the legal requirements involved in disaster preparedness and relief.

Critically, DHS must immediately address areas of potential ambiguity or perceived confusion—who declares an emergency, who leads the response and recovery efforts, how are resources managed—and we must create an expedited, transparent, and effective contracting and contract oversight process.

*Id.*

55    42 U.S.C. §§ 5121–5205 (2000).

56    Whitley et al., *supra* note 43, at 4–6.

As he explains, the historic relationship between the federal, state, and local governments is best described as a "pull" approach, in which the federal government presumes that states and localities can cope independently with a disaster unless they specifically request (or pull) resources from the federal government.[57] This view of federalism in disaster response—that state officials are directly responsible for the health and safety of their citizens and that federal assistance is supplementary only—has long been the general rule, although the role has evolved toward greater expectations of federal assistance.[58] Although this approach works in the majority of instances, Whitley argues that disasters of Katrina's magnitude show that federal policy must enable a "push" approach where needed, in which the federal government intervenes to provide assistance even without a direct request by the state or local government.[59] After all, he explains, "[t]he 'pull' approach simply cannot work when the state and local governments are, as they were after Katrina, without communication, without the ability to assess the extent of damages or needs, and without even adequate personnel to make requests for everything needed."[60] Although Whitley assigns a fair share of blame to state and local governments for their inadequate response, he holds the federal government especially accountable for failing to "promptly trigger the necessary federal legal authorities to begin the process of implementing federal assistance in the immediate aftermath of the storms," when the state and local authorities were so incapacitated that they could not possibly have followed the rituals anticipated by the Stafford Act or the NRP.[61] "Under such a catastrophic scenario," Whitley concludes, "the federal government, without being asked, must intervene more promptly in the immediate aftermath of an event."[62]

Even before Hurricane Katrina hit the Gulf Coast, NRP drafters were aware that state and local governments might become overwhelmed during the course of a catastrophic emergency.[63] When Katrina hit, they had nearly finalized a "Catastrophic Incident Annex" to the NRP, enabling a push approach to address these concerns.[64] However, this is a politically complicated innovation because it contradicts the relevant language of the Stafford Act, which authorizes federal disaster assistance to the states, sets forth the primary role of state and local responders, and clarifies the supplementary nature of federal support.[65] Whitley suggests that the Stafford Act may also need to be amended to enable a push

---

57  *Id.* at 4.
58  *Id.*
59  *Id.*
60  *Id.*
61  *Id.* at 7.
62  *Id.*
63  *Id.* at 4.
64  *Id.*
65  *Id.*

approach in catastrophic circumstances.[66] In the meantime, the Katrina experience recently motivated passage of a new federal law that enables the President to deploy the military in response to natural disasters and other major domestic emergencies without consent of the states involved.[67]

Although Whitley's blow-by-blow account of the post-Katrina failures are chilling, he also praises the great acts of generosity and self-sacrifice by those involved in the relief effort, commending members of the U.S. Coast Guard, FEMA, the National Guard, and first responders and law enforcement officers for their particularly heroic efforts to save lives and offer comfort to victims.[68] His seasoned observation of the details of the Katrina response indicate that failures were not the result of callous or careless behavior by individuals, but were institutional failures—namely, the rules or perceived rules of law that convinced decision-makers not to proceed with the "push" response that was clearly necessary out of fear that doing so would, in essence, violate the Constitution.

*2. The President, the Governor, the Mayor, and the Stafford Act*     Federalism concerns were not limited to managerial choices in the field but pervaded the response effort up to the highest levels. News reports indicated that "[f]or days, Bush's top advisers argued over legal niceties about who was in charge,"[69] that "[i]nterviews with officials in Washington and Louisiana show that as the situation grew worse, they were wrangling with questions of federal/state authority,"[70] and that "the crisis in New Orleans deepened because of a virtual standoff between hesitant federal officials and besieged authorities in Louisiana."[71] The issues that most snarled the response effort were uncertainty about the point at which the federal government should stop waiting for instructions on how to assist the state and take initiative via its superior command capacity (through the deployment of U.S. military or federalized National Guard troops),[72] and after that, confusion about who would then be in charge.

---

66   *Id.*

67   John Warner National Defense Authorization Act for Fiscal Year 2007, Pub. L. No. 109-364, 120 Stat. 2083 (2006) [hereinafter Warner Act]; *see also* Michael Greenberger, *Yes, Virginia: The President Can Deploy Federal Troops to Prevent the Loss of a Major American City from a Devastating Natural Catastrophe* 1–2 (U. OF MD. LEGAL STUDIES RESEARCH PAPER NO. 2006-37), *available at* http://ssrn.com/abstract=946207 (arguing that the new law neither adds to nor subtracts from the President's existing powers but merely clarifies them after uncertainty suggested during the Katrina emergency).

68   Whitley et al., *supra* note 43, at 3.

69   Evan Thomas et al., *The Lost City*, NEWSWEEK, Sept. 12, 2005, at 41, 48.

70   Lipton et al., *Political Issues*, *supra* note 53, at A1.

71   Lipton et al., *Breakdowns*, *supra* note 53, at §1; *see id.* (reporting that "interviews with dozens of officials" supported this contention).

72   *See* Thomas et al., *supra* note 69, at 48–49 ("Beginning early in the week, Justice Department lawyers presented arguments for federalizing the Guard, but Defense Department lawyers fretted about untrained 19-year-olds trying to enforce local laws . . . .").

Even as it became clear that federal assistance was necessary, uncertainty unfolded among all three levels of government as to who should be in control of the troops to be deployed.[73] Apparently desperate for results, New Orleans Mayor Ray Nagin supported federalizing the response,[74] while Louisiana Governor Kathleen Babineaux Blanco balked, and President George W. Bush, hesitant to offend federalism principles in this interjurisdictional no man's land, waited for clarity.[75] In one infamous exchange four days into the crisis at a strategy session aboard Air Force One, the distraught Mayor slammed the conference table with his hand and asked the President "to cut through this and do what it takes to have a more-controlled command structure. If that means federalizing it, let's do it."[76] Mayor Nagin recommended the Pentagon's "on-scene commander," Lieutenant General Russel Honoré, to lead the flailing relief effort on behalf of the federal government.[77] According to another meeting participant, President Bush turned to Governor Blanco and said, "[w]ell, what do you think of that, Governor?"[78] But Governor Blanco declined to discuss the matter except in a private meeting with the President, which apparently followed the strategy session.[79] However, there was still no agreement over one week later,[80] leaving idle the assistance of an estimated 100,000 National Guard troops accessible on short notice in neighboring states.[81] News accounts suggest that Governor Blanco did ask the President for 40,000 federal troops, but did not agree to surrender oversight of the relief effort to the federal government.[82]

---

73   Thomas et al., *supra* note 47, at 40.

74   *Id.*

75   *See id.* The troops of each state's National Guard report to their Governor unless they are "federalized" by Presidential order in accordance with the terms of the Stafford Act. *See* 42 U.S.C. §§ 5191–5192 (2000) (authorizing the President to declare disaster emergencies and direct federal government response).

76   Thomas et al., *supra* note 47, at 40.

77   *Id.*

78   *Id.*

79   *Id.*

80   *Id.*

81   John M. Broder, *Guard Units' New Mission: From Combat to Flood Duty*, N.Y. TIMES, Aug. 30, 2005, at A13.

82   *See* Karen Tumulty et al., *4 Places Where the System Broke Down: The Governor*, TIME, Sept. 19, 2005, § 2, at 34. *Time* reported:

Further tangling the post-Katrina disaster effort was a struggle for power. On the Friday after the hurricane, as the Governor met with Bush aboard Air Force One on the tarmac of the New Orleans airport, the President broached a sensitive question: Would Blanco relinquish control of local law enforcement and the 13,268 National Guard troops from 29 states that fall under her command? . . . [S]he thought the request had a political motive. It would allow Washington to come in and claim credit for a relief operation that was finally beginning to show progress.

Had Governor Blanco surrendered her claim to control over the relief effort,[83] President Bush would have been able to reconcile the urgency of providing needed federal assistance with the federalism principles that he believed foreclosed such authorization in the interim.[84] Nevertheless, contemporaneous news accounts indicate that the Justice Department's Office of Legal Counsel researched the matter and "concluded that the federal government had authority to move in even over the objection of local officials."[85] Indeed, many commentators—including some close to the Bush Administration, such as former Deputy Assistant Attorney General John Yoo—argued vigorously that the President did not need the Governor's consent to federalize the response in light of available jurisdictional hooks in the Stafford Act, including state incapacity and federal obligation.[86] In addition to the President's authority to unilaterally federalize a State's National Guard in time of insurrection or war,[87] the Act authorizes the President to coordinate *all* disaster relief, including the use of Federal and State assets, in a time of crisis whenever "primary responsibility for response rests with the United States because the

---

Blanco asked for 24 hours to consider it, but as she was meeting at midnight that Friday night with advisers, [Chief of Staff Andrew] Card called and told her to look for a fax. It was a letter and memorandum of understanding under which she would turn over control of her troops. Blanco refused to sign it.

*Id.*; *see also Katrina Aftermath, Louisiana: Don't Want You on My Dance Card*, AMERICAN POLITICAL NETWORK, THE HOTLINE, Sept. 8, 2005, at 7 (discussing Governor Blanco's rejection of the White House proposal for federal control of troops in Louisiana).

83    It remains unclear why Blanco did not, given that the state resources at her disposal had proved insufficient to manage the relief effort independently. Viewed most generously, it may be that she was reluctant to turn control over to a federal government that had so far shown nothing but incompetence in its own handling of the disaster. Viewed less generously, her decision to refuse federal aid in the face of state incapacity tyrannically exacerbated the suffering of her own citizens by contributing to the delay. If she refused to relinquish control on federalism grounds while being unable to provide the needed resources independently, then her view of federalism warrants just as much criticism as that of the federal government. *See supra* note 52 and accompanying text (discussing Michael Brown's testimony on the role of federalism considerations during the response effort).

84    Under both the Stafford Act and the NRP, the President may federalize emergency response at the request of a state's governor. *See supra* notes 46 & 75 and accompanying text.

85    Greenberger, *supra* note 67, at 11 (internal quotation marks omitted).

86    John Yoo, Editorial, *Trigger Power*, L.A. TIMES, Oct. 2, 2005, at M5; *see also* Greenberger, *supra* note 67, at 14–19 (arguing that the President had clear authority to intervene even before passage of the Warner Act); Candidus Dougherty, While the Government Fiddled Around, The Big Easy Drowned: How the *Posse Comitatus* Act Became the Government's Alibi for the Hurricane Katrina Disaster 39 (Jan. 1, 2006) (unpublished manuscript, *available at* http://ssrn.com/abstract=938249) (arguing that the Posse Comitatus Act did not bar the deployment of federal troops as part of the Katrina relief effort because it does not prohibit the military from providing humanitarian aid).

87    Insurrection Act, 10 U.S.C. §§ 331–335 (2000).

emergency involves a subject area for which, under the Constitution or laws of the United States, the United States exercises exclusive or preeminent responsibility and authority."[88] But what exactly does that mean? What counts as "a subject area for which, under the Constitution or laws of the United States, the United States exercises exclusive or *preeminent responsibility and authority*"?[89]

No court has interpreted this provision of the Stafford Act, because it has never arisen in a justiciable controversy.[90] But it goes to the heart of the federalism quandary: what does the Constitution tell us about when the United States exercises "preeminent responsibility and authority"? Although John Yoo is convinced that the text authorizes at least some measure of federal disaster response without a gubernatorial request, the question is unsettled. This uncertainty makes President Bush's decision *not* to invoke his potential authority, especially in the face of such hideous human suffering and public pressure to act,[91] all the more significant.

Indeed, President Bush's reluctance to respond more proactively was not well received by the public,[92] prompting his subsequent request that Congress study

---

88    42 U.S.C. § 5191(b) (2000). Unlike 42 U.S.C. § 5170, this section does not require the consent of a given state's Governor, though it does require as much consultation with the Governor as is practicable. 42 U.S.C. § 5191(b). The Stafford Act leaves the determination of when the United States exercises preeminent responsibility or authority up for interpretation, though commentators like Yoo have suggested that the particular circumstances after Katrina would have warranted unilateral federal action. *See* Yoo, *supra* note 86, at M5 (determining that Katrina would have qualified as a national emergency and that "[o]nce a national emergency has been declared, the president can send troops to provide assistance and restore order").

89    42 U.S.C. § 5191(b) (emphasis added).

90    The Warner Act recently affirmed that the President may unilaterally deploy federal troops, including National Guard troops in federal service, to respond to a major domestic emergency such as a natural disaster. *See supra* note 67 and accompanying text. However, the Warner Act does not provide additional bases of authority to federalize a state's National Guard in the first place, leaving the Stafford Act issue unresolved. *See* Warner Act, Pub. L. No. 109-364, § 1076, 120 Stat. 2083, 2404 (2006) (to be codified at 10 U.S.C. § 333) (adding circumstances in which "[t]he President may employ the armed forces, including the National Guard in federal service").

91    For example, Anchor Brian Williams questioned Michael Brown:
Why can't some of the Chinook helicopters and Black Hawks that we have heard flying over for days and days and days simply lower pallets of water, meals ready to eat, medical supplies, right into downtown New Orleans? ["]Where is the aid?["] It's the question people keep asking us on camera!
*NBC Nightly News: FEMA Director Michael Brown Discusses Relief Efforts in Hurricane Zone* (NBC television broadcast Sept. 1, 2005) [hereinafter NBC Nightly News].

92    *E.g.*, Michael A. Fletcher & Richard Morin, *Bush's Approval Rating Drops to New Low in Wake of Storm*, WASH. POST, Sept. 13, 2005, at A8 ("The bungled response to the hurricane has helped drag down Bush's job-approval rating, which now stands at 42 percent—the lowest of his presidency—in the Post-ABC poll and down three points since

proposals for guidance on federal initiative in future scenarios.[93] However, what is most significant about the President's decision is *why* he declined to exercise the potential Stafford Act authority in the first place, given such overwhelming political pressure to do so and his demonstrated confidence asserting untested federal executive authority in other realms.[94] One patent explanation for the President's hesitancy to explore all potential avenues of authority during the most devastating natural disaster in U.S. history is the profound influence of strict-separationist idealism. Federalizing the Louisiana National Guard and subjecting state and city police to federal command would have blurred the very lines of regulatory authority that New Federalism so endeavors to preserve.[95] The best

---

the hurricane hit two weeks ago."). Many members of the U.S. House of Representatives issued press releases emphasizing a popularly held sentiment about the primary role that the Federal Government should serve in disaster response and in providing aid to Katrina victims. *See, e.g.*, Press Release, Representative Marion Berry, Berry Issues Statement on Presidential Address (Sept. 15, 2005), *available at* http://www.house.gov/berry/pressreleases/archive/katrina3.html ("One of the primary roles of the federal government is to step in during times of national emergency."); Press Release, Representative Elijah E. Cummings, Cummings: Brown Demonstrates Blurred Hindsight (Sept. 27, 2005), *available at* http://www.house.gov/cummings/press/05sep27a.htm ("Mr. Brown continues to blame state and local officials, many of whom were storm victims themselves, while denying the primary role of the federal government in helping its own citizens survive a catastrophe."); Press Release, Representative Jan Schakowsky, Schakowsky Statement on the Approval of $10.5 Billion in Emergency Supplemental Appropriations for Hurricane Victims (Sept. 2, 2005), *available at* http://www.house.gov/schakowsky/PressRelease_9_2_05_KatrinaAid. html ("[I]t is the primary role of the federal government to aid these victims."). *Newsweek Magazine*'s *Special Report: After Katrina* "drew more than 1,000 letters," most taking the federal government to task for its "inept response to the catastrophe." *Mail Call: In the Wake of a Devastating Hurricane*, NEWSWEEK, Sept. 26, 2005, at 18.

93    *See, e.g.*, Shane & Shanker, *supra* note 49, at A1 (noting that the hurricane response touched off "a national debate about whether in the future the Pentagon should take charge immediately after catastrophes," and that President Bush had requested that Congress evaluate the question).

94    President Bush is often noted (both with praise and criticism) for expanding federal executive authority beyond that exercised by any previous administration in U.S. history. *See, e.g.*, Jeffrey Rosen, *Bush's Leviathan State: Power of One*, THE NEW REPUBLIC, July 24, 2006, at 8 ("One of the defining principles of the Bush administration has been a belief in unfettered executive power. . . . A conservative ideology that had always been devoted to limiting government power has been transformed into the largest expansion of executive power since FDR."); Press Release, Senator Patrick Leahy, Statement On Presidential Signing Statements (July 25, 2006), *available at* http://leahy.senate.gov/press/200607/072506a.html ("Whether it is torture, warrantless eavesdropping on American citizens, or the unlawful detention of military prisoners, this Republican-led Congress has been willing to turn a blind eye and rubber-stamp the questionable actions of this Administration, regardless of the consequences to our Constitution or civil liberties.").

95    For example, Scott L. Silliman, Executive Director of Duke University School of Law's Center on Law, Ethics and National Security, believes that delays were caused

alternative explanation—and one equally troubling—is that the White House relied on New Federalism rhetoric for political cover in avoiding any involvement with the unfolding mess.[96] Either way, that New Federalism ideals could stall effective governance at such a key moment or provide reliable cover to so monumental an abdication suggests their infirmity.

In the end, reasonable people may disagree on how best to apportion blame between the amply culpable local, state, and federal authorities for the failed response, subsequently heralded as "a national disgrace."[97] That said, it remains difficult to digest the confirmed reports that after fifteen-foot floodwaters swept through the Jackson Barracks headquarters of the Louisiana National Guard Headquarters—severing communication lines, flooding high-water trucks, and converting the entire nerve center force into 375 more New Orleans refugees in need of a water rescue[98]—White House officials stalled in Washington, debating how the finer principles of constitutional federalism dictated the scope of federal intervention.[99] In their defense, the debate was at least warranted by a faithful interpretation of the federalism model advanced by the sitting Supreme Court. But it raises the fair question, in light of the stakes and the results that can flow from that model—is this really the federalism we intended?

*3. The Price of Failure* While the President's senior advisers fiddled with federalism, New Orleans drowned. The details of the debacle are by now painfully well-known to most Americans, but they bear repeating to highlight the scope of the failed response. Over a thousand residents perished in their homes and neighborhoods,[100] and up to thirty-four died in the makeshift mass shelters at the New Orleans Superdome and convention center,[101] where some 39,000 evacuees were encamped without adequate food, water, power, or sanitary facilities for up

---

not by the limitations of the Posse Comitatus Act, which generally precludes the use of federal troops for domestic security concerns, but by confusion over the lines of authority between President Bush and Governor Blanco: "I think the problem was you had two heads of state . . . each having the authority, but one waiting for the other to act." Anne Plummer, *Loosening Restrictions on the Military Enforcing Civil Law Unwise, Say Critics*, Cong. Q. Wkly., Sept. 24, 2005, at 2550 (internal quotation marks omitted).

96    *See id.* Silliman's interpretation, of course, suggests another possible explanation for the administration's reluctance to intervene despite an arguable legal basis for doing so: the desire to pass the hot potato and avoid responsibility for an intractable situation. *See Tug of War, supra* note 1, at 588–91.

97    *E.g.*, Lewis, *supra* note 42, at 52.

98    Shane & Shanker, *supra* note 49, at A1.

99    *See supra* note 53 and accompanying text.

100    *Katrina's Official Death Toll Tops 1,000*, CNN.com, Sept. 21, 2005, http://www.cnn.com/2005/US/09/21/katrina.impact.

101    Lipton et al., *Breakdowns, supra* note 53, at A1 (quoting official reports of thirty-four deaths: ten at the Superdome and twenty-four at the convention center).

to seven days.[102] Two-thirds of the occupants were women, children, or elderly, many of them infirm, and they huddled in darkness and 100-degree temperatures amidst the unbearable stench of human waste covering the floors and the ceiling debris fallen from holes torn from the roof by the storm.[103] Unchecked lawless behavior terrorized citizens and local law enforcement alike, both within the emergency shelters and on the flooded city streets.[104] The near total collapse of landline, satellite, and cell-phone communications hindered the ability of local law enforcement and the Louisiana National Guard to coordinate a response—even available radio channels were so jammed with traffic that they became useless.[105]

The chaotic rescue and evacuation efforts impacted families as well, as the National Center for Missing and Exploited Children reported in mid-September 2005 that 1,831 children from Louisiana, Alabama, and Mississippi were reported as missing in the aftermath of the storm, and that weeks later, only 360 of these cases had been resolved.[106] At least a million evacuees took shelter in other cities and states,[107] and by March 2006 the federal government had committed $6.9 billion in shelter and direct financial assistance to Gulf Coast residents affected

---

102    *Id.* Food and water supplies stashed at the planned emergency shelter of the Superdome ran out within the first few days after Katrina made landfall. *Id.* After the Superdome had filled beyond all capacity, an additional 15,000 refugees were directed to the convention center, where there were no food or water supplies. *Id.*; *see also* John Riley & Craig Gordon, *Katrina—What Went Wrong*, NEWSDAY, Sept. 3, 2005, at A4 (describing the deplorable conditions in the convention center).

103    Lipton et al., *Breakdowns*, *supra* note 53, at A1 (citing Chief Lonnie C. Swain, an assistant police superintendent who oversaw ninety police officers on patrol at the Superdome).

104    *See id.* (quoting Captain Jeffrey Winn, head of the convention center's police SWAT team: "The only way I can describe it is as a completely lawless situation.").

105    Shane & Shanker, *supra* note 49, at A1.

106    Barbara Kantrowitz & Karen Breslau, *Some Are Found, All Are Lost*, NEWSWEEK, Sept. 19, 2005, at 51. Young children were often separated from parents during chaotic boat rescues and bus evacuations. *Id.* at 52.

107    *See* Lester R. Brown, *Global Warming Forcing U.S. Coastal Population to Move Inland*, EARTH POL'Y INST., Aug. 16, 2006, http://www.earth-policy.org/Updates/2006/Update57.htm (explaining that Hurricane Katrina forced one million people to move inland from the afflicted coastal cities); *see also* Eric Lipton, *Storm and Crisis: Hurricane Evacuees Face Eviction Threats at Both Their Old Homes and New*, N.Y. TIMES, Nov. 4, 2005, at A20 (discussing the large influx of displaced Katrina victims to Texas). For a graphical depiction of Katrina refugee displacement, see Kantrowitz & Breslau, *supra* note 106, at 53. Refugees have fled to forty-nine different states and the District of Columbia. *See* Press Release, White House, Fact Sheet: Gulf Coast Update: Hurricane Relief, Recovery, and Rebuilding Continues (Mar. 8, 2006) [hereinafter Gulf Coast Fact Sheet], *available at* http://www.whitehouse.gov/news/releases/2006/03/20060308-8.html (noting the federal aid flowing to local education agencies in forty-nine states and the District of Columbia for displaced school children).

by the hurricane.[108] Countless thousands of starving and injured companion animals continued to roam the streets or languish trapped within the homes of evacuated owners for weeks following the storm,[109] most perishing before rescue but not before ghastly suffering.[110]

Damage to oil infrastructure was the worst ever experienced by the industry.[111] More than nine million gallons were reported spilled,[112] and gas prices skyrocketed to as high as $6 per gallon in the following weeks.[113] Chemical spills, rotting remains, and flooding resulted in environmental hazards ranging from land-based toxic sludge to poisoned water supplies that will continue to threaten human health and safety into the foreseeable future.[114] Approximately $88 billion in federal aid has already been allocated toward relief, recovery, and rebuilding efforts, and an additional $20 billion has been requested to assist a variety of federal agencies in their continuing relief efforts.[115] These moneys have been earmarked for programs including unemployment assistance,[116] community disaster loans to local

---

108    Gulf Coast Fact Sheet, *supra* note 107. This is more than "double the combined total of Individuals and Households Assistance Program (IHP) dollars provided for six major U.S. natural disasters occurring since 1992." *Id.*

109    *See, e.g.*, Oscar Corral, *Stranded Pets Facing Starvation*, MIAMI HERALD, Sept. 5, 2005, at A13 (noting that many pets were abandoned because their owners could not bring them on evacuation buses); Norma Mendoza, *Task Force Members Describe Devastation in New Orleans*, EDWARDSVILLE INTELLIGENCER, Oct. 11, 2005, at 1, 3 ("Another sad sight was the dogs that were everywhere, strays and abandoned pets that rescue workers wouldn't allow people to bring with them. Some died, trapped in the houses where they were left. Others were starving and the officers had nothing to give them.").

110    *See, e.g., Photo Gallery: Pets, Hurricane Katrina's Other Victims*, NAT'L GEOGRAPHIC.COM, Sept. 8, 2005, http://news.nationalgeographic.com/news/2005/09/0908_050908_katrina_pets.html (illustrating the anguish of animals abandoned in Katrina's wrath); *cf.* Karlyn Barker & Nia-Malika Henderson, *Plight of Stranded Animals Worsening Daily*, WASH. POST, Sept. 8, 2005, at B4 (estimating that thousands of animals abandoned by their owners after Katrina were in peril).

111    *See* Pam Radtke Russell, *Gulf Platform Damage Still Being Assessed*, NEWHOUSE NEWS SERV., Mar. 23, 2006 (on file with author) (explaining that the damage to oil and gas platforms from Katrina was the worst ever seen in the Gulf of Mexico, and that the harm caused by rigs was equally noteworthy).

112    Mike Taibbi, *Oil Coats Homes, Water After Katrina*, MSNBC.COM, Nov. 8, 2005, http://www.msnbc.msn.com/id/9972220.

113    Robert J. Samuelson, *Hitting the Economy*, NEWSWEEK, Sept. 12, 2005, at 54.

114    *See* Thomas et al., *supra* note 47, at 34–35 (listing environmental hazards affecting public health).

115    Gulf Coast Fact Sheet, *supra* note 107. As high as this figure seems, it nevertheless falls short of the $150 billion of federal aid that experts had predicted would be necessary for recovery efforts. Nina J. Easton, *Katrina Aid Falls Short of Promises*, BOSTON GLOBE, Nov. 27, 2005, at A1.

116    *See* Press Release, FEMA, By the Numbers: FEMA Recovery Update in Louisiana (Mar. 24, 2006), *available at* http://www.fema.gov/news/newsrelease.fema?id=24505

governments,[117] housing assistance,[118] and public assistance projects.[119] Separate grants have also been awarded, including a $1.6 billion special congressional appropriation to the Department of Education for public and private schools where relocated students enrolled.[120]

Americans watched their televisions (and increasingly agitated journalists watched on the scene) in disbelief as day after day passed before anything resembling an organized disaster response was assembled in the devastated City of New Orleans.[121] Public outrage brimmed over in the days and weeks following the crisis, exemplified by one news story's observation that "[t]he descent of the Superdome from haven to a fetid, crime-infested hellhole by the time mass evacuations began Thursday was emblematic of what appeared to many to be a government failure of epic proportions last week, leaving experts and ordinary citizens alike puzzled and infuriated."[122]

Of course, much of the devastation that Gulf Coast residents suffered from the winds and rain of Katrina cannot be blamed on bad disaster management. Setting aside the degree to which anthropogenic climate change contributes to the intensity of hurricanes like Katrina,[123] hurricanes are a force of nature that we have long learned to fear. River and wetland management choices along the Mississippi Delta exacerbated the flooding that proved the worst of New Orleans'

---

(allocating $165 million to disaster unemployment assistance).

117   *See id.* (allocating $700 million in loans to local governments in need of assistance).

118   FEMA has already dispersed checks in the amount of $3.5 billion for rental assistance and home restoration. *Id.*

119   Over $1.9 billion has already been set aside for such public assistance undertakings. *Id.*

120   Gulf Coast Fact Sheet, *supra* note 107.

121   Even journalists of ordinarily studied neutrality found themselves challenging official accounts of the relief effort. For example, in an interview with FEMA Director Michael Brown three days into the crisis, NBC Nightly News anchor Brian Williams incredulously demanded to know why federal Chinook and Blackhawk helicopters circling the area could not be used to deliver food, water, and medical supplies to the encamped evacuees. *See* NBC Nightly News, *supra* note 91 ("[']Where is the aid?['] It's the question people keep asking us on camera!"). In response, Brown indicated that the federal government had only just become aware of the thousands of desperate refugees that day. *Id.*

122   Riley & Gordon, *supra* note 102, at A4.

123   *Compare* Stefan Rahmstorf et al., *Hurricanes and Global Warming–Is There a Connection?*, REALCLIMATE, Sept. 2, 2005, http://www.realclimate.org/index.php?p=181 (suggesting that man-made increases in greenhouse gases have, at least in part, led to a rise in ocean temperatures, which tends to cause more destructive hurricanes like Katrina), *with* James K. Glassman, *Katrina and Disgusting Exploitation*, TCS DAILY, Aug. 31, 2005, http://www.tcsdaily.com/article.aspx?id=083105JKG (refusing to acknowledge a nexus between global warming and the severity of Hurricane Katrina).

battles,[124] and Americans are right to ask for better long-term planning from the local, state, and federal authorities responsible for these activities.[125] Still, it was the bungled humanitarian relief effort—the disorganized response that stranded the sick and injured, separated young children from their parents, and left the most vulnerable members of society struggling to survive amidst prolonged *Lord of the Flies* conditions[126]—that triggered public outrage.

*4. Coda: Which Federalism?* Given the proven ability of the United States to respond quickly and effectively in the face of natural disaster (for example, our immediate and ambitious relief effort in response to the South Asian tsunami just nine months earlier[127]), what could possibly account for this spectacular failure of

---

124  *See* Erin Ryan, *New Orleans, the Chesapeake, and the Future of Environmental Assessment: Overcoming the Natural Resources Law of Unintended Consequences*, 40 U. RICH. L. REV. 981, 990–97 (2006) (describing the natural resource management choices made along the Mississippi River that made New Orleans particularly vulnerable to Hurricane Katrina's storm surge).

125  *Cf.* John Schwartz, *Army Builders Accept Blame Over Flooding*, N.Y. TIMES, June 2, 2006, at A1 (reporting that an Army Corps of Engineers' study concluded that the design of the New Orleans levees was flawed and incapable of handling a storm the strength of Katrina).

126  *See, e.g., Britons Describe Hurricane Ordeal*, BBC NEWS, Sept. 6, 2005, http://news.bbc.co.uk/1/hi/uk/4214746.stm (recounting the putrid conditions in the Superdome); *see also* Kantrowitz & Breslau, *supra* note 106, at 51–52 (describing one family that was separated when rescue helicopters dropped the children off at one location and rescue boats brought the parents to another); Evan Thomas, *Taken by Storm*, NEWSWEEK, Dec. 26, 2005/Jan. 2, 2006, at 47, 56 (recounting the same episode); Thomas et al., *supra* note 69, at 44–45 (comparing the images of helpless families and children begging for food and water to third-world conditions in Mogadishu or Port-au-Prince).

127  *See* Brigadier General John Allen, Principal Director of Asia and Pacific Affairs, Office of the Secretary of Defense, "Update—U.S. Government Relief Efforts in Asia," Foreign Press Center Briefing, Washington, D.C. (Jan. 3, 2005), *available at* http://www.pacom.mil/speeches/sst2005/050103-wh-presstranscript.shtml ("Within minutes of our notification of this disaster, we began military planning to assist in the U.S. Governmental response to this crisis . . . . Within hours, U.S. forces began to move to the affected area."); BUREAU OF INT'L INFO. PROGRAMS, U.S. DEP'T OF STATE, GOING THE DISTANCE: THE U.S. TSUNAMI RELIEF EFFORT 2005, at 1 (2005), http://usinfo.state.gov/products/pubs/tsunami/tsunami.pdf (reporting that, at the height of the relief effort, "more than 15,000 U.S. military personnel were involved in providing relief support in the affected region. Twenty-five ships and ninety-four aircraft were participating in the effort. The U.S. military had delivered about 2.2 million pounds of relief supplies to affected nations . . . ."); *see also* Ralph A. Cossa, President of the Pacific Forum Center for Strategic and International Studies, *South Asian Tsunami: U.S. Military Provides "Logistical Backbone" for Relief Operation*, EJOURNAL USA: FOREIGN POLICY AGENDA (Nov. 2004), http://usinfo.state.gov/journals/itps/1104/ijpe/cossa.htm (noting, in ironic contrast to the later Katrina relief effort, that "[w]hile the numbers of forces dedicated to the relief effort and the extent of

governance? In the face of such unimaginable domestic despair, prompting ordinary Americans from the four corners of the nation to arrive at New Orleans' doorstep with whatever they had to offer, why couldn't the United States government properly protect, feed, and evacuate its own?

In his post-storm Congressional testimony, former FEMA director Michael Brown provided perhaps the best answer, and in so doing invokes several of the important federalism issues with which we began this part. In his poignant defense of his agency's performance on federalism grounds, he explained:

> Princip[les] of federalism should not be lost in a short-term desire to react to a natural disaster of catastrophic proportions, for if that concept is lost, the advantages of having a robust state and local emergency management system will lead not only to waste of taxpayer dollars at the federal level, but will inherently drive decision-making best left to the local and state level, to a centralized federal government, which inherently cannot understand the unique needs of each community across this nation.[128]

Brown's statement is important for three reasons. First, he correctly articulates a central problem of federalism: structural constraints are only meaningful if they are followed in difficult times as well as easy times. For Brown, allowing the federal government to cross federalism's proverbial line in the sand to satisfy a short-term desire would undermine the very principles of constitutional government. But this brings us to the second important point in Brown's statement, which is his invocation of the fallacy perpetuated by New Federalism rhetoric that strict-separationist dual sovereignty is *itself* federalism, as opposed to one vision among alternatives. Although earlier federal intervention might have violated the tenets of the strict-separationist ideal, it might have been an acceptable move within an alternative conception of federalism (such as one that acknowledges the interjurisdictional gray area).

This brings us to the third important reference point in Brown's statement—and as it happens, back to the core federalism question raised here—namely, that of *which federalism*? If there is a legitimate interpretive choice among alternatives, we should choose the model that best enables the kind of governance that serves the values we ascribe to government. For Brown, the regulatory impulse "to react to a natural disaster of catastrophic proportions" is little more than a "short-term desire,"[129] a crassly self-satisfying move in the foreground of a much greater drama about the grand diffusion of separately sovereign power. But to what end is

---

aid they provided were impressive, the most invaluable U.S. contribution focused around another Defense Department unique capability: command, control, communications, and coordination. These attributes, critical in wartime, proved equally critical in ensuring an effective, coordinated response.").

128   *See* Brown Statement, *supra* note 52, at 3.
129   *Id.*

power so divided, if neither one nor the other level of government can intervene to prevent the most galling (and continuing) episode of domestic human suffering in this lifetime? Is Michael Brown's FEMA the kind of federal government that we want? Or might it suggest the value of a different model of federalism, one that can afford meaningful constraints without requiring a like sacrifice?

In the end, we must remember that clear errors were made by federal, state, and local authorities that had nothing to do with federalism (for example, New Orleans failed to consider the plight of many citizens without the means or strength to evacuate themselves,[130] and the Army Corps of Engineers later acknowledged that levees protecting the City had not been designed to withstand the combination of known soil subsidence patterns[131] and projected levee-top overflow during a storm of Katrina's magnitude[132]). Still, we should be deeply troubled by accounts like Michael Brown's, which suggest that the most devastating post-storm errors—those crystallized in the delayed and uncoordinated relief effort—flowed from the good-faith but ill-fated vehemence with which our leaders hewed to a principled reading of the constitutional balance of state and federal power.

## III. Katrina and the Interjurisdictional Gray Area

Against this backdrop of a federalism jurisprudence neatly cleaved between the truly national and the truly local, this piece asks how "Our Federalism" can better account for the tricky regulatory matters that straddle the boundary between them. Interjurisdictional regulatory problems—ranging from the environment to telecommunications to national security—simultaneously implicate areas of such

---

130    Joe Whitley observes that

[w]hile more than 1.2 million people were successfully evacuated from coastal areas before Katrina hit, tens of thousands of people were not, including citizens from two of Louisiana's most populous localities, New Orleans and Jefferson Parishes. Despite the eventual declaration of a mandatory evacuation on Sunday before landfall, New Orleans officials were unable to provide adequate transportation to evacuate the population.

Whitley et al., *supra* note 43, at 6.

131    *See* Ryan, *supra* note 124, at 990–97 (noting how channelization of the Mississippi River has led to soil subsidence in the Delta and explaining its implications for New Orleans during Hurricane Katrina).

132    Schwartz, *supra* note 125, at A1. The Corps' 6,113-page report was remarkably candid about the failed levee system:

The region's network of levees, floodwalls, pumps and gates lacked any built-in resilience that would have allowed the system to remain standing and provide protection even if water flowed over the tops of levees and floodwalls . . . . Flaws in the levee design that allowed breaches in the city's drainage canals were not foreseen, and those floodwalls failed even though the storm waters did not rise above the level that the walls were designed to hold.

national and local obligation or expertise that their resolution depends on exercise of authority by both a federal and a state actor. Identifying this third sphere of interjurisdictional concern should facilitate the development of a more stable American federalism by revealing where the strict-separationist premise of New Federalism fails. Where the New Federalism seeks to distinguish the local from the national, interjurisdictional problems monkey-wrench the system by being simultaneously *both*. This is so either because neither side has all the jurisdiction it needs to effectively solve the problem,[133] or because compelling circumstances make a partnership approach necessary to solve the problem *de facto* even if the federal government could theoretically preempt all local jurisdiction *de jure*.[134]

The legal concept of an interjurisdictional problem is nothing new, having been recognized in the United States at least since the early border-crossing cases involving interstate litigation,[135] criminal law enforcement,[136] air pollution,[137] water pollution,[138] waterway management,[139] and species protection.[140] However, the advancing reach of local impacts in the post-industrial era has also given rise to interjurisdictional problems that the Framers could never have foreseen—including

---

133    For example, this is arguably the case with regard to the problem of stormwater pollution, which stems both from land uses regulated by municipal governments and water uses regulated by the federal government. *See Tug of War, supra* note 1, at 576–80.

134    In other words, in this type of interjurisdictional regulatory problem, though the national government could theoretically preempt local involvement as a legal matter, the regulatory target so implicates an area of local concern or expertise that to do so would obstruct, rather than facilitate, meaningful resolution of the problem (as regarding such national security matters as the National Response Plan).

135    *E.g.*, Erie R.R. Co. v. Tompkins, 304 U.S. 64 (1938) (finding that federal courts hearing state law claims under diversity jurisdiction are to apply the substantive laws of those states and not federal common law).

136    *E.g.*, Wayne A. Logan, *Creating a "Hydra in Government": Federal Recourse to State Law in Crime Fighting*, 86 B.U. L. Rev. 65, 66–67 (2006) (examining the federal government's use of state law "to help effectuate its burgeoning criminal justice authority" while simultaneously "infus[ing] federal law with the normative judgments of the respective states").

137    *E.g.*, Gerald F. Hess, *The Trail Smelter, the Columbia River, and the Extraterritorial Application of CERCLA*, 18 Geo. Int'l Envtl. L. Rev. 1, 2–4 (2005) (discussing the arbitration decisions in the 1930s and early 1940s between Canada and the U.S. regarding the Trail Smelter, a facility near the border of British Columbia that pumped sulphur dioxide into Washington State).

138    *E.g.*, City of Milwaukee v. Illinois, 451 U.S. 304, 317–19 (1981) (finding that an interstate sewage discharge claim should be resolved under the Federal Water Pollution Control Act, rather than by federal common law).

139    Willson v. Black-Bird Creek Marsh Co., 27 U.S. (2 Pet.) 245, 251–52 (1829) (acknowledging overlapping state and federal concern in upholding the legality of a state-authorized dam through a waterway subject to the federal navigational servitude).

140    *E.g.*, Migratory Bird Treaty Act, 16 U.S.C. §§ 703–711 (2000) (prohibiting interstate taking, killing, or transporting migratory birds, and their eggs, parts, and nests).

such powerful environmental problems as stormwater pollution,[141] greenhouse gas emissions,[142] and mass extinctions,[143] but also such non-environmental problems as telecommunications law,[144] public health crises (e.g., bird flu),[145] and localized threats to national security and infrastructure (such as failures of the power grid[146] or Internet backbone[147]). Moreover, the growing economic interdependence that accompanied us into the new millennium has transformed many problems that might once have been purely local into the interjurisdictional variety.[148] Products liability is such a realm, drawing scholarly attention to the "undertheorized attempts of federal courts (particularly the Supreme Court) to mediate the tensions between

141    *E.g.*, John R. Nolon, *Katrina's Lament: Reconstructing Federalism*, 23 PACE ENVTL. L. REV. 987, 987–91 (2006) (examining the overlapping state and federal regulatory jurisdiction of stormwater runoff); Donald J. Kochan, *Runoff and Reality: Externalities, Economics, and Traceability Problems in Urban Runoff Regulation*, 9 CHAPMAN L. REV. 409, 414–19, 427–28 (2006) (outlining regulation of stormwater pollution and the problems of traceability).

142    *E.g.*, Associated Press, *Agreement Close for Multistate Pollution Reduction Plan*, MAINETODAY.COM, Sept. 21, 2005, http://news.mainetoday.com/apwire/D8COLE481-263. shtml (discussing the Regional Greenhouse Gas Initiative).

143    *E.g.*, Endangered Species Act of 1973, 16 U.S.C. §§ 1531–1544 (2000) (banning the "taking" of threatened or listed species).

144    *E.g.*, Philip J. Weiser, *Towards a Constitutional Architecture for Cooperative Federalism*, 79 N.C. L. REV. 663, 675–77 (2001) (discussing interjurisdictional regulatory problems arising under the Telecommunications Act of 1996).

145    *E.g.*, Elisabeth Rosenthal, *Recent Spread of Bird Flu Confounds Experts*, N.Y. TIMES, Mar. 6, 2006, at A6 (discussing the potential global scope of the bird flu pandemic).

146    *E.g.*, Seth Schiesel, *In Frayed Networks, Common Threads*, N.Y. TIMES, Aug. 21, 2003, at G1 (examining the vulnerabilities of the vast, interconnected power networks that led to the summer 2003 blackout); *Power Returns to Most Areas Hit by Blackout*, CNN. COM, Aug. 15, 2003, http://www.cnn.com/2003/US/08/15/power.outage (quoting New York Governor George Pataki's statement that the summer 2003 blackout was "the largest blackout in the history of America").

147    *E.g.*, David McGuire & Brian Krebs, *Large-Scale Attack Cripples Internet Backbone*, WASH. POST, Oct. 23, 2002, at E5 (describing a coordinated attack on computers that serve as master directories for most computer networks and websites around the world).

148    *See* Samuel Issacharoff & Catherine M. Sharkey, *Backdoor Federalization*, 53 UCLA L. REV. 1353, 1410–12 (2006) (discussing the increase in federalization of areas traditionally regulated by state law). For example, if a hurricane of similar strength to Katrina hit New Orleans a century earlier, it would have triggered fewer national interests than it does today, since the nerve center of oil and gas infrastructure that now exists seaward of New Orleans was nonexistent, and the Port of New Orleans was less central to the nation's economy. *See* Oliver Houck, *Can We Save New Orleans?*, 19 TUL. ENVTL. L.J. 1, 17–18 (2006) (explaining the development of oil and gas infrastructure in Louisiana from the early 1900s to present); *see also* Simon Romero, *A Barren Port Waits Eagerly For Its People*, N.Y. TIMES, Oct. 6, 2005, at C1 (noting the significance of the Port of New Orleans to the national economy).

the claimed commitment to the states as sovereign overseers of the quotidian affairs of their citizens and the reality that the lives of citizens are increasingly accountable to broader market commands."[149] Public servants at the national, state, and municipal levels are working overtime to address modern problems that defy jurisdictional boundaries—but the strict-separationist premise associated with the New Federalism ideal leaves them unclear on the rules for solving them.[150]

------

149    Issacharoff & Sharkey, *supra* note 148, at 1358. Other recent federalism scholars have also grappled with the concept of interjursidictionality. *See, e.g.*, Robert A. Schapiro, *Toward a Theory of Interactive Federalism*, 91 Iowa L. Rev. 243, 248–49 (2005) (proposing the concept of polyphonic federalism, where the focus is placed upon the interaction between state and federal authority, rather than upon where the two spheres diverge); Robert A. Schapiro, *Polyphonic Federalism: State Constitutions in the Federal Courts*, 87 Cal. L. Rev. 1409, 1416–17 (1999), (applying the polyphonic concept to a defense of federal interpretations of state constitutions); William W. Buzbee, *Contextual Environmental Federalism*, 14 N.Y.U. Envtl. L.J. 108, 108–09 (2005) (noting the benefits of regulatory overlap and cooperative federalism structures); William W. Buzbee, *Recognizing the Regulatory Commons: A Theory of Regulatory Gaps*, 89 Iowa L. Rev. 1, 8–14 (2003) (examining how the "regulatory commons problem" can generate regulatory gaps for interjurisdictional problems like urban sprawl and global warming); Jody Freeman, *Collaborative Governance in the Administrative State*, 45 UCLA L. Rev. 1, 4–8 (1997) (proposing a normative model of collaborative governance that involves cooperation between agencies and government in the administrative process); and Kirsten H. Engel, *Harnessing the Benefits of Dynamic Federalism in Environmental Law*, 56 Emory L.J. 155 (2006) (arguing that the static allocation of regulatory authority to *either* the state *or* federal government obstructs good environmental management, and that broadly overlapping state and federal regulatory jurisdiction is needed).

150    In proposing the category of "interjurisdictional regulatory problem," I should note first what I am *not* proposing to do. Although I believe that we can meaningfully discuss regulatory problems in general terms, I offer no unifying theory about the features of problems that make them more or less susceptible to regulatory solutions, other than to note that I am generally referring to such classic regulatory targets as market failures, negative externalities, and collective action problems that respond favorably to intervention. Reasonable minds may differ about the margin between the set of problems resolvable by government and the set of those that are not, but this definition enables a conversation about the best decision rules for government actors in a federal system regardless of that margin. In other words, to continue the conversation from here, we need only agree that there is such a thing as "regulatory problems" in some shape or form, allowing individuals to substitute different values for the variables in an otherwise stable equation.

Similarly, reasonable minds may disagree on the absolute boundaries between legitimate local and national regulatory *concern*, and this is ultimately the more important problem. It is, of course, the central federalism problem itself, and the fact that we have failed to achieve consensus on this point thus far suggests that it will not be easily forthcoming even if we can agree to acknowledge the existence of some set of interjurisdictional problems. I return to this problem in Part V of the full article, where I propose the outlines of a jurisprudential standard to assist in differentiating between legitimate interjurisdictional crossover and unjustifiable breach. Here, however, I put off debate about the margins to

As a nation, we may lack consensus about the extent to which local regulation should be held vicariously accountable under the Endangered Species Act (ESA),[151] or to which the federal government should be able to regulate gay marriage.[152] But few now argue that the federal government should not play a role in disaster management (an area of regulatory authority traditionally assigned to the states), or that state law enforcement should not play a role in domestic efforts to prevent terrorist attacks initiated abroad (a realm in which the federal government might, if absurdly, preempt state participation as a matter of international affairs).[153] Similarly, the federal government is more often criticized for failing to address the bird flu threat[154] than it is for intruding on a classic realm of the state police power, and few argue that the federal government should assume top-to-bottom control over intrastate administration of the Clean Air and Clean Water Acts, which would

---

make the case for the more basic proposition that there are at least some problems that truly implicate both local and national regulatory obligations—in a way that warrants attention from both.

151   The most famous example of such "vicarious" liability for takes prohibited by the ESA arose in *Strahan v. Coxe*, in which a state agency was held responsible for illegal takings of endangered whales because it authorized the placement of fixed gear for commercial fishing operations near the whales' spring feeding grounds. 127 F.3d 155, 161–66 (1st Cir. 1997). A more controversial instance arose in *Loggerhead Turtle v. Council of Volusia County*, in which the Eleventh Circuit ordered a county government agency to better regulate nighttime lighting on beaches where endangered loggerhead turtles hatched. 148 F.3d 1231, 1258 (11th Cir. 1998). In *Loggerhead Turtle*, the problem was that young turtles instinctively head from the beach sands where they hatched toward the ocean, following the reflection of the moonlight in the water, but the bright lights from beachside development caused excessive hatchling mortality by encouraging the turtles to head in the wrong direction. *Id.* at 1234–36.

152   Current proposals for a federal constitutional amendment banning the states from recognizing gay marriages sometimes proceed from arguments about border-crossing harms. *E.g.*, 152 Cong. Rec. S5517 (daily ed. June 7, 2006) (statement of Sen. Byrd) (discussing the state role in defining marriage and family matters and noting that the federal government's respect for these laws "is the essence of federalism").

153   *Cf.* ACLU of N.J., Inc. v. County of Hudson, 799 A.2d 629, 654–55 (N.J. Super. Ct. App. Div. 2002) (allowing a federal regulation requiring that the identities of terrorist suspects be kept secret to preempt a preexisting state law requiring that their identities be disclosed). The court observed that "while the State possesses sovereign authority over the operation of its jails, it may not operate them, in respect of INS detainees, in any way that derogates the federal government's exclusive and expressed interest in regulating aliens." *Id.*

154   James Gerstenzang, *Bird Flu Warning Would Ravage U.S., White House Warns*, L.A. Times, May 4, 2006, at A6 (noting that as the Bush Administration presented its bird flu report, Senator Edward Kennedy issued a scathing report of his own, criticizing the administration for failing to prepare the country for a possible flu pandemic).

vastly increase the size of the federal bureaucracy in an ironic move to protect the boundary between state and federal authority.[155]

Within this framework, we can understand the Katrina crisis as a colossal interjurisdictional regulatory problem, one demanding the unique capacities of multiple levels of government. Especially in hindsight, it is hard to imagine a serious argument that preparation and response should have proceeded at an exclusively national or local level. Nevertheless, in accordance with the strict-separationist model, the White House viewed the Katrina response as a properly state regulatory affair, declining to take more aggressive federal initiative because it viewed avoiding interference with (let alone commandeering) state resources as its highest obligation.[156] Yet nothing could have proved this view more tragically simplistic than our actual experience in the aftermath of the hurricane.

Katrina was clearly a local problem, demanding the protection of public health and safety and the maintenance of domestic law and order that lie at the heart of traditional state function.[157] State regulatory concern was implicated in the dispatch of first responders with localized expertise, the provision of humanitarian aid for intrastate evacuees, and the protection and salvage of state infrastructure and private property. However, to the extent that the crisis implicated the channels of interstate commerce, the national economy, and the care of interstate evacuees, it was also a matter of national concern. The Port of New Orleans is the largest shipping port in the United States (measured by tonnage handled),[158] and a sizeable percentage of our domestic energy supplies are pumped, delivered, or shipped via its channels.[159] In addition, a network of 20,000 miles of oil and gas distribution lines embedded in the New Orleans wetlands provide critical supplies

---

155    By contrast, some have argued that the federal government should devolve more of such regulatory responsibility to the states. *See, e.g.*, Jonathan H. Adler, *Jurisdictional Mismatch in Environmental Federalism*, 14 N.Y.U. ENVTL. L.J. 130, 135 (2005) ("Because most environmental problems are local or regional in nature, there is a strong case that most . . . environmental problems should be addressed at the state and local level." (footnote omitted)). Despite these arguments, however, few propose the abolition of the federal Clean Air Act and Clean Water Act, which fulfill a classic centralized regulatory role of preventing negative externalities and remedying collective action problems.

156    *See Tug of War, supra* note 1, at 527–32.

157    *See* 16A AM. JUR. 2D *Constitutional Law* § 313 (2006) (noting that the "state cannot surrender, abdicate, or abridge its police power").

158    Rip Watson, *New Orleans Port Opens to Relief Ships After Katrina*, BLOOMBERG. COM, Sept. 6, 2005, http://www.bloomberg.com/apps/news?pid=10000082&sid=adNXIjd n4Z8Q.

159    Thanks to the convenient proximity of rich carbon-based fuels in the Gulf of Mexico to the Port of New Orleans, this region is perhaps the most important energy hub in the continental United States, supplying nearly twenty percent of domestic demand for oil and natural gas. Robert Viguerie, *Coastal Erosion: Crisis in Louisiana's Wetlands*, 51 LA. B.J. 85, 86 (2003).

to the rest of the nation,[160] lines so vital that the federal government tapped into the national oil reserves to make up for the shortfall when the network went offline.[161] Residents left homeless and destitute in the wake of the storm soon became refugees requiring assistance in countless other states.[162] Federal responsibility in the crisis may also attach to the federal role in constructing what the Army Corps of Engineers now itself concedes were structurally faulty levees.[163] Finally, it has even been argued that the anarchy following Katrina rendered federal intervention necessary to fulfill the Constitution's Guarantee Clause,[164] which, in guaranteeing each state "a Republican Form of Government" implicitly promised federal action to preserve at least *some* functioning governance in New Orleans when state and local government had collapsed.[165]

Thus, responding to Katrina was indeed the state's obligation, but it was also the nation's obligation. Despite the NRP's promise to protect lives, the relief effort failed the thousands of residents who died in their neighborhoods and nursing homes and the thirty-four who died in the Superdome and convention center.[166] Hundreds of thousands of evacuees sought shelter and employment in cities and towns across the nation, and federal expenditures on emergency housing for them amount to millions of dollars each day. Oil spills and damaged infrastructure spiked the price of fuel nationwide, triggering fears ranging from a national recession to an increase in domestic terrorist activity. With up to twenty-five percent of New Orleans' housing stock condemned,[167] an epidemic of crime that has persisted more

---

160    LaCoast, Stemming the Tide: The Mississippi River Delta and the Davis Pond Freshwater Diversion Project, http://www.lacoast.gov/programs/Davis Pond/stemming-the-tide.htm (last visited Nov. 13, 2008).

161    Jad Mouawad & Vikas Bajaj, *Gulf Oil Operations Remain in Disarray*, N.Y. Times, Sept. 2, 2005, at C1.

162    *See supra* notes 107–108 and accompanying text.

163    *See* Schwartz, *supra* note 125 (recounting reports that the Army Corps conceded that the levee designs were flawed).

164    U.S. Const. art. IV, § 4.

165    Greenberger, *supra* note 67, at 23.

166    *See supra* notes 100–101 and accompanying text.

167    *See* Adam Nossiter, *Thousands of Demolitions Near, New Orleans Braces for New Pain*, N.Y. Times, Oct. 23, 2005, § 1 (noting that over 50,000 of the city's 180,000 homes could be demolished).

than a year after the storm,[168] and environmental hazards threatening health and safety into the foreseeable future,[169] there is no quick end to the crisis in sight.

In other words, everyone had a stake—but as we now well know, the bifurcated disaster response itself proved disastrous. As the stories of failure after failure in the relief effort unfolded, culpability fell on city, state, and federal agencies alike. The City of New Orleans probably should have considered how the 100,000 New Orleans residents without motor vehicles would be able to heed Mayor Nagin's evacuation command. The State of Louisiana probably should have considered the wisdom of moving the National Guard headquarters that would coordinate hurricane response to higher ground before the storm. The federal government apparently failed to heed National Weather Service warnings about the scope of the storm and failed to deploy FEMA resources appropriately before the storm. The federal government probably should have intervened sooner when it became clear (at least to the average American watching the nightly news) that local efforts to confront the hurricane aftermath were insufficient, and when it finally did intervene, it should have been able to provide a more effective chain of command to facilitate decision-making.

From the constitutional perspective, it is these last failures that are most troubling, given reports about the White House debate over the federalism implications of taking initiative[170] and former FEMA Director Michael Brown's congressional testimony explaining the reluctant federal response (disingenuously or not) in overtly New Federalist terms.[171] The New Federalism decisions themselves may not have erected an explicit doctrinal barrier to the interjurisdictional response needed after Katrina,[172] but they define a trajectory pointing state and federal leadership toward the strict-separationist extreme that either convinced or confused them about the available regulatory choices. The fact that the crisis was a legitimate matter of state concern did not foreclose the fact that it was also a matter of legitimate federal concern, demanding proactive federal intervention from within the federalism order.

---

168     *See* Brandon L. Garrett & Tania Tetlow, *Criminal Justice Collapse: The Constitution After Hurricane Katrina*, 56 Duke L.J. 127, 135–54 (2006) (describing the collapse of the criminal justice system in post-Katrina New Orleans); Adam Nossiter, *Storm Left New Orleans Ripe for Violence*, N.Y. Times, Jan. 11, 2007, at A24 ("The storm of violence that has burst over this city since New Year's Day can be traced in part to dysfunctional law enforcement institutions, aggravated by a natural disaster that turned the physical and social landscape of New Orleans into an ideal terrain for criminals.").

169     *See* EPA, Response to 2005 Hurricanes: Frequent Questions, http://www.epa. gov/katrina/faqs.htm (last visited Mar. 15, 2007) (providing a forum to address a host of continuing health and safety related issues for the residents of the New Orleans area).

170     *See Tug of War*, *supra* note 1, at 527–32.

171     *See supra* notes 52–53 and accompanying text.

172     That said, the anticommandeering rule of *New York* and *Printz* may well have discouraged the White House from "federalizing" the Louisiana National Guard without gubernatorial consent.

The Katrina debacle illustrated the risks of applying a binary decision rule in interjurisdictional contexts—characterizing matters as "either/or": if national, then not local; if local, then not national.[173] Taken to its extreme, this approach obstructs effective governance by assigning jurisdiction over a matter requiring both a local and national response to *either* state *or* federal agents exclusively, and then zealously guarding the boundary against defensible (even desirable) crossover by the other. But this is a nonsensical approach when the problem requires both local and national competencies. The strict-separationist model regards regulatory activity as permissible if it fits neatly within the state or federal box anticipated by its test, and impermissible if it does not. But what if the problem is not with the activity, but with the limitations of a simple, two-box test?

If nothing else, Katrina has taught us that interjurisdictional regulatory problems require us, quite literally, to think outside the New Federalism boxes. Indeed, Michael Brown memorably intoned (from squarely within the box) that the "princip[les] of federalism should not be lost in a short-term desire to react to a natural disaster of catastrophic proportions," fretting that a more proactive federal response would have undermined the very foundations of dual sovereignty.[174] His testimony sadly demonstrates that the New Federalism failed Katrina victims not for lack of good intentions, but for lack of imagination.

Now that the 39,000 refugees have left the "Third World hellhole" that became New Orleans in the first few days after the storm,[175] it is easier to find sympathy for how White House officials became mired in the federalism problems suggested by the response. After all, they were fairly interpreting the trajectory of the Supreme Court's recent federalism rulings,[176] and thus hesitated to invoke potential Stafford Act authority to intrude upon the state's primary role as provider of intrastate relief and law enforcement services. But the interjurisdictional nature of the Katrina emergency demonstrates how a problem shaped beyond the comprehension of the strict-separationist model can cause the entire system to crash. Indeed, interjurisdictional problems spawn circumstances that exacerbate the inherent tension between underlying federalism values, with which the New Federalism is ill-equipped to handle. Although symptoms of this mismatch were evident in foundering regulatory responses to less mediagenic interjurisdictional problems preceding Katrina (e.g., the disposal of low-level radioactive waste and the management of respiratory disease in Los Angeles), the Katrina debacle brought home to the nation a clear message: a legal framework built around a

---

173    *See* Robert A. Schapiro & William W. Buzbee, *Unidimensional Federalism: Power and Perspective in Commerce Clause Adjudication*, 88 CORNELL L. REV. 1199, 1203–05 (2003) (arguing that the Rehnquist Court's narrow federalism perspective threatens to impermissibly impinge on proper federal legislative power).

174    Brown Statement, *supra* note 52, at 3.

175    Thomas et al., *supra* note 47, at 40.

176    *See Tug of War, supra* note 1, at 554–63 (discussing the distinct spheres of state and federal power in the New Federalism).

theory that does not track the real-world targets of regulatory response is unstable and unsustainable.

It also suggested an alternative, at least in the Katrina response, that most Americans collectively imagined was possible. In this vision, the federal government would have assessed claims by the emergency to its own regulatory responsibility, and then weighed the regulatory crossover alternative (here, proactive federal intervention) against each of the federalism values at stake— the reasons for our federal system of government in the first place. It would have considered the severity of the problem, the capacity of the state and local governments to respond, and the relative risks to dual sovereignty checks and balances of crossing into the interjurisdictional gray area. The state and local governments would have made a similar evaluation, to the extent of their capacity. Most Americans apparently believed that the federal interest in saving the lives and relieving the human suffering of its own citizens far overwhelmed the risks to inter-sovereign diplomacy, but in any event, a conclusion would have been reached more efficiently and decisively if freed from the paralysis provoked by the New Federalism approach.[177]

This paralysis reflects perhaps the most serious trap of binary thinking promoted by the New Federalism, which is its essential suggestion that we must choose between _either_ federalism _or_ interjurisdictional problem-solving. Either we are faithful to the constitutional ideal of dual sovereignty, or we can effectively grapple with the collective action problems that we ask regulation to help us control. New Federalism frames this as the choice by positing the check-and-balance value as synonymous with federalism in general. But as important as they are, checks and balances are only _one_ of the principles of good government that undergird American federalism. Indeed, there are a host of others—accountability, localism, problem-solving—all in tension with one another. The interpretive model of federalism that we choose determines how we mediate this tension, and New Federalism's solution is to privilege checks and balances over all others. So does faithfulness to federalism require that we forsake interjurisdictional problem-solving? It depends on the operative federalism model. New Federalism suggests so, but this chapter suggests not.

Instead, the Court's future federalism jurisprudence should draw from a model of federalism that continues to protect our important interest in the balance of state and federal power while also affording the flexibility necessary for government at all levels to meaningfully address the problems we entrust to their care. To the extent that the New Federalism model cannot accommodate the dimensions of the interjurisdictional gray area, then it must be adjusted until it can, enabling more effective governance in accordance with a more robust theoretical model. Whether an act of regulatory crossover should be considered a constitutional violation should depend on a consideration of all federalism values that lead us to

---

177   _See supra_ note 92 and accompanying text (reviewing public disapproval of the federal response).

the system of dual sovereignty symbolized by the Tenth Amendment, not just the strict separation of state and federal powers for its own sake. Once again, it is not a choice about federalism or not, but rather *which* model of federalism realizes the best balance of the values that motivate federalism to begin with.[178]

## Acknowledgements

For their assistance on the full article (of which this chapter is an excerpt), I am deeply indebted to Bill Van Alstyne, Richard Lazarus, Erwin Chemerinsky, Vicki Jackson, Neal Devins, Michael Stein, Tony Arnold, David Barron, John Vile, and Laura Heymann for their insightful comments, and as well to Ned Ryan, Eric Kades, Dave Douglas, Michele Gillman, Nancy Combs, Rich Hynes, Eric Chason, and Linda Malone for their guidance during my early phases of research. This project would not have been possible without the expert research assistance of Jessica Deering, Syed Masood, Janet McCrae, Katy Mikols, Catherine Rylyk, Tara St. Angelo, Matthew Whipple, and especially Tal Kedem, and the hard work of the *Maryland Law Review* editors who helped prepare it for publication. Finally, I am thankful to Robin Paul Malloy and the other participants in the workshop on *Law and Recovery from Disaster* for their insights during our meeting.

---

178    The full length article argues that, to remedy the theoretical problems left unresolved by cooperative federalism and the pragmatic ones caused by New Federalism, the Court should adopt a model of Balanced Federalism that better mediates between competing federalism values and provides greater guidance for regulatory decision-making in the interjurisdictional gray area. Where the New Federalism asks the Tenth Amendment to police a stylized boundary between state and federal authority from crossover by either side, Balanced Federalism asks the Tenth Amendment to patrol regulatory activity within the gray area for impermissible compromises of fundamental federalism values. The article concludes by introducing the outlines of a jurisprudential standard for interpreting Tenth Amendment claims within a model of Balanced Federalism dual sovereignty that affords both checks and balances. *See* Erin Ryan, *Federalism and the Tug of War Within: Seeking Checks and Balance in the Interjurisdictional Gray Area*, 66 MD. L. REV. 503, 644–65 (2007).

# Table of Cases

# Bibliography

## Books, News, Articles

ABRAHAM, KENNETH S., DISTRIBUTING RISK: INSURANCE, LEGAL THEORY, AND PUBLIC POLICY (1986).

ABRAMS, CHARLES, FORBIDDEN NEIGHBORS (1955).

Adler, Jonathan H., *Jurisdictional Mismatch in Environmental Federalism*, 14 N.Y.U. ENVTL. L.J. 130, 135 (2005).

Aguirre, B.E., *Dialectics of Vulnerability and Resilience*, 14 GEO. J. ON POVERTY L. & POL'Y 39 (2007).

Alexander, Frank S., *Land Bank Strategies for Renewing Urban Land*, 14 J. AFFORDABLE HOUS. & COMMUNITY DEV. L. 140 (2005).

Alexander, Frank S., *Tax Liens, Tax Sales and Due Process*, 75 IND. L.J. 747 (2000).

Alexander et al., Frank S., *New Orleans Technical Assessment and Assistance Report: Recommended Actions to Facilitate Prevention, Acquisition, and Disposition of New Orleans' Blighted, Abandoned, and Tax Adjudicated Properties*, Feb. 21, 2005.

ALEXANDER, GREGORY, COMMODITY & PROPERTY (1979).

Alexandre, Michèle, *Love Don't Live Here Anymore: Economic Incentives for More Equitable Models of Urban Redevelopment*, 35 B.C. ENVTL. AFF. L. REV. 1 (2007).

Alstyne, William Van, *Interpreting This Constitution: The Unhelpful Contributions of Special Theories of Judicial Review*, 35 U. FLA. L. REV. 209 (1983).

AM. ACAD. OF ACTUARIES, PUBLIC POLICY MONOGRAPH, P/C TERRORISM INSURANCE COVERAGE: WHERE DO WE GO POST-TERRORISM RISK INSURANCE ACT? 12 (2004).

AMERICAN LAW OF PROPERTY, Vol. 5, § 20.11 (ed. James Casner) (1952).

Ammons, M. Paige, *Private Governance for All: A Desirable Outcome or a Cause for Concern?* 9 N.Y.U. J. LEGIS. & PUB. POL'Y 503 (2005).

ANDERSON, MARY B. & PETER J. WOODROW, RISING FROM THE ASHES: DEVELOPMENT STRATEGIES IN TIMES OF DISASTER (1998).

Arnold, Craig A., *Ignoring the Rural Underclass: The Biases of Federal Housing Policy*, 2 STAN. L. & POL'Y REV. 191 (1990).

Baldwin, Timothy, *The Constitutional Right to Travel: Are Some Forms of Transportation More Equal than Others?*, 1 NW. J.L. & SOC. POL'Y 213 (2006).

Banerjee, Neela, *In New Orleans, Rebuilding With Faith*, N.Y. TIMES, Oct. 26, 2007.

BANKS, ERIK, ALTERNATIVE RISK TRANSFER: INTEGRATING RISK MANAGEMENT THROUGH INSURANCE, REINSURANCE AND THE CAPITAL MARKETS (2004).

BANKS, ERIK, CATASTROPHIC RISK: ANALYSIS AND MANAGEMENT (2005).

Barker, Karlyn & Nia-Malika Henderson, *Plight of Stranded Animals Worsening Daily*, WASH. POST, Sept. 8, 2005, at B4.

Barron, David J., *Fighting Federalism with Federalism: If It's Not Just a Battle Between Federalists and Nationalists, What Is It?*, 74 FORDHAM L. REV. 2081 (2006).

Bassett, Debra Lyn, *Distancing Rural Poverty*, 13 GEO. J. POVERTY L. & POL'Y 3 (2006).

Bassett, Debra Lyn, *The Hidden Bias in Diversity Jurisdiction*, 81 WASH. U. L.Q. 119 (2003).

Bassett, Debra Lyn, *The Politics of the Rural Vote*, 35 ARIZ. ST. L.J. 743 (2003).

Bassett, Debra Lyn, *The Rural Venue*, 57 ALA. L. REV. 939 (2006).

Bassett, Debra Lyn, *Ruralism*, 88 IOWA L. REV. 273 (2003).

BECK, ULRICH, RISK SOCIETY: TOWARD A NEW MODERNITY 36 (1986).

BERGER, RAOUL, GOVERNMENT BY JUDICIARY (1997).

Berman, Paul Schiff, *Towards a Cosmopolitan Vision of Conflict of Laws: Redefining Governmental Interests in a Global Era*, 153 U. PA. L. REV. 1819 (2005).

Bernier, Barbara L., *The Praxis of Church and State in the (Under) development of Women's Religion from France to the New World*, 7 WM. & MARY J. WOMEN & L. 683 (2001).

BERNSTEIN, PETER L., AGAINST THE GODS: THE REMARKABLE STORY OF RISK (1996).

Beydoun, Khaled Ali, *Without Color of Law: The Losing Race Against Color Blindness in Michigan*, 12 MICH. J. RACE & L. 465 (2007).

Birkmaier, Ulrike & Camille Codoni, *World Insurance in 2003: Insurance Industry on the Road to Recovery*, in SIGMA 2004, at 33 (Swiss Re, Sigma No. 3/2004, 2004).

BLAIKIE, PIERS, TERRY CANNON, IAN DAVIS & BEN WISNER, AT RISK: NATURAL HAZARDS, PEOPLE'S VULNERABILITY AND DISASTERS 9 (1994).

Bohacek, Erin, *A Disastrous Effect: Hurricane Katrina's Impact on Louisiana Landlord-Tenant Law and the Need for Legislative and Judicial Action*, 52 LOY. L. REV. 877 (2006).

Bohn, James G. & Brian J. Hall, *The Moral Hazard of Insuring the Insurers*, in THE FINANCING OF CATASTROPHIC RISK (KENNETH A. FROOT ED., 1999).

Bolin, R. & L. Stanford, *The Northridge Earthquake: Community-Based Approaches at Unmet Recovery Needs*, 22 DISASTERS 21 (1998).

Bork, Robert H., *The Constitution, Original Intent, and Economic Rights*, 23 SAN DIEGO L. REV. 823 (1986).

BRAUNER, CHRISTIAN, THE RISK LANDSCAPE OF THE FUTURE 15 (Swiss Re 2004).

Bray, James H., Michael F. Enright & John Rogers, *Collaboration With Primary Care Physicians*, in PRACTICING PSYCHOLOGY IN RURAL SETTINGS: HOSPITAL PRIVILEGES AND COLLABORATIVE CARE (Jerry A. Morris ed., 1997).

BRINKLEY, DOUGLAS, THE GREAT DELUGE: HURRICANE KATRINA, NEW ORLEANS, AND THE MISSISSIPPI GULF COAST (2006).

Broder, John M., *Guard Units' New Mission: From Combat to Flood Duty*, N.Y. TIMES, Aug. 30, 2005, at A13.

Brown, Carol Necole & Serena M. Williams, *The Houses That Eminent Domain and Housing Tax Credits Built: Imagining a Better New Orleans*, 34 FORDHAM URB. L.J. 689 (2007).

Buchanan, James M., *The Samaritan's Dilemma*, in ALTRUISM, MORALITY, AND ECONOMIC THEORY (Edmund S. Phelps ed., 1975).

Bullard, Robert D., *Addressing Urban Transportation Equity in the United States*, 31 FORDHAM URB. L.J. 1183 (2004).

Bumiller, Elisabeth, *In New Orleans, Bush Speaks With Optimism but Sees Little of Ruin*, N.Y. TIMES, Jan. 13, 2006, at A12.

Buzbee, William W., *Contextual Environmental Federalism*, 14 N.Y.U. ENVTL. L.J. 108 (2005).

Buzbee, William W., *Recognizing the Regulatory Commons: A Theory of Regulatory Gaps*, 89 IOWA L. REV. 1 (2003).

Byrne, J. Peter & Michael Diamond, *Affordable Housing, Land Tenure, and Urban Policy: The Matrix Revealed*, 34 FORDHAM URB. L.J. 527 (2007).

CALABRESI, GUIDO, THE COSTS OF ACCIDENTS: A LEGAL AND ECONOMIC ANALYSIS (1970).

CAMPANELLA, RICHARD, GEOGRAPHIES OF NEW ORLEANS: URBAN FABRICS BEFORE THE STORM (2006).

CAREY, CORRINE, HUMAN RIGHTS WATCH, NO SECOND CHANCE: PEOPLE WITH CRIMINAL RECORDS DENIED ACCESS TO PUBLIC HOUSING (2004).

CENTER FOR PROGRESSIVE REFORM, AN UNNATURAL DISASTER: THE AFTERMATH OF HURRICANE KATRINA 34 (2005).

CHING, BARBARA & GERALD W. CREED, KNOWING YOUR PLACE: RURAL IDENTITY AND CULTURAL HIERARCHY (1997).

City of New Orleans, City Announces First 17 Target Recovery Zones, Mayors Office of Comm'ns (Mar. 29, 2007).

Coase, Ronald H., *The Nature of the Firm*, 4 ECONOMICA 386 (1937).

COMMITTEE FOR A BETTER NEW ORLEANS, A BLUEPRINT FOR A BETTER NEW ORLEANS (2001).

Corral, Oscar, *Stranded Pets Facing Starvation*, MIAMI HERALD, Sept. 5, 2005, at A13.

Cotter, David A., *Addressing Person and Place to Alleviate Rural Poverty*, in PERSPECTIVES ON POVERTY, POL'Y & PLACE, RUPRI Rural Poverty Res. Ctr. (2003).

Craig-Taylor, Phyllis, *To Be Free: Liberty, Citizenship, Property, and Race*, 14 HARV. BLACKLETTER L.J. 45 (1998).

CRIPPEN, DAN L., CONG. BUDGET OFFICE, A CBO STUDY: FEDERAL REINSURANCE FOR DISASTERS (Cong. Budget Office 2002).

Cummins, J. David, Neil Doherty & Anita Lo, *Can Insurers Pay for the "Big One":
Measuring the Capacity of the Insurance Market to Respond to Catastrophic
Losses*, 26 J. BANKING & FIN. 557 (2002).

Dagan, Hanoch & Michael Heller, *The Liberal Commons*, 110 YALE L.J. 549 (2001).

D'AGOSTINO, DAVI M., CATASTROPHE INSURANCE RISKS: THE ROLE OF RISK-LINKED SECURITIES AND FACTORS AFFECTING THEIR USE, GENERAL ACCOUNTING OFFICE (GAO) No. 02-941 (2002).

Darden, Joe T., *The Effect of World War I on Black Occupational and Residential
Segregation: The case of Pittsburgh*, 18 J. OF BLACK STUDIES 3, 308 (1988).

Dash, Eric & David Leonhardt, *Invasion of Reluctant Renters; So Many Evacuees
and, Luckily, So Many Apartments in Cities of Refuge*, N.Y. TIMES, Sept. 16, 2005, at C1.

DAVIDSON, OSHA GRAY, BROKEN HEARTLAND: THE RISE OF AMERICA'S RURAL GHETTO (1996).

DAVIS, EDWIN A. & RALEIGH SUAREZ, LOUISIANA: THE PELICAN STATE (5th ed. 1985).

Dean, Robert G., *New Orleans and the Wetlands of Central Louisiana*, 36 THE BRIDGE 35, 39 (2006).

Deavers, Kenneth L. & Robert A. Hoppe, *The Rural Poor: The Past as Prologue*,
*in* RURAL POLICIES FOR THE 1990S (Cornelia B. Flora & James A. Christenson eds., 1991).

DeLeon, Patrick H., Mary Wakefield and Kristofer J. Hagglund, *The Behavioral
Health Care Needs of Rural Communities in the 21st Century*, *in* RURAL BEHAVIORAL HEALTH CARE: AN INTERDISCIPLINARY GUIDE (B. Hudnall Stamm ed., 2003).

*Discrimination in Sale or Rental Terms and Services*, 15 AM. JUR. 2D CIVIL RIGHTS, § 392 (2007).

DIXON, LLOYD & RACHEL KAGANOFF STERN, COMPENSATION FOR LOSSES FROM THE 9/11 ATTACKS (RAND 2004).

Donze, Frank, *Low-Profile Agency Gains Blight-Bust Powers: Unlikely Agency
Key to Rebirth*, TIMES-PICAYUNE (NEW ORLEANS), Oct. 11, 2006.

Drew, Christopher, *In New Orleans, Rust in the Wheels of Justice*, N.Y. TIMES, Nov. 21, 2006, at A1.

Dudziak, Mary L., *The Court and Social Context in Civil Rights History*, 72 U. CHI. L. REV. 429 (2005).

Dutton, Jane, *The Processing of Crisis and Non-Crisis Strategic Issues*, 23 J. MGMT. STUD. 501 (1988).

Easton, Nina J., *Katrina Aid Falls Short of Promises*, BOSTON GLOBE, Nov. 27, 2005, at A1.

Eaton, Leslie, *Judge Steps in for Poor Inmates Without Justice Since Hurricane*,
N.Y. TIMES, May 23, 2006, at A1.

Editorial, *Reforming Foreign Assistance*, WASH. POST, Jan. 3, 2006, at A16.

Elliott, Dominic, Kim Harris & Steve Baron, *Crisis Management and Services Marketing*, 19 J. SERVICES MARKETING 336 (2005).

Elliott, Dominic & Martina McGuinness, *Public Inquiries: Panacea or Placebo?*, 10 J. CONTINGENCIES & CRISIS MGMT. 14 (2002).

Engel, Kristen H, *Harnessing the Benefits of Dynamic Federalism in Environmental Law*, 56 EMORY L.J. 155 (2006).

*Ensuring Economic Security in the Face of Terrorism: A Public-Private Partnership*, AM. INS. ASS'N ADVOCATE, Mar. 3, 2005, at 3.

Epstein, Richard, *Notice and Freedom of Contract in the Law of Servitudes*, 55 S. CAL. L. REV. 1353 (1982).

Farber, Daniel A., *Disaster Law and Inequality*, 25 LAW & INEQ. 297 (2007).

FARBER, DANIEL A. & JIM CHEN, DISASTERS AND THE LAW: KATRINA AND BEYOND (2006).

Feld, Barry C., *Race, Politics and Juvenile Justice: The Warren Court and the Conservative "Backlash,"* 87 MINN. L. REV. 1447 (2003).

Filosa, Gwen & Michelle Hunter, *Rental Quandary: Scarce Units, Costly Repairs and Surging Rents Hit Tenants and Landlords Hard*, TIMES-PICAYUNE (NEW ORLEANS), Dec. 12, 2005.

FINK, STEVEN, CRISIS MANAGEMENT: PLANNING FOR THE INEVITABLE (1986).

Finley, Robert M., *Fixing a Hole Where the Rain Gets in: The Case for a National Homeowner's Insurance Plan*, 14 GEO. J. ON POVERTY L. & POL'Y 155 (2007).

FITCHEN, JANET M., ENDANGERED SPACES, ENDURING PLACES: CHANGE, IDENTITY, AND SURVIVAL IN RURAL AMERICA (1991).

Fletcher, Michael A. & Richard Morin, *Bush's Approval Rating Drops to New Low in Wake of Storm*, WASH. POST, Sept. 13, 2005, at A8.

Frankel, Tamar & Joseph W. LaPlume, *Securitizing Insurance Risk*, 19 ANN. REV. BANKING L. 203 (2000).

Franzese, Paula & Steven Siegal, *Trust and Community: The Common Interest Community as Metaphor and Paradox*, 72 Mo. L. Rev. 1111 (2007).

Freeman, Jody, *Collaborative Governance in the Administrative State*, 45 UCLA L. REV. 1 (1997).

Frieden, Lex, *Involve People with Disabilities in Relief Plans: Let's Learn from Our Mistakes Before the Next Disaster Strikes*, CLARION-LEDGER, Jan. 7, 2006.

FRIEDMAN, MILTON R. & PATRICK A. RANDOLPH, JR., FRIEDMAN ON LEASES §§ 9.1– 9.12 (5th ed. 2004).

GABE, THOMAS, GENE FALK & MAGGIE MCCARTY, HURRICANE KATRINA: SOCIAL-DEMOGRAPHIC CHARACTERISTICS OF IMPACTED AREAS 18 (Nov. 4, 2005) (CRS Order Code RL33141).

Garrett, Brandon L. & Tania Tetlow, *Criminal Justice Collapse: The Constitution After Hurricane Katrina*, 56 DUKE L.J. 127 (2006).

Gerstenzang, James, *Bird Flu Warning Would Ravage U.S., White House Warns*, L.A. TIMES, May 4, 2006, at A6.

Goyet, Claude de Ville de and André Griekspoor, *Natural Disasters, The Best Friend of Poverty*, 14 GEO. J. POVERTY L. & POL'Y 61 (2007).

GRODZINS, MORTON, THE AMERICAN SYSTEM (Daniel J. Elazar ed., 1966).

Guy, Clifford & Mary Duckett, *Small Retailers in an Inner City Community: A Case Study of Adamsdown, Cardiff*, 31 INT'L J. RETAIL & DISTRIBUTION MGMT. 401 (2003).

Haar, Charles M., *Wanted: Two Federal Levers for Urban Land Use – Land Banks and Urbank: Paper submitted to Subcomm. on Housing Panels, of H. Comm. on Banking and Currency* (1971).

Hale, Joanne E., Ronald E. Dulek & David P. Hale, *Crisis Response Communication Challenges: Building Theory from Qualitative Data*, 42 J. BUS. COM. 112 (2005).

Hammer, David, *Relief Far Off for La. Rental Owners*, TIMES-PICAYUNE (NEW ORLEANS), Jan. 4, 2007.

HARVARD MEDICAL SCHOOL, THE CENTER FOR HEALTH AND THE GLOBAL ENVIRONMENT, CLIMATE CHANGE FUTURES: HEALTH, ECOLOGICAL AND ECONOMIC DIMENSIONS 4 (Paul R. Epstein & Evan Mills eds., 2005).

Helfenstein, Rainer & Thomas Holzheu, *Securitization—New Opportunities for Insurers and Investors*, in SIGMA 2006, at 24 (Swiss Re, Sigma No. 7/2006, 2006).

Henckaerts, Jean-Marie & Louise Doswald-Beck, 1 CUSTOMARY INTERNATIONAL HUMANITARIAN LAW 489 (Cambridge U. Press 2005).

Hermann, Charles F., *Some Consequences of Crises Which Limit the Viability of Organizations*, 8 ADMIN. SCI. Q. 61 (1963).

Hess, Gerald F., *The Trail Smelter, the Columbia River, and the Extraterritorial Application of CERCLA*, 18 GEO. INT'L ENVTL. L. REV. 1, 2–4 (2005).

Hills, Alice, *Seduced by Recovery: The Consequences of Misunderstanding Disaster*, 6 J. CONTINGENCIES & CRISIS MGMT 162 (1998).

Hirst, Eliza, *The Housing Crisis for Victims of Domestic Violence: Disparate Impact Claims and Other Housing Protection for Victims of Domestic Violence*, 10 GEO. J. ON POVERTY L. & POL'Y 131 (2003).

Houck, Oliver, *Can We Save New Orleans?*, 19 TUL. ENVTL. L.J. 1 (2006).

HUBBARD, R. GLENN & BRUCE DEAL, THE ECONOMIC EFFECTS OF FEDERAL PARTICIPATION IN TERRORISM RISK (2004).

*HUD Approves $4.2 B for Louisiana's "Road Home" Rebuilding Program*, USA TODAY, July 11, 2006.

Hylton, Keith N. & Vincent D. Rougeau, *Lending Discrimination: Economic Theory, Econometric Evidence, and the Community Reinvestment Act*, 85 GEO. L.J. 237 (1996).

*Improving Housing Policy and Practice* (Mtumishi St. Julien, November 2001).

Issacharoff, Samual & Catherine M. Sharkey, *Backdoor Federalization*, 53 UCLA L. REV. 1353 (2006).

JACKSON, KENNETH T., CRABGRASS FRONTIER: THE SUBURBANIZATION OF THE UNITED STATES (1985).

Jackson, Vicki C., *Federalism and the Uses and Limits of Law: Printz and Principle?*, 111 Harv. L. Rev. 2180 (1998).

Jimenez, Mary, *Bossier Civic Center Closes Special Needs Shelter*, Shreveport Times, Oct. 7, 2005, at 1A.

Johnson, Marcia, *Addressing Housing Needs in the Post Katrina Gulf Coast*, 31 T. Marshall L. Rev. 327 (2006).

Kantrowitz, Barbara & Karen Breslau, *Some Are Found, All Are Lost*, Newsweek, Sept. 19, 2005, at 51.

*Katrina Aftermath, Louisiana: Don't Want You on My Dance Card*, American Political Network, The Hotline, Sept. 8, 2005, at 7.

Kimball, Spencer L. & Herbert S. Denenberg, Insurance, Government, and Social Policy (1969).

Kirchhoff, Bruce A., Entrepreneurship and Dynamic Capitalism: The Economies of Business Firm Formation and Growth 9 (1994).

Kleindorfer, Paul R. & Howard C. Kunreuther, *Challenges Facing the Insurance Industry in Managing Catastrophic Risks*, in The Financing of Catastrophic Risk (Kenneth A. Froot ed., 1999).

Kochan, Donald J., *Runoff and Reality: Externalities, Economics, and Traceability Problems in Urban Runoff Regulation*, 9 Chapman L. Rev. 409 (2006).

Kravis, Irvin B. & Michael W.S. Davenport, *The Political Arithmetic of International Burden Sharing*, 71 J. Pol. Econ. 309 (1963).

Krugman, Paul, *The Effectiveness Thing*, N.Y. Times, Feb. 6, 2006, at A23.

Krupa, Michelle, *Doubt Next Door*, Times-Picayune (New Orleans), Aug. 26, 2007 at A1.

Kuba, Sue A. & Mary Beth Kenkel, *The Wellness of Women: Implications for the Rural Health Care Provider*, in Practicing Psychology in Rural Settings: Hospital Privileges and Collaborative Care (Jerry A. Morris ed., 1997).

Kunreuther, Howard, *The Case for Comprehensive Disaster Insurance*, 11 J. Law & Econ. 133 (1968).

La Fetra, Deborah J., *A Moving Target: Property Owners' Duty to Prevent Criminal Acts on the Premises*, 28 Whittier L. Rev. 409 (2006).

Laycock, Douglas, *Protecting Liberty in a Federal System: The US Experience*, in Patterns of Regionalism and Federalism: Lessons for the UK (Jörg Fedtke & Basil S. Markesinis eds., 2006).

Lazarus, Richard J., The Making of Environmental Law (2004).

Levingston, Kirsten D., *Denying Housing to Those with Criminal Records Will Perpetuate Cycles of Crime*, Christian Sci. Monitor, Mar. 8, 2006, at 9.

Levmore, Saul, *Coalitions and Quakes: Disaster Relief and Its Prevention*, 3 U. Chi. L. School Roundtable 1 (1996).

Levmore, Saul & Kyle D. Logue, *Insuring Against Terrorism—and Crime*, 102 Mich. L. Rev. 268 (2003).

Lewis, Christopher M. & Kevin C. Murdock, *Alternative Means of Redistributing Catastrophic Risk in a National Risk-Management System*, in The Financing of Catastrophic Risk (Kenneth A. Froot ed., 1999).

Lewis, John, *"This is a National Disgrace,"* NEWSWEEK, Sept. 12, 2005, at 52.

Lewis, Michael, *The National Catastrophe Casino*, N.Y. TIMES (MAGAZINE), Aug. 26, 2007, at 28.

Lipton, Eric, *Storm and Crisis: Hurricane Evacuees Face Eviction Threats at Both Their Old Homes and New*, N.Y. TIMES, Nov. 4, 2005, at A20.

Lipton et al., Eric, *Storm and Crisis: Breakdowns Marked Path from Hurricane to Anarchy*, N.Y. TIMES, Sept. 11, 2005, § 1.

Lipton et al., Eric, *Storm and Crisis: Political Issues Snarled Plans for Troop Aid*, N.Y. TIMES, Sept. 9, 2005, at A1.

LIPTON, MICHAEL, WHY POOR PEOPLE STAY POOR: URBAN BIAS IN WORLD DEVELOPMENT (1976).

LOCKWOOD, C.C., DISCOVERING LOUISIANA (1986).

Logan, Wayne A., *Creating a "Hydra in Government": Federal Recourse to State Law in Crime Fighting*, 86 B.U. L. REV. 65 (2006).

Lovett, John A., *A Bend in the Road: Easement Pliability in the New Restatement (Third) of Property: Servitudes*, 38 CONN. L. REV. 1 (2005).

Lovett, John A., *Doctrines of Waste in a Landscape of Waste*, 72 MO. L. REV. 1209 (2007).

Lovett, John A., *Property and Radically Changed Circumstances: Hurricane Katrina and Beyond*, 74 TENN. L. REV. 463 (2007).

Lovett, John A., *Rebuilding a Region: Housing Recovery Efforts in the Wake of Katrina and Rita*, 20 PROB. & PROP. 49 (2006).

Mahoney, Martha, *Law and Racial Geography: Public Housing and the Economy in New Orleans*, 42 STAN. L. REV. 12 (1990).

*Mail Call: In the Wake of a Devastating Hurricane*, NEWSWEEK, Sept. 26, 2005, at 18.

Malloy, Robin Paul, *The Secondary Mortgage Market: A Catalyst for Change in Real Estate Transactions*, 39 SW. L.J. 991 (1986).

MALLOY, ROBIN PAUL & JAMES CHARLES SMITH, REAL ESTATE TRANSACTIONS: PROBLEMS, CASES AND MATERIALS (3d ed. 2007).

MAPPING VULNERABILITY: DISASTERS, DEVELOPMENT AND PEOPLE (Greg Bankoff et al. eds., 2003).

MARCH, CANDIDA, INES SMYTH & MAITRAYEE MUKHOPADHYAY, A GUIDE TO GENDER ANALYSIS FRAMEWORKS (1999).

Martin, Charles L., *Blending Services and Crises: A Few Questions and Observations*, 19 J. SERVICES MARKETING 346 (2005).

Maute, Judith L., *Response: The Value of Legal Archaeology*, 2000 UTAH L. REV. 223.

McGuire, David & Brian Krebs, *Large-Scale Attack Cripples Internet Backbone*, WASH. POST, Oct. 23, 2002, at E5.

Medina, Jennifer, *Storm and Crisis: Voices from the Storm: Stuck in a Shelter, and Left Asking "Why?,"* N.Y. TIMES, Oct. 5, 2005, at A25.

Meese III, Edwin, *Toward a Jurisprudence of Original Intent*, 11 HARV. J.L. & PUB. POL'Y 5, 7 (1988).

Mendoza, Norma, *Task Force Members Describe Devastation in New Orleans*, EDWARDSVILLE INTELLIGENCER, Oct. 11, 2005, at 1.

Mertus, Julie A., WAR'S OFFENSIVE ON WOMEN (2000).

Mitchell, Thomas W., *From Reconstruction to Deconstruction: Undermining Black Landownership, Political Independence, and Community Through Partition Sales of Tenancies in Common*, 95 Nw. U. L. Rev. 505 (2001).

Moran, Kate, *No Boom, No Bust*, TIMES-PICAYUNE (NEW ORLEANS), Mar. 5, 2008, at C-8.

Morris, Jerry A., *The Rural Psychologist in the Hospital Emergency Room*, *in* PRACTICING PSYCHOLOGY IN RURAL SETTINGS: HOSPITAL PRIVILEGES AND COLLABORATIVE CARE (Jerry A. Morris ed., 1997).

Morton, Lois Wright, *Spatial Patterns of Rural Mortality*, *in* CRITICAL ISSUES IN RURAL HEALTH (Nina Glasgow et al. eds., 2004).

Mouawad, Jad & Vikas Bajaj, *Gulf Oil Operations Remain in Disarray*, N.Y. TIMES, Sept. 2, 2005, at C1.

Mowbray, Rebecca, *Insurance Outlook Gets Brighter*, TIMES-PICAYUNE (NEW ORLEANS), Sept. 3, 2007.

Mowbray, Rebecca, *Reason for Hope*, TIMES-PICAYUNE (NEW ORLEANS), Aug. 12, 2007.

Munzer, Stephen R. & James W. Nickel, *Does the Constitution Mean What It Always Meant?*, 77 COLUM. L. REV. 1029 (1977).

Murray, J. Dennis & Peter A. Keller, *Psychology and Rural America: Current Status and Future Directions*, 46 AM. PSYCHOLOGIST 220 (1991).

Nagin Transition Team: R. Stephanie Bruno & Wayne Neveu, *Blighted Housing Task Force Report* (2002).

National Center for Children in Poverty, *Child Poverty in States Hit by Hurricane Katrina*, *in* CHILD POVERTY IN 21ST CENTURY AM. (2005).

NBC Nightly News, FEMA Director Michael Brown Discusses Relief Efforts in Hurricane Zone (NBC television broadcast Sept. 1, 2005).

Nelson, Grant S. & Dale A. Whitman, REAL ESTATE FINANCE LAW (4th ed. 2001).

Nelson, Grant S. & Dale Whitman, REAL ESTATE TRANSFER, FINANCE AND DEVELOPMENT: CASES AND MATERIALS (7th ed. 2006).

Newton, Milton B., ATLAS OF LOUISIANA (1972).

Niehuss, Marvin H., *Alteration or Replacement of Buildings by Long-Term Lessee*, 30 MICH. L. REV. 386 (1932).

Nolon, John R., *Katrina's Lament: Reconstructing Federalism*, 23 PACE ENVTL. L. REV. 987 (2006).

Nossiter, Adam, *Storm Left New Orleans Ripe for Violence*, N.Y. TIMES, Jan. 11, 2007, at A24.

Nossiter, Adam, *Thousands of Demolitions Near, New Orleans Braces for New Pain*, N.Y. TIMES, Oct. 23, 2005, at 1.

Orth, John V., *Relocating Easements: A Response to Professor French*, 38 REAL PROP. PROB. & TR. J. 643 (2004).

Overby, A. Brooke, *Mortgage Foreclosure in Post-Katrina New Orleans*, 48 B.C. L. Rev. 851 (2007).

Overton, Spencer, *Race, Privilege and Campaign Finance*, 79 N.C. L. Rev. 1541 (2001).

Peacock, Walter Gillis & Chris Girard, *Ethnic and Racial Inequalities in Hurricane Damage and Insurance Settlements*, in Hurricane Andrew: Ethnicity, Gender and the Sociology of Disasters (Walter Gillis Peacock et al. eds., 1997).

Pearson, Christine M. & Judith A. Clair, *Reframing Crisis Management*, 23 Acad. Mgmt. Rev. 59 (1998).

Peñalver, Eduardo, *Property as Entrance*, 91 U.Va. L. Rev. 1889 (2005).

Perry, Stephen C., *The Relationship Between Written Business Plans and the Failure of Small Businesses in the U.S.*, 39 Int'l J. Retail & Distribution Mgmt. 201 (2000).

Pidgeon et al., Nick, The Social Amplification of Risk (2003).

Ploss, George, *America's Real "Prisoner's Dilemma,"* U. Wire, Mar. 27, 2007.

Plummer, Anne, *Loosening Restrictions on the Military Enforcing Civil Law Unwise, Say Critics*, Cong. Q. Wkly., Sept. 24, 2005.

Porro, Bruno & Werner Schad, *The Risk Landscape of the Future*, Swiss Re (2004).

Porter, Katherine, *Going Broke the Hard Way: The Economics of Rural Failure*, 2005 Wis. L. Rev. 969.

Posner, Richard A., Catastrophe: Risk and Response (2004).

Post, Robert, *Theories of Constitutional Interpretation*, in Representations 13 (1990).

Pub. Affairs Research Council of Louisiana, *Guide to the Constitutional Amendments* (Sept. 8, 2006).

Purdy, Jedediah, *The American Transformation of Waste Doctrine: A Pluralist Interpretation*, 91 Cornell L. Rev. 653 (2006).

Quarantelli, Enrico L., *Disaster Crisis Management: A Summary of Research Findings*, 25 J. Mgmt. Stud. 373 (1988).

Quigley, William P., *Obstacle to Opportunity: Housing That Working and Poor People Can Afford in New Orleans since Katrina*, 42 Wake Forest L. Rev. 393 (2007).

Randolph, Patrick, *A Mortgagee's Interest in Casualty Loss Proceeds, Evolving Rules and Risks*, 32 Real Prop. Prob. & Tr. 1 (1997).

Rehnquist, William H., *The Notion of a Living Constitution*, 54 Tex. L. Rev. 693 (1976).

*Renters in New Orleans See Prices Rise 39 Percent*, N.Y. Times, Sept. 17, 2006.

Restatement (Third) of Property (2000).

Rhee, Robert J., *Catastrophic Risk and Governance After Hurricane Katrina: A Postscript to Terrorism Risk in a Post-9/11 Economy*, 38 Ariz. St. L.J. 581 (2006).

Rhee, Robert J., *The Effect of Risk on Legal Valuation*, 78 U. Colo. L. Rev. 193 (2007).

Rhee, Robert J., *A Price Theory of Legal Bargaining: An Inquiry into the Selection of Settlement and Litigation Under Uncertainty*, 56 EMORY L.J. 619 (2006).

Robert J. Rhee, *Terrorism Risk in a Post-9/11 Economy: The Convergence of Capital Markets, Insurance, and Government Action*, 37 ARIZ. ST. L.J. 435 (2005).

Rhee, Robert J., *Tort Arbitrage*, 60 FLA. L. REV. 125 (2008).

Riley, John & Craig Gordon, *Katrina—What Went Wrong*, NEWSDAY, Sept. 3, 2005, at A4.

Robbins, D. Keith, Louis J. Pantuosco, Darrell F. Parker & Barbara K. Fuller, *An Empirical Assessment of the Contribution of Small Business Employment to U.S. State Economic Performance*, 15 SMALL BUS. ECON. 293 (2001).

Roberts, Deon, *Real Estate Expert: N.O. Population Will Recover Slowly*, NEW ORLEANS CITY BUS., Feb. 1, 2006.

Robinson, Glen O., *Explaining Contingent Rights: The Puzzle of Obsolete Covenants*, 91 COLUM. L. REV. 546 (1991).

Romero, Simon, *A Barren Port Waits Eagerly For Its People*, N.Y. TIMES, Oct. 6, 2005, at C1.

Rose, Carol, *Servitudes, Security and Assent: Some Comments on Professors French and Reichman*, 55 S. CAL. L. REV. 1403 (1982).

Rosen, Jeffrey, *Bush's Leviathan State: Power of One*, THE NEW REPUBLIC, July 24, 2006, at 8.

Rosenthal, Elisabeth, *Recent Spread of Bird Flu Confounds Experts*, N.Y. TIMES, Mar. 6, 2006, at A6.

ROTHBARD, MURRAY N., FOR A NEW LIBERTY: THE LIBERTARIAN MANIFESTO (rev. ed. 1978).

Rubin, Edward L., *The Fundamentality and Irrelevance of Federalism*, 13 GA. ST. U. L. REV. 1009 (1997).

Rubin, Edward L. & Malcolm Feeley, *Federalism: Some Notes on a National Neurosis*, 41 UCLA L. REV. 903 (1994).

Runyan, Rodney C., *Small Business in the Face of Crisis: Identifying Barriers to Recovery from a Natural Disaster*, 14 J. CONTINGENCIES & CRISIS MGMT. 12 (2006).

Runyan, Rodney C. & Patricia Huddleston, *Getting Customers Downtown: The Role of Branding in Achieving Success for Central Business Districts*, 15 J. PRODUCT & BRAND MGMT. 48 (2006).

RURAL SOC. SOC'Y TASK FORCE ON PERSISTENT RURAL POVERTY, PERSISTENT POVERTY IN RURAL AMERICA (1993).

Russell, Gordon, *On Their Own: In the Absence of Clear Direction, New Orleanians Are Rebuilding a Patchwork City*, TIMES-PICAYUNE (NEW ORLEANS), Aug. 27, 2006.

Russell, Pam Radtke, *Gulf Platform Damage Still Being Assessed*, NEWHOUSE NEWS SERV., Mar. 23, 2006.

Ryan, Erin, *Federalism and the Tug of War Within: Seeking Checks and Balance in the Interjurisdictional Gray Area*, 66 MD. L. REV. 503 (2007).

Ryan, Erin, *New Orleans, the Chesapeake, and the Future of Environmental Assessment: Overcoming the Natural Resources Law of Unintended Consequences*, 40 U. RICH. L. REV. 981 (2006).

Samuelson, Robert J., *Hitting the Economy*, NEWSWEEK, Sept. 12, 2005, at 54.

Saulny, Susan & Gary Rivlin, *Little Aid Coming to Displaced New Orleans Renters; Homeowners are Seeing Lion's Share of Post-Katrina Help*, N.Y. TIMES, Sept. 17, 2006.

SAXON, LYLE, FABULOUS NEW ORLEANS (1952).

Scales, Adam F., *A Nation of Policyholders: Governmental and Market Failure in Flood Insurance*, 26 MISS. C. L. REV. 3 (2007).

SCALIA, ANTONIN, A MATTER OF INTERPRETATION: FEDERAL COURTS AND THE LAW (1997).

Scalia, Antonin, *Originalism: The Lesser Evil*, 57 U. CIN. L. REV. 849 (1989).

Schapiro, Robert A., *Polyphonic Federalism: State Constitutions in the Federal Courts*, 87 CAL. L. REV. 1409 (1999).

Schapiro, Robert A., *Toward a Theory of Interactive Federalism*, 91 Iowa L. Rev. 243 (2005).

Schapiro, Robert A. & William W. Buzbee, *Unidimensional Federalism: Power and Perspective in Commerce Clause Adjudication*, 88 CORNELL L. REV. 1199 (2003).

Schiesel, Seth, *In Frayed Networks, Common Threads*, N.Y. TIMES, Aug. 21, 2003, at G1.

Schwartz, John, *Army Builders Accept Blame Over Flooding*, N.Y. TIMES, June 2, 2006, at A1.

Seicshnaydre, Stacy E., *The More Things Change, the More They Stay the Same: In Search of a Just Public Housing Policy Post-Katrina*, 81 TUL. L. REV. 1263 (2007).

Seidule, Nicholas, A Fly in the Soup Bowl: Using the State-Created Danger Doctrine to Find Liability Against the State of Louisiana for the Katrina Disaster (unpublished manuscript, on file with The Nova Law Review).

Shane, Scott & Thom Shanker, *When Storm Hit, National Guard Was Deluged Too*, N.Y. TIMES, Sept. 28, 2005, at A1.

SHAPO, MARSHALL S., COMPENSATION FOR VICTIMS OF TERRORISM 44–88 (2005).

SHILLER, ROBERT J., THE NEW FINANCIAL ORDER: RISK IN THE 21ST CENTURY (2003).

Siegel, Reva B., *She the People: The Nineteenth Amendment, Sex Equality, Federalism, and the Family*, 115 HARV. L. REV. 947 (2002).

SILVERMAN, DAVID, INTERPRETING QUALITATIVE DATA: METHODS FOR ANALYZING TALK, TEXT AND INTERACTION (1993).

Singer, Joseph William, *After the Flood: Equality and Humanity in Property Regimes*, 52 LOY. L. REV. 243 (2006).

SLATER, COURTENAY M. & MARTHA G. DAVIS, STATE PROFILES: THE POPULATION AND ECONOMY OF EACH U.S. STATE (1999).

Smith, Andrene, *Different World: Financial Determinants of Well-Being in New Orleans in Black and White*, 14 GEO. J. ON POVERTY L. & POL'Y 179 (2007).

Smith, Denis, *Beyond Contingency Planning: Towards a Model of Crisis Management*, 4 INDUS. CRISIS Q. 263 (1990).

Smith, Denis, *Business (Not) as Usual: Crisis Management, Service Recovery and the Vulnerability of Organizations*, 19 J. SERVICES MARKETING 309 (2005).

Smith, James C., *Disaster Planning and Public Housing: Lessons Learned from Katrina*, RE-DEVELOPMENT AFTER A MAJOR DISASTER in the Law, Property, and Society book series of Ashgate Publishing (series editor, Robin Paul Malloy) (forthcoming).

Smith, Peter J. *Sources of Federalism: An Empirical Analysis of the Court's Quest for Original Meaning*, 52 UCLA L. REV. 217 (2004).

Stamm et al., B. Hudnall, *Introduction*, *in* RURAL BEHAVIORAL HEALTH CARE: AN INTERDISCIPLINARY GUIDE (B. Hudnall Stamm ed., 2003).

STEINBERG, TED, ACTS OF GOD: THE UNNATURAL HISTORY OF NATURAL DISASTER IN AMERICA (2000).

STOEBUCK, WILLIAM A. & DALE A. WHITMAN, THE LAW OF PROPERTY (3d ed. 2000).

Summers, John O., *Guidelines for Conducting Research and Publishing in Marketing: From Conceptualization Through the Review Process*, 29 J. ACAD. MARKETING SCI. 405 (2001).

Taylor, Spencer M., *Insuring Against the Natural Catastrophe After Katrina*, 20 NAT. RESOURCES & ENV'T 26 (2006).

TERRORISM AND INSURANCE 3 (Swiss Re 1993).

Thomas, Evan, *Taken by Storm*, NEWSWEEK, Dec. 26, 2005/Jan. 2, 2006, at 47.

Thomas et al., Evan, *How Bush Blew It*, NEWSWEEK, Sept. 19, 2005, at 30.

Thomas et al., Evan, *The Lost City*, NEWSWEEK, Sept. 12, 2005, at 41.

Thomas, Greg, *Rental Rates Fall with Demand*, TIMES-PICAYUNE (NEW ORLEANS), Sept. 9, 2007 at A1.

Thomas, Greg, *Riverfront Power Plant Gets Initial OK for Tax Breaks*, TIMES-PICAYUNE (NEW ORLEANS), Aug. 15, 2007 at A1.

Tickamyer, Ann R. & Cynthia M. Duncan, *Poverty and Opportunity Structure in Rural America*, 16 ANN. REV. SOC. 67 (1990).

TIFFANY, REAL PROPERTY, VOL. 2 (3d ed. 1939).

Tomlinson, Sherrie Armstrong, *No New Orleanians Left Behind: An Examination of the Disparate Impact of Hurricane Katrina on Minorities*, 38 CONN. L. REV. 1153 (2006).

Tritt, Cheryl A., *Telecommunications Future*, 852 PLI/Pat 85 (2005).

Tumulty et al., Karen, *4 Places Where the System Broke Down: The Governor*, TIME, Sept. 19, 2005, at 34.

TURNER, ET. AL, MICHAEL A., RECOVERY, RENEWAL AND RESILIENCY: GULF COAST SMALL BUSINESSES TWO YEARS LATER, POLITICAL & ECONOMIC RESEARCH COUNCIL (2007).

VALE, LAWRENCE J. & THOMAS J. CAMPANELLA, THE RESILIENT CITY: HOW MODERN CITIES RECOVER FROM DISASTER (2005).

Viguerie, Robert, *Coastal Erosion: Crisis in Louisiana's Wetlands*, 51 LA. B.J. 85 (2003).

Warren, John K., *Restoring Responsibility and Accountability in Disaster Relief*, 31 Wm. & Mary Envtl. L. & Pol'y Rev. 893 (2007).

Waterstone, Michael E. & Michael Ashley Stein, *Emergency Preparedness and People with Disabilities*, 30 Mental & Physical Disability L. Rep. 338 (2006).

Watner, Coleman, *People still Moving into New Orleans*, Times-Picayune (New Orleans), Nov. 14, 2007, at A1.

Weber, Bruce & Leif Jensen, *Poverty and Place: A Critical Review of Rural Poverty Literature*, RUPRI Rural Poverty Res. Ctr., Working Paper Series (2004).

Webster's Ninth New Collegiate Dictionary (1983).

Weiser, Philip J. *Towards a Constitutional Architecture for Cooperative Federalism*, 79 N.C. L. Rev. 663 (2001).

Weisheit et al., Ralph A., Crime and Policing in Rural and Small-Town America 2 (2d ed. 1999).

White, James Boyd, *Law as Language: Reading Law and Reading Literature*, 60 Tex. L. Rev. 415 (1982).

Whitley et al., Joe, *Homeland Security After Hurricane Katrina: Where Do We Go from Here?*, 20 Nat. Resources & Env't 1 (2006).

Wilcox, Rob, *Housing in Post-Katrina New Orleans: Legal Rights and Recourses for Displaced African-American Residents*, 2 N.W. J. L. & Soc. Pol'y 105 (2007).

Williams, Suzanne, The Oxfam Gender Training Manual (1994).

Wyatt, Marva Jo, *Ports, Politicians and the Public Trust: The Los Angeles Port Funds Controversy Comes Face to Face with Federal Law*, 9 U.S.F. Mar. L.J. 357 (1997).

Yoo, John, *Trigger Power*, L.A. Times, Oct. 2, 2005, at M5.

Zanetti et al., Auriela, *Natural Catastrophes and Man-Made Disasters in 2003*, in Sigma 2004, at 38 (Swiss Re, Sigma No. 1/2004, 2004).

Zulack, Mary Marsh, *If You Prompt Them, They Will Rule: The Warranty of Habitability Meets the New Court Information Systems*, 40 J. Marshall L. Rev. 395 (2007).

**Government Documents**

Access to Criminal Records and Information, 24 C.F.R. § 5 (2006).

Air Transportation Safety and System Stabilization Act, 49 U.S.C. § 40101 (2003).

Ark. Code Ann. § 14-54-1705 (2006).

BAPCPA Act of 2005, 11 U.S.C. §§ 101–1502.

Cong. Budget Office, The Federal Government's Spending and Tax Actions in Response to the 2005 Gulf Coast Hurricanes (2007).

Congressional Budget Office, Congress of the United States, Publ'n No. 2940, Federal Reinsurance for Terrorism Risks: Issues in Reauthorization 1 (2007).

Consumer Protections, Fla. Stat. § 501.005 (2006).

Disaster Relief and Emergency Assistance Amendments of 1988, 42 U.S.C. §§ 3601–3619 (2000).

Elimination of Barriers for Katrina Victims Act, H.R. 4213, 109th Cong. (2005–2006).

Exec. Order No. 13,347, 69 Fed. Reg. 44,573 (July 22, 2004).

Fair and Accurate Credit Transactions Act of 2003, 15 U.S.C. §1681.

Federal Tort Claims Act, 28 U.S.C. § 2680 (2006).

Geneva Convention Relative to the Protection of Civilian Persons in Time of War, 6 U.S.T. 3516 (1949).

Geneva Convention Relative to the Treatment of Prisoners of War, 6 U.S.T. 3316 (1949).

H.B. 516, 2006 Reg. Sess (La.).

H.R. 4704, 109th Cong. § 2 (2006).

Individuals with Disabilities in Emergency Preparedness, Exec. Order No. 13347 (2004).

Insurrection Act, 10 U.S.C. §§ 331–335 (2000).

King, Rawle, *National Flood Insurance Program: Treasury Borrowing in the Aftermath of Hurricane Katrina*, Congressional Research Service, June 6, 2006, at 2.

La. Acts 666 (2006).

La. Acts 851 & 859 (amending La. Const.) (2006).

La. Civ. Code Ann. (West. 2004).

La. Const. art. I.

La. Const. art. VI.

La. Const. art. VII.

La. Rev. Stat. Ann. (2006).

La. Rev. Stat. Ann. (West Supp. 2007).

Migratory Bird Treaty Act, 16 U.S.C. §§ 703–711 (2000).

Military Commissions Act of 2006, Pub. L. No. 109-366, 120 Stat. 2600 (2006).

Miss. Code Ann. (West 1999).

National Flood Insurance Act of 1968, Pub. L. No. 90-448, 82 Stat. 572 (2000).

New Orleans (La.), Ordinance 22499 (Feb. 1, 2007).

N.Y. Real Prop. Act. Law § 803 (McKinney 1979).

Office of Emergency Preparedness (La), *Southeast La. Hurricane Evacuation and Sheltering Plan* (2000).

Orszag, Peter R., Cong. Budget Office, letter to Hon. John M. Spratt, Chairman, H. Budget Comm., The Federal Government's Spending and Tax Actions in Response to the 2005 Gulf Coast Hurricanes 7 (Aug. 1, 2007).

Pub. L. No. 89-298, § 204, 79 Stat. 1073 (1965).

Regs. for Revision of the Water Pollution Control Program Addressing Storm Water Discharges, 64 Fed. Reg. 68 (1999).

S. 2124, 109th Cong. § 1 (2005).

St. Bernard Parish Council, LA., ORD. 670-09-06 (2006).

St. Bernard Parish Council, LA., ORD. 697-12-06 (2006).

Standards for PHA tenant selection criteria, 24 C.F.R. § 960.203 (2006).

Terrorism Risk Insurance Act of 2002, Pub. L. No. 107-297, 116 Stat. 2322 (2002).

Terrorism Risk Insurance Extension Act of 2005, Pub. L. No. 109-144, 119 Stat. 2660 (2005).

Terrorism Risk Insurance Program Reauthorization Act of 2007, Pub. L. No. 110-160, 121 Stat. 1839 (2007).

U.S. Census, General Housing Characteristics (2000).

U.S. CONST. art. I, § 8.

U.S. CONST. art. IV, § 4.

U.S. CONST. art. VI, cl. 2.

U.S. CONST. amend. X.

U.S. CONST. amend. XIII.

U.S. CONST. amend. XIV.

U.S. CONST. amend. XVI.

U.S. Dep't of Agric., Econ. Res. Serv., Rural Dev. Res. Report No. 100, *Rural Poverty at a Glance* 4 (2004).

U.S. Dep't of Homeland Sec., *Hurricane Katrina: The Role of the Federal Emergency Management Agency: Hearing Before the H. Select Bipartisan Comm. to Investigate the Preparation for and Response to Hurricane Katrina, in* NATIONAL RESPONSE PLAN, 109th Cong. (2005).

U.S. Dep't of Homeland Sec., National Response Plan 6 (2004).

U.S. GEN. ACCOUNTING OFFICE, PUBL'N NO. GAO-03-1033, CATASTROPHIC INSURANCE RISKS: STATUS OF EFFORTS TO SECURITIZE NATURAL CATASTROPHE AND TERRORISM RISK 1 (2003).

U.S. GEN. ACCOUNT. OFFICE, PUBL'N NO. GAO-04-307, TERRORISM INSURANCE: IMPLEMENTATION OF THE TERRORISM RISK INSURANCE ACT OF 2002 28 (2004).

U.S. GOV'T ACCOUNTABILITY OFFICE, PUBL'N NO. GAO-06-119, FEDERAL EMERGENCY MANAGEMENT AGENCY: IMPROVEMENTS NEEDED TO ENHANCE OVERSIGHT AND MANAGEMENT OF THE NATIONAL FLOOD INSURANCE PROGRAM (2005).

U.S. GOV'T ACCOUNTABILITY OFFICE, PUBL'N NO. GAO-06-174T, FEDERAL EMERGENCY MANAGEMENT AGENCY: CHALLENGES FACING THE NATIONAL FLOOD INSURANCE PROGRAM (2005).

U.S. GOV'T ACCOUNTABILITY OFFICE, PUBL'N NO. GAO-06-183T, FEDERAL EMERGENCY MANAGEMENT AGENCY: OVERSIGHT AND MANAGEMENT OF THE NATIONAL FLOOD INSURANCE PROGRAM 2 (2005).

U.S. GOV'T ACCOUNTABILITY OFFICE, PUBL'N NO. GAO-06-322T, HURRICANE PROTECTION: STATUTORY AND REGULATORY FRAMEWORK FOR LEVEE MAINTENANCE AND EMERGENCY RESPONSE FOR THE LAKE PONTCHARTRAIN PROJECT 4 (2005).

U.S. GOV'T ACCOUNTABILITY OFFICE, PUBL'N NO. GAO-07-88, DISASTER ASSISTANCE: BETTER PLANNING NEEDED FOR HOUSING VICTIMS OF CATASTROPHIC DISASTERS 9 (2007).

U.S. GOV'T ACCOUNTABILITY OFFICE, PUBL'N NO. GAO-07-991T, NATIONAL FLOOD INSURANCE PROGRAM: PRELIMINARY VIEWS ON FEMA'S ABILITY TO ENSURE ACCURATE PAYMENTS ON HURRICANE-DAMAGED PROPERTIES 6 (2007).

U.S. GOV'T ACCOUNTABILITY OFFICE, PUBL'N NO. GAO-07-1078, NATIONAL FLOOD INSURANCE PROGRAM: FEMA'S MANAGEMENT AND OVERSIGHT OF PAYMENTS FOR INSURANCE COMPANY SERVICES SHOULD BE IMPROVED 1 (2007).

U.S. GOV'T ACCOUNTABILITY OFFICE, PUBL'N NO. GAO-07-1079, GULF COAST REBUILDING: OBSERVATIONS ON FEDERAL FINANCIAL IMPLICATIONS 14 (2007).

U.S. HOUSE OF REPRESENTATIVES, A FAILURE OF INITIATIVE: FINAL REP. OF THE SELECT BIPARTISAN COMM. TO INVESTIGATE THE PREPARATION FOR AND RESPONSE TO HURRICANE KATRINA, H.R. Rep No. 109-377 (2006).

U.S. TREASURY DEPARTMENT, BOARD OF GOVERNORS OF THE FED. RESERVE, SECURITIES AND EXCHANGE COMM'N & COMMODITY FUTURES TRADING COMM'N, TERRORISM RISK INSURANCE: REPORT OF THE PRESIDENT'S WORKING GROUP ON FINANCIAL MARKETS (2006).

Warner, John, National Defense Authorization Act for Fiscal Year 2007, Pub. L. No. 109-364, 10 U.S.C. § 333 (2006).

## Websites

ACORN, REBUILDING AFTER HURRICANE KATRINA: ACORN PLANNING PRINCIPLES, http://www.acorn.org/fileadmin/KatrinaRelief/report/Planning_Principles.pdf.

ALEXANDER, FRANK S., LAND BANK AUTHORITIES: A GUIDE FOR THE CREATION AND OPERATION OF LOCAL LAND BANKS 5–7 (Local Initiatives Support Corp. 2005), Apr. 1, 2005, http://www.lisc.org/content/publications/detail/793.

Allen, John, Office of the Secretary of Defense, Update—U.S. Government Relief Efforts in Asia, Foreign Press Center, Jan. 3, 2005, http://www.pacom.mil/speeches/sst2005/050103-wh-presstranscript.shtml.

AM. FRIENDS SERVICE COMMITTEE, http://www.afsc.org.

Am. Pub. Transp. Ass'n, Public Transportation: Wherever Life Takes You, http://www.publictransportation.org/.

Anderson, Dan R., *The National Flood Insurance Program—Problems and Potential*, 41 J. RISK & INS. 579 (1974), http://links.jstor.org/sici?sici=0022-4367%28197412%2941%3A4%3C579%3ATNFIPP%3E2.0.CO%3B2-F.

Argoff, Jeanne & Harilyn Rousso, *Hardest Hit and Least Protected*, FOUND. NEWS & COMMENTARY, Nov./Dec. 2005, http://foundationnews.org/CME/article.cfm?ID=3489.

Associated Press, *Agreement Close for Multistate Pollution Reduction Plan*, MAINETODAY.COM, Sept. 21, 2005, http://news.mainetoday.com/apwire/D8COLE481-263.shtml.

Atkins, Dan & Christie Guisti, *The Confluence of Poverty and Disability*, http://www.housingforall.org/rop0304%20poverty%20and%20disability.pdf.

Beeson, Elizabeth & Marty Strange, Why Rural Matters: The Need for Every State to Take Action on Rural Education (2000), http://www.mrea-mt.org/rural_matters.html.

Bernier, Brad & Linda Gonzales, Issues in Rural Independent Living 56, *available at* http://eric.ed.gov/ERICDocs/data/ericdocs2/content_storage_01/0000000b/80/24/92/4f.pdf.

Berry, Marion, Berry Issues Statement on Presidential Address, Sept. 15, 2005, http://www.house.gov/berry/pressreleases/archive/katrina3.html.

*Britons Describe Hurricane Ordeal*, BBC News, Sept. 6, 2005, http://news.bbc.co.uk/1/hi/uk/4214746.stm.

The Brookings Inst. Metro. Pol'y Program, New Orleans After the Storm: Lessons from the Past, a Plan for the Future 20 (2005), http://www.brookings.edu/metro/pubs/20051012_NewOrleans.pdf.

Brown, Lester R., *Global Warming Forcing U.S. Coastal Population to Move Inland*, Earth Pol'y Inst. (2006), http://www.earth-policy.org/Updates/2006/Update57.htm.

Bureau of Governmental Research, Cementing Imbalance: A Post-Katrina Analysis of the Regional Distribution of Subsidized Rental Housing 2 (2007), *available at* http://www.bgr.org.

Bureau of Governmental Research, The Road Home Rental Housing Program: Consequences for New Orleans 11 (2006), http://www.bgr.org/Consequences_for_N.O._091506.pdf.

Bureau of Int'l Info., Programs, U.S. Dep't of State, Going the Distance: The U.S. Tsunami Relief Effort 2005, http://usinfo.state.gov/products/pubs/tsunami/tsunami.pdf.

Cannizaro, Steve, *St. Bernard Parish Government, Parish Council Proposing Major Changes to Rental Property Ordinance*, Dec. 7, 2006, http://www.sbpg.net/dec0506f.html.

Chen, Jim, posting to http://jurisdynamics. blogspot.com/2006/10/emergent-new-orleans-cybernetic-urban.html (Oct. 13, 2006, 8:38 EST) (blog entry entitled *Emergent New Orleans: Cybernetic Urban Planning and Some Self-Organizing Alternatives*).

Chen, Michelle, *Housing Watchdogs Call Post-Katrina Ordinance*, The New Standard Oct. 6, 2006, http://newstandardnews.net/content/index.cfm/items/3731.

Chen, Michelle, *New Orleans' Displaced Struggle for Housing, Jobs, Neighborhoods*, The New Standard, Oct. 21, 2005, http://newstandardnews.net/content/index.cfm/items/2514.

Church World Service, http://www.churchworldservice.org.

City-data.com, *New Orleans: Geography and Climate*, http://www.city-data.com/us-cities/The-South/New-Orleans-Geography-and-Climate.html.

CLARK, ANNIE & KALIMA ROSE, POLICY LINK, BRINGING LOUISIANA RENTERS HOME, June 2007, http://www.policylink.org/Communities/Louisiana/resources.html.

Code of Conduct for the International Red Cross and Red Crescent Movement and NGOs in Disaster Relief (1995), http://www.icrc.org/Web/Eng/siteeng0.nsf/html/57JMNB.

Comm. To Investigate the Preparation for and Response to Hurricane Katrina, *A Failure of Initiative*, 109th Cong., (Comm. Print 2006) http://www.katrina.house.gov/full_katrina_report.htm.

Convention on the Rights of Persons with Disabilities, G.A. Res. 61/106, U.N. Doc. A/RES/61/106, Dec. 13, 2006, http://www.un.org/esa/socdev/enable/rights/convtexte.htm.

COSGRAVE, JOHN, SYNTHESIS REPORT: EXPANDED SUMMARY: JOINT EVALUATION OF THE INTERNATIONAL RESPONSE TO THE INDIAN OCEAN TSUNAMI (Tsunami Evaluation Commission 2007), http://www.tsunami-evaluation.org/NR/rdonlyres/2E8A3262-0320-4656-BC81-EE0B46B54CAA/0/SynthRep.pdf.

Cossa, Ralph A., President of the Pacific Forum Center for Strategic and International Studies, *South Asian Tsunami: U.S. Military Provides 'Logistical Backbone' for Relief Operation*, EJOURNAL USA: FOREIGN POLICY AGENDA (Nov. 2004), http://usinfo.state.gov/journals/itps/1104/ijpe/cossa.htm.

Cummings, Elijah E., Brown Demonstrates Blurred Hindsight, Sept. 27, 2005, http://www.house.gov/cummings/press/05sep27a.htm.

Cutter, Susan L. *The Geography of Social Vulnerability: Race, Class, and Catastrophe*, http://understandingkatrina.ssrc.org/Cutter (Sept. 23, 2005).

Dep't of Homeland Sec., *Hurricane Katrina: What Government is Doing*, http://www.dhs.gov/xprepresp/programs/gc_1157649340100.shtm.

DEP'T OF INJURIES AND VIOLENCE PREVENTION, WORLD HEALTH ORGANIZATION, DISASTERS, DISABILITY, AND REHABILITATION (2005), http://www.who.int/violence_injury_prevention/other_injury/disaster_disability2.pdf.

DISABILITY RIGHTS SECTION, CIVIL RIGHTS DIVISION, U.S. DEPARTMENT OF JUSTICE, AN ADA GUIDE FOR LOCAL GOVERNMENTS: MAKING COMMUNITY EMERGENCY PREPAREDNESS AND RESPONSE PROGRAMS ACCESSIBLE TO PEOPLE WITH DISABILITIES (last update Aug. 5, 2006), *available at* http://www.ada.gov/emerprepguidescrn.pdf.

Dougherty, Candidus, While the Government Fiddled Around, The Big Easy Drowned: How the *Posse Comitatus* Act Became the Government's Alibi for the Hurricane Katrina Disaster (unpublished manuscript), http://ssrn.com/abstract=938249.

Drabenstott, Mark & Katharine H. Sheaff, Exploring Policy Options for a New Rural America: A Conference Summary (2001), http://www.kc.frb.org/PUBLICAT/Exploring/RC01DRAB.pdf.

Elimination of Barriers for Katrina Victims Act, H.R. 4213, 109th Cong. (2005), *available at* http://www.govtrack.us/congress/ billtext.xpd?bill=h109-4213.

EPA, Response to 2005 Hurricanes: Frequent Questions, http://www.epa.gov/katrina/faqs.htm.

FEMA, 2 Years Later: Federal Funds for Gulf Coast Recovery Exceed $8.3 Billion, Aug. 24, 2007, http://www.fema.gov/news/newsrelease.fema?id=39209.

FEMA, By the Numbers: FEMA Recovery Update in Louisiana, Mar. 24, 2006, http://www.fema.gov/news/newsrelease.fema?id=24505.

FEMA, Disaster Assistance Available from FEMA, http://www.fema.gov/assistance/process/assistance.shtm#0.

FEMA, Do I Qualify for "Housing Needs" Assistance?, http://www.fema.gov/assistance/process/qualify_housing.shtm.

FEMA, FEMA Assistance for Hurricane Rita recovery tops $2 billion, Sept. 24, 2007, http://www.fema.gov/news/newsrelease.fema?id=40949.

FEMA, *Katrina and Rita Breakdown of Manufactured Housing Units as of 8/14/07*, http://www.fema.gov/txt/hazard/hurricane/2005katrina/gulf_manufactured_housing_by_type.rtf.

FEMA, National Flood Insurance Program: Summary of Coverage, http://www.fema.gov/pdf/nfip/summary_cov.pdf.

Filosa, Gwen, *Bias Found in Rental Market*, TIMES-PICAYUNE (NEW ORLEANS), Apr. 25, 2007, *available at* http://www.nola.com/topnews/2007/04/bias-found-in-rental-market.html.

Freshwater, David, *Rural America at the Turn of the Century: One Analyst's Perspective*, RURAL AMERICA (2000), http://www.ers.usda.gov/publications/ruralamerica/sep2000/sep2000c.pdf.

Frickel, Scott, *Our Toxic Gumbo: Recipe for a Politics of Environmental Knowledge*, http://understandingkatrina.ssrc.org/Frickel (Oct. 6, 2005).

Frieden, Lex, Letter to Fred Hiatt, Editorial Page Editor, WASH. POST, Jan. 27, 2006, *available at* http://www.ncd.gov/newsroom/correspondence/2006/hiatt_01-27-06.htm.

Gale, Fred & Dennis Brown, *How Important Is Airport Access for Rural Businesses?*, 15 RURAL AMERICA 16 (2000), http://www.ers.usda.gov/publications/ruralamerica/sep2000/sep2000e.pdf.

Gamm, Larry, Sarah Stone & Stephanie Pittman, *Mental Health and Mental Disorders—A Rural Challenge*, http://www.srph.tamhsc.edu/centers/rhp2010/08Volume1mentalhealth.htm.

The Gavel, Joint Hearing on the National Flood Insurance System, June 12, 2007, http://www.speaker.gov/blog/?p=476.

GCR Metropolitan New Orleans Population Estimate, *available at* http://www.gcrprofessional.com/Pro_NewsRelease.htm?NewsID=18.

GEORGE, LANCE & MILANA BARR, MOVING HOME: MANUFACTURED HOUSING IN RURAL AMERICA (Housing Assistance Council, 2005), http://www.knowledgeplex.org/showdoc.html?id=137748.

Glasgow, Nina, *Older Americans' Patterns of Driving and Using Other Transportation*, 15 RURAL AMERICA 26 (2000), http://www.ers.usda.gov/publications/ruralamerica/sep2000/sep2000f.pdf.

Glassman, James K., *Katrina and Disgusting Exploitation*, TCS DAILY, Aug. 31, 2005, http://www.tcsdaily.com/article.aspx?id=083105JKG.

Greater New Orleans Community Data Center, St. Bernard Parish: People & Household Characteristics, http://www.gnocdc.org/st_bernard/people.html.

Greater New Orleans Fair Housing Action Center, News Release, Fair Housing Centers File Suit Against St. Bernard Parish; Announces New Conference Regarding Lawsuit, Oct. 3, 2006, http://gnofairhousing.org/pdfs/10-03-06-pressreleaselawsuit-StBernard.pdf.

Greenberger, Michael, *Yes, Virginia: The President Can Deploy Federal Troops to Prevent the Loss of a Major American City from a Devastating Natural Catastrophe*, U. OF MD. LEGAL STUDIES, http://ssrn.com/abstract=946207.

Grossman, David A. *Flood Insurance: Can a Feasible Program Be Created?*, 34 LAND ECON. 352, Nov. 1958, http://links.jstor.org/sici?sici=0023-7639%2819195811%2934%3A4%3C352%3AFICAFP%3E2.0.CO%3B2-7.

Guinn, Patricia L., *Hurricane Katrina: Analysis of the Impact on the Insurance Industry* (2005), www.towersperrin.com/tillinghast/publications/reports/Hurricane_Katrina/katrina.pdf.

The Henry J. Kaiser Family Foundation, The Washington Post/Kaiser Family Foundation/Harvard University Survey of Hurricane Katrina Evacuees, http://www.kff.org/newsmedia/washpost.

Hohns, Joe, *Sen. Lott's Home Destroyed by Katrina*, CNN, Sept. 4, 2005, http://www.cnn.com/2005/POLITICS/08/30/katrina.lott.

Holt Int'l Children's Services, http://www.holtintl.org.

HOUSING ASSISTANCE COUNCIL, TAKING STOCK: RURAL PEOPLE, POVERTY, AND HOUSING AT THE TURN OF THE 21ST CENTURY 20–21 (2002), http://ruralhome.org/pubs/hsganalysis/ts2000/index.htm.

HOWLEY, CRAIG, THE RURAL SCHOOL BUS RIDE IN FIVE STATES: A REPORT TO THE RURAL SCHOOL AND COMMUNITY TRUST at i (2001), http://oak.cats.ohiou.edu/~howleyc/bus2.htm.

Humanitarian Accountability Partnership, *The Humanitarian Accountability Report 2005* (2005), http://www.hapinternational.org.

Information on Disability for Empowerment, Advocacy and Support, *Katrina Disability Information*, Feb. 2007, http://katrinadisability.info.

InterAction PVO Standards, Disability Amendments, http://www.interaction.org/pvostandards/index.html.

International Disability Rights Monitor, *Disability and Tsunami Relief Efforts in India, Indonesia and Thailand* (2005), http://www.ideanet.org/cir/uploads/File/TsunamiReport.pdf.

ISO, *PCS Catastrophe Serial Numbers*, http://www.iso.com/products/2800/prod2802.html.

JIMERSON, LORNA, SLOW MOTION: TRAVELING BY SCHOOL BUS IN CONSOLIDATED DISTRICTS IN WEST VIRGINIA 7 (Rural School and Community Trust 2007), http://www.ruraledu.org/site/lookup.asp?c=beJMIZOCIrH&b=2589073.

Johnson, Kenneth, *Demographic Trends in Rural and Small Town America*, in 1 REPORTS ON RURAL AMERICA 7 (U. of New Hampshire, Carsey Institute, Issue

No. 1, 2006), http://www.carseyinstitute.unh.edu/documents/Demographics_complete_file.pdf.

*Katrina Damage Estimate Hits $125B*, USA TODAY, http://www.usatoday.com/money/economy/2005-09-09-katrina-damage_x.htm.

*Katrina's Official Death Toll Tops 1,000*, CNN.COM, Sept. 21, 2005, http://www.cnn.com/2005/US/09/21/katrina.impact.

Kaufman, Phil R., *Rural Poor Have Less Access to Supermarkets, Large Grocery Stores*, 13 RURAL DEV. PERSPECTIVES 19 (1999), http://www.ers.usda.gov/publications/rdp/rdp1098/rdp1098c.pdf.

Kellogg Found., *Perceptions of Rural America* (2001), http://www.wkkf.org/pubs/FoodRur/pub2973.pdf.

Kellogg Found., *Perceptions of Rural America: Media Coverage* (2003), *available at* http://www.wkkf.org/Pubs/FoodRur/MediaCoverage_00253_03795.pdf.

KOBE, KATHERINE, SMALL BUSINESS ADMINISTRATION, THE SMALL BUSINESS SHARE OF GDP: 1998–2004, http://www.sba.gov/advo/research/rs299tot.pdf.

LaCoast, Stemming the Tide: The Mississippi River Delta and the Davis Pond Freshwater Diversion Project, http://www.lacoast.gov/ programs/DavisPond/stemming-the-tide.htm.

Lang, Susan S. *Federal Policies Keep People with Disabilities in a "Poverty Trap," Say Cornell Experts in Urging Major Reforms*, CORNELL UNIV. NEWS SERV., Aug. 31, 2005, http://www.news.cornell.edu/stories/Aug05/disability.poverty.ssl.html.

Latter & Blum Inc. Realtors Report, *available at* http://www.realestate.uno.edu.

Lawyer's Committee for Civil Rights, St. Bernard Parish Agrees to Halt Discriminatory Zoning Rule, Nov. 13, 2006, http://www.lawyerscommittee.org/2005website/publications/press/press111306.html.

Leahy, Patrick, Statement on Presidential Signing Statements, July 25, 2006, *available at* http://leahy.senate.gov/press/200607/072506a.html.

Lee, Anita, *U.S. Rep. Gene Taylor Sees Fraud In Insurer Denials; He Suspects NFIP, Taxpayers Are Being Cheated*, SUN HERALD, Oct. 24, 2006, http://www.accessmylibrary.com/comsite5/bin/comsite5.pl?page=library&item_id=0286-15729307 (registration required).

Letter from Lex Frieden, then-Chairperson of the National Council on Disability, to Fred Hiatt, Editorial Page Editor, The Washington Post (Jan. 27, 2006), *available at* http://www.ncd.gov/newsroom/correspondence/2006/hiatt_01-27-06.htm.

Lipton, Eric, *Key Documents Regarding the Government Response to Katrina*, N.Y. TIMES, http://www.nytimes.com/ref/national/nationalspecial/10katrina-docs.html.

LIU, AMY & ALLISON PLYER, THE NEW ORLEANS INDEX: SECOND ANNIVERSARY SPECIAL EDITION, A REVIEW OF KEY INDICATORS OF RECOVERY TWO YEARS AFTER KATRINA (Aug. 2007), http://www.gnocdc.org/.

Louisiana Dep't of Public Safety and Corrections, *Parole Board Dockets*, http://www.corrections.state.la.us/Offices/paroleboard/paroledockets.htm.

Louisiana Plans, Long-Term Recovery Planning, St. Bernard Parish, http://www. louisianaspeaks-parishplans.org/IndParishHomepage.cfm?EntID=13.

Louisiana Recovery Authority, Homeowners, http://www.road2la.org/ homeowner.

Louisiana Recovery Authority, *The Road Home Homeowner Policies* (Version 4.0, April 15, 2007), *available at* http://www.road2la.org/homeowner/resources. htm#policies.

Louisiana Recovery Authority, The Road Home Program, http://www.road2la. org/about-us.

Louisiana Recovery Authority, The Road Home Program: Latest Statistics, *Weekly Detailed Statistics as of April 30, 2007*, *available at* http://www.road2la.org/ newsroom/stats.htm.

McNabb, Donnald & Louis E. "Lee" Madère, Jr., *A History of New Orleans*, http:// www.madere.com/history.html.

Mercy Corps, http://www.mercycorps.org.

Miller, Kathleen K. & Bruce A. Weber, *How Do Persistent Poverty Dynamics and Demographics Vary Across the Rural-Urban Continuum?*, MEASURING RURAL DIVERSITY, Jan. 2004, http://srdc.msstate.edu/measuring/series/miller_weber. pdf.

*Missing Stories From Katrina Coverage: Survivors Locked Up in Makeshift Jail*, THE PRAXIS PROJECT, Sept. 6, 2005, http://www.thepraxisproject.org/tools/ YMC_katrina.doc.

Mobility Int'l USA, http://www.miusa.org.

Morton, Lois Wright & Troy C. Blanchard, *Starved for Access: Life in Rural America's Food Deserts*, RURAL REALITIES (2007), http://www.ruralsociology. org/pubs/RuralRealities/Issue4.html.

Mowbray, Rebecca, *Procedural Changes Speeded Insurance Payouts, But May Have Allowed Abuses*, TIMES-PICAYUNE (NEW ORLEANS), June 11, 2007, http:// blog.nola.com/times-picayune/2007/06/procedural_changes_speeded_ins. html.

National Council on Disability, *The Needs of People with Psychiatric Disabilities During and After Hurricanes Katrina and Rita: Position Paper and Recommendations*, July 7, 2006, http://www.ncd.gov/newsroom/ publications/2006/peopleneeds.htm.

National Council on Disability, *Saving Lives: Including People with Disabilities in Emergency Planning*, Apr. 2005, http://www.ncd.gov/newsroom/ publications/2005/saving_lives.htm.

National Council on Disability Public Consultations, *Homeland Security, Emergency Preparedness, Disaster Relief and Recovery*, May 31, 2007, http:// www.ncd.gov/newsroom/publications/2007/ncd_consultant_05-31-07.htm.

National Hurricane Center, Hurricane Preparedness, http://www.nhc.noaa.gov/ HAW2/english/storm_surge.shtml.

NAT'L LOW INCOME HOUS. COAL., PRELIMINARY ESTIMATE 9-22-05, HURRICANE KATRINA'S IMPACT ON LOW INCOME HOUSING UNITS ESTIMATED 302,000 UNITS LOST OR DAMAGED, 71% LOW INCOME (2005), http://nlihc.org/doc/05-02.pdf.

National Rural Network, *Why Rural Matters II: The Rural Impact of the Administration's FY07 Budget Proposal* (2006), http://www.rupri.org/ruralPolicy/publications/2007budgetanalysis.pdf.

New Orleans Redevelopment Authority, http://www.noraworks.org.

Nitschke, Lori, *Manufactured Homes a Big Factor in Rural Homeownership in U.S.*, POPULATION REFERENCE BUREAU (2004), *available at* http://www.prb.org/Articles/ 2004/ManufacturedHomesaBigFactorinRuralHomeownershipinUS.aspx.

People's Hurricane Relief Fund and Oversight Coalition, Tenants Rights Working Group, www.peopleshurricane.org.

*Photo Gallery: Pets, Hurricane Katrina's Other Victims*, NATIONAL GEOGRAPHIC. COM, Sept. 8, 2005, http://news.nationalgeographic.com/news/2005/09/0908_050908_katrina_pets.html.

PIKE, JENNIFER, GULF GOV. REPORTS: SPENDING FEDERAL DISASTER AID 2 (Nelson A. Rockefeller Inst. of Gov. and the Pub. Affairs Research Council of Louisiana 2007), *available at* www.rockinst.org/gulfgov.

*Power Returns to Most Areas Hit by Blackout*, CNN.COM, Aug. 15, 2003, http://www.cnn.com/2003/US/08/15/power.outage.

Proceedings of the Council of the Parish of St. Bernard, State of Louisiana, http://www.sbpg.net.

Rahmstorf et al., Stefan, *Hurricanes and Global Warming—Is There a Connection?*, REALCLIMATE, Sept. 2, 2005, http://www.realclimate.org/index.php?p=181.

The Road Home, *Overview of Small Rental Property Program*, http://www.road2la.org/rental/overview.htm.

The Road Home, Rental Property Owners Encouraged to Apply to "The Road Home" Small Rental Property Program, http://www.road2la.org/news_releases/rental_launch_012907.htm.

ROCKEFELLER FOUNDATION, NEW ORLEANS: PLANNING FOR A BETTER FUTURE 3 (2006), http://www.rockfound.org/library/no_better_future.pdf.

Rosenbloom, Philip, *Homeowners, and Tenants Too: Mobile Homeowners Face Unique, Yet Familiar, Challenges*, NAT'L HOUS. INST. (2000), http://www.nhi.org/online/issues/112/rosenbloom.html.

Rowley, Thomas D., *Rural Disabled Struggle for Independence*, RURAL MONITOR NEWSLETTER 1 (Fall 2003), *available at* http://www.raconline.org/newsletter/web/Fall03_vol10-2.html.

Rural Poverty Res. Ctr., *What are Persistent Poverty Counties?*, *available at* http://www.rprconline.org.

Rural School & Cmty. Trust, *Hidden Rural Realities of Hurricane Katrina*, RURAL POLICY MATTERS (The Rural School and Community Trust, Randolph, Vermont) Sept. 2006, *available at* http://www.ruraledu.org/site/c.beJMIZOCIrH/

b.2059003/apps/nl/content.asp?content_id=%7B50A94578-EBF2-4B5F-ACD7-DEB4C04C541B%7D&notoc=1.

Saenz, Rogelio & Walter G. Peacock, *Rural People, Rural Places: The Hidden Costs of Hurricane Katrina*, RURAL REALITIES, http://www.ruralsociology.org/pubs/RuralRealities/Issue1.html.

SAMUELS, PAUL & DEBBIE MUKAMAL, LEGAL ACTION CENTER, AFTER PRISON: ROADBLOCKS TO REENTRY: A REPORT ON STATE LEGAL BARRIERS FACING PEOPLE WITH CRIMINAL RECORDS (Legal Action Center 2004), http://www.lac.org/lac/upload/lacreport/LAC_PrintReport.pdf.

Schakowsky, Jan, Statement on the Approval of $10.5 Billion in Emergency Supplemental Appropriations for Hurricane Victims, Sept. 2, 2005, http://www.house.gov/schakowsky/PressRelease_9_2_05_KatrinaAid.html.

Sebok, Anthony J., *The Response to the Disaster in New Orleans: Will There Be a Compensation Program Similar to the 9/11 Victims' Fund?*, Sept. 5, 2005, http://writ.news.findlaw.com/sebok/20050905.html.

The Small Rental Property Program, http://www.road2la.org/rental/overview.htm.

Sothern, Billy, *A Question of Blood*, THE NATION, Mar. 27, 2007, http://www.thenation.com/doc/20070409/sothern.

Sphere Project, *Humanitarian Charter and Minimum Standards in Disaster Response* (2004), http://www.sphereproject.org.

Stommes, Eileen S. & Dennis M. Brown, *Transportation in Rural America: Issues for the 21st Century*, 16 RURAL AMERICA 4 (2002), http://www.ers.usda.gov/publications/ruralamerica/ra164/ra164b.pdf.

Taibbi, Mike, *Oil Coats Homes, Water After Katrina*, MSNBC.COM, Nov. 8, 2005, http://www.msnbc.msn.com/id/9972220.

Trickle Up, http://www.trickleup.org.

TVA RURAL STUDIES, OTA FOLLOW-UP CONFERENCE REPORT: RURAL AMERICA AT THE CROSSROADS 4 (2001), http://www.rural.org/workshops/rural_telecom/OTA_followup_report.pdf.

The Unified New Orleans Plan, http://unifiedneworleansplan.com.

U.N. Dev. Programme, Millennium Development Goals: A Compact Among Nations to End Human Poverty, Human Development Report 2003, http://hdr,undp.org/reports/global/2003/.

United Nations High Commissioner for Refugees, http://www.unhcr.org/protect.html.

Univ. of Montana Rural Inst., *Rural Facts: Update on the Demography of Rural Disability Part One: Rural and Urban*, Apr. 2005, http://rtc.ruralinstitute.umt.edu/RuDis/RuDemography.htm.

Univ. of Wis., Center for Community Econ. Dev., *Transportation Barriers to Employment of Low-Income People* (1998), http://www.aae.wisc.edu/pubs/cenews/docs/ce258.txt.

U.S. AGENCY FOR INT'L DEV., AAPD 05-07, USAID ACQUISITION AND ASSISTANCE POLICY DIRECTIVE (DISABILITY POLICY ON NEW CONSTRUCTION) (2005), http:// www.usaid.gov/about_usaid/disability/.

U.S. AGENCY FOR INT'L DEV., USAID DISABILITY POLICY PAPER (1997), http://pdf. dec.org/pdf_docs/PDABQ631.pdf.

U.S. Agency for Int'l Dev., *USAID Disability Policy – Assistance* (2004), *available at* http://www.usaid.gov/about_usaid/disability.

U.S. Census Bureau, Census 2000 Urban and Rural Classification, http://www. census.gov/geo/www/ua/ua_2k.html.

U.S. Dep't of Agric., *Rural Income, Poverty, and Welfare: Rural Poverty*, ECON. RES. SERV., Nov. 10, 2004, http://www.ers.usda.gov/briefing/IncomePovertyWelfare/ ruralpoverty.

U.S. DEP'T OF HOMELAND SECURITY, NATIONAL RESPONSE PLAN (2004), http://www. dhs.gov/xlibrary/assets/NRPbaseplan.pdf.

U.S. DEP'T OF HOMELAND SECURITY OFF. FOR CIVIL RIGHTS AND CIVIL LIBERTIES, INDIVIDUALS WITH DISABILITIES IN EMERGENCY PREPAREDNESS (2005), http://www. dhs.gov/xlibrary/assets/CRCL_IWDEP_AnnualReport_2005.pdf.

U.S. Dep't of Hous. & Urban Dev. Office of Policy Dev. & Res., *Funding for Recovery in the Hurricanes' Wake, Part I*, RESEARCH WORKS (Oct. 2006), *available at* www.huduser.org/periodicals/Researchworks.html.

U.S. Dep't of Hous. & Urban Dev., Office of Policy Dev. & Res., *Funding for Recovery in the Hurricanes' Wake, Part II*, RESEARCH WORKS (Oct. & Nov. 2006), *available at* www.huduser.org/periodicals/Researchworks.html.

U.S. Dept. of Hous. & Urban Dev., Office of Policy, Dev. & Res., *The Impact of Hurricanes Katrina, Rita and Wilma on the Gulf Coast Housing Stock, in* U.S. Housing Market Conditions (2006), *available at* www.huduser.org/periodicals/ ushmc/spring06/USHML_06Q1_ch1.pdf.

U.S. Dep't of Hous. & Urban Dev., Office of Policy Dev. & Research, RESEARCH WORKS, www.huduser.org.

U.S. Dep't of Hous. & Urban Dev., U.S. Housing Market Conditions, OFFICE OF POLICY DEV. & RESEARCH, May 2006, http://www.huduser.org/periodicals/ ushmc/spring06/USHMC_06Q1.doc.

U.S. Dep't of Justice, *Blacks Were Almost Three Times More Likely Than Hispanics and Five Times More Likely Than Whites to Be in Jail*, http://www.ojp.usdoj. gov/bjs/glance/jailrair.htm.

U.S. Dep't of Justice, Bureau of Justice Statistics, Profile of Jail Inmates (2002), *available at* http://www.ojp.usdoj.gov/bjs/pub/pdf/pji02.pdf.

Watson, Rip, *New Orleans Port Opens to Relief Ships After Katrina*, BLOOMBERG. COM, Sept. 6, 2005, http://www.bloomberg.com/apps/news?pid=10000082&si d=adNXIjdn4Z8Q.

Waveland to Wasteland, http://www.femaforgotwaveland.com.

Wellington, Darryl Lorenzo, *New Orleans: A Right to Return?* DISSENT, Fall 2006, http://www.dissentmagazine.org.article/?article=695&print=1.

White House, Fact Sheet: Gulf Coast Update: Hurricane Relief, Recovery, and Rebuilding Continues, Mar. 8, 2006, http://www.whitehouse.gov/news/releases/2006/03/20060308-8.html.

WHITE HOUSE, THE FEDERAL RESPONSE TO HURRICANE KATRINA: LESSONS LEARNED (2006), http://www.whitehouse.gov/reports/katrina-lessons-learned.pdf.

Younge, Gary, *New Orleans Forsaken*, THE NATION, Aug. 31, 2006, http://www.thenation.com/doc/20060918/younge.

# Index